S0-DYT-060

Leaders of America

Capsule Biographies of Over 260 Famous Personalities

ILLUSTRATED BY KERN PEDERSON

COUNTRY BEAUTIFUL
Waukesha, Wisconsin

Dedicated to my wife, Evey;
Steve, Gary, Jeff, Kathy, Vi, Kris, Suzy and Kirk

 Manufactured in the United States of America. Film processed by Crown Color Corporation, Fox Lake, Ill.

Library of Congress Cataloging in Publication Data

Pederson, Kern O.
Leaders of America.

Includes index.
1. United States—Biography. I. Title.
E176.P36 920'.073 75-786
ISBN 0-87294-073-X

CONTENTS

People are listed in chronological sequence, according to the year of their birth.

Winslow Homer

Amelia Earhart

Tyrus Raymond "Ty" Cobb

Edward "Duke" Ellington

TWENTIETH CENTURY

1588 - 1649
John Winthrop
COLONIAL PURITAN STATESMAN AND FIRST GOVERNOR OF THE MASSACHUSETTS BAY COLONY
HE WAS BORN AT EDWARDSTONE, SUFFOLK, ENGLAND.
WINTHROP SAILED FROM SOUTHAMPTON, ENGLAND, IN 1630, ABOARD THE "ARBELLA" WHICH WAS PART OF A FLEET CARRYING 700 MEN, WOMEN AND CHILDREN. THIS WAS THE FIRST LARGE GROUP OF PURITANS WHO SETTLED AT THE PRESENT SITE OF BOSTON TO FORM A "BIBLE COMMONWEALTH." TEN YRS. LATER, DURING THE GREAT MIGRATION PERIOD, 200 SHIPS BROUGHT 20,000 SETTLERS TO MASSACHUSETTS BAY. ADVOCATE OF NEW ENGLAND CONFEDERATION.
GIVE ME YOUR IDEAS AND I WILL WORK WITH YOU!
HE SERVED AS GOVERNOR OF THE COLONY ALMOST CONTINUALLY FROM 1629 TO HIS DEATH.
I'LL PUT THESE AWAY FOR THE FUTURE.
THE FIRST TWO VOLUMES OF HIS MANUSCRIPT JOURNAL (1630-49) WERE PUBLISHED IN FULL AS "THE HISTORY OF NEW ENGLAND" IN 1825-26.
KERN

1591- 1643

Anne M. Hutchinson

RELIGIOUS LEADER IN COLONIAL AMERICA AND SYMBOL OF THE RIGHT OF RELIGIOUS DISSENT

SHE CAME TO MASSACHUSETTS BAY WITH HER HUSBAND AND FAMILY IN 1634. ANNE HUTCHINSON WAS VERY POPULAR BECAUSE OF HER KINDNESS AND GENEROUS CARE OF THE SICK. ***SHE ORGANIZED MEETINGS WHERE SHE OPENLY PREACHED THE DOCTRINE OF SALVATION THROUGH DIVINE GRACE AND LOVE RATHER THAN BY WORKS, CHALLENGING ORTHODOX PURITAN DOCTRINE OF MASS. BAY COLONY.***

SHE WAS BORN IN ALFORD, LINCOLNSHIRE, ENGLAND.

UNDER THE CIRCUMSTANCES I CANNOT ALLOW YOU TO STAY.

I WELCOME YOU TO OUR COLONY.
WE THANK YOU!

ANNE LEFT WITH HER FAMILY, IN 1638 FOR ROGER WILLIAMS' NEW SETTLEMENT IN NARRAGANSETT BAY. ***SHE FOUNDED PORTSMOUTH, RHODE ISLAND.***

JOHN WINTHROP OPPOSED HER IDEAS. ***SHE WAS BROUGHT TO TRIAL AND EXPELLED FROM THE CHURCH IN 1638 FOR HERESY. SHE REFUSED TO MAKE A PUBLIC RECANTATION.***

KERN

1592 - 1672

Peter Stuyvesant

DUTCH DIRECTOR-GENERAL OF NEW NETHERLAND, NOW NEW YORK

IN 1646, STUYVESANT WAS APPOINTED THE DIRECTOR-GENERAL OF NEW NETHERLAND. ***HE WAS A VIGOROUS AND PROGRESSIVE LEADER. HE CURBED THE SALE OF LIQUOR TO THE INDIANS, ARRANGED BOUNDARIES BETWEEN THE ENGLISH AND DUTCH TERRITORIES, ENFORCED THE OBSERVANCE OF THE SABBATH, AND TAXED IMPORTS TO BUILD PUBLIC WORKS.***

HE WAS BORN IN SCHERPENZEEL, FRIESLAND, HOLLAND.

THE PEOPLE ARE DEMANDING SELF GOVERNMENT.
OUR CITY IS FINALLY PROSPERING!
LET'S HOPE IT CONTINUES!

INSPITE OF HIS REFORMS HE WAS DICTATORIAL. ***HE YIELDED ONLY UNDER PRESSURE TO THE DEMANDS OF THE PEOPLE FOR SELF GOVERNMENT IN NEW AMSTERDAM.***

STUYVESANT DID MUCH FOR THE COMMERCIAL PROSPERITY OF THE CITY OF NEW AMSTERDAM WHICH RECEIVED ITS NAME IN 1653.

KERN

1603-1683
Roger Williams
PURITAN CLERGYMAN, FOUNDER OF THE COLONY OF RHODE ISLAND AND ADVOCATE OF RELIGIOUS FREEDOM
HE WAS BORN IN LONDON, ENGLAND.
WILLIAMS CAME TO BOSTON IN 1631. IN 1633, HE BECAME MINISTER OF THE CHURCH AT SALEM. HE WAS BANISHED IN 1635 BECAUSE OF HIS BELIEFS. WITH A FEW FAITHFUL FOLLOWERS, WILLIAMS WENT TO NARRAGANSETT BAY WHERE HE BOUGHT LANDS FROM THE LOCAL INDIAN CHIEFS, AND FOUNDED THE CITY OF PROVIDENCE, RHODE ISLAND, IN 1636. HE ESTABLISHED A GOVERNMENT FOUNDED ON COMPLETE RELIGIOUS TOLERATION, WHICH CONTRIBUTED GREATLY TO THE PRINCIPLE OF SEPARATION OF CHURCH AND STATE IN THE COLONY AND LATER IN THE U.S.
THIS IS A RIGHT OF THE PEOPLE!
HE COMPILED A DICTIONARY OF THE INDIAN LANGUAGE FOR THE MISSIONARIES TO USE AS THEY WORKED AMONG THEM. THE INDIANS' TRUST IN HIM HELPED PRESERVE THE PEACE FOR ALL NEW ENGLAND.
HE WAS THE FIRST CRUSADER FOR COMPLETE RELIGIOUS TOLERATION IN AMERICA.
KERN

1637 - 1675

Father Jacques Marquette

HE WAS A DILIGENT MISSIONARY WHOSE WORK AMONG THE INDIANS AND EXPLORATIONS ARE RECOGNIZED ALL OVER THE WORLD. HE ESTABLISHED THE EXISTENCE OF A WATERWAY FROM THE ST. LAWRENCE TO THE GULF OF MEXICO IN HIS VOYAGE DOWN THE MISSISSIPPI.

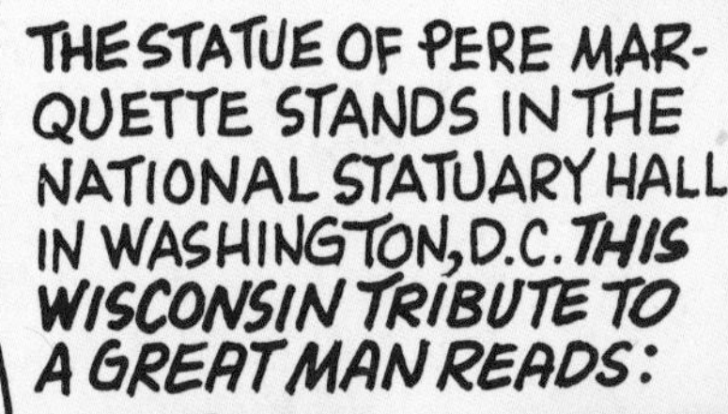

THE STATUE OF PERE MARQUETTE STANDS IN THE NATIONAL STATUARY HALL IN WASHINGTON, D.C. THIS WISCONSIN TRIBUTE TO A GREAT MAN READS:

JAMES MARQUETTE S.J. WHO WITH LOUIS JOLLIET DISCOVERED THE MISSISSIPPI RIVER AT PRAIRIE DU CHIEN, WIS. **JUNE 17, 1673.**

BORN IN LEON, FRANCE, HE LANDED AT QUEBEC IN 1666.

MARQUETTE HAD GREAT INFLUENCE OVER THE INDIANS *BECAUSE HE LEARNED THEIR LANGUAGE* AND CUSTOMS.

FR. MARQUETTE GAINED THE RESPECT OF THE INDIANS, AND ***TRAVELED AMONG THEM BY JUST CARRYING A PEACE PIPE!***

KERN

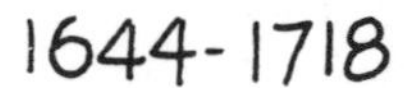

William Penn

FAMOUS ENGLISH QUAKER WHO FOUNDED
THE COLONY OF PENNSYLVANIA

WHILE STUDYING AT OXFORD, ENGLAND, PENN CONVERTED TO QUAKERISM. HE WAS SENT TO PRISON 3 TIMES AS A QUAKER PREACHER AND WRITER. ***DURING HIS FIRST IMPRISONMENT PENN WROTE "NO CROSS, NO CROWN," HIS MOST FAMOUS BOOK ON CHRISTIANITY. IN 1680, CHARLES II GRANTED HIM ALL THE NEW WORLD TERRITORY WEST OF THE DELAWARE RIVER BETWEEN NEW YORK AND MARYLAND IN LIEU OF AN $80,000 DEBT THE KING OWED HIS FATHER. HERE THE QUAKERS MOVED IN BY THE THOUSANDS TO LIVE IN PEACE AND FREEDOM.***

HE WAS BORN IN LONDON, ENGLAND.

IN OCT. 1682, HE MADE HIS FAMOUS TREATY WITH THE INDIAN TRIBES. ***HE PLANNED AND NAMED PHILADELPHIA WHICH MEANS "THE CITY OF BROTHERLY LOVE" AND FOR 2 YRS. GOVERNED IT WISELY AND WELL.***

THE KING ASKED THAT THE COLONY'S NAME HONOR PENN'S FATHER. ***THIS IS NOW PENNSYLVANIA, WHICH MEANS "PENN'S WOODS."***

1645-1700
Louis Jolliet
FRENCH-CANADIAN EXPLORER AND FUR TRADER
JOLLIET, WITH FR. MARQUETTE AND 5 BOATMEN, CROSSED GREEN BAY, TRAVELED UP THE FOX RIVER, PORTAGED TO THE WISCONSIN RIVER, FLOATED DOWN UNTIL THEY REACHED THE MISSISSIPPI RIVER JUNE 17, 1673. THEY PADDLED DOWN IT AS FAR AS THE ARKANSAS RIVER WHERE THEY TURNED BACK BECAUSE OF THEIR FEAR OF THE SPANIARDS!
HE WAS BORN IN QUEBEC PROVINCE, CANADA.
LAKE SUPERIOR
FORT MACKINAC
LAKE HURON
FOX R.
WIS. RIVER
MISS. R.
LAKE MICHIGAN
PRAIRIE DU CHIEN
ILLINOIS R.
ARK. RIVER
JOLLIET AND MARQUETTE'S ROUTE
KERN
JOLLIET ALSO EXPLORED THE LABRADOR AND HUDSON BAY REGIONS. IN 1697, HE WAS MADE CANADIAN ROYAL HYDROGRAPHER.
IT IS BELIEVED THEY WERE THE FIRST WHITE MEN TO SEE THE UPPER WATERS OF THE GREAT RIVER.

1663 - 1728

Cotton Mather

AMERICAN CONGREGATIONAL CLERGYMAN, WRITER AND WITCHCRAFT INVESTIGATOR

HE SUCCEEDED HIS FATHER, INCREASE, AS PURITAN PASTOR OF BOSTON WHERE HE SERVED FROM 1685 UNTIL HIS DEATH. MATHER WAS THE MOST PROLIFIC OF PURITAN WRITERS, AND A CONSERVATIVE UPHOLDER OF PURITAN THEOCRACY. ***ALTHOUGH HE SUPPORTED WITCHCRAFT TRIALS HE DID NOT BELIEVE IN STRONG PUNISHMENT FOR WITCHES.***

HE WAS BORN IN BOSTON, MASS. AND EDUCATED AT HARVARD.

AN AVID PROMOTER OF LEARNING, HE PUBLISHED OVER 400 WORKS ON ***HISTORY, SCIENCE, BIOGRAPHY AND THEOLOGY. HIS LIBRARY CONTAINED 3,000 VOLUMES.***

IN 1721 HE CRUSADED FOR SMALLPOX INOCULATIONS AND DID MUCH TO CHANGE PUBLIC OPINION AGAINST BEING INOCULATED.

KERN

1703-1758
Jonathan Edwards
EARLY AMERICAN THEOLOGIAN
WE MUST HAVE STERNER RELIGIOUS DISCIPLINE!
EDWARDS WROTE AN ESSAY, "THE NATURE OF THE SOUL," WHEN HE WAS 10 YRS. OLD. HE RECEIVED A.B. AND A.M. DEGREES FROM YALE UNIVERSITY. IN 1727, HE WAS ORDAINED AND CALLED TO ASSIST HIS GRANDFATHER IN THE LARGE AND WEALTHY CHURCH OF NORTHAMPTON, WHERE HE BECAME PASTOR IN 1729. EDWARDS WAS A FIRM BELIEVER IN CALVINISM AND THE DOCTRINE OF PREDESTINATION. HE WAS AN OUTSTANDING PULPIT ORATOR. HIS SERMONS RESULTED IN A GREAT NUMBER OF CONVERSIONS. A RELIGIOUS REVIVAL, PART OF THE "GREAT AWAKENING," CAME TO HIS CHURCH IN 1734. HIS SERMON, "SINNERS IN THE HANDS OF AN ANGRY GOD," WAS PREACHED DURING THIS REVIVAL. HIS REFUSAL TO GIVE COMMUNION TO UNCONVERTED CHURCH MEMBERS CAUSED HIS DISMISSAL IN 1750.
HE WAS BORN IN EAST WINDSOR, CONN.
GREETINGS! I HAVE COME TO TALK TO YOU.
CONGRATULATIONS, JONATHAN, YOU WILL BE A GREAT PRESIDENT.
HE WENT TO STOCKBRIDGE, MASS., WHERE HE WAS PASTOR AND MISSIONARY TO THE HOUSATONIC INDIANS. WHILE THERE HE WROTE HIS MOST IMPORTANT WORK, "FREEDOM OF THE WILL," WHICH IS ONE OF THE MOST FAMOUS THEOLOGICAL WORKS EVER WRITTEN IN THE U.S. SOME OF HIS OTHER WORKS ARE "TREATISE ON THE RELIGIOUS AFFECTIONS" AND "DOCTRINE OF ORIGINAL SIN."
IN 1757, HE BECAME PRESIDENT OF THE COLLEGE OF NEW JERSEY (NOW PRINCETON). 5 WKS. LATER HE DIED FROM AN INOCULATION AGAINST SMALLPOX.
KERN

1706-1790

Benjamin Franklin

STATESMAN, DIPLOMAT, EDITOR AND SCIENTIST

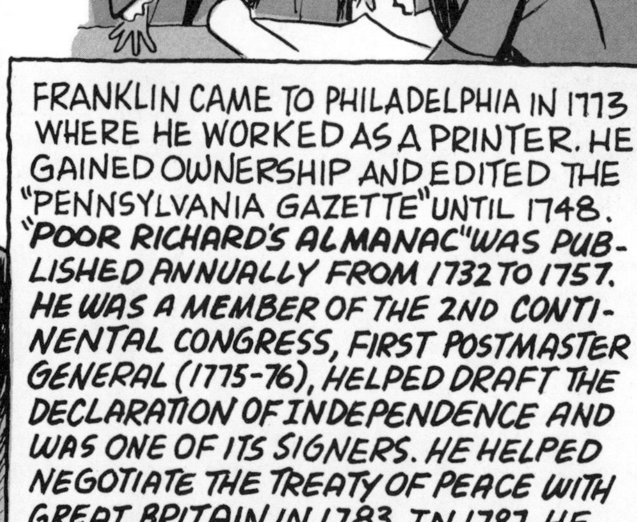

FRANKLIN CAME TO PHILADELPHIA IN 1773 WHERE HE WORKED AS A PRINTER. HE GAINED OWNERSHIP AND EDITED THE "PENNSYLVANIA GAZETTE" UNTIL 1748. "POOR RICHARD'S ALMANAC" WAS PUBLISHED ANNUALLY FROM 1732 TO 1757. HE WAS A MEMBER OF THE 2ND CONTINENTAL CONGRESS, FIRST POSTMASTER GENERAL (1775-76), HELPED DRAFT THE DECLARATION OF INDEPENDENCE AND WAS ONE OF ITS SIGNERS. HE HELPED NEGOTIATE THE TREATY OF PEACE WITH GREAT BRITAIN IN 1783. IN 1787, HE WAS A MEMBER OF THE CONSTITUTIONAL CONVENTION.

HE WAS BORN IN BOSTON, MASS.
HIS STOVE GAVE MORE HEAT AND SAVED ON FUEL.

FRANKLIN WON INTERNATIONAL FAME AS A SCIENTIST AND INVENTOR. HE INVENTED THE FRANKLIN STOVE AND PERFORMED THE KITE EXPERIMENT ***TO IDENTIFY LIGHTNING AND ELECTRICITY***.

YOU CAN BE THE FIRST TO USE MY NEW CIRCULATING LIBRARY.

HE FOUNDED PHILADELPHIA'S FIRST FIRE CO., A CIRCULATING LIBRARY AND A ACADEMY WHICH WAS THE *BEGINNING OF THE UNIVERSITY OF PA.*

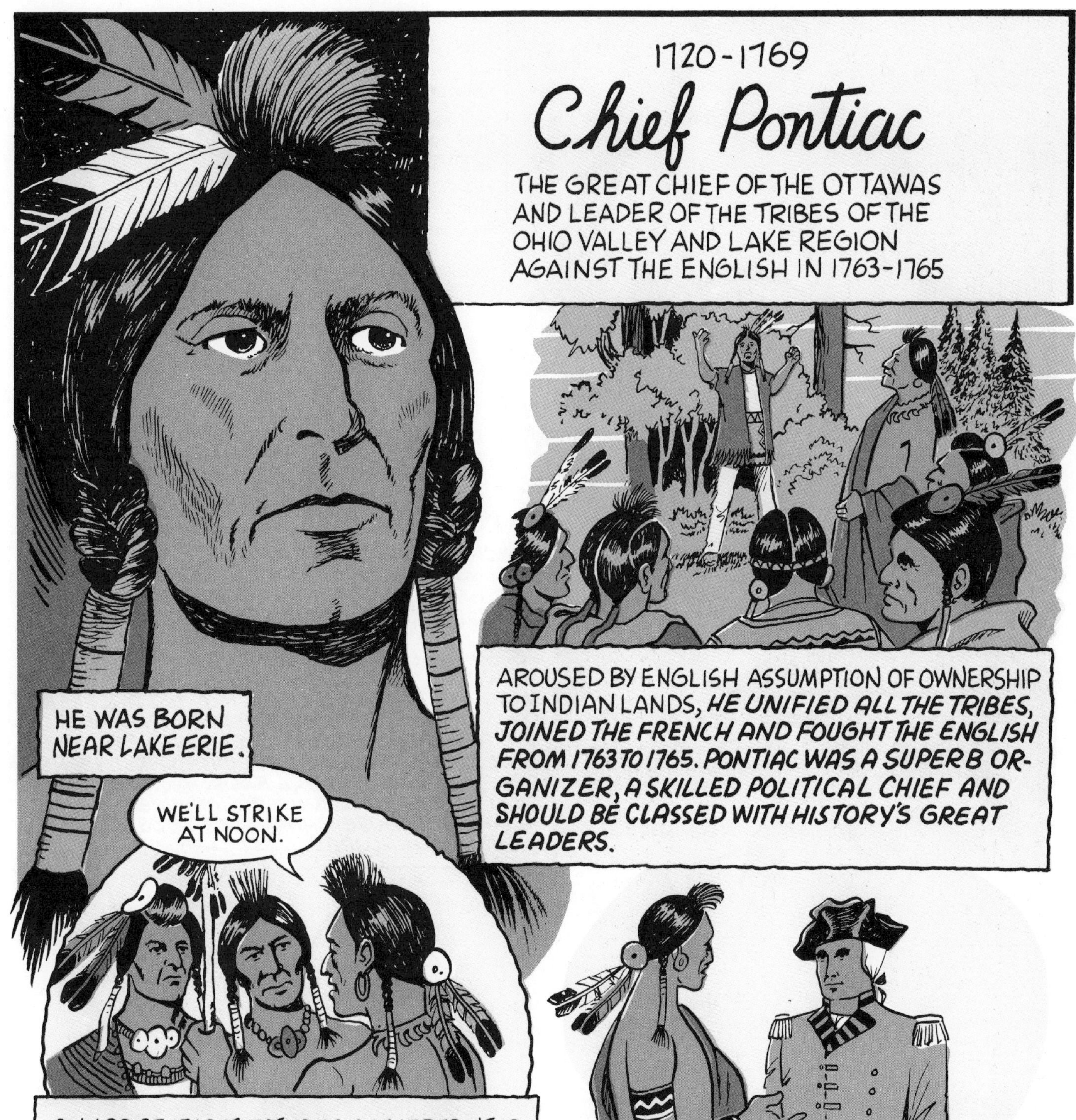
1720-1769
Chief Pontiac
THE GREAT CHIEF OF THE OTTAWAS AND LEADER OF THE TRIBES OF THE OHIO VALLEY AND LAKE REGION AGAINST THE ENGLISH IN 1763-1765
HE WAS BORN NEAR LAKE ERIE.
AROUSED BY ENGLISH ASSUMPTION OF OWNERSHIP TO INDIAN LANDS, HE UNIFIED ALL THE TRIBES, JOINED THE FRENCH AND FOUGHT THE ENGLISH FROM 1763 TO 1765. PONTIAC WAS A SUPERB ORGANIZER, A SKILLED POLITICAL CHIEF AND SHOULD BE CLASSED WITH HISTORY'S GREAT LEADERS.
WE'LL STRIKE AT NOON.
ON APR. 27, 1763, THE TRIBES GATHERED NEAR DETROIT TO HEAR PONTIAC'S PLAN TO CAPTURE THE ENGLISH FORT. A 5-MONTH SIEGE BEGAN, BUT THE ENGLISH AND FRENCH SIGNED A PEACE TREATY, THEREBY ALL AID TO PONTIAC WAS CUT OFF AND HE HAD TO SIGN A TREATY WITH THE ENGLISH AT OSWEGO, N.Y.
NEVER BEFORE HAD AN INDIAN OF NORTH AMERICA LED SO MANY TRIBES AS DID PONTIAC. HE ALWAYS WANTED WHAT WAS BEST FOR HIS PEOPLE!
KERU

1725 - 1792
George Mason
REVOLUTIONARY LEADER, AUTHOR OF VIRGINIA DECLARATION OF RIGHTS AND DELEGATE TO THE CONSTITUTIONAL CONVENTION
YOUR IDEAS IN THIS DOCUMENT ARE SPLENDID, GEORGE.
HE WAS BORN IN FAIRFAX COUNTY, VA.
MASON RECEIVED HIS EDUCATION FROM TUTORS, INCLUDING HIS STUDY OF LAW. HE REFUSED MANY PUBLIC OFFICES, BUT FINALLY AGREED TO BE A MEMBER OF THE THIRD VIRGINIA CONVENTION WHERE HE WROTE THE DECLARATION OF RIGHTS. THOMAS JEFFERSON USED IDEAS FROM THIS DOCUMENT WHEN HE WROTE THE DECLARATION OF INDEPENDENCE. MASON WAS IN FAVOR OF THE PROPOSED FEDERAL CONSTITUTION, BUT OBJECTED TO COMPROMISES ON THE TARIFF AND SLAVERY QUESTIONS. HE BELIEVED THAT SLAVES SHOULD BE EDUCATED FIRST, THEN SET FREE, BUT ON A GRADUAL BASIS. HE REFUSED TO SIGN THE FEDERAL CONSTITUTION WHEN IT WAS ADOPTED BECAUSE MANY OF HIS SUGGESTIONS WERE NOT INCLUDED.
WILL YOU BE GOING INTO THIS AREA, GEORGE?
YES, I PLAN TO CLAIM ALL THE LAND BETWEEN THE MISSISSIPPI RIVER AND THE ALLEGHENY MOUNTAINS.
MISSISSIPPI RIVER
WITHOUT A BILL OF RIGHTS WE ARE DOOMED!
MASON HELPED EXTEND THE WESTERN BORDERS OF THE U.S. BY SPONSORING GEORGE ROGERS CLARK'S EXPEDITION TO THE NORTHWEST TERRITORIES.
KERN
HE WANTED THE CONSTITUTION TO INCLUDE A BILL OF RIGHTS, WHICH WAS NOT ADDED UNTIL AFTER THE CONSTITUTION WAS ADOPTED.

1732 - 1799

George Washington

AMERICAN SOLDIER, STATESMAN, *FIRST PRESIDENT OF THE UNITED STATES (1789-97) AND FATHER OF OUR COUNTRY*

VALLEY FORGE DURING THE WINTER OF 1777-78

WASHINGTON WAS 15 YRS. OLD WHEN HE BECAME AN ASSISTANT SURVEYOR. AT 19 HE WAS A MAJOR IN THE VIRGINIA MILITIA. AT 23 HE WAS THE LEADER OF VIRGINIA'S ARMY. *IN 1775, HE ACCEPTED THE COMMAND OF THE CONTINENTAL ARMY. BECAUSE OF HIS GREAT COURAGE, HE HELD HIS TROOPS TOGETHER THROUGH EVERY HARDSHIP UNTIL FREEDOM FOR THE COLONIES WAS WON IN THE REVOLUTIONARY WAR.*

HE WAS BORN ON A FARM NEAR FREDERICKSBURG, VIRGINIA.

DURING HIS ADMINISTRATION, THE *TREASURY, WAR, STATE DEPT'S AND THE SUPREME COURT WERE ESTABLISHED. THE FIRST 10 AMENDMENTS TO THE CONSTITUTION WERE ADOPTED IN 1791.*

HIS MOST BRILLIANT ACHIEVEMENT WAS HIS SECRET AND SPEEDY MARCH FROM HUDSON TO CHESAPEAKE BAY *WHERE HE FORCED CORNWALLIS TO SURRENDER AT YORKTOWN OCT. 19, 1781, THUS ENDING THE WAR.*

KERN

1734 - 1820

Daniel Boone

THE MOST FAMOUS PIONEER OF COLONIAL TIMES

BOONE, THE EXPLORER, WENT INTO THE UNKNOWN FORESTS AND LAND OF KENTUCKY, BLAZING TRAILS TO LEAD THE SETTLERS THERE. ***HIS WILDERNESS ROAD OVER THE ALLEGHENY MTS. BECAME ONE OF THE MOST IMPORTANT ROUTES TO THE WEST. BY 1800 THOUSANDS OF SETTLERS HAD TRAVELED WESTWARD OVER THIS ROUTE.***

HE WAS BORN NEAR THE PRESENT SITE OF READING, PA.

IN 1769, HE WAS CAPTURED BY THE SHAWNEE INDIANS. ***CHIEF BLACKFISH ADOPTED HIM INTO THE TRIBE. HE WAS GREATLY ADMIRED FOR HIS SKILL AS A HUNTER AND WOODSMAN. BOONE SOON ESCAPED AND MADE HIS WAY BACK TO HIS PEOPLE.***

BOONE BUILT A FORT BY THE KENTUCKY RIVER NEAR THE ***WILDERNESS ROAD AND CALLED IT BOONESBORO.***

KERN

1735-1818

Paul Revere

AMERICAN PATRIOT AND EXPERT CRAFTSMAN

HE WENT TO SCHOOL IN BOSTON AND LEARNED THE SILVERSMITH TRADE. HAVING BECOME INTERESTED IN THE MOVEMENT FOR INDEPENDENCE, ***REVERE PARTICIPATED IN THE BOSTON TEA PARTY AND WORKED HARD FOR THE RATIFICATION OF THE CONSTITUTION. HE WAS THE FIRST AMERICAN TO DISCOVER THE PROCESS FOR ROLLING SHEET COPPER, AND BUILT THE FIRST COPPER ROLLING MILL IN THE U.S. HE CAST BRONZE CANNON FOR THE ARMY AND LATER CHURCH BELLS WHICH ARE STILL USED IN NEW ENGLAND.***

AFTER THE WAR, REVERE WENT BACK TO HIS SILVERSMITH TRADE IN BOSTON. ***MANY OF HIS WORKS ARE REGARDED AS MASTERPIECES, AND ARE PRIZED TODAY BY MUSEUMS AND COLLECTORS.***

ON APR. 18-19, 1775, ***REVERE MADE HIS MEMORABLE RIDE TO LEXINGTON TO WARN HANCOCK AND ADAMS OF THEIR DANGER, AND TO ROUSE THE MINUTEMEN TO ARMS.***

KERN

1735 - 1826

John Adams

PATRIOT, LEGISLATOR, FIRST VICE-PRESIDENT (1789-97) AND ***SECOND*** PRESIDENT OF THE UNITED STATES (1797-01)

THIS WILL BE A LASTING PEACE.

ADAMS GRADUATED FROM HARVARD IN 1755. THREE YEARS LATER HE WAS ADMITTED TO THE BAR. AS A DELEGATE TO THE FIRST AND SECOND CONTINENTAL CONGRESS, HE RECOMMENDED WASHINGTON FOR COMMANDER OF THE ARMY. ***ADAMS DEFENDED AND GUIDED THE DECLARATION OF INDEPENDENCE IN ITS PASSAGE THROUGH CONGRESS. IN 1783, HE WORKED WITH FRANKLIN AND JAY NEGOTIATING THE PARIS PEACE TREATY WITH GREAT BRITAIN. ADAMS STAYED ON TO SERVE AS U.S. MINISTER (1785-1788). IN 1796, HE WAS ELECTED PRESIDENT TO SUCCEED GEORGE WASHINGTON. ADAMS WAS THE FIRST PRESIDENT TO LIVE IN THE WHITE HOUSE. HE MOVED INTO THE INCOMPLETE MANSION IN 1800.***

HE WAS BORN IN QUINCY, MASS.

CONGRATULATIONS, SON.

ADAMS LIVED TO SEE HIS SON, JOHN QUINCY, BECOME THE NATION'S ***SIXTH PRESIDENT!***

DURING ADAMS' TERM, THE SHIPS, ***"UNITED STATES," "CONSTITUTION" AND "CONSTELLATION" WERE THE FIRST OF A NEW U.S. NAVY. BY 1799 THE U.S. HAD A FLEET OF 49 SHIPS.***

KERN

1736-1799
Patrick Henry
REVOLUTIONARY LEADER, ORATOR, PATRIOT, STATESMAN, MEMBER OF THE CONTINENTAL CONGRESS AND GOVERNOR OF VIRGINIA
HENRY WAS LICENSED TO PRACTICE LAW IN 1760 AND SOON BECAME ONE OF THE LEADING LAWYERS IN WESTERN VIRGINIA. HE WAS A DELEGATE TO THE FIRST CONTINENTAL CONGRESS BETWEEN 1774-1776. THROUGH HIS EFFORTS THE BILL OF RIGHTS WAS ADOPTED AS THE FIRST TEN AMENDMENTS TO THE CONSTITUTION.
HE WAS BORN IN HANOVER COUNTY, VIRGINIA.
HENRY WAS OFFERED MANY GOVERNMENTAL JOBS INCLUDING U.S. SENATOR IN 1794, U.S. SEC. OF STATE AND CHIEF JUSTICE OF THE U.S. SUPREME COURT IN 1795, BUT DECLINED SO HE COULD CONTINUE HIS LAW PRACTICE.
KERN
ON MAR. 23, 1775, IN A SPEECH RESISTING BRITISH POLICY HE DECLARED, "I KNOW NOT WHAT COURSE OTHERS WILL TAKE, BUT AS FOR ME, GIVE ME LIBERTY OR GIVE ME DEATH!"

1737 – 1793
John Hancock
PRESIDENT OF THE CONTINENTAL CONGRESS FROM 1775 TO 1777, AND THE FIRST GOVERNOR OF MASSACHUSETTS
I DEMAND MY SHIP BACK!
HANCOCK GRADUATED FROM HARVARD IN 1754. HE HEADED A BOSTON MERCANTILE HOUSE IN 1764. HE FIRST HAD TROUBLE WITH THE BRITISH GOVERNMENT IN 1768 WHEN CUSTOM OFFICERS SEIZED HIS SHIP "LIBERTY" FOR UNLOADING A CARGO OF WINE WITHOUT PAYING IMPORT DUTIES. HE VIGOROUSLY RESISTED, THEREBY GAINING WIDE POPULARITY AMONG ANTI-BRITISH LEADERS IN MASSACHUSETTS.
HE WAS BORN IN QUINCY, MASS.
John Hancock
HANCOCK WAS THE FIRST SIGNER OF THE DECLARATION OF INDEPENDENCE ON JULY 4, 1776. THE OTHER DELEGATES SIGNED LATER.
GENTLEMEN, WE MUST GO FORWARD!
HE WAS THE FIRST GOV. OF MASSACHUSETTS FROM 1780 TO 1785, AND AGAIN FROM 1787 UNTIL HIS DEATH IN 1793.
KERN

1737 - 1809

Thomas Paine

REVOLUTIONARY AGITATOR, AUTHOR AND PHILOSOPHER

PAINE CAME TO PHILADELPHIA IN 1774 WHERE HE WROTE ARTICLES FOR "*THE PENNSYLVANIA MAGAZINE*" *IN 1776, HE PUBLISHED HIS PAMPHLET CALLED "COMMON SENSE" WHICH ARGUED FOR COMPLETE AND IMMEDIATE INDEPENDENCE. 120,000 COPIES OF HIS PAMPHLET WERE SOLD IN THE FIRST THREE MONTHS. THE TOTAL SALE WAS 500,000 COPIES. IN "THE RIGHTS OF MAN" PAINE DEFENDED THE REPUBLICAN FORM OF GOVERNMENT AND THE FRENCH REVOLUTION.*

HE WAS BORN IN THETFORD, NORFOLK, ENGLAND.

HE WROTE THE "*CRISIS*" PAPERS WHICH STATED IN PART "*THESE ARE TIMES THAT TRY MEN'S SOULS. THE SUMMER SOLDIER AND THE SUNSHINE PATRIOT WILL IN THIS CRISIS SHRINK FROM THE SERVICE OF THEIR COUNTRY.*" *THIS PAMPHLET WAS ORDERED READ TO THE REVOLUTIONARY TROOPS, BECAUSE OF ITS ELOQUENT PATRIOTISM.*

HERE'S MY REPORT.

HE SERVED AS *SECRETARY OF THE COMMITTEE ON FOREIGN AFFAIRS OF THE CONTINENTAL CONGRESS. PAINE LIVED HIS LAST YEARS IN POVERTY AND OBSCURITY.*

KERN

1738 - 1815

John Singleton Copley

AMERICA'S FIRST GREAT PAINTER

HE WAS BORN IN BOSTON, MASS.

HE STUDIED PAINTING FROM HIS STEPFATHER, A WELL-KNOWN PAINTER AND ENGRAVER. FROM 1757 UNTIL HE WENT TO LONDON IN 1775 HE PAINTED MANY EMINENT PEOPLE, ***INCLUDING GEORGE WASHINGTON, JOHN HANCOCK AND SAMUEL ADAMS. WHILE LIVING IN LONDON HE BECAME AN ASSOCIATE MEMBER OF THE ROYAL ACADEMY AND 2 YRS. LATER WAS ADMITTED TO FULL MEMBERSHIP. SOME OF HIS HISTORICAL PAINTINGS WHICH BROUGHT HIM FAME WERE "DEATH OF CHATHAM," "DEATH OF MAJOR PIERSON" AND "SEIGE AND RELIEF OF GIBRALTAR."***

THIS PORTRAIT OF GOV. THOMAS MIFFLIN AND HIS WIFE WAS PAINTED BEFORE HIS TRIP TO EUROPE IN 1774. ***IT HAS BEEN COMPARED TO THE WORK OF VERMEER FOR ITS CAREFUL ATTENTION TO SMALL DETAILS.***

HIS REMARKABLE PORTRAITS OF MEMBERS OF COLONIAL SOCIETY INCLUDE ***MRS. THOMAS BOYLSTON, PAUL REVERE, WILLIAM PENN AND MRS. EZEKIEL GOLDTHWAIT. ANOTHER OF HIS MEMORABLE PAINTINGS IS "WATSON AND THE SHARK."***

KERN

1742 - 1786
Nathanael Greene
AMERICAN REVOLUTIONARY GENERAL
YOU ARE A CREDIT TO OUR GREAT NATION!
GREENE WAS BROUGHT UP IN A QUAKER FAMILY. BECAUSE HE SHOWED INTEREST IN MILITARY AFFAIRS THE PACIFIST CHURCH EXPELLED HIM. A MEMBER OF THE RHODE ISLAND LEGISLATURE, HE SAW THE COMING CONFLICT BETWEEN THE AMERICAN COLONIES AND GREAT BRITAIN. IN 1775, HE WAS APPOINTED BRIG. GENERAL IN THE CONTINENTAL ARMY AND TOOK AN ACTIVE PART IN THE SEIGE OF BOSTON. AFTER WINNING PRAISES FROM GEORGE WASHINGTON, HE WAS MADE A MAJOR GENERAL AND COMMANDED THE ARMY OF OCCUPATION IN BOSTON. GREENE FOUGHT IN THE BATTLES OF TRENTON, BRANDYWINE AND GERMANTOWN AND SERVED AT VALLEY FORGE. NEXT TO GEORGE WASHINGTON, HISTORIANS RANK HIM AS ONE OF OUR GREAT MILITARY STRATEGISTS OF THE AMERICAN REVOLUTION.
HE WAS BORN IN WARWICK, R.I.
THIS STATUE STANDS IN RHODE ISLAND'S CAPITOL.
IN 1869 R.I. PLACED A STATUE OF GREENE IN STATUARY HALL, WASH., D.C.
HERE'S YOUR DEED TO THIS BEAUTIFUL PLANTATION, GENERAL.
I AM MOST GRATEFUL TO THE PEOPLE OF GEORGIA.
IN 1780, GREENE REPLACED GEN. GATES, WHOSE ARMY HAD BEEN SEVERELY BEATEN AT CAMDEN, S.C. BECAUSE OF GREENE'S BRILLIANT MANEUVERS HIS ARMY PUSHED THE BRITISH BACK INTO CHARLESTON AND SAVANNAH, GA. FOR THIS VICTORY GEORGIA GAVE HIM A PLANTATION WHERE HE RETIRED IN 1785.
KERN

1743 - 1826

Thomas Jefferson

SCIENTIST, ARCHITECT, ADVOCATE OF RELIGIOUS FREEDOM, APOSTLE OF AGRARIAN DEMOCRACY, GOVERNOR, SEC. OF STATE, VICE-PRESIDENT AND ***THIRD*** PRESIDENT OF THE UNITED STATES (1801-09)

I NEED YOUR SUPPORT FOR MY LAND ORDINANCE BILL.

JEFFERSON GRADUATED FROM THE COLLEGE OF WILLIAM AND MARY IN 1762. HE STUDIED LAW AND WAS ADMITTED TO THE BAR IN 1767. WHILE IN CONGRESS FROM 1783-84, ***HE DRAFTED THE LAND ORDINANCE, WHICH WAS THE BASIS FOR THE ORGANIZATION OF THE TERRITORIES.*** HE FOLLOWED FRANKLIN AS ***MINISTER TO FRANCE, AND WAS WASHINGTON'S FIRST SEC. OF STATE. IN 1880, HE TIED WITH AARON BURR IN ELECTORAL VOTES FOR THE PRESIDENCY. WITH HAMILTON'S SUPPORT, THE HOUSE OF REPRESENTATIVES CHOSE JEFFERSON PRESIDENT. HIS ADMINISTRATION WAS ONE OF SIMPLICITY AND ECONOMY.***

HE WAS 33 YRS. OLD ***WHEN HE AUTHORED THE DECLARATION OF INDEPENDENCE. THIS WAS THE MOST IMPORTANT PIECE OF WRITING IN AMERICAN HISTORY.***

KERN

THE GREATEST EVENT IN HIS ADMINISTRATION WAS ***THE PURCHASE OF LOUISIANA FROM FRANCE FOR $15,000,000. THE AREA, OVER 800,000 SQUARE MILES, WAS PURCHASED FOR LESS THAN 3¢ AN ACRE. THIS LAND DOUBLED THE AREA OF THE UNITED STATES!***

1745 - 1816
Francis Asbury
A FOUNDER AND BISHOP OF THE METHODIST EPISCOPAL CHURCH IN THE UNITED STATES
HE WAS BORN IN HAMSTEAD BRIDGE, ENGLAND.
IN 1771, ASBURY WAS SENT FROM ENGLAND AS A MISSIONARY TO AMERICA. HE WAS THE FIRST METHODIST BISHOP CONSECRATED IN AMERICA, IN 1784. IT IS ESTIMATED THAT HE TRAVELED 270,000 MILES, MOSTLY ON HORSEBACK, TO BRING HIS RELIGION TO THE PEOPLE. HE ESTABLISHED THE CIRCUIT RIDER SYSTEM AS AN IMPORTANT PART OF AMERICAN RELIGIOUS LIFE.
ASBURY RANKS WITH JOHN WESLEY, THE GREAT ENGLISH RELIGIOUS REFORMER, IN THE METHODIST MOVEMENT OF HIS TIME.
HE PREACHED 16,500 SERMONS AND ORDAINED MORE THAN 4,000 MINISTERS.
KERN

1745 - 1829

John Jay

DIPLOMAT, STATESMAN, AUTHOR AND FIRST CHIEF JUSTICE OF THE SUPREME COURT, SERVING FROM 1790 TO 1795

ENGLAND AND AMERICA MUST WORK TOGETHER.

HE WAS BORN IN NEW YORK CITY.

JAY WAS EDUCATED AT KING'S COLLEGE (NOW COLUMBIA UNIVERSITY) AND ADMITTED TO THE BAR IN 1768. ***HE WAS A MEMBER OF THE FIRST AND SECOND CONTINENTAL CONGRESS. JAY WAS A MEMBER OF THE U.S. DELEGATION TO PARIS IN 1783 TO NEGOTIATE PEACE WITH ENGLAND AFTER THE AMERICANS HAD DEFEATED THE ENGLISH IN THE REVOLUTIONARY WAR.*** IN 1794, ***HE WAS SENT TO ENGLAND TO SETTLE SERIOUS DIFFERENCES. ALTHOUGH HE HAD TO GIVE CONCESSIONS HIS "JAY'S TREATY" AVERTED WAR AT THAT TIME.***

JOHN, YOU ARE THE ONE I WANT FOR THE SUPREME COURT.

THIS IS A SURPRISE!

GEORGE WASHINGTON APPOINTED HIM ***CHIEF JUSTICE OF THE SUPREME COURT. JAY HAD THE UNDERSTANDING OF WHAT WAS NEEDED TO KEEP THE COUNTRY GOING DURING ITS VERY DIFFICULT EARLY YEARS.***

JAY RETURNED FROM ENGLAND AFTER COMPLETING "***JAY'S TREATY***" TO FIND TO HIS SURPRISE THAT HE HAD BEEN ELECTED GOVERNOR OF NEW YORK STATE. ***HE RESIGNED FROM THE SUPREME COURT TO SERVE AS GOVERNOR FROM 1795 TO 1801.***

KERN

1747-1792
John Paul Jones
NAVAL OFFICER IN THE REVOLUTIONARY WAR
AT THE BEGINNING OF THE REVOLUTIONARY WAR, JONES WAS COMMISSIONED A SENIOR LIEUTENANT OF THE AMERICAN FLAGSHIP "ALFRED." IN 1776, HE WAS PROMOTED TO CAPTAIN, COMMANDING THE "PROVIDENCE", THE "ALFRED" AND THE "RANGER". HE CRUISED THE WEST INDIES AND THE COAST OF GREAT BRITAIN FROM 1776 TO 1778, CAPTURING AND DESTROYING BRITISH SHIPS.
HE WAS BORN IN KIRKBEAN, KIRKCUDBRIGHTSHIRE, SCOTLAND.
SOME DAY YOU WILL COMMAND A SHIP.
JOHN PAUL WAS 12 YRS. OLD WHEN HE SAILED AS A CABIN BOY TO FREDERICKSBURG, VA. IN 1773, HE ADDED THE SURNAME JONES, AFTER A FRIEND WILLIE JONES, WHO HAD BEEN KIND TO HIM.
KERN
WHILE COMMANDING THE "BONHOMME RICHARD" IN 1779, HE FOUGHT THE FAMOUS BATTLE WITH THE BRITISH MAN-OF-WAR, "SERAPIS." THE BRITISH SHIP WAS CAPTURED. JONES' SHIP WAS SO BADLY DAMAGED THAT IT SANK TWO DAYS LATER.

CONGRESSMAN, SECRETARY OF STATE AND **FOURTH** PRESIDENT OF THE UNITED STATES (1809-17)

MADISON WAS EDUCATED AT THE COLLEGE OF NEW JERSEY (*NOW PRINCETON UNIVERSITY*). ***HE PUT FORTH EVERY EFFORT FOR THE INDEPENDENCE OF THE COLONIES. HE WAS ELECTED TO THE CONSTITUTIONAL CONVENTION AT PHILADELPHIA IN 1787, WHERE HE PLAYED A VITAL PART IN THE ADOPTION OF THE CONSTITUTION. THIS EARNED HIM THE TITLE "THE FATHER OF OUR CONSTITUTION."***

HE WAS BORN IN PORT CONWAY, VIRGINIA.

THIS IS MY LEGACY TO FUTURE GENERATIONS.
KERN

AS A CONGRESSMAN (1789-97), ***HE WAS THE CHIEF AUTHOR OF THE FIRST 10 AMENDMENTS TO THE CONSTITUTION, KNOWN AS "THE BILL OF RIGHTS."***

MADISON AND HIS WIFE DOLLY WERE FORCED TO LEAVE THE WHITE HOUSE WHEN THE BRITISH LOOTED AND BURNED IT ALONG WITH THE CAPITOL DURING THE WAR OF 1812. ***DOLLY SAVED THE DECLARATION OF INDEPENDENCE AND A VALUABLE PORTRAIT OF WASHINGTON.***

1752-1818

George Rogers Clark

AMERICAN REVOLUTIONARY OFFICER AND FRONTIERSMAN

CLARK CONQUERED THE NORTHWEST AND EXPLORED THE OHIO AND KENTUCKY RIVERS FROM 1772 TO 1774. WHEN THE REVOLUTIONARY WAR BROKE OUT, HE WAS A MAJOR IN CHARGE OF THE DEFENSE OF KENTUCKY. **IN A HEROIC WINTER MARCH OF 180 MILES, HE CAPTURED STRATEGIC VINCENNES, FORCING LT. GOV. HENRY HAMILTON TO SURRENDER IN FEB. 1779. CLARK CONTINUED TO FIGHT THE ENGLISH FOR THE REMAINDER OF THE WAR. FOR HIS LOYALTY HE WAS MADE A BRIGADIER GENERAL.**

HE WAS BORN IN CHARLOTTESVILLE, VIRGINIA.

THIS WILL GIVE AMERICA A BIG BOOST IN LAND AREA.

AFTER THE WAR, HE BECAME INTERESTED IN **INDIAN HISTORY AND ARCHAEOLOGY.**

CLARK'S CONQUEST OF THE NORTHWEST ENABLED THE U.S. GOVERNMENT IN THE PEACE NEGOTIATIONS OF 1782-83, TO **CLAIM ALL THE LAND BETWEEN THE MISSISSIPPI RIVER AND THE ALLEGHENY MOUNTAINS.**

KERN

1755-1804

Alexander Hamilton

AMERICAN STATESMAN, ***FIRST*** U.S. SECRETARY OF THE TREASURY AND SIGNER OF THE CONSTITUTION

I HOPE YOU WILL ACCEPT THIS VERY IMPORTANT POSITION.

HAMILTON WROTE MANY PAMPHLETS FOR THE PATRIOTIC CAUSE. HE BECAME A CAPTAIN IN THE ARTILLERY AND SERVED WITH DISTINCTION. ***WASHINGTON MADE HIM HIS AID-DE-CAMP AND PRIVATE SECRETARY. THROUGH THE "FEDERALIST PAPERS" HE DID MUCH TO GET THE CONSTITUTION RATIFIED. FROM 1789-1795 HAMILTON WAS APPOINTED FIRST SEC. OF THE TREASURY AND ESTABLISHED THE BANK OF THE U.S. HE FAVORED A STRONG CENTRAL GOVERNMENT AND ACCURATELY VISUALIZED FUTURE AMERICA AS A HEALTHY INDUSTRIAL LAND.***

HE WAS BORN ON THE WEST INDIAN ISLAND OF NEVIS.
THANK YOU, GENTLEMEN. I MUST DECLINE.

HE WAS FATALLY SHOT IN A DUEL WITH AARON BURR IN WEEHAWKEN, N.Y., ***AND DIED THE NEXT DAY.***

HAMILTON RESIGNED AS SEC. OF THE TREASURY IN 1795. ***HE WAS OFFERED AN APPOINTMENT AS CHIEF JUSTICE OF THE SUPREME COURT BUT HE DECLINED AND RETURNED TO HIS LAW PRACTICE IN NEW YORK.***

KERN

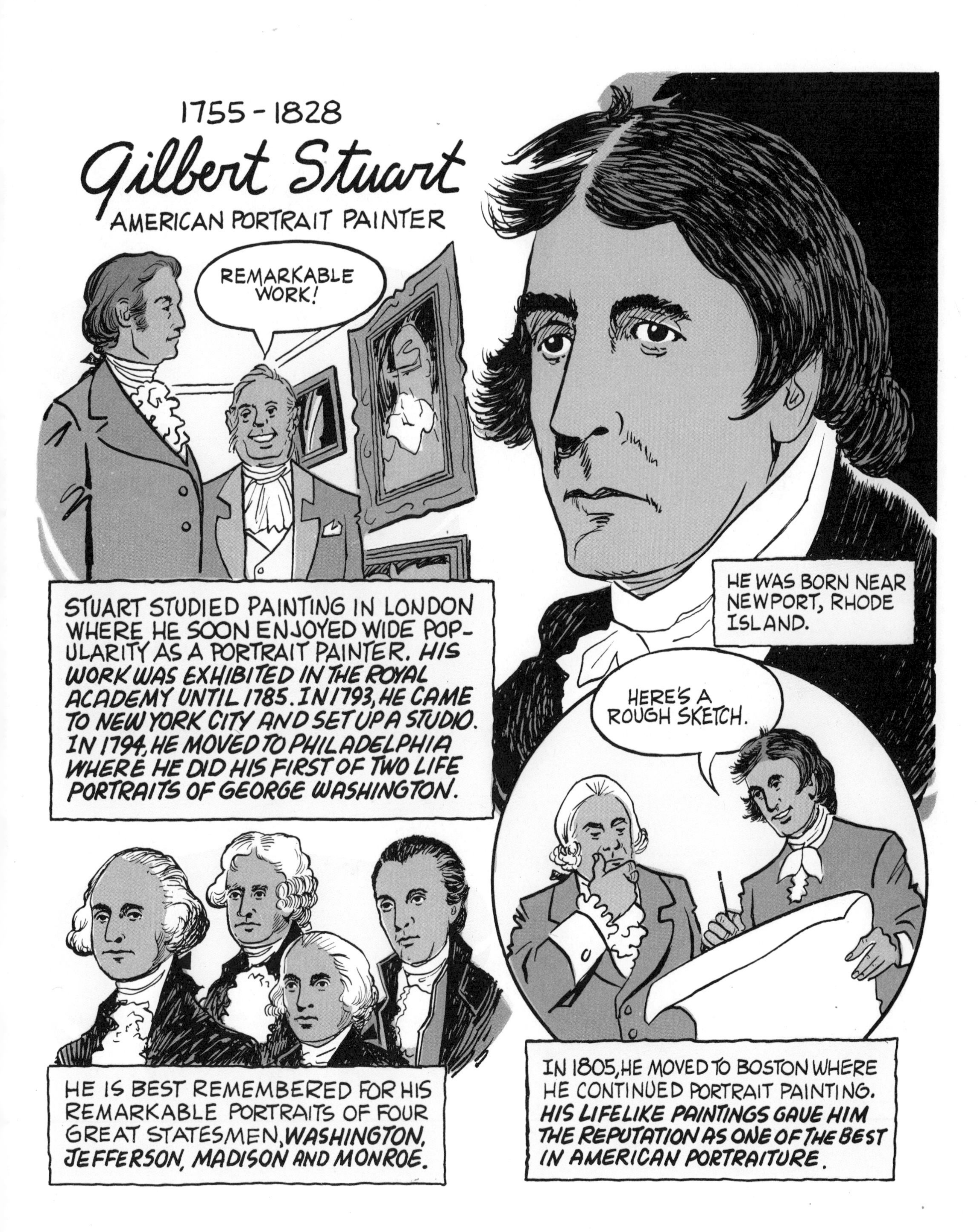
1755 - 1828
Gilbert Stuart
AMERICAN PORTRAIT PAINTER
REMARKABLE WORK!
HE WAS BORN NEAR NEWPORT, RHODE ISLAND.
STUART STUDIED PAINTING IN LONDON WHERE HE SOON ENJOYED WIDE POPULARITY AS A PORTRAIT PAINTER. HIS WORK WAS EXHIBITED IN THE ROYAL ACADEMY UNTIL 1785. IN 1793, HE CAME TO NEW YORK CITY AND SET UP A STUDIO. IN 1794, HE MOVED TO PHILADELPHIA WHERE HE DID HIS FIRST OF TWO LIFE PORTRAITS OF GEORGE WASHINGTON.
HERE'S A ROUGH SKETCH.
HE IS BEST REMEMBERED FOR HIS REMARKABLE PORTRAITS OF FOUR GREAT STATESMEN, WASHINGTON, JEFFERSON, MADISON AND MONROE.
IN 1805, HE MOVED TO BOSTON WHERE HE CONTINUED PORTRAIT PAINTING. HIS LIFELIKE PAINTINGS GAVE HIM THE REPUTATION AS ONE OF THE BEST IN AMERICAN PORTRAITURE.

1755 - 1835

John Marshall

DIPLOMAT, SEC. OF STATE UNDER JOHN ADAMS, AND CHIEF JUSTICE OF THE U.S. SUPREME COURT (1801-35)

THE SUPREME COURT CAN DECLARE LAWS UNCONSTITUTIONAL.

HE SERVED IN THE AMERICAN REVOLUTION, FIRST AS A LIEUTENANT, AND THEN AS A CAPTAIN IN THE CONTINENTAL ARMY. MARSHALL STUDIED LAW AT WILLIAM AND MARY COLLEGE AND BEGAN PRACTICE IN 1783. ***HE WAS A DELEGATE TO THE STATE CONVENTION WHICH RATIFIED THE FEDERAL CONSTITUTION IN 1788. WHILE CHIEF JUSTICE OF THE SUPREME COURT, HE MADE IT THE INDISPUTABLE RIGHT OF THE SUPREME COURT TO REVIEW FEDERAL AND STATE LAWS.***

HE WAS BORN IN MIDLAND, VIRGINIA.

WE MUST ESTABLISH GOOD RELATIONSHIPS BETWEEN THE THREE BRANCHES OF GOVERNMENT.

I BELIEVE IN A STRONG FEDERAL GOVERNMENT SO WE CAN ACT EFFECTIVELY AS A NATION.

WHEN MARSHALL BECAME CHIEF JUSTICE IN 1801, ***THE SUPREME COURT WAS WEAK AND INEFFECTIVE. AT THE TIME OF HIS DEATH 34 YRS. LATER, THE COURT HAD BECOME A VIGOROUS BRANCH OF OUR GOVERNMENT.***

MARSHALL WAS KNOWN AS "***THE GREAT CHIEF JUSTICE.***" ***HE SERVED FOR 34 YRS. AND ESTABLISHED THE HIGH PRESTIGE THE COURT NOW HOLDS.***

KERN

1758-1831

James Monroe

AMERICAN STATESMAN AND ***FIFTH*** PRESIDENT OF THE UNITED STATES (1817-25)

MONROE DISTINGUISHED HIMSELF IN THE CONTINENTAL ARMY RISING FROM A LIEUTENANT TO A LT. COLONEL. HE STUDIED LAW UNDER JEFFERSON'S GUIDANCE. ***MONROE SERVED IN CONGRESS, WAS U.S. SENATOR FROM VIRGINIA, U.S. MINISTER TO FRANCE, GOV. OF VIRGINIA, U.S. MINISTER TO GREAT BRITAIN, U.S. SEC. OF STATE, AND U.S. SEC. OF WAR BEFORE BECOMING THE FIFTH U.S. PRESIDENT. MONROE'S ADMINISTRATION WAS KNOWN AS THE "ERA OF GOOD FEELING."***

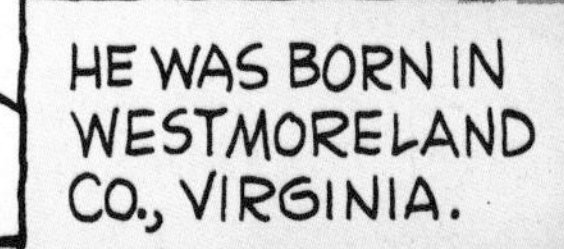
HE WAS BORN IN WESTMORELAND CO., VIRGINIA.

DURING HIS ADMINISTRATION THE FIRST STEAMSHIP CROSSED THE ATLANTIC IN 1819, FLORIDA WAS PURCHASED FROM SPAIN IN 1821, THE FIRST PUBLIC SCHOOL WAS STARTED AND 5 STATES JOINED THE UNION FROM 1817 TO 1821.

THE MONROE DOCTRINE, HIS GREATEST ACHIEVEMENT, WAS PROCLAIMED IN 1823. THIS DOCTRINE WAS A WARNING TO EUROPEAN POWERS TO KEEP HANDS OFF THE AMERICAS.

1758-1843

Noah Webster

AMERICAN EDUCATOR, JOURNALIST, FOUNDER OF AMHERST COLLEGE AND THE COMPILER OF THE ***ORIGINAL "WEBSTER'S DICTIONARY."***

AFTER GRADUATING FROM YALE, HE STUDIED LAW AND WAS ADMITTED TO THE BAR AT HARTFORD WHERE HE PRACTICED FROM 1789 TO 1793. ***WHILE TEACHING SCHOOL IN 1782 HE COMPILED A SPELLING BOOK, A GRAMMAR BOOK AND FINALLY A READER FOR SCHOOL CHILDREN. BY 1890, TWO MILLION SPELLING BOOKS HAD BEEN SOLD.***

HE WAS BORN IN WEST HARTFORD, CONNECTICUT.

WEBSTER CAMPAIGNED FOR THE FIRST COPYRIGHT LAWS AND WROTE MANY POLITICAL PAMPHLETS AS A MEMBER OF THE FEDERALIST PARTY. ***HE WAS A PIONEER IN THE FIELD OF LEXICOGRAPHY.***

CONGRATULATIONS, NOAH, FOR ONE OF HISTORY'S GREATEST CONTRIBUTIONS!

HE PUBLISHED HIS FIRST DICTIONARY IN 1806. IN 1828, HE PUBLISHED 2 VOLS. CALLED ***"AN AMERICAN DICTIONARY OF THE ENGLISH LANGUAGE." THIS EDITION WAS ENLARGED FOR AN EDITION INCLUDING 12,000 WORDS AND 40,000 DEFINITIONS THAT HAD NEVER APPEARED IN A DICTIONARY BEFORE.***

KERN

1763-1844
Charles Bulfinch
NOTED EARLY AMERICAN ARCHITECT
BULFINCH WAS A GRADUATE OF HARVARD UNIVERSITY. FROM 1785-87 HE TRAVELED ABROAD TO STUDY ARCHITECTURE. IN 1783 HE DESIGNED THE FIRST PLAYHOUSE ERECTED IN NEW ENGLAND, THE OLD FEDERAL ST. THEATER IN BOSTON. HE PLANNED THE STATE HOUSE IN BOSTON WHICH WAS FINISHED IN 1798. OTHER BUILDINGS BULFINCH DESIGNED WERE THE SUFFOLK COUNTY COURTHOUSE IN BOSTON, THE UNIVERSITY HALL IN CAMBRIDGE, THE CITY HALL AT HARTFORD, CONN., THE MASSACHUSETTS GENERAL HOSPITAL AND THE LEAN ASYLUM IN SUMMERVILLE. BULFINCH SERVED FOR 20YRS. AS CHAIRMAN OF THE BOARD OF SELECTMEN OF BOSTON. THIS OFFICE CORRESPONDED WITH THE MAYOR'S OFFICE OF TODAY.
HE WAS BORN IN BOSTON, MASS.
WE'LL START CONSTRUCTING THE ROTUNDA IMMEDIATELY.
IN 1817 HE SUCCEEDED BENJAMIN LATROBE AS ARCHITECT OF THE CAPITOL IN WASH., D.C. THE ROTUNDA WAS BUILT FROM HIS OWN DRAWINGS AFTER PLANS SUGGESTED BY LATROBE. BULFINCH DESIGNED THE WEST APPROACHES AND THE PORTICO. THE BUILDING WAS COMPLETED IN 1830.
THESE BOW FRONT HOUSES WERE BUILT FROM BULFINCH'S PLANS.
IN ITS DAY IT WAS THE MOST IMPROVED OF MODERN ELEGANCE.
MANY HOMES ON BOSTON'S FAMOUS BEACON HILL WERE DESIGNED BY BULFINCH. HIS WORK DIRECTLY INFLUENCED THE FEDERAL STYLE.
KERN

1763 - 1848

John Jacob Astor

FUR TRADER, MERCHANT AND FINANCIER

ASTOR CAME TO NEW YORK CITY IN 1783 AND WENT INTO THE FUR BUSINESS, DEALING DIRECTLY WITH THE INDIANS. ***HE ORGANIZED THE AMERICAN FUR COMPANY IN 1808 AND ESTABLISHED TRADING POSTS ALONG THE MISSOURI AND COLUMBIA RIVERS. AFTER THE WAR OF 1812 HE SHIPPED HIS FURS TO MANY FOREIGN COUNTRIES, NOTABLY CHINA. ASTOR BOUGHT LARGE TRACTS OF LAND ON MANHATTAN ISLAND WHICH LATER BECAME THE CENTER OF NEW YORK CITY.***

HE WAS BORN IN WALDORF, GERMANY.

THIS LIBRARY WILL BENEFIT ALL OF THE PEOPLE.

WHEN ASTOR DIED IN 1848, HE WAS ***THE RICHEST MAN IN AMERICA. HIS FORTUNE WAS ESTIMATED AT $30,000,000. HE GAVE $400,000 FOR THE ESTABLISHMENT OF THE NEW YORK PUBLIC LIBRARY.***

IN 1811, HE BUILT ASTORIA AT THE MOUTH OF THE COLUMBIA RIVER ON THE PACIFIC COAST, ***BUT LOST IT DURING THE WAR OF 1812. THROUGHOUT THE WAR HE WAS TRADING WITH THE BRITISH IN THE GREAT LAKES REGION.***

KERN

1764-1820

Benjamin H. Latrobe

ARCHITECT AND CIVIL ENGINEER

THANKS FOR APPROVING MY PLANS.

LATROBE CAME TO THE U.S. IN 1796. ***HE WAS ONE OF THE FINEST ARCHITECTS OF THE EARLY 19th CENTURY.*** IN 1798, HE MOVED TO PHILADELPHIA WHERE HE DESIGNED ***THE BANK OF PENNSYLVANIA, THE FIRST GREEK REVIVAL BUILDING IN THE U.S. HE BUILT THE ROMAN CATHOLIC BALTIMORE CATHEDRAL, THE FIRST CATHEDRAL IN THE U.S. AS AN ENGINEER HE DESIGNED THE PHILADELPHIA WATER SUPPLY SYSTEM, THE FIRST IN THE COUNTRY.***

HE WAS BORN AT FULNECK, YORKSHIRE, ENGLAND.

I APPOINT YOU TO THIS JOB BECAUSE I KNOW YOU CAN DO IT!

IN 1803, JEFFERSON APPOINTED HIM ***SURVEYOR OF PUBLIC BUILDINGS IN WASHINGTON. HE DESIGNED THE SOUTH WING OF THE CAPITOL AND MADE ALTERATIONS IN THE WHITE HOUSE.***

IN 1812, LATROBE WENT TO PITTSBURGH TO DESIGN STEAMBOATS, ***BUT WAS CALLED BACK TO WASHINGTON IN 1815 TO REBUILD THE CAPITOL AFTER THE BRITISH HAD BURNED IT.***

1765- 1815

Robert Fulton

AMERICAN CIVIL ENGINEER, INVENTOR AND PIONEER IN STEAM NAVIGATION

FULTON SHIFTED HIS INTEREST FROM PAINTING TO SCIENCE AND ENGINEERING WHEN HE WAS 28 YRS. OLD. ***HE INVENTED AN INCLINED PLANE FOR RAISING AND LOWERING CANAL BOATS, A POWER SHOVEL FOR DIGGING CANAL CHANNELS, A MACHINE FOR SAWING MARBLE, A FLAX SPINNING MACHINE, AND A DEVICE FOR TWISTING HEMP INTO ROPE. AFTER EXPERIMENTING WITH STEAM-DRIVEN BOATS HE LAUNCHED THE "CLERMONT" ON THE HUDSON RIVER IN 1807 AND WENT TO ALBANY AND BACK TO NEW YORK IN 5 DAYS!***

HE WAS BORN ON A FARM NEAR LITTLE BRITAIN, PENNSYLVANIA.
THAT'S MY PLAN, MR. SECRETARY.

IN 1814-15 HE CONSTRUCTED THE ***FIRST STEAM-PROPELLED WARSHIP FOR THE U.S. GOVERNMENT, THE 38-TON VESSEL CALLED "THE FULTON."***

AS A YOUNG MAN, HE PAINTED PORTRAITS AND LANDSCAPES. IN 1787, HE WENT TO ENGLAND AND STUDIED PAINTING UNTIL 1793.

KERN

1765–1825

Eli Whitney

AMERICAN INVENTOR, FAMOUS FOR HIS INVENTION OF ***THE COTTON GIN, AND PIONEER FIREARMS MANUFACTURER***

WHEN HE WAS A BOY HE BECAME FAMILIAR WITH MECHANICS IN HIS FATHER'S METAL SHOP. IN 1792, HE WENT TO GEORGIA WHERE HE WORKED ON A COTTON PLANTATION. ***IT WAS HERE WHERE HE INVENTED A MACHINE FOR SEPARATING COTTON SEED FROM THE FIBER. HE ESTABLISHED A PLANT IN NEW HAVEN, CONN., BUT GAVE IT UP BECAUSE OF COSTS TO PROTECT HIS PATENT RIGHTS. ALTHOUGH HIS COTTON GIN WAS ONE OF THE MOST IMPORTANT INVENTIONS CONNECTED WITH COTTON MANUFACTURE, HE MADE VERY LITTLE MONEY FROM IT.***

HE WAS BORN IN WESTBORO, MASS.

THE COTTON GIN WAS SO SUCCESSFUL THAT THE NUMBER OF POUNDS OF COTTON SENT TO EUROPE ROSE FROM **200,000 TO 6 MILLION!**

KERN

IN 1798, HE SET UP A SUCCESSFUL FACTORY IN WHITNEYVILLE, CONN., TO MANUFACTURE ***FIREARMS FOR THE GOVERNMENT. WHITNEY DESIGNED AND BUILT MACHINERY FOR PRODUCING GUNS WITH STANDARDIZED PRECISION PARTS.***

1767-1845
Andrew Jackson
CONGRESSMAN, SENATOR, GENERAL AND SEVENTH PRESIDENT OF THE UNITED STATES (1829-37)
PUT HIM IN JAIL NOW!
ANDY WAS 13 YRS. OLD WHEN HE FOUGHT AS A BOY MILITIAMAN IN THE REVOLUTIONARY WAR. THE BRITISH CAPTURED HIM AND PUT HIM IN PRISON. AFTER THE WAR HE STUDIED LAW IN SALISBURY, NORTH CAROLINA, AND WAS ADMITTED TO THE BAR IN 1787. JACKSON GAINED FAME DURING THE WAR OF 1812 WITH HIS VICTORY AT THE BATTLE OF NEW ORLEANS, THE BIGGEST BATTLE ON THE CONTINENT AT THIS TIME. JACKSON LOST LESS THAN 20 MEN AND THE BRITISH LOST OVER 2,000!
HE WAS BORN NEAR THE BORDER TOWN OF WAXHAW, NORTH CAROLINA.
I WOULD LIKE TO HAVE YOU JOIN MY CABINET.
WHEN JACKSON WAS PRESIDENT, HE APPOINTED HIS POLITICAL FRIENDS AS A REWARD FOR THEIR SUPPORT. THIS WAS KNOWN AS "THE SPOILS SYSTEM." DESPITE PUBLIC CRITICISM HIS POPULARITY REMAINED GREAT.
DURING THE WAR OF 1812, HE WALKED SO A WOUNDED SOLDIER COULD RIDE HIS HORSE. HIS MEN SAID HE WAS TOUGH AS "OLD HICKORY." THE NAME OLD HICKORY STUCK WITH HIM.
KERN

1767-1848

John Quincy Adams

SENATOR, FIRST U.S. MINISTER TO RUSSIA, U.S. MINISTER TO ENGLAND, SECRETARY OF STATE AND ***SIXTH*** PRESIDENT OF THE UNITED STATES (1825-29)

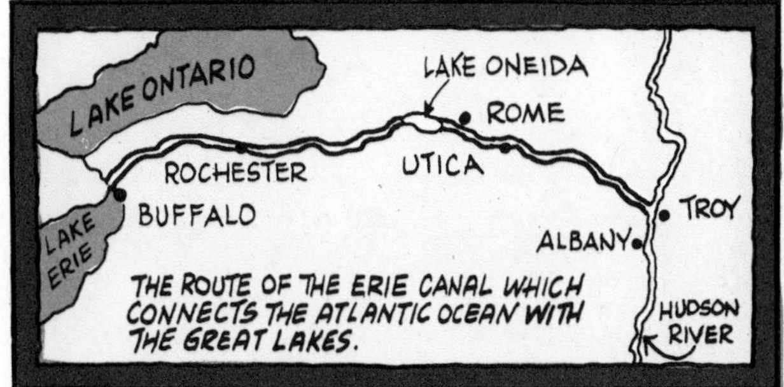

HE WAS BORN IN BRAINTREE (NOW QUINCY), MASS.
THIS PROBLEM MUST BE SOLVED!
HE WAS THE LEADER IN THE NEGOTIATIONS WHEN THE TREATY OF GHENT WAS DRAWN UP. THIS TREATY ENDED THE WAR OF 1812.

THE ROUTE OF THE ERIE CANAL WHICH CONNECTS THE ATLANTIC OCEAN WITH THE GREAT LAKES.

ADAMS, THE SON OF ***JOHN ADAMS, THE 2nd PRESIDENT,*** WAS EXPOSED TO POLITICS AT AN EARLY AGE. ***WHEN HE WAS 14 YRS. OLD HE WAS THE PRIVATE SECRETARY TO FRANCIS DASCA, AMERICA'S FIRST AMBASSADOR TO RUSSIA.*** ADAMS GRADUATED FROM HARVARD AND PRACTICED LAW IN BOSTON. ***DURING HIS ADMINISTRATION THE ERIE CANAL WAS COMPLETED AND THE BALTIMORE AND OHIO RAILROAD WAS STARTED. ADAMS LATER BECAME AN OUTSTANDING CONGRESSMAN.***

I AM A FIRM BELIEVER IN FREE SPEECH AND THE RIGHT OF PETITION.
JOHN QUINCY, THE BIBLE READER, WAS THE ONLY SON OF A PRESIDENT TO BECOME PRESIDENT!
KERN

1768 - 1813

Chief Tecumseh

THE GREAT SHAWNEE INDIAN LEADER

HE WAS BORN NEAR OLDTOWN, OHIO.

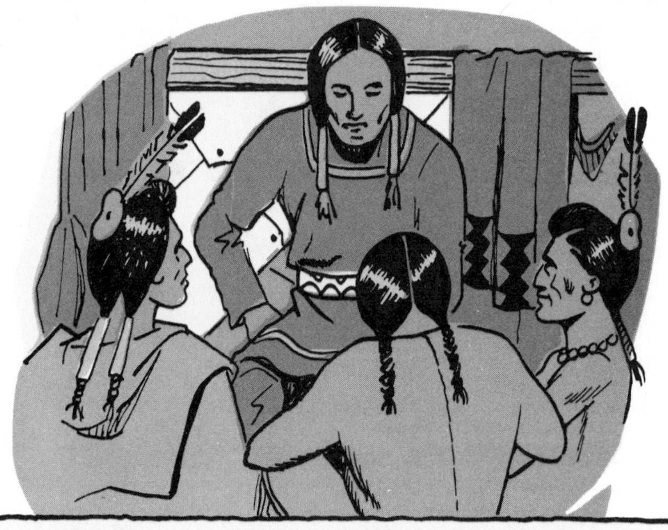

TECUMSEH CONCEIVED THE IDEA OF FORMING A ***GENUINE INDIAN CONFEDERACY AND WAS DETERMINED TO HOLD THE OHIO RIVER AS A PERMANENT INDIAN BORDER. IN 4 SHORT YEARS HE HAD MADE UNUSUAL PROGRESS IN FORMING A BASIS FOR A LASTING TRIBAL UNION.***

HE VISITED INDIANS FROM WISCONSIN TO FLORIDA, EXPRESSING HIS IDEAS FOR A ***STRONG CONFEDERACY. HIS PROPOSALS WERE EAGERLY ACCEPTED BY THE YOUNG BRAVES!***

THIS DEFEAT ENDS OUR DREAM OF A CONFEDERACY.

ON NOV. 7, 1811, WHILE TECUMSEH WAS AWAY, HIS BROTHER, ***"THE PROPHET," FOUGHT A HASTY BATTLE WITH THE AMERICANS UNDER GEN. WM. HARRISON AT TIPPECANOE. LOSSES WERE EVEN ON BOTH SIDES. THE INDIANS WERE FORCED TO RETREAT AND TECUMSEH'S VISION OF A CONFEDERACY CRUMBLED AWAY.***

KERN

1770-1838

William Clark

PRESIDENT JEFFERSON PICKED CAPT. LEWIS TO BE THE COMMANDER OF THE OVERLAND EXPEDITION TO THE PACIFIC. LEWIS ASKED CAPT. CLARK TO JOIN HIM AND SHARE AUTHORITY. THEY LEFT ST. LOUIS IN THE SPRING OF 1804, WORKED THEIR WAY TO THE HEADWATERS OF THE MISSOURI, CROSSED THE ROCKY MTS. AND FLOATED DOWN THE COLUMBIA RIVER TO THE BLUE PACIFIC, THEN RETURNED THE NEXT YEAR.

THEY WERE GUIDED BY SACAGAWEA, A SHOSHONI GIRL. THERE ARE SAID TO BE MORE STATUES ERECTED TO HER HONOR THAN ANY OTHER WOMAN IN AMERICAN HISTORY!

HE WAS BORN IN CAROLINE CO., VA.

THEY LED THE FIRST EXPLORATION OF THE "GREAT WEST" - 1804-1806.

1774-1809

Meriwether Lewis

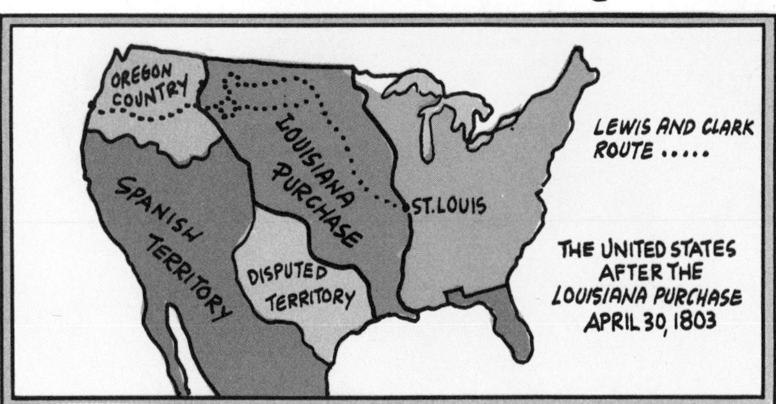

THE LEWIS AND CLARK EXPEDITION OPENED THE EYES OF THE NATION TO THE GREAT VALUE OF THE LOUISIANA PURCHASE. THIS EXPEDITION ALSO GAVE THE UNITED STATES ANOTHER CLAIM TO THE BEAUTIFUL REGION CALLED OREGON.

HE WAS BORN NEAR CHARLOTTESVILLE, VA.

1773 - 1841

William H. Harrison

SOLDIER, STATESMAN AND ***NINTH*** PRESIDENT OF THE UNITED STATES (MAR. 4, 1841 - APR. 4, 1841)

HE WAS BORN IN BERKELEY, CHARLES CITY CO., VIRGINIA.

THE WESTERN LANDS SHOULD BE DIVIDED SO THE POOR CAN BUY THEM.

HARRISON BEGAN HIS MEDICAL STUDIES IN RICHMOND IN 1790. HE LEFT A YEAR LATER AND JOINED THE ARMY WHERE HE SERVED UNTIL 1798. ***WHEN HE WAS 26 YRS. OLD, PRES. JOHN ADAMS APPOINTED HIM SEC. OF THE NORTHWEST TERRITORY. HE BECAME A DELEGATE IN CONGRESS OF THE TERRITORY AND WAS THE FIRST TERRITORIAL DELEGATE TO SIT IN CONGRESS. FROM 1800-12 HE WAS GOV. OF THE NEWLY CREATED INDIANA TERRITORY. IN 1812 HE DEFEATED THE SHAWNEE INDIANS AT THE BATTLE OF TIPPECANOE.***

TIPPECANOE AND TYLER TOO!

TIPPECANOE AND TYLER TOO

DURING THE CAMPAIGN OF 1840, THE FAMOUS SLOGAN "***TIPPECANOE AND TYLER TOO***" ***WAS USED TO ELECT HARRISON PRESIDENT AND TYLER VICE-PRESIDENT. THEY WON BY 234 ELECTORAL VOTES TO VAN BUREN'S 60. 1,000,000 MORE PEOPLE WENT TO THE POLLS IN 1840 THAN IN 1836.***

KERN

GENTLEMEN, I DEMAND COMPLETE HONESTY IN MY ADMINISTRATION.

HARRISON, THE EXCELLENT MILITARY LEADER AND HONEST ADMINISTRATOR, WAS THE ***OLDEST MAN EVER TO BE ELECTED PRESIDENT. HE WAS 68! HE WAS THE FIRST PRESIDENT TO DIE IN OFFICE, AND HIS TERM WAS THE SHORTEST IN AMERICAN HISTORY, ONLY 30 DAYS.***

1777 - 1852

Henry Clay

CONGRESSMAN, SENATOR, SEC. OF STATE AND **ONE OF THE FOREMOST STATESMEN OF HIS TIME**

GENTLEMEN, WE MUST THINK WHAT IS BEST FOR OUR COUNTRY.

CLAY WAS 18 YRS. OLD WHEN HE STUDIED LAW IN THE OFFICE OF THE ATTORNEY GENERAL IN RICHMOND, VA., AND 20, WHEN HE WAS ADMITTED TO THE BAR. ***HE EARNED A REPUTATION AS A GREAT ORATOR AND JURY LAWYER. WHILE IN CONGRESS HE FOUGHT FOR A LARGE ARMY AND LED A CAMPAIGN FOR THE WAR OF 1812. IN 1814, HE WAS ONE OF THE NEGOTIATORS FOR PEACE WITH GREAT BRITAIN, KNOWN AS THE TREATY OF GHENT.***

HE WAS BORN IN HANOVER CO., VIRGINIA.

HE URGED RECOGNITION OF THE SOUTH AMERICAN REPUBLICS IN 1817 AND WAS INFLUENTIAL IN FRAMING ***THE MISSOURI COMPROMISE OF 1820. IN 1824, CLAY WAS A CANDIDATE FOR PRESIDENT. HE WAS 4th IN THE NUMBER OF ELECTORAL VOTES RECEIVED SO HE GAVE HIS SUPPORT TO JOHN QUINCY ADAMS. LATER ADAMS APPOINTED HIM SEC. OF STATE.***

I AM A FIRM BELIEVER IN FEDERAL AID FOR INTERNAL IMPROVEMENTS.
KERN

CLAY WORKED HARD TO REDUCE TENSIONS BETWEEN THE NORTHERN AND SOUTHERN STATES. ***HIS COMPROMISE OF 1850 POSTPONED THE OUTBREAK OF THE CIVIL WAR FOR 10 YEARS. HE WAS CALLED "THE GREAT PACIFICATOR."***

1779 - 1813

Zebulon M. Pike

AMERICAN SOLDIER AND EARLY EXPLORER OF LARGE AREAS OF THE OLD WEST

HE WAS BORN IN TRENTON, N.J.
GENTLEMEN, WE WILL HAVE TO RESORT TO NEW TACTICS.

WHEN HE WAS 15 YRS. OLD HE WAS A CADET IN HIS FATHER'S REGIMENT. 5 YRS. LATER HE BECAME A FIRST LIEUTENANT. *IN 1805, PIKE WAS SENT ON AN EXPEDITION TO DISCOVER THE SOURCE OF THE MISSISSIPPI RIVER. ALTHOUGH HE FAILED TO FIND THE EXACT SPOT WHERE THE RIVER BEGAN, HE DID MAKE EXCELLENT MAPS AND BROUGHT BACK VALUABLE INFORMATION ABOUT THE INDIAN TRIBES IN THE AREA.*

HE WAS A COLONEL DURING THE WAR OF 1812 AND DIRECTED OPERATIONS AROUND TORONTO, CANADA.

KERN

PIKES PEAK IN COLORADO WAS NAMED FOR HIM. *HE DISCOVERED THE MOUNTAIN WHILE EXPLORING THE RED AND ARKANSAS RIVERS IN 1806.*

1779-1843

Francis Scott Key

LAWYER, POET AND AUTHOR OF "***THE STAR SPANGLED BANNER,***" THE NATIONAL ANTHEM OF THE U.S.

DURING THE WAR OF 1812, KEY WATCHED THE BRITISH BOMBARDMENT OF FORT MCHENRY, THE MOST IMPORTANT FORT AT BALTIMORE. ***THE SIGHT OF THE AMERICAN FLAG STILL FLYING OVER THE FORT THE NEXT MORNING INSPIRED HIM TO WRITE "THE STAR SPANGLED BANNER". THE POEM, SET TO MUSIC, BECAME THE NATIONAL ANTHEM BY AN ACT OF CONGRESS IN 1931. THE ARMY AND NAVY HAD RECOGNIZED THE SONG AS THE NATIONAL ANTHEM LONG BEFORE CONGRESS ADOPTED IT.***

HE WAS BORN IN CARROLL COUNTY, MARYLAND.

I HAVE BEEN SENT TO HELP SOLVE YOUR PROBLEMS.

HE PRACTICED LAW IN MARYLAND AND THE DISTRICT OF COLUMBIA. IN 1835, PRESIDENT JACKSON SENT HIM TO SETTLE A LAND DISPUTE WITH THE ***CREEK INDIANS.***

IT'S A PLEASURE TO SIGN THIS PROCLAMATION.

THE GOVERNMENT HAS GRANTED PERMISSION FOR THE FLAG TO FLY 24 HRS. A DAY OVER ***FT. MCHENRY AND KEY'S GRAVE AT FREDERICK, MARYLAND, AS A CONTINUAL SYMBOL OF AMERICAN PATRIOTISM. THE FLAG IS LOWERED ONLY DURING STORMY WEATHER.***

1779 - 1845

Joseph Story

DISTINGUISHED 19TH-CENTURY JURIST

THE JOB IS YOURS, JOSEPH.
THANK YOU, MR. PRESIDENT.

AFTER GRADUATING FROM HARVARD, STORY STUDIED LAW AND PRACTICED IN SALEM, MASS. IN 1808, HE ENTERED CONGRESS. ***IN 1811, PRESIDENT MADISON APPOINTED HIM ASSOCIATE JUSTICE OF THE U.S. SUPREME COURT. HE SERVED IN THIS POSITION WITH GREAT CREDIT FOR 34 YRS. STRONGLY OPPOSED TO SLAVERY, STORY WAS VERY UNPOPULAR WITH THE SOUTHERN STATES. HE DISTINGUISHED HIMSELF WITH A DECISION ESTABLISHING THE COURT'S POWER TO REVIEW ISSUES OF CONSTITUTIONAL LAW RAISED IN STATE CASES. HE STOOD FOR JUST POWERS FOR THE UNION WITHOUT INTERFERENCE WITH THE RIGHTS OF THE STATE.***

HE WAS BORN IN MARBLEHEAD, MASS.
Constitutional conflicts

I USE YOUR BOOKS IN MY CLASSES, MR. STORY. THEY ARE GREAT!

HIS BOOKS HAVE HAD GREAT INFLUENCE ON AMERICAN LEGAL EDUCATION. SOME OF HIS VALUABLE WORKS ARE ***"COMMENTARIES ON THE CONSTITUTION OF THE UNITED STATES" AND "THE CONFLICT OF LAWS."***

KERN

IN 1829, STORY BECAME A PROFESSOR OF LAW AT HARVARD UNIVERSITY. ***HE HELD THIS POSITION WHILE CONTINUING TO SERVE AS A JUDGE OF THE SUPREME COURT.***

1782-1850

John C. Calhoun

AMERICAN STATESMAN, ORATOR AND ONE OF THE MOST IMPORTANT SUPPORTERS OF **THE STATES RIGHTS DOCTRINE**

CALHOUN GRADUATED FROM YALE IN 1804 AND WAS ADMITTED TO THE BAR IN 1807. HE WAS A STRONG NATIONALIST IN FAVOR OF A LARGE ARMY AND NAVY. FROM 1817-25 HE WAS SEC. OF WAR UNDER PRES. MONROE. **HE ASSUMED THE OFFICE OF VICE-PRESIDENT, TO WHICH HE HAD BEEN ELECTED IN 1824. REELECTED IN 1828, HE SERVED WITH PRES. JACKSON. FROM 1832-44 CALHOUN WAS IN THE U.S. SENATE. IN 1844, PRES. TYLER CHOSE HIM TO BE HIS SEC. OF WAR. IN 1845, HE REENTERED THE SENATE WHERE HE REMAINED UNTIL HIS DEATH.**

I APPEAL TO YOUR GOOD SENSE!

CALHOUN TOOK A PROMINENT PART IN NATIONAL AFFAIRS FOR **40 YEARS. HE WAS A MAJOR POLITICAL FIGURE BEFORE THE CIVIL WAR.**

HE WAS BORN NEAR ABBEVILLE, S.C.

I AM AGAINST GIVING TOP JOBS TO YOUR POLITICAL FRIENDS, SO I AM RESIGNING!

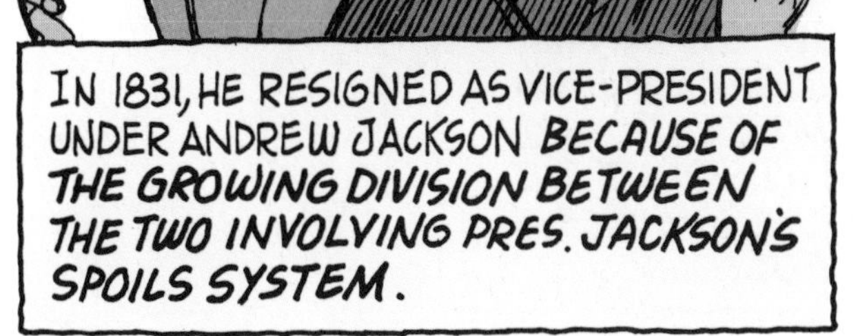

IN 1831, HE RESIGNED AS VICE-PRESIDENT UNDER ANDREW JACKSON **BECAUSE OF THE GROWING DIVISION BETWEEN THE TWO INVOLVING PRES. JACKSON'S SPOILS SYSTEM.**

KERN

1782 - 1852

Daniel Webster

ONE OF THE MOST PROMINENT ORATORS AND STATESMEN IN AMERICAN HISTORY

WE MUST STAY TOGETHER!

WEBSTER GRADUATED FROM DARTMOUTH COLLEGE, STUDIED LAW AND WAS ADMITTED TO THE BAR IN 1805. HE PRACTICED LAW IN BOSTON FOR 7 YRS. ***WEBSTER WAS A CHAMPION OF THE CONSTITUTION, THE UNION AND THE GROWING INDUSTRIAL INTERESTS OF THE NORTH. IT WAS WEBSTER MORE THAN ANY OTHER MAN WHO HELD THE UNION TOGETHER WHEN IT WAS AT A POINT OF BREAKING UP. TYPICAL OF HIS LOYALTY TO THE COUNTRY, HE WAS IN FAVOR OF THE COMPROMISE OF 1850, A STAND WHICH BROUGHT HIM MANY ENEMIES.***

HE WAS BORN IN FRANKLIN, N.H.

HE SERVED BRILLIANTLY AS A U.S. SENATOR. WEBSTER WAS SEC. OF STATE UNDER PRES. WM. HARRISON, WHEN HE NEGOTIATED THE MAINE BOUNDARY DISPUTE WITH ENGLAND. HE WAS SEC. OF STATE UNDER PRES. FILLMORE. ***IN 1852 HE TRIED TO GET THE WHIG NOMINATION FOR PRESIDENT BUT WAS UNSUCCESSFUL.***

I AM IN FAVOR OF RENEWING THE CHARTER OF THE UNITED STATES BANK.
KERN

ONE OF WEBSTER'S FAMOUS SPEECHES IN DEFENSE OF THE CONSTITUTION ENDED WITH THESE WORDS: ***"LIBERTY AND UNION, NOW AND FOREVER, ONE AND INSEPARABLE." THIS SPEECH DID MORE TO UNIFY THE COUNTRY THAN ANY OTHER ORATION OF ITS TIME.***

1782 - 1862

Martin Van Buren

SECRETARY OF STATE, VICE-PRESIDENT AND **EIGHTH** PRESIDENT OF THE UNITED STATES (1837-41)

THIS MEETING WILL COME TO ORDER.

VAN BUREN WAS 17 YEARS OLD WHEN HE BORROWED $40, WENT TO NEW YORK CITY AND STUDIED LAW. ADMITTED TO THE BAR IN 1803, HE MOVED STEADILY UPWARD IN POLITICS. HE WAS ELECTED U.S. SENATOR IN 1821 AND LED THE FIGHT TO **ABOLISH DEBTORS' PRISON. VAN BUREN WAS SEC. OF STATE UNDER PRES. JACKSON, AND IN 1832, JACKSON CHOSE HIM AS HIS VICE-PRESIDENT. THEY WON AN OVERWHELMING VICTORY. WHEN AN ASSASSINATION ATTEMPT WAS MADE ON JACKSON'S LIFE, VAN BUREN CARRIED TWO LOADED PISTOLS WITH HIM WHEN HE PRESIDED OVER THE SENATE. IN 1836, HE WON A DECISIVE VICTORY OVER WM. H. HARRISON FOR THE PRESIDENCY.**

HE WAS BORN IN KINDERHOOK, N.Y.

CLOSED

PANIC

BANKS CLOSED!

DURING HIS ADMINISTRATION, GOODYEAR DISCOVERED **THE VULCANIZED PROCESS, THE FIRST BASEBALL GAME WAS PLAYED IN COOPERSTOWN, N.Y., THE NATIONAL TREASURY WAS ESTABLISHED IN WASH., D.C., AND SAMUEL MORSE PATENTED HIS TELEGRAPH.**

HE WAS IN OFFICE FOR ONLY 36 DAYS WHEN THE NATION WAS STRUCK WITH **A FINANCIAL DEPRESSION KNOWN AS THE PANIC OF 1837. BANKS CLOSED AND HUNDREDS FAILED. THIS WAS DUE TO THE JACKSON MONEY POLICY WHICH VAN BUREN HAD SUPPORTED.**

1782 - 1866

Lewis Cass

AMERICAN STATESMAN WHO WAS DIRECTLY INVOLVED WITH INDIAN AFFAIRS FOR 18 YEARS

AFTER FIGHTING IN THE WAR OF 1812, CASS WAS APPOINTED BY PRESIDENT MADISON TO BE **GOVERNOR GENERAL OF THE TERRITORY OF MICHIGAN AND SERVED THERE FROM 1813-31. HE MADE 22 TREATIES WITH THE INDIANS, BUILT ROADS AND ORGANIZED LOCAL GOVERNMENTS. LARGE TRACTS OF LAND WERE THEN OPEN FOR SETTLEMENT.** IN 1848, HE RECEIVED THE DEMOCRATIC NOMINATION FOR THE PRESIDENCY, **BUT WAS DEFEATED BY ZACHARY TAYLOR**. CASS SERVED IN THE **U.S. SENATE FROM 1845-56.**

HE WAS BORN IN EXETER, NEW HAMSPHIRE.

GOOD NEWS. YOUR BOOK IS SELLING VERY WELL.

HE WROTE A BOOK ON **THE HISTORY AND LANGUAGES OF THE U.S. INDIANS. CASS WAS OFTEN CALLED "THE FATHER OF THE OLD NORTHWEST."**

KERN

IN HIS DISTINGUISHED PUBLIC CAREER, HE WAS A **GENERAL, A GOVERNOR, A CABINET OFFICER, A DIPLOMAT, A SENATOR AND A PRESIDENTIAL CANDIDATE.**

1783 - 1859

Washington Irving

THE FIRST CREATIVE AMERICAN WRITER TO WIN INTERNATIONAL FAME

IRVING LEFT SCHOOL WHEN HE WAS 16YRS. OLD AND ENTERED A LAW OFFICE WHERE HE STUDIED AND EVENTUALLY WAS ADMITTED TO THE BAR. IRVING TRAVELED IN EUROPE FOR 2YRS. WHERE HE ENJOYED ART, LITERATURE AND EUROPEAN CUSTOMS. ***UNDER THE PSEUDONYM OF KNICKERBOCKER HE WROTE THE "HISTORY OF NEW YORK" IN 1809, A SATIRICAL ACCOUNT OF NEW YORK DURING THE PERIOD OF DUTCH OCCUPATION. IN 1820, HE ACHIEVED GREAT SUCCESS WITH HIS "SKETCH BOOK," A COLLECTION OF SHORT STORIES. TWO OF THE STORIES, "RIP VAN WINKLE" AND "THE LEGEND OF SLEEPY HOLLOW," ARE CLASSICS OF AMERICAN LITERATURE.***

HE WAS BORN IN NEW YORK CITY.

I AM HAPPY TO LEARN THAT PEOPLE ARE BEGINNING TO READ SHORT STORIES.

I CAN'T THINK OF A BETTER MAN FOR THIS JOB.
THANK YOU, MR. PRESIDENT.

IN 1842 IRVING WAS APPOINTED ***MINISTER TO SPAIN, SERVING FOR 4 YEARS.***

KERN

IRVING WAS THE DISCOVERER OF THE EFFECTIVENESS OF THE ***SHORT STORY.*** HE WROTE ***"THE BRACEBRIDGE HALL," "TALES OF A TRAVELER," "OLIVER GOLDSMITH" AND "THE LIFE OF WASHINGTON."***

1784 - 1850

Zachary Taylor

FARMER, SOLDIER AND THE *TWELFTH* PRESIDENT OF THE UNITED STATES (1849-50)

THE INTERIOR DEPT. WILL TAKE CARE OF INDIAN AFFAIRS, CENSUS, PATENTS, PENSIONS AND PUBLIC LANDS.

DURING HIS PRESIDENTIAL TERM, THE DEPARTMENT OF INTERIOR WAS CREATED, THE OVERLAND MAIL SERVICE WAS BEGUN AND THE BITTER ***CONGRESSIONAL DEBATE ON SLAVERY KNOWN AS THE COMPROMISE OF 1850 STARTED.*** HE DIED FROM SUNSTROKE WHILE ATTENDING CEREMONIES ON JULY 4, 1850, FOR THE CORNERSTONE LAYING OF THE WASHINGTON MONUMENT. ***TAYLOR SERVED AS PRESIDENT FOR ONLY 16 MONTHS.***

HE WAS BORN NEAR BARBOURVILLE, VA.

YOU DESERVE CONGRATULATIONS FOR YOUR FINE MILITARY RECORD.

TAYLOR BECAME A NATIONAL HERO DURING HIS MEXICAN WAR VICTORIES IN THE 1840'S.

A BORN LEADER AND A DETERMINED FIGHTER, HE WAS KNOWN AS ***"OLD ROUGH AND READY"*** DURING HIS 40 YEARS AS A ***FRONTIER SOLDIER. HE HAD A LIFELONG RECORD OF MILITARY VICTORIES WITHOUT A SINGLE DEFEAT.***

1785 - 1819

Oliver Hazard Perry

THE FAMOUS NAVAL OFFICER NOTED FOR HIS HEROISM IN THE WAR OF 1812

COMMENCE FIRING!

PERRY ATTENDED PRIVATE SCHOOLS AND WAS ONLY 14 YRS. OLD WHEN HE SERVED UNDER HIS FATHER IN THE WEST INDIES DURING THE NAVAL WAR WITH FRANCE. **IN 1807, HE WAS PUT IN CHARGE OF GUNBOATS AT NEWPORT. DURING THE WAR OF 1812 PERRY WAS BUSY BUILDING A FLEET OF WAR SHIPS ON LAKE ERIE. IN SEPT. 1813, HE MET THE BRITISH FLEET. THEY FOUGHT FOR 3 HOURS. AFTER PERRY'S FLAGSHIP "LAWRENCE" WAS DESTROYED, HE WAS ROWED TO THE "NIAGARA", TORE THROUGH THE BRITISH LINES, AND AFTER 8 MINUTES HE WON THE BATTLE!**

HE WAS BORN IN SOUTH KINGSTON, RHODE ISLAND.

SEND THIS MESSAGE NOW!!

WE THANK YOU FOR YOUR HEROISM.

PERRY WAS PROMOTED TO CAPTAIN FOR HIS LAKE ERIE VICTORY AND WAS GIVEN A **GOLD MEDAL AND THE THANKS OF CONGRESS!**

KERN

PERRY'S FAMOUS MESSAGE "**WE HAVE MET THE ENEMY AND THEY ARE OURS, TWO SHIPS, TWO BRIGS, ONE SCHOONER AND ONE SLOOP" WAS SENT TO GEN. WM. HENRY HARRISON, MILITARY COMMANDER OF THE WEST.**

1785- 1851
John James Audubon
FAMOUS NATURALIST AND PAINTER OF BIRDS AND OTHER WILDLIFE

THESE ARE THE FINEST BIRD DRAWINGS I HAVE EVER SEEN!

AUDUBON LIVED ON AN ESTATE CALLED MILL GROVE NEAR PHILADELPHIA WHERE HE SPENT HIS TIME DRAWING BIRDS. HE MADE SEVERAL ATTEMPTS IN A BUSINESS CAREER BUT FAILED. ***IN 1820, HE WANTED TO PUBLISH A COLLECTION OF HIS PAINTINGS OF AMERICAN BIRDS, BUT NO AMERICAN PUBLISHER WAS INTERESTED SO HE WENT TO ENGLAND WHERE HIS WORK CREATED A SENSATION AND "BIRDS OF AMERICA" WAS PUBLISHED. THIS BOOK CONTAINED 87 PARTS WITH 435 LIFE-SIZED COLORED ENGRAVINGS MADE FROM HIS WATER COLORS. AUDUBON THEN CAME BACK TO THE U.S. AND PUBLISHED AMERICAN EDITIONS OF HIS WILDLIFE PAINTINGS.***

HE WAS BORN AT LES CAYES, HAITI.

THIS SOCIETY IS DEDICATED TO A GREAT ARTIST.

AUDUBON TRAVELED IN ALL ACCESSIBLE PARTS OF THE UNITED STATES AND CANADA FROM 1830 TO 1842 TO FIND NEW MATERIAL FOR HIS PAINTINGS.

KERN

THE NATIONAL AUDUBON SOCIETY, NAMED FOR HIM, IS THE OLDEST NATIONAL CONSERVATION ORGANIZATION IN NORTH AMERICA. IT WAS FOUNDED IN 1905.

1785-1853

William Beaumont

U.S. ARMY SURGEON AND PIONEER IN THE STUDY OF THE HUMAN STOMACH

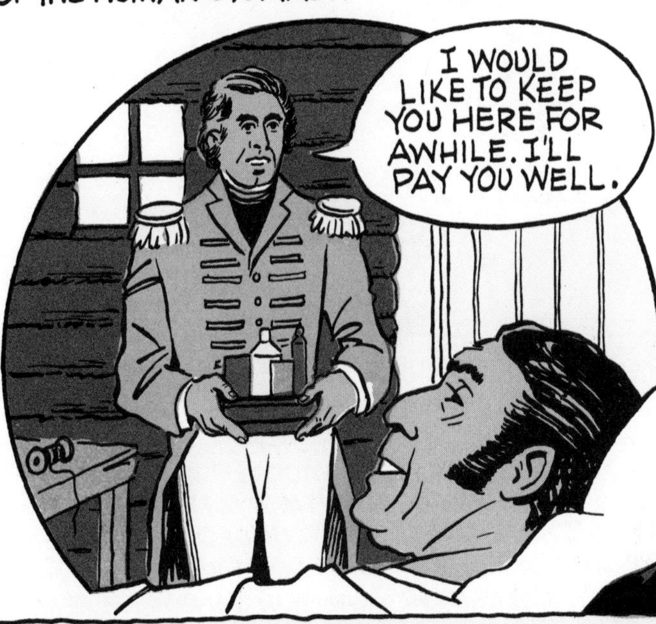

I WOULD LIKE TO KEEP YOU HERE FOR AWHILE. I'LL PAY YOU WELL.

HE WAS BORN AT LEBANON, CONN.

DR. BEAUMONT TREATED ALEX ST. MARTIN FOR A SERIOUS STOMACH WOUND WHILE HE WAS ON MACKINAC ISLAND IN JUNE 1822. ST. MARTIN'S WOUND HEALED EXCEPT FOR A SMALL OPENING WHICH WAS COVERED WITH A FOLD OF FLESH. BY PUSHING THE FLESH ASIDE, DR. BEAUMONT COULD LOOK DIRECTLY INTO ST. MARTIN'S STOMACH AND OBSERVE ITS MOTION WHEN FOOD WAS PUT IN AND PULLED OUT. BEAUMONT HAD AN EXCELLENT OPPORTUNITY FOR EXPERIMENTING ON THE GASTRIC JUICES AND THE PROCESS OF DIGESTION. DR. BEAUMONT WAS THE FIRST TO DESCRIBE HOW THE STOMACH DIGESTED FOOD, AND THE FIRST TO PROVE THAT VIOLENT ANGER DISTURBED DIGESTION. HE OBSERVED THAT OVEREATING DELAYS DIGESTION, AND THAT VEGETABLES WERE LESS EASILY DIGESTED THAN ANIMAL FOOD.

BEAUMONT'S EXPERIMENTS AND OBSERVATIONS, PUBLISHED IN 1833, ARE REGARDED AS **THE GREATEST SINGLE CONTRIBUTION TO THE KNOWLEDGE OF DIGESTION.**

A MEMORIAL PLAQUE WAS ERECTED TO DR. BEAUMONT AT PRAIRIE DU CHIEN, WIS., IN 1931.

KERN

1787 - 1870
Emma Hart Willard
AMERICAN PIONEER IN HIGHER EDUCATION FOR WOMEN
WOMEN MUST HAVE THE CHANCE TO IMPROVE THEMSELVES.
SHE BEGAN TEACHING SCHOOL WHEN SHE WAS 16 YRS. OLD. AFTER HER MARRIAGE, DR. JOHN WILLARD HELPED HER ESTABLISH A GIRLS' BOARDING SCHOOL AT MIDDLEBURY, VT. HERE SHE INTRODUCED MANY NEW METHODS OF INSTRUCTION. LATER SHE FOUNDED A GIRLS' SEMINARY AT WATERTOWN, N.Y. IT WAS MOVED TO TROY, N.Y. IN HER "PLAN FOR IMPROVING FEMALE EDUCATION" AND IN HER SCHOOLS, SHE PROMOTED EQUAL EDUCATION AND OPPORTUNITIES FOR WOMEN. SHE ALSO HELPED FOUND A TRAINING SCHOOL FOR WOMEN TEACHERS IN GREECE.
SHE WAS BORN IN BERLIN, CONN.
WE'RE SO HAPPY TO HAVE YOU SPEAK TO US.
WE FINALLY GOT AROUND TO HONOR A GREAT LADY.
SHE WROTE A BOOK OF POEMS. ONE OF HERS IS THE WELL KNOWN "ROCKED IN THE CRADLE OF THE DEEP". SHE TRAVELED IN NEW YORK STATE, THE SOUTH AND THE WEST, PROMOTING HIGHER EDUCATION FOR WOMEN.
KERN
IN 1895, A STATUE WAS UNVEILED IN TROY, N.Y., TO HER MEMORY, AND IN 1905, SHE WAS ELECTED TO THE HALL OF FAME FOR OUTSTANDING AMERICANS AT NEW YORK UNIVERSITY.

1789-1851

James F. Cooper

AMERICAN AUTHOR KNOWN FOR HIS EXCITING STORIES ABOUT FRONTIER LIFE

THERE'S A CHARACTER FOR YOUR STORIES, JIM.

COOPER WAS ONE YEAR OLD WHEN HIS PARENTS MOVED TO EAST CENTRAL NEW YORK STATE. HE ATTENDED YALE BUT WAS ASKED TO LEAVE IN HIS THIRD YEAR BECAUSE HE WAS A POOR STUDENT. ***HE THEN JOINED THE NAVY WHICH GAVE HIM VALUABLE MATERIAL FOR HIS NOVELS. IN 1823, HE COMPLETED "THE PIONEER," THE FIRST OF 5 NOVELS KNOWN AS THE "LEATHERSTOCKING" SERIES. ABOUT FRONTIER WILDERNESS LIFE. "THE LAST OF THE MOHICANS," WRITTEN IN 1826, WAS A ROMANTIC NOVEL OF LIFE AMONG THE AMERICAN INDIANS. THIS NOVEL IS REGARDED AS HIS GREATEST ACHIEVEMENT. "THE PRAIRIE," "THE PATHFINDER" AND "THE DEERSLAYER" COMPLETED THE "LEATHERSTOCKING TALES."***

YOUR BOOK IS AN INSTANT SUCCESS.

IN 1821, HE PUBLISHED ***"THE SPY"*** AT HIS OWN EXPENSE. ***THIS NOVEL, A ROMANTIC STORY OF THE AMERICAN REVOLUTION, WAS AN IMMEDIATE SUCCESS.***

KERN

HE WAS BORN IN BURLINGTON, N.J.

SOME OF HIS WELLKNOWN CHARACTERS WERE ***LONGKNIFE, THE PIONEER HUNTER, AND UNCAS AND CHINGACHGOOK, INDIAN SON AND FATHER IN "THE LAST OF THE MOHICANS."***

1790-1862
John Tyler
GOVERNOR, SENATOR, VICE-PRESIDENT AND TENTH PRESIDENT OF THE UNITED STATES (1841-45)
IT LOOKS LIKE YOU ARE MY MAN, JOHN.
THANK YOU, HENRY.
HE GRADUATED FROM WILLIAM AND MARY COLLEGE, STUDIED LAW WITH HIS FATHER, A DISTINGUISHED JUDGE, AND WAS ADMITTED TO THE BAR IN 1809. AT 26 TYLER WAS A CONGRESSMAN, AT 35 GOVERNOR OF VIRGINIA AND AT 37 A SENATOR. TYLER WAS ELECTED VICE-PRESIDENT WITH PRES. WM. HENRY HARRISON IN THE FAMOUS "TIPPECANOE AND TYLER TOO" CAMPAIGN. THIRTY DAYS LATER TYLER WAS PRESIDENT UPON THE UNEXPECTED DEATH OF THE OLD WAR HERO WM. HENRY HARRISON.
HE WAS BORN IN CHARLES CITY CO., VIRGINIA.

DURING TYLER'S ADMINISTRATION THE ***FIRST TELEGRAPH LINE WAS CONSTRUCTED, A TREATY WAS SIGNED OPENING UP TRADE WITH CHINA, FLORIDA JOINED THE UNION AND PIONEERS MOVED WESTWARD ALONG THE OREGON TRAIL.***

TYLER WAS THE ***FIRST PRESIDENT TO HAVE IMPEACHMENT PROCEEDINGS INTRODUCED BY LEADERS IN CONGRESS. THE VOTE FAILED 27 TO 83.*** ON HIS LAST DAY IN OFFICE CONGRESS OVERRODE ONE OF HIS VETOES. ***THIS WAS THE FIRST TIME IN HISTORY THAT A PRESIDENTIAL VETO HAD BEEN OVERRIDDEN.***

KERN

1791-1868
James Buchanan

CONGRESSMAN, SENATOR, DIPLOMAT, SEC. OF STATE AND ***FIFTEENTH*** PRESIDENT OF THE UNITED STATES (1857-61)

WE MUST SIGN A TREATY FOR OUR NATION'S WELFARE.

BUCHANAN GRADUATED WITH TOP HONORS FROM DICKINSON COLLEGE IN 1809, THEN STUDIED LAW IN LANCASTER, PA. AFTER SERVING AS A PRIVATE IN THE WAR OF 1812, ***HE WAS ELECTED TO CONGRESS. IN 1831, BUCHANAN WAS APPOINTED MINISTER TO RUSSIA, WHERE HE NEGOTIATED THE FIRST TREATY BETWEEN THE TWO COUNTRIES.***

HE WAS BORN AT STONYBATTER, FRANKLIN CO., PA.

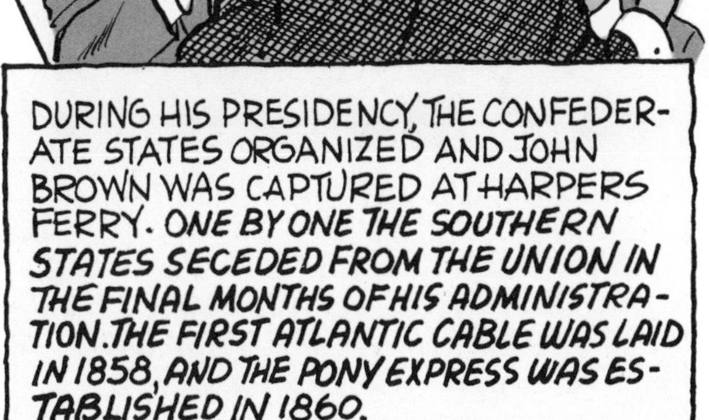

I'LL SECEDE FROM THE UNION, AND YOU CAN'T DO A THING ABOUT IT!

DURING HIS PRESIDENCY, THE CONFEDERATE STATES ORGANIZED AND JOHN BROWN WAS CAPTURED AT HARPERS FERRY. ***ONE BY ONE THE SOUTHERN STATES SECEDED FROM THE UNION IN THE FINAL MONTHS OF HIS ADMINISTRATION. THE FIRST ATLANTIC CABLE WAS LAID IN 1858, AND THE PONY EXPRESS WAS ESTABLISHED IN 1860.***

I MUST HAVE THIS SPEECH READY FOR TOMORROW.

BUCHANAN WAS THE ONLY PRESIDENT WHO NEVER MARRIED. ***HE DEVOTED HIS LIFE TO PUBLIC SERVICE.***

KERN

1791 - 1872
Samuel F. B. Morse
AMERICAN ARTIST AND INVENTOR OF THE TELEGRAPH
WHAT HATH GOD WROUGHT
AFTER GRADUATING FROM YALE COLLEGE IN 1810, HE WENT TO ENGLAND TO FURTHER HIS ART STUDIES. HE BECAME A VERY SUCCESSFUL PORTRAIT PAINTER AND SCULPTOR. WHILE A PROFESSOR OF ART AT NEW YORK UNIVERSITY, HE BECAME INTERESTED IN CHEMICAL AND ELECTRICAL EXPERIMENTS. HE DEVELOPED EQUIPMENT FOR A MAGNETIC TELEGRAPH AND A CODE FOR HIS TELEGRAPH INSTRUMENT. IN 1843, CONGRESS APPROPRIATED $30,000 TO BUILD A TELEGRAPH LINE BETWEEN WASHINGTON AND BALTIMORE. WHEN THIS LINE WAS INSTALLED MAY 24, 1844, MORSE SENT THESE WORDS: "WHAT HATH GOD WROUGHT!" BY 1860, EVERY STATE IN THE UNION WAS USING HIS INVENTION.
HE WAS BORN IN CHARLESTOWN, MASS.
WE WANT YOU TO ACCEPT THIS CASH AWARD FOR YOUR OUTSTANDING WORK.
A VERY FINE SKETCH.
KERN

HE WAS RECOGNIZED AS ONE OF THE BEST EARLY AMERICAN PORTRAIT PAINTERS. HE HELPED ORGANIZE THE NATIONAL ACADEMY OF DESIGN AND SERVED AS ITS FIRST PRESIDENT IN 1826.

MORSE WON FAME AND WEALTH WITH HIS INVENTIONS. A NUMBER OF EUROPEAN COUNTRIES UNITED AND GAVE HIM A CASH AWARD OF 400,000 FRANCS. THE TELEGRAPH OPERATORS' OF AMERICA HONORED HIM WITH A STATUE WHILE HE WAS STILL LIVING.

1791-1883

Peter Cooper

AMERICAN INVENTOR, MANUFACTURER AND PHILANTHROPIST

I APPRECIATE YOUR HELP, PETER.

HE HAD LITTLE SCHOOLING, BUT SHOWED GREAT MECHANICAL SKILL. WHEN HE WAS 17 HE WORKED FOR A NEW YORK COACHMAKER FOR $25 A YR. AND BOARD. **COOPER SAVED ENOUGH MONEY TO MANUFACTURE CLOTH SHEARING MACHINES. HE WAS 33 WHEN HE OWNED A GLUE AND ISINGLASS FACTORY. LATER HE BUILT THE LARGEST ROLLING MILL IN THE U.S. AT THE TIME WHERE THE FIRST STRUCTURAL IRON FOR FIREPROOF BUILDINGS WAS ROLLED. COOPER WAS A BIG FINANCIAL SUPPORTER OF CYRUS FIELD'S ATLANTIC CABLE PROJECT. HE FOUNDED COOPER UNION IN NEW YORK CITY TO HELP WORKING PEOPLE GET AN EDUCATION. COOPER USED MUCH OF HIS WEALTH TO HELP HIS FELLOW MAN.**

HE WAS BORN IN NEW YORK CITY, N.Y.
WE ARE VERY GRATEFUL FOR YOUR GREAT HELP.

IN 1870, HE RECEIVED **THE BESSEMER GOLD MEDAL FROM THE IRON AND STEEL INSTITUTE OF GREAT BRITAIN FOR DEVELOPING THE AMERICAN IRON TRADE. IN 1876, HE WAS THE PRESIDENTIAL CANDIDATE OF THE GREENBACK PARTY.**

THERE IT IS!

IN 1829-30, HE DESIGNED AND BUILT ONE OF **THE FIRST STEAM LOCOMOTIVES IN AMERICA, THE ONE-HORSEPOWER "TOM THUMB."**

KERN

1793-1863

Samuel Houston

AMERICAN SOLDIER, POLITICAL LEADER AND THE MAIN FORCE IN THE FIGHT OF TEXAS FOR INDEPENDENCE FROM MEXICO

I WILL TAKE COMMAND IMMEDIATELY!

HOUSTON LIVED WITH THE CHEROKEE INDIANS FOR 3 YRS. BEFORE SERVING IN THE ARMY UNDER ANDREW JACKSON DURING THE WAR OF 1812. HE STUDIED LAW IN NASHVILLE, TENN., AND WAS ADMITTED TO THE BAR. AFTER SERVING AS A CONGRESSMAN AND GOVERNOR OF TENN., JACKSON SENT HIM TO TEXAS TO NEGOTIATE A TREATY WITH THE INDIANS FOR THE PROTECTION OF THE AMERICAN TRADERS. HE DECIDED TO STAY IN TEXAS. ***IN NOV. 1835, HE WAS ELECTED COMMANDER OF THE TEXAS ARMY IN THE TEXAS REVOLUTION AGAINST MEXICO. HIS CAPTURE OF SANTA ANNA WON TEXAS THEIR INDEPENDENCE. IN 1836, HOUSTON WAS ELECTED THE FIRST PRESIDENT OF THE NEW REPUBLIC OF TEXAS.***

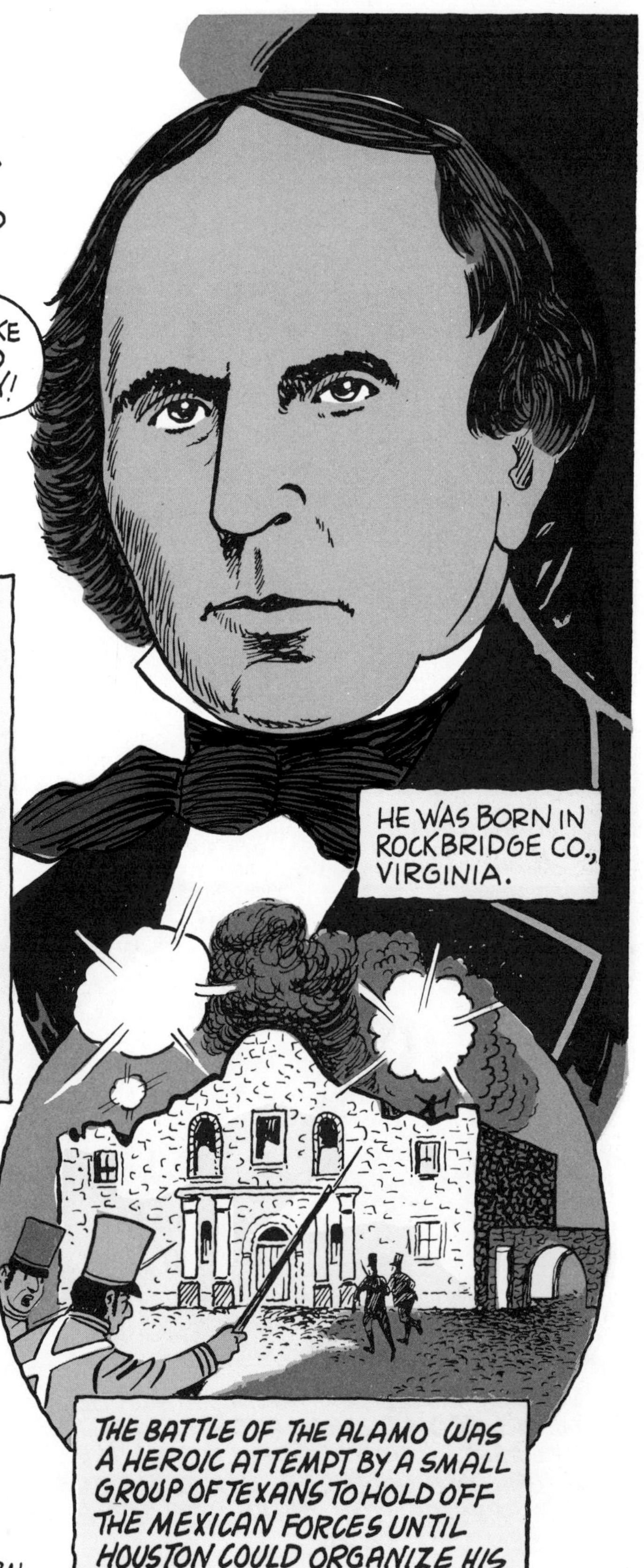

HE WAS BORN IN ROCKBRIDGE CO., VIRGINIA.

THE BATTLE OF THE ALAMO WAS A HEROIC ATTEMPT BY A SMALL GROUP OF TEXANS TO HOLD OFF THE MEXICAN FORCES UNTIL HOUSTON COULD ORGANIZE HIS ARMY.

TEXAS STAYS IN THE UNION!

FROM 1846-59 HE WAS U.S. SENATOR FROM TEXAS. IN 1859, HE WAS ELECTED GOVERNOR. ***DURING THE CIVIL WAR HE REFUSED TO TAKE TEXAS OUT OF THE UNION, SO WAS REMOVED FROM OFFICE IN 1861.***

KERN

1794 - 1877
Cornelius Vanderbilt
AMERICAN FINANCIER, SHIPPING MAGNATE AND THE FIRST PRESIDENT OF THE NEW YORK CENTRAL RAILROAD
THE FOUNDER OF THE FAMILY FORTUNE, VANDERBILT WAS THE LEADING STEAMSHIP OWNER IN THE COUNTRY AND BY 1850 HAD A MONOPOLY. THE "COMMODORE," AS HE WAS CALLED, STARTED STEAMSHIP ROUTES TO EUROPE AND SAN FRANCISCO. WHEN HE SOLD OUT, HIS INTERESTS NETTED HIM MORE THAN $1,000,000. AT THE AGE OF 70, DURING THE CIVIL WAR HE BEGAN TO INVEST IN RAILROADS, OWNING LINES AS FAR WEST AS CHICAGO. WHEN HE DIED IN 1877 HE LEFT A FORTUNE OF ABOUT $100,000,000. HE CONTRIBUTED $1,000,000 FOR THE ESTABLISHMENT OF VANDERBILT UNIVERSITY AT NASHVILLE, TENN.
HE WAS BORN IN STATEN ISLAND, N.Y.
YOU ARE WELCOME TO USE MY SHIP.
THANK YOU, MR. VANDERBILT.
HE WAS 16 YEARS OLD WHEN HE OWNED HIS FIRST SMALL SHIP WHICH SAILED BETWEEN STATEN ISLAND AND NEW YORK CITY.
KERN
DURING THE CIVIL WAR HE DONATED HIS PRIVATE STEAMSHIP TO THE U.S. GOVERNMENT.

1794-1878
William C. Bryant
"FATHER OF AMERICAN POETS," JOURNALIST AND LAWYER
PUT THIS EDITORIAL ON THE FRONT PAGE.
BRYANT WAS ADMITTED TO THE BAR IN 1815 AND PRACTICED LAW FOR 10 YEARS. IN 1825, HE MOVED TO NEW YORK CITY AND BECAME ASSOCIATE EDITOR OF THE NEW YORK "EVENING POST." LATER HE WAS MADE THE EDITOR-IN-CHIEF, SERVING FOR OVER 50 YRS. BRYANT GAINED PROMINENCE AS A STRAIGHTFORWARD EDITORIAL WRITER. ONE OF HIS GREATEST JOYS WAS THE DOWNFALL OF SLAVERY. THE FIRST AMERICAN POET TO BECOME WELL KNOWN, HE DIED FROM SUNSTROKE WHILE DELIVERING AN ADDRESS IN NEW YORK CITY'S CENTRAL PARK.
HE WAS BORN IN CUMMINGHAM, MASS.
YOUNG MAN, THIS IS A FINE POEM.
THE BEAUTIES OF NATURE INSPIRED MANY OF HIS POEMS - "THANATOPSIS", "TO A WATERFOWL", "THE DEATH OF THE FLOWERS" AND "TO THE FRINGED GENTIAN."
KERN
HIS INTEREST IN LITERATURE BEGAN AT AN EARLY AGE. HIS FIRST POEM WAS PUBLISHED BY A COUNTRY NEWSPAPER WHEN HE WAS 10. "THANATOPSIS," THE FIRST GREAT AMERICAN POEM, WAS WRITTEN WHEN HE WAS 17!

1795 - 1849

James K. Polk

LAWYER, CONGRESSMAN, GOVERNOR AND **ELEVENTH** PRESIDENT OF THE UNITED STATES (1845-49)

U.S. NAVAL ACADEMY ESTABLISHED AT ANNAPOLIS, 1845.

POLK WAS ALMOST NATIONALLY UNKNOWN WHEN HE BECAME AMERICA'S FIRST "DARK HORSE" PRESIDENTIAL CANDIDATE IN 1844. HE DEFEATED HENRY CLAY. ***DURING POLK'S ADMINISTRATION, THE POSTAGE STAMP WAS INTRODUCED, THE U.S. ACADEMY WAS ESTABLISHED (NAVY) AT ANNAPOLIS, THE SMITHSONIAN INSTITUTE WAS ESTABLISHED, GOLD WAS DISCOVERED IN CALIFORNIA AND THE OREGON TREATY WAS NEGOTIATED WITH GREAT BRITAIN. FEW PRESIDENTS EVER WORKED HARDER THAN POLK. HE DIED 6 MONTHS AFTER LEAVING OFFICE.***

HE WAS BORN IN MECKLENBURG CO., NORTH CAROLINA.

STATES WHICH CAME INTO THE UNION

TEXAS 1845
IOWA 1846
WISCONSIN .. 1848

THE GADSDEN PURCHASE, 1853

THE VICTORY IN THE MEXICAN WAR GAVE THE U.S. A VAST TERRITORY WHICH IS NOW ***ARIZONA, CALIFORNIA, NEVADA, NEW MEXICO, UTAH AND PART OF WYOMING.***

nihil videō quod timeam... ("I SEE NOTHING TO FEAR.")

HE GRADUATED FROM THE UNIVERSITY OF NORTH CAROLINA AT THE TOP OF HIS CLASS, DELIVERING HIS ***GRADUATION ADDRESS IN LATIN!***

KERN

1796 - 1859

Horace Mann

LAWYER, CONGRESSMAN, COLLEGE PRESIDENT AND ONE OF AMERICA'S LEADING EDUCATORS

THESE LAWS MUST BE PASSED.

DURING HIS TERM IN THE MASSACHUSETTS LEGISLATURE, HE HELPED ENACT LAWS PROHIBITING **THE SALE OF ALCOHOLIC BEVERAGES AND LOTTERY TICKETS, ESTABLISHED STATE HOSPITALS FOR THE INSANE AND CREATED THE FIRST BOARD OF EDUCATION IN THE UNITED STATES. IN 1837, HE LEFT POLITICS TO DEVOTE THE REST OF HIS LIFE TO IMPROVING SCHOOLS.**

HE WAS BORN IN FRANKLIN, MASS.
HORACE MANN WAS ONE OF THE GREAT MEN OF EDUCATION.
KERN

EDUCATION IS THE KEY TO SUCCESS.

MANN PLAYED A LEADING ROLE IN ESTABLISHING **THE ELEMENTARY SCHOOL SYSTEM IN THE U.S. AND AROUSED PUBLIC INTEREST IN EDUCATION. HE HAS BEEN CALLED "THE FATHER OF COMMON SCHOOLS."**

IN 1900 HE WAS ELECTED TO NEW YORK UNIVERSITY'S **HALL OF FAME TO HONOR GREAT AMERICANS.**

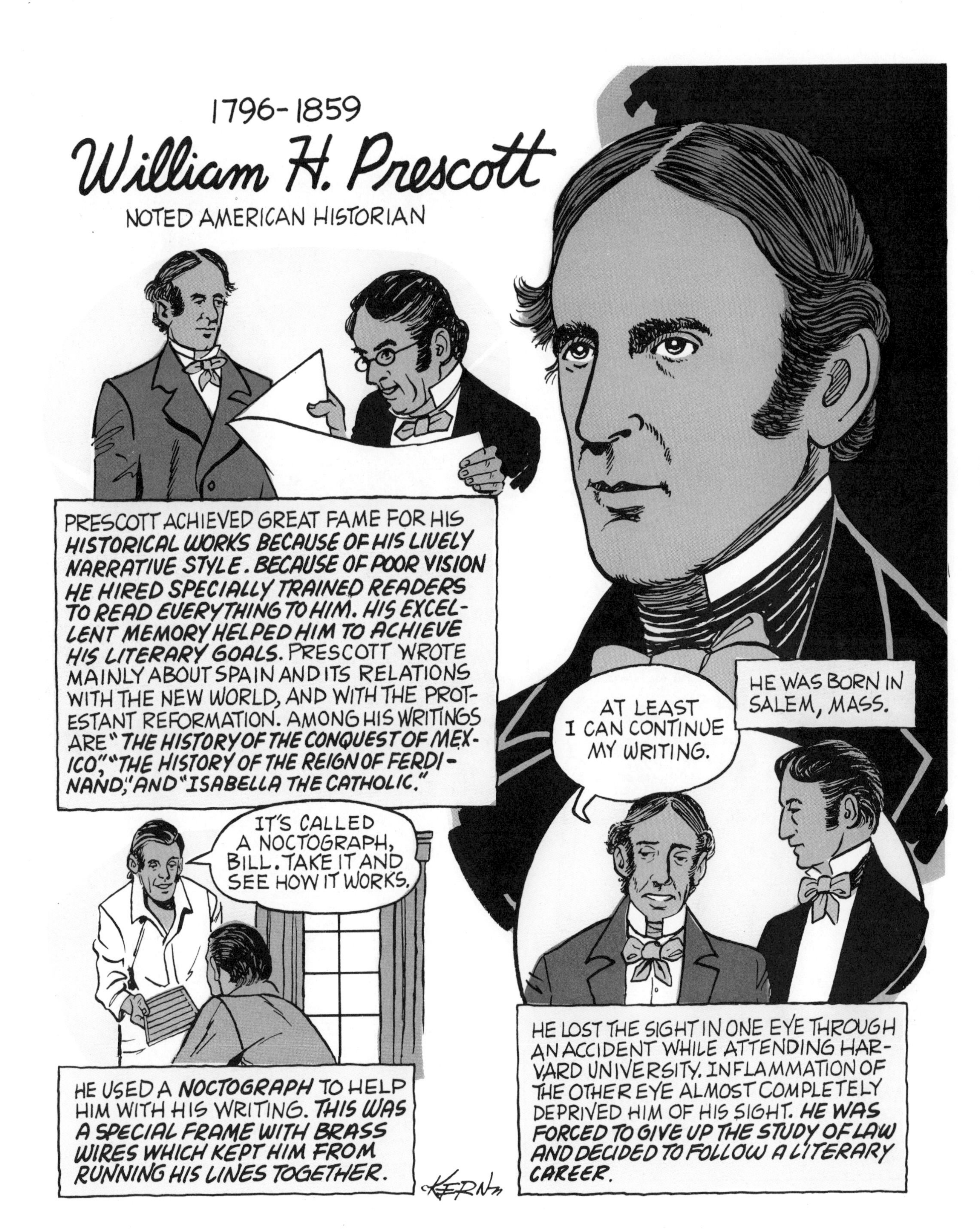
1796-1859
William H. Prescott
NOTED AMERICAN HISTORIAN
PRESCOTT ACHIEVED GREAT FAME FOR HIS HISTORICAL WORKS BECAUSE OF HIS LIVELY NARRATIVE STYLE. BECAUSE OF POOR VISION HE HIRED SPECIALLY TRAINED READERS TO READ EVERYTHING TO HIM. HIS EXCELLENT MEMORY HELPED HIM TO ACHIEVE HIS LITERARY GOALS. PRESCOTT WROTE MAINLY ABOUT SPAIN AND ITS RELATIONS WITH THE NEW WORLD, AND WITH THE PROTESTANT REFORMATION. AMONG HIS WRITINGS ARE "THE HISTORY OF THE CONQUEST OF MEXICO", "THE HISTORY OF THE REIGN OF FERDINAND," AND "ISABELLA THE CATHOLIC."
HE WAS BORN IN SALEM, MASS.
AT LEAST I CAN CONTINUE MY WRITING.
IT'S CALLED A NOCTOGRAPH, BILL. TAKE IT AND SEE HOW IT WORKS.
HE USED A NOCTOGRAPH TO HELP HIM WITH HIS WRITING. THIS WAS A SPECIAL FRAME WITH BRASS WIRES WHICH KEPT HIM FROM RUNNING HIS LINES TOGETHER.
HE LOST THE SIGHT IN ONE EYE THROUGH AN ACCIDENT WHILE ATTENDING HARVARD UNIVERSITY. INFLAMMATION OF THE OTHER EYE ALMOST COMPLETELY DEPRIVED HIM OF HIS SIGHT. HE WAS FORCED TO GIVE UP THE STUDY OF LAW AND DECIDED TO FOLLOW A LITERARY CAREER.
KERN

1796-1872

George Catlin

AMERICAN PAINTER, WRITER AND EXPLORER

HE WAS BORN IN WILKES-BARRE, PA.

REMARKABLE!

HIS PAINTINGS, WHICH HANG IN THE AMERICAN MUSEUM OF NATURAL HISTORY, NEW YORK CITY, AND THE NATIONAL GALLERY, WASHINGTON, D.C., ***HAVE GREAT HISTORIC VALUE.***

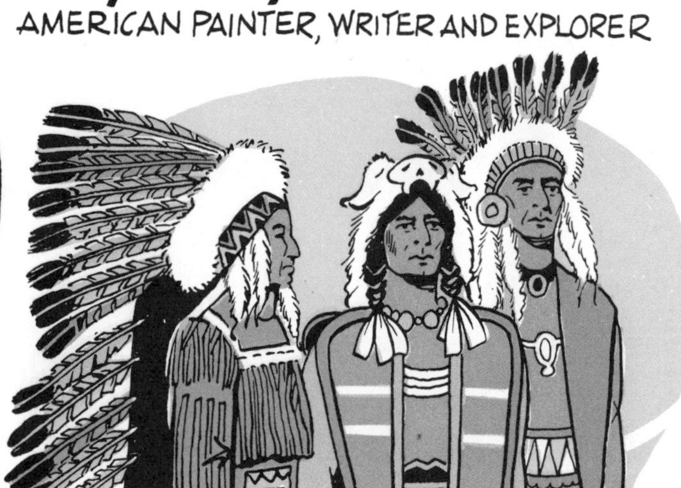

CATLIN PRACTICED LAW IN PHILADELPHIA BEFORE HE BECAME A SELF-TAUGHT ARTIST. ***AWARE THAT THE INDIANS' NATURAL STATE WAS NEARING ITS END, HE DEVOTED HIMSELF TO THE STUDY OF THE PRIMITIVE INDIAN TRIBES OF THE AMERICAS. GAINING THEIR ACCEPTANCE AS NO OTHER WHITE MAN DID, HE MADE PAINTINGS ABOUT THEIR HABITS AND CUSTOMS. MUCH OF OUR PRESENT-DAY KNOWLEDGE ABOUT INDIANS COMES FROM HIS BOOKS "MANNERS, CUSTOMS, AND CONDITIONS OF THE NORTH AMERICAN INDIANS" AND "LAST RAMBLES AMONG THE ROCKIES AND ANDES."*** AFTER A LONG SUCCESSFUL CAREER, HE BECAME DEPRESSED BY GROWING PUBLIC INDIFFERENCE TO HIS ART AND HIS INDIANS. ***HE WENT BANKRUPT AND DIED A BROKEN MAN.***

CATLIN SPENT 10 YRS. IN THE MIDWEST PAINTING THE INDIANS IN ALL THEIR SPLENDOR. ***HE HAS GIVEN US ONE OF THE GREATEST ARTISTIC RECORDS.***

KERN

1797 - 1878

Joseph Henry

AMERICAN PHYSICIST FAMOUS FOR HIS DISCOVERIES IN ELECTROMAGNETISM

HE WAS BORN IN ALBANY, N.Y.

WHILE TEACHING AT ALBANY ACADEMY, HE BEGAN EXPERIMENTING IN ELECTROMAGNETISM. ***HIS FIRST IMPORTANT WORK WAS THE IMPROVEMENT OF THE ELECTROMAGNET. IN 1831, HENRY CONSTRUCTED THE FIRST PRACTICAL ELECTROMAGNETIC TELEGRAPH AND THE FIRST ELECTRIC MOTOR.*** HE WAS ACTIVE IN FOUNDING THE NATIONAL ACADEMY OF SCIENCES AND WAS SELECTED PRESIDENT IN 1867.

I AM NOT AN INVENTOR. I ONLY DEMONSTRATE A SCIENTIFIC PRINCIPLE. OTHER MEN CAN APPLY IT TO A PRACTICAL INVENTION.

HENRY'S EXPERIMENTS PLAYED AN IMPORTANT PART IN THE DEVELOPMENT OF THE ***TELEPHONE, TELEGRAPH, RADIO AND DYNAMO.***

HE WAS THE ***FIRST DIRECTOR OF THE SMITHSONIAN INSTITUTE,*** WHERE HE USED THE TELEGRAPH TO TRANSMIT WEATHER REPORTS. ***HIS SUCCESSFUL WORK AT THE INSTITUTION LED TO THE CREATION OF THE U.S. WEATHER BUREAU.***

1800 - 1860

Charles Goodyear

AMERICAN INVENTOR AND PIONEER OF THE RUBBER INDUSTRY

GOODYEAR HAD NO FORMAL EDUCATION. HE WAS IN THE HARDWARE BUSINESS WITH HIS FATHER, BUT IT FAILED. **EVEN WHILE HE WAS IN DEBTORS' PRISON HE TRIED TO IMPROVE THE PROCESS FOR CURING INDIA RUBBER. AFTER MANY FAILURES, HE FINALLY WAS SUCCESSFUL IN VULCANIZING RUBBER. HE BORROWED $50,000 TO PERFECT HIS PROCESS, AND GOT HIS PATENT IN 1844. FINANCIAL OBLIGATIONS FORCED HIM TO SELL HIS PATENT RIGHTS FOR A SMALL SUM. HE WENT TO EUROPE FROM 1851-59 AND ESTABLISHED A RUBBER BUSINESS, BUT POOR HEALTH, INCREASING DEBTS AND UNSUCCESSFUL LAWSUITS WERE TOO MUCH FOR HIM. HE DIED IN POVERTY.**

HE WAS BORN IN NEW HAVEN, CONN.

HE PATENTED A RUBBER PROCESS IN 1837 WHICH HE USED IN MAKING **SHOES, TABLECLOTHS AND PIANO COVERS.**

IN 1839, GOODYEAR ACCIDENTLY DROPPED A **RUBBER AND SULFUR MIXTURE ON A HOT STOVE. THE RUBBER DID NOT MELT. THIS LED TO THE DISCOVERY OF THE VULCANIZING PROCESS.**

1800-1874

Millard Fillmore

CONGRESSMAN, VICE-PRESIDENT AND ***THIRTEENTH*** PRESIDENT OF THE UNITED STATES (1850-53)

WE MUST ESTABLISH TRADE WITH JAPAN.

I'LL DO MY BEST, MR. PRESIDENT.

VICE-PRESIDENT WITH ZACHARY TAYLOR, FILLMORE BECAME PRESIDENT WHEN TAYLOR DIED IN 1850. PRES. FILLMORE SIGNED THE ***"COMPROMISE OF 1850" WHICH ABOLISHED SLAVERY IN THE DISTRICT OF COLUMBIA, ADMITTED CALIFORNIA TO THE UNION AS A FREE STATE AND TIGHTENED LAWS CONCERNING FUGITIVE SLAVES FOR THE PROTECTION OF SLAVE OWNERS.*** IN 1852, HE SENT COMMODORE MATTHEW PERRY TO JAPAN, AN EXPEDITION WHICH LATER RESULTED IN THE OPENING OF JAPANESE PORTS TO TRADE.

HE WAS BORN IN CAYUGA COUNTY LOCATED NEAR LOCKE, NEW YORK.
MORSE NEEDS THIS MONEY FOR HIS UNUSUAL INVENTION.

WHILE SERVING AS A CONGRESSMAN, HE WAS VERY HELPFUL IN GETTING A **$30,000** ***GRANT FOR SAMUEL MORSE SO HE COULD DEVELOP HIS TELEGRAPH.***

IN 1851, WHEN THE LIBRARY OF CONGRESS BURNED, PRESIDENT FILLMORE AND HIS CABINET FORMED A BUCKET BRIGADE AND HELPED ***PUT OUT THE FIRE!***

1801 - 1870

David G. Farragut

FAMOUS AMERICAN NAVAL HERO

I AM AT YOUR SERVICE, SIR.

FARRAGUT FOUGHT THE BRITISH SHIPS IN 1814. DURING THE MEXICAN WAR, HE COMMANDED SHIPS UNDER COMMODORE PERRY. ***AT THE OUTBREAK OF THE CIVIL WAR, HE OFFERED HIS SERVICES TO THE FEDERAL GOVERNMENT. HE WAS IN COMMAND OF THE WEST GULF BLOCKADING SQUADRON AND IN APR. 1862, CAPTURED NEW ORLEANS. HE BLOCKADED VICKSBURG AND SECURED THE SURRENDER OF FORTS MORGAN AND GAINES AT THE ENTRANCE OF MOBILE BAY.*** HE WAS ONE OF THE FIRST TO BE ELECTED TO THE AMERICAN ***HALL OF FAME.***

HE WAS BORN NEAR KNOXVILLE, TENN.

WE THANK YOU, ADMIRAL.

CONGRESS CREATED, ESPECIALLY FOR HIM, THE RANK OF ***VICE-ADMIRAL IN 1864 AND ADMIRAL IN 1866 FOR HIS OUTSTANDING SERVICE!***

FARRAGUT WON FAME AT THE ***BATTLE OF MOBILE BAY DURING THE CIVIL WAR WITH HIS SLOGAN*** "DAMN THE TORPEDOES! FULL STEAM AHEAD!"

KERN

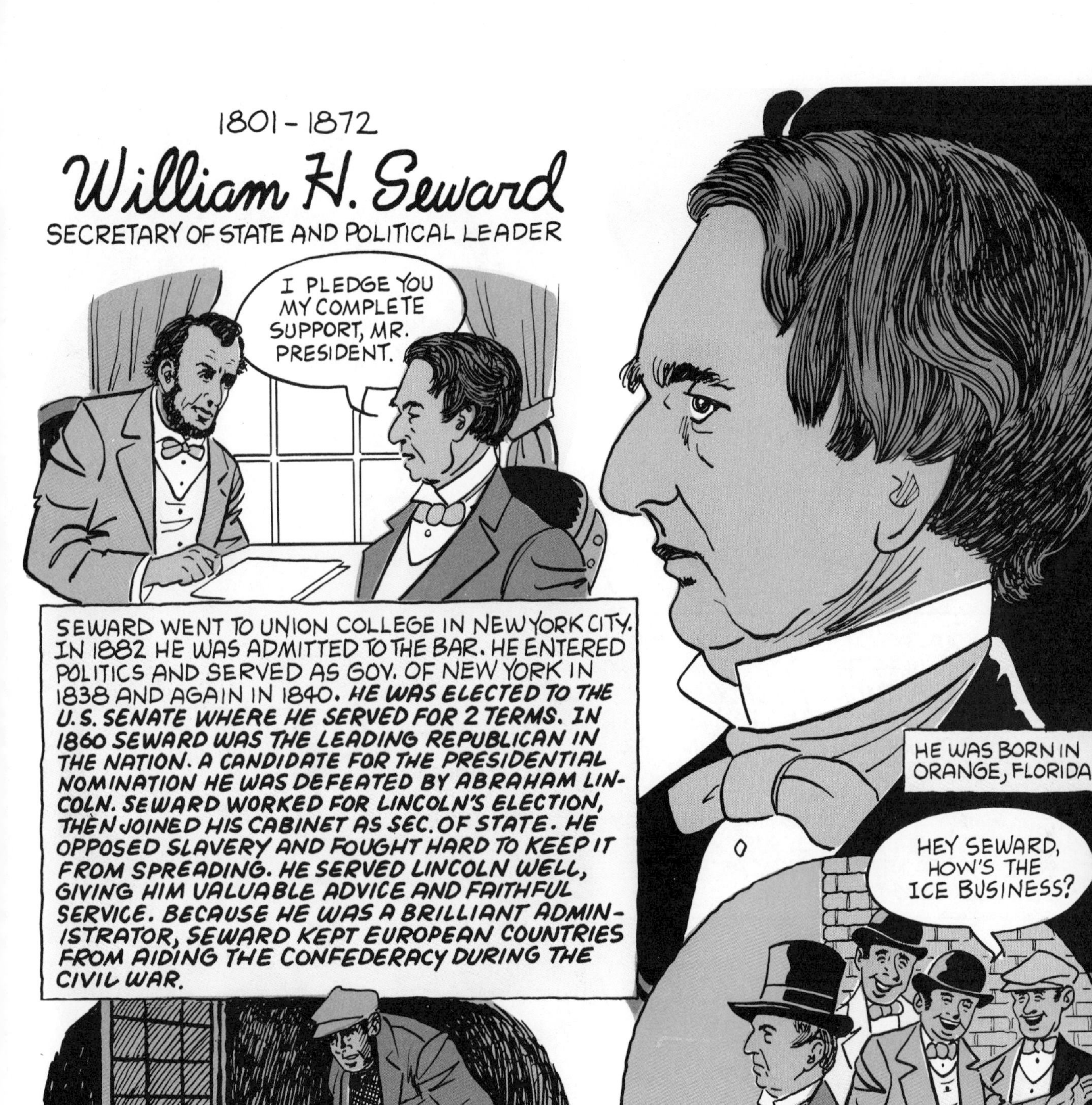

SEWARD WAS WOUNDED BY AN ACCOMPLICE OF BOOTH ON THE NIGHT OF LINCOLN'S ASSASSINATION. **HE RECOVERED AND CONTINUED AS SEC. OF STATE UNDER PRES. ANDREW JOHNSON.**

ONE OF SEWARD'S IMPORTANT ACCOMPLISHMENTS WAS THE PURCHASE OF **ALASKA FROM RUSSIA. AT THE TIME IT WAS CALLED "SEWARD'S FOLLY" AND "SEWARD'S ICE BOX." ALASKA PROVED VERY VALUABLE TO THE U.S. IT BECAME THE 49th STATE IN 1958.**

1801 - 1877

Brigham Young

AMERICAN MORMON LEADER

BRIGHAM YOUNG SETTLED IN MONROE COUNTY, NEW YORK, 40 MILES FROM JOSEPH SMITH WHO FOUNDED THE **MORMON CHURCH**. YOUNG BECAME INTERESTED IN MORMONISM AND AFTER 2 YRS. OF STUDY JOINED THE CHURCH IN 1832. ***WHEN SMITH DIED, YOUNG BECAME THE SECOND PRESIDENT AND BRILLIANT LEADER OF THE MORMON CHURCH OR AS IT IS PROPERLY CALLED*** "THE CHURCH OF JESUS CHRIST OF LATTER-DAY SAINTS." ***HE SPENT THE REST OF HIS LIFE SERVING THE CHURCH.***

YOUNG TRAVELED THROUGHOUT THE EASTERN PART OF THE UNITED STATES TO CONVERT PEOPLE. ***HE WAS THE MOST SUCCESSFUL MISSIONARY AT THAT TIME.***

©KERN

HE WAS BORN IN WHITINGHAM, VT.

I HOPE YOU CAN SERVE AS THE TERRITORIAL GOVERNOR.

I WILL SERVE TO THE BEST OF MY ABILITY, MR. PRESIDENT.

IN THE WINTER OF 1846, YOUNG AND 143 FOLLOWERS SET OUT ON THEIR LONG AND DIFFICULT JOURNEY WEST. ***THEY ARRIVED IN THE VALLEY OF THE GREAT SALT LAKE IN UTAH, JULY 1847. PRES. FILLMORE APPOINTED HIM GOVERNOR OF THE TERRITORY OF UTAH IN 1850.***

1803 - 1882

Ralph Waldo Emerson

INFLUENTIAL POET, ESSAYIST AND PHILOSOPHER

YOU ARE NOW LICENSED TO PREACH.

HE GRADUATED FROM HARVARD AT 18 AND IN 1826 WAS LICENSED TO BE A UNITARIAN MINISTER OF THE SECOND CHURCH OF BOSTON. RESIGNING IN 1832, HE WENT TO CONCORD, MASS. TO WRITE AND LECTURE. **HE WROTE "ENGLISH TRAITS",** A BRILLIANT BOOK ON TRAVEL. OTHER IMPORTANT WORKS WERE "**REPRESENTATIVE MEN**" AND THE "**CONDUCT OF LIFE**." **THE FIRST STANZA FROM HIS CONCORD HYMN IS INSCRIBED AT THE BASE OF THE MINUTE MAN STATUE AT CONCORD.**

"BY THE RUDE BRIDGE THAT ARCHED THE FLOOD,
THEIR FLAG TO APRIL'S BREEZE UNFURLED,
HERE ONCE THE EMBATTLED FARMERS STOOD,
AND FIRED THE SHOT HEARD ROUND THE WORLD."

HE WAS BORN IN BOSTON, MASS.

I WANT TO THANK YOU FOR GIVING ME NEW COURAGE IN LIFE.

IN 1836, HE PUBLISHED HIS FIRST BOOK CALLED "**NATURE**." **THIS BOOK EXPRESSED THE INFLUENCE OF NATURE ON MAN. IT HAS COME TO BE REGARDED AS HIS MOST ORIGINAL AND SIGNIFICANT WORK.**

EMERSON WROTE "**TO AWAKE IN MAN AND TO RAISE THE FEELING OF HIS WORTH.**" HIS WRITINGS INSPIRED MANY READERS WITH NEW COURAGE TO BE THEMSELVES. **EMERSON'S DOCTRINE OF TRANSCENDENTALISM WAS A PLEA FOR FREEDOM OF THE INDIVIDUAL FROM MAN-MADE RESTRAINTS.**

1804 - 1864
Nathaniel Hawthorne
DISTINGUISHED NOVELIST AND STORY WRITER
HAWTHORNE GRADUATED FROM BOWDOIN COLLEGE IN 1825. TWO OF HIS CLOSEST FRIENDS WERE HENRY W. LONGFELLOW AND FRANKLIN PIERCE WHO LATER BECAME OUR 14th PRESIDENT. FOR MANY YEARS HIS WRITINGS RECEIVED NO RECOGNITION. HE WORKED IN THE BOSTON CUSTOM HOUSE TO EARN A LIVING, THEN TWO YEARS LATER HE RETURNED TO WRITING. HE WROTE "THE HOUSE OF SEVEN GABLES", "THE WONDER BOOK" AND "THE SNOW IMAGE." THE "BLITHEDALE ROMANCE" WAS INSPIRED BY HIS ADVENTURE IN COOPERATIVE LIVING AT BROOK FARM NEAR BOSTON. WHILE TRAVELING WITH FRANKLIN PIERCE IN 1864, HAWTHORNE DIED AND WAS BURIED AT CONCORD NEAR THOREAU AND EMERSON.
HE WAS BORN IN SALEM, MASS.
I WISH YOU A SAFE TRIP, NATHANIEL.
THANK YOU, FRANKLIN.
PRES. PIERCE SENT HIM TO LIVERPOOL, ENGLAND, AS THE U.S. CONSUL IN 1853. HE HELD THIS POST FOR 4 YRS. HAWTHORNE THEN WENT TO ITALY WHERE HE WROTE "THE MARBLE FAUN." ON HIS RETURN TO THE U.S. HE WROTE "OUR OLD HOME," HIS IMPRESSIONS OF ENGLAND.

THIS IS A REMARKABLE BOOK.
The Scarlet Le
HAWTHORNE WON FAME WHEN "THE SCARLET LETTER" WAS PUBLISHED IN 1850. THIS WORK HAS BECOME ONE OF THE CLASSICS OF AMERICAN LITERATURE.
KERN

1804-1869

Franklin Pierce

CONGRESSMAN, U.S. SENATOR, GOVERNOR AND **FOURTEENTH** PRESIDENT OF THE UNITED STATES (1853-57)

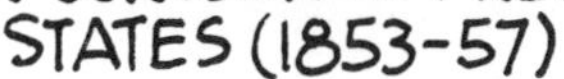

AS A CONGRESSMAN, I INTEND TO SUPPORT JACKSON'S POLICIES.

PIERCE WAS EDUCATED AT BOWDOIN COLLEGE MAINE, WHERE HE GRADUATED WITH HONORS IN 1824. **HE STUDIED LAW AND OPENED A LAW OFFICE IN CONCORD, NEW HAMPSHIRE. FROM 1833-37 HE WAS A MEMBER OF THE HOUSE OF REPRESENTATIVES, AND SUPPORTED THE POLICIES OF ANDREW JACKSON. HE WAS ELECTED U.S. SENATOR IN 1837 BUT RESIGNED IN 1842. DURING THE MEXICAN WAR, HE ENLISTED IN THE U.S. ARMY AND WAS SOON PROMOTED TO A BRIGADIER GENERAL.**

HE WAS BORN IN HILLSBORO, N.H.

WELCOME TO OUR COUNTRY.
THANK YOU, AND GREETINGS FROM MY PRESIDENT.

DURING HIS ADMINISTRATION, **COMMODORE PERRY OPENED JAPAN TO AMERICAN TRADE, THE NATIONAL DEBT WAS REDUCED FROM 60 TO 11 MILLION, AND THE GADSDEN PURCHASE ADDED 45,535 SQ. MI. TO THE TERRITORY OF THE UNITED STATES.**

I THINK THIS BILL IS A STEP IN THE RIGHT DIRECTION.

PIERCE SIGNED **THE KANSAS-NEBRASKA ACT WHICH CREATED 2 NEW WESTERN TERRITORIES. HERE SETTLERS WERE ALLOWED TO DECIDE THE SLAVERY QUESTION BY THEMSELVES AND BLOODY BATTLES OCCURRED AS THE OPPOSING FORCES FOUGHT FOR CONTROL.**

KERN

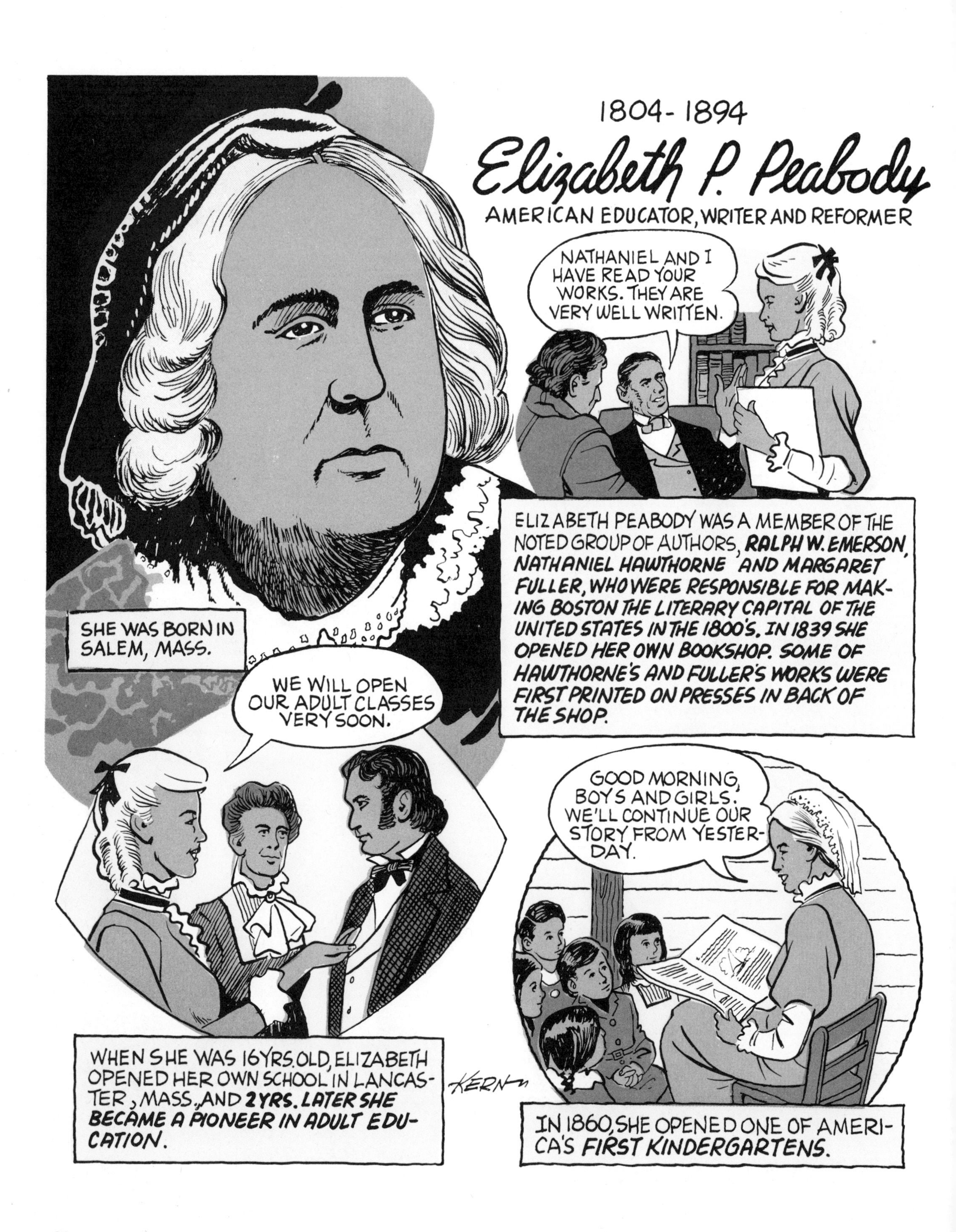
1804-1894
Elizabeth P. Peabody
AMERICAN EDUCATOR, WRITER AND REFORMER
NATHANIEL AND I HAVE READ YOUR WORKS. THEY ARE VERY WELL WRITTEN.
ELIZABETH PEABODY WAS A MEMBER OF THE NOTED GROUP OF AUTHORS, RALPH W. EMERSON, NATHANIEL HAWTHORNE AND MARGARET FULLER, WHO WERE RESPONSIBLE FOR MAKING BOSTON THE LITERARY CAPITAL OF THE UNITED STATES IN THE 1800'S. IN 1839 SHE OPENED HER OWN BOOKSHOP. SOME OF HAWTHORNE'S AND FULLER'S WORKS WERE FIRST PRINTED ON PRESSES IN BACK OF THE SHOP.
SHE WAS BORN IN SALEM, MASS.
WE WILL OPEN OUR ADULT CLASSES VERY SOON.
WHEN SHE WAS 16YRS.OLD, ELIZABETH OPENED HER OWN SCHOOL IN LANCASTER, MASS., AND 2YRS. LATER SHE BECAME A PIONEER IN ADULT EDUCATION.
GOOD MORNING, BOYS AND GIRLS. WE'LL CONTINUE OUR STORY FROM YESTERDAY.
IN 1860, SHE OPENED ONE OF AMERICA'S FIRST KINDERGARTENS.
KERN

1806 - 1869

John Augustus Roebling

CIVIL ENGINEER AND INDUSTRIALIST

ROEBLING CAME TO THE U.S. IN 1831. ***HE WAS A PIONEER IN THE USE AND MANUFACTURE OF STEEL CABLE IN THE BUILDING OF STEEL SUSPENSION BRIDGES. AFTER BUILDING MANY U.S. BRIDGES, HE WAS CHOSEN THE CHIEF ENGINEER FOR THE BROOKLYN BRIDGE PROJECT, BUT DIED FROM A FOOT INJURY BEFORE IT WAS FINISHED.***

THIS BRIDGE WAS ***THE WORLD'S FIRST GREAT SUSPENSION BRIDGE. IT IS 1,595 FEET LONG AND COST $15,000,000.***

HE WAS BORN IN MÜHLHAUSEN, GERMANY.

1837 - 1926

Washington A. Roebling

CIVIL ENGINEER AND INDUSTRIALIST

I'LL TAKE CARE OF ALL OF YOUR INSTRUCTIONS.

THANK YOU, SAM.

ROEBLING GRADUATED FROM POLYTECHNIC INSTITUTE, TROY, N.Y. ***HE SERVED WITH DISTINCTION AS AN ENGINEER WITH THE UNION ARMY (1861-65). AFTER THE WAR HE JOINED HIS FATHER, JOHN, IN HIS BRIDGE CONSTRUCTION PROJECTS. AFTER JOHN'S DEATH, THE ENTIRE DIRECTION OF THE BROOKLYN BRIDGE WAS HIS. HE WORKED SO HARD THAT HIS HEALTH BROKE DOWN AND HE HAD TO SUPERVISE THE ENTIRE PROJECT FROM HIS BEDROOM, UNTIL THE BRIDGE WAS COMPLETED IN 1883.***

HE WAS BORN IN SAXONBURG, PA.

KERN

1807-1870
Robert E. Lee
COMMANDER-IN-CHIEF OF THE ARMIES OF THE SOUTH IN THE CIVIL WAR
LEE'S TROOPS BADE THEIR BELOVED LEADER A SILENT FAREWELL.
LEE WAS 22 WHEN HE GRADUATED SECOND IN HIS CLASS FROM WEST POINT. HE DISTINGUISHED HIMSELF IN THE MEXICAN WAR, WINNING 3 PROMOTIONS. HIS COMMANDING GENERAL WINFIELD SCOTT, CALLED HIM "THE GREATEST MILITARY GENIUS IN AMERICA." LATER AS THE COMMANDING GENERAL OF THE SOUTHERN FORCES, HIS BRILLIANT MILITARY STRATEGY WAS OVERCOME ONLY BY THE UNION'S SUPERIOR MANPOWER AND RESOURCES. DEPRIVED OF HIS PROPERTY AFTER THE CIVIL WAR, HE REFUSED FINANCIAL AID AND ACCEPTED THE PRESIDENCY OF WASHINGTON COLLEGE (NOW CALLED WASHINGTON AND LEE UNIVERSITY) AT LEXINGTON, VIRGINIA.
HE WAS BORN IN STRATFORD, VA.
I NEED YOU, ROBERT.
THANK YOU, MR. PRESIDENT, BUT I MUST DECLINE.
IN EARLY 1861 PRES. LINCOLN OFFERED LEE THE FIELD COMMAND OF THE UNION FORCES, BUT LEE DECLINED. HE OPPOSED THE BREAKUP OF THE UNION BUT FELT HE HAD TO BE LOYAL TO THE SOUTHERN STATES.
THE CIVIL WAR ENDED APR. 9, 1865, WHEN LEE SURRENDERED TO GENERAL ULYSSES GRANT AT THE APPOMATTOX COURT HOUSE.

1807-1873
Louis Agassiz
SWISS-AMERICAN ZOOLOGIST AND GEOLOGIST
IT'S A FOREGONE CONCLUSION THAT ANIMAL SPECIES DO NOT CHANGE.
HE WAS BORN IN MOTIERS, SWITZERLAND.
HE STUDIED AT THE UNIVERSITIES OF ZURICH, HEIDELBERG AND MUNICH, GRADUATING WITH DEGREES IN MEDICINE AND PHILOSOPHY. HE BECAME WELL KNOWN FOR HIS STUDY OF FOSSIL FORMS OF FISHES. IN 1848 HE WAS APPOINTED PROFESSOR OF NATURAL HISTORY AT HARVARD UNIVERSITY, WHERE HE FOUNDED THE MUSEUM OF NATURAL HISTORY, NOW KNOWN AS AGASSIZ MUSEUM. HE ESTABLISHED A ZOOLOGICAL LABORATORY ON AN ISLAND OFF THE COAST OF MASS. TO TRAIN TEACHERS OF NATURAL HISTORY. AGASSIZ CRITICIZED DARWIN'S THEORIES ON EVOLUTION BECAUSE HE BELIEVED THAT ANIMAL SPECIES DO NOT CHANGE.
HIS ENTHUSIASM, CLEAR THOUGHTS AND ELOQUENCE MADE HIM AN EXCELLENT TEACHER. HE ATTRACTED STUDENTS WHO THEMSELVES BECAME EMINENT BIOLOGISTS.
IN HIS LATER YEARS AT HARVARD, HE DEVOTED HIS TIME TO LECTURING AND EXPLORATIONS. HE EXPLORED THE LAKE SUPERIOR REGION AND THE FLORIDA CORAL REEFS. HE WROTE THE 4 VOLUMES OF "CONTRIBUTIONS TO THE NATURAL HISTORY TO THE UNITED STATES."
KERU

1807-1882
Henry W. Longfellow
ONE OF AMERICA'S MOST DISTINGUISHED POETS AND SCHOLARS
WE'LL MISS YOU HERE AT HARVARD, HENRY.
HE WAS EDUCATED AT BOWDOIN COLLEGE IN BRUNSWICK, MAINE, AND STUDIED IN FRANCE, ITALY, SPAIN AND GERMANY. HE WAS A PROFESSOR OF MODERN LANGUAGES AT BOWDOIN FOR 6YRS. AND AT HARVARD UNIVERSITY FOR 9 YRS. IN 1854 LONGFELLOW DEVOTED HIMSELF EXCLUSIVELY TO WRITING. HE WAS ONE OF THE MOST POPULAR AND BEST LOVED POETS OF HIS TIME. MORE THAN 300,000 COPIES OF HIS BOOKS OF VERSE WERE SOLD. SOME OF HIS BEST KNOWN POEMS WERE "THE VILLAGE BLACKSMITH," "PAUL REVERES RIDE," "THE WRECK OF THE HESPERUS," "HIAWATHA" AND "THE COURTSHIP OF MILES STANDISH."
HE WAS BORN IN PORTLAND, MAINE.
KEEP UP THE GOOD WORK, YOUNG MAN.
HIS FIRST POEM, "THE BATTLE OF LOVELL'S POND," WAS PUBLISHED IN THE "PORTLAND GAZETTE" WHEN HE WAS 13YRS. OLD.
THANK YOU, HENRY, FOR ALL YOUR HELP.
GLAD TO BE OF HELP, JOHN.
A VERY SINCERE AND KIND MAN, LONGFELLOW ALWAYS HAD TIME TO HELP ANYONE WHO CALLED ON HIM.
KERN

1808-1875

Andrew Johnson

CONGRESSMAN, GOVERNOR, SENATOR, VICE-PRESIDENT AND **SEVENTEENTH** PRESIDENT OF THE UNITED STATES (1865-69)

HE WAS BORN IN RALEIGH, N. C.
LET'S STICK TOGETHER AND FIGHT.

WE ARE AT YOUR SERVICE, MR. PRESIDENT.

WHEN JOHNSON WAS 10 YRS. OLD, HE WAS APPRENTICED TO A TAILOR, AND IN 8 YRS. HE HAD HIS OWN SHOP. ***HIS WIFE TAUGHT HIM WRITING AND ARITHMETIC. AFTER 10 YRS. IN LOCAL POLITICS, JOHNSON SERVED AS U.S. REPRESENTATIVE, GOV. OF TENNESSEE AND AS A U.S. SENATOR. LINCOLN APPOINTED HIM MILITARY GOV. OF TENNESSEE (1862-64). ELECTED VICE-PRESIDENT WITH LINCOLN IN 1865, HE TOOK OFFICE 6 WKS. LATER WHEN LINCOLN WAS ASSASSINATED. JOHNSON TRIED TO CARRY OUT LINCOLN'S PROGRAM OF KIND AND GENEROUS TREATMENT OF THE SOUTH BUT CONGRESS BLOCKED EVERY MOVE HE MADE.***

NEBRASKA JOINED THE UNION IN 1867.

JOHNSON DEFIED A VERY UNFRIENDLY CONGRESS BY VETOING BILLS WHICH WOULD PUNISH THE SOUTH. ***BITTER FEELINGS AROSE WHEN JOHNSON DISMISSED SEC. OF WAR STANTON WITHOUT THE SENATE'S CONSENT. THE HOUSE VOTED FOR JOHNSON'S IMPEACHMENT 128-47, BUT THE SENATE FAILED BY ONE VOTE TO REMOVE HIM FROM OFFICE!***

KERN

DURING JOHNSON'S ADMINISTRATION, ***ALASKA WAS PURCHASED, THE 13th AND 14th AMENDMENTS TO THE CONSTITUTION WERE ADOPTED, FREEING ALL REMAINING SLAVES AND MAKING THEM CITIZENS. NEBRASKA JOINED THE UNION.***

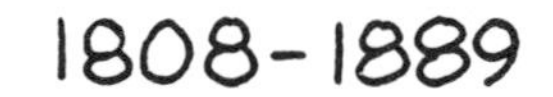

Jefferson Davis

PRESIDENT OF THE CONFEDERATE STATES DURING THE CIVIL WAR

I EMPLORE YOU, DO NOT SECEDE!

A WEST POINT GRADUATE, DAVIS HAD A WIDE EXPERIENCE AS A STATESMAN, CONGRESSMAN, SENATOR, CABINET MEMBER AND SOLDIER. **AS A SECOND TERM SENATOR, HE BECAME THE SPOKESMAN FOR THE SOUTHERN POINT OF VIEW. OPPOSED TO THE IDEA OF SECESSION, HE TRIED TO KEEP THE SOUTHERN STATES IN THE UNION. WHEN MISSISSIPPI SECEDED, HE RESIGNED FROM THE SENATE. ON FEB. 18, 1861, HE WAS MADE PRESIDENT OF THE CONFEDERATE STATES. HE WAS NOT POPULAR WITH THE PEOPLE DURING THE WAR YEARS, BUT EVENTUALLY WON THEIR RESPECT AND AFFECTION AFTER THE WAR BECAUSE OF HIS LIFELONG DEFENSE OF THE SOUTHERN CAUSE.**

HE WAS BORN IN TODD CO., KY.

THIS BOOK GIVES A LOOK AT THE PROBLEMS WE HAD TO FACE.

DAVIS SPENT HIS LAST DAYS WRITING AND STUDYING IN HIS HOME AT BILOXI, MISS. IN 1881, HE PUBLISHED "***THE RISE AND FALL OF THE CONFEDERATE GOVERNMENT.***"

I'M READY TO GO WITH YOU.

IN 1866, ***DAVIS WAS INDICTED FOR TREASON, THEN RELEASED ON $100,000 BAIL. THE NEXT YEAR THE TRIAL WAS DROPPED BY THE FEDERAL GOVERNMENT.***

1809 - 1849

Edgar Allan Poe

WORLD-RENOWNED SHORT STORY WRITER AND POET

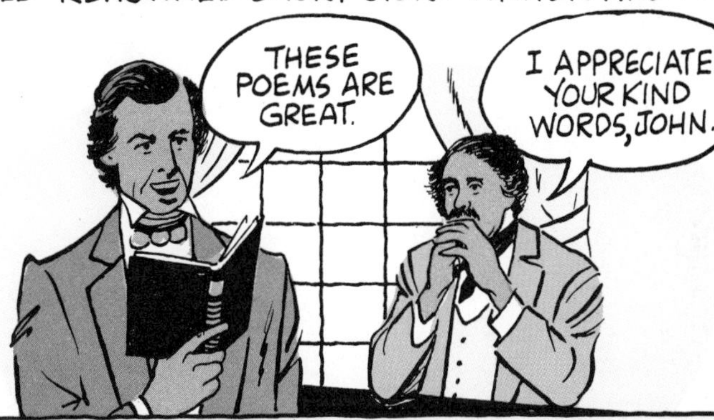

THESE POEMS ARE GREAT.
I APPRECIATE YOUR KIND WORDS, JOHN.

POE'S POEMS "THE RAVEN" AND "ANNABEL LEE" RANK HIM AMONG THE FINEST POETS AMERICA HAS PRODUCED. HIS WORK SHOWS ROMANTIC IMAGINATION AND ORIGINALITY. POE'S FAVORITE SUBJECT WAS DEATH AND HIS WRITINGS WERE MYSTERIOUS AND MORBID. HE SUFFERED ILL HEALTH AND MISFORTUNE MOST OF HIS LIFE. SOME OF HIS NOTED STORIES, "THE PURLOINED LETTER," "THE FALL OF THE HOUSE OF USHER," "THE CASK OF AMONTILLADO" AND "THE PIT AND THE PENDULUM," WERE PRINTED IN MANY LANGUAGES.

HE WAS BORN IN BOSTON, MASS.

POE'S GRAVE IN BALTIMORE IS ONE OF AMERICA'S LITERARY SHRINES. HE WAS ELECTED TO THE HALL OF FAME AT NEW YORK UNIVERSITY IN 1910.

WE ARE HAPPY TO HAVE YOU ON OUR STAFF, EDGAR.

IN 1835, POE JOINED THE STAFF OF THE "SOUTHERN LITERARY MESSENGER" AS A WRITER. THE CIRCULATION INCREASED 7 TIMES BECAUSE OF POE'S STORIES, POEMS AND LITERARY REVIEWS.

1809 - 1865

Abraham Lincoln

CONGRESSMAN, SOLDIER, DEBATER AND *SIXTEENTH* PRESIDENT OF THE UNITED STATES (1861-65)

"ABE" LINCOLN WAS 7 YRS. OLD WHEN HE MOVED FROM KENTUCKY TO INDIANA WITH HIS PARENTS. *ONLY A YEAR OF HIS YOUTH WAS SPENT IN SCHOOL. LINCOLN HIRED OUT AS A LABORER WHEN HE WAS 16 YRS. OLD FOR 25¢ A DAY. WHEN HE WAS 21, HE MOVED TO ILLINOIS. HE GOT HIS LICENSE TO PRACTICE LAW IN 1836. HE WAS ELECTED U.S. REPRESENTATIVE FROM ILLINOIS (1847-49). LINCOLN WON NATIONAL PROMINENCE, DEBATING STEPHEN DOUGLAS ON THE SLAVERY ISSUE. KNOWN AS "HONEST ABE," THIS HUMBLE, GENTLE, WITTY AND DYNAMIC MAN WAS ONE OF AMERICA'S GREATEST PRESIDENTS. HE SERVED FOR 4 YRS., 6 WKS. BEFORE HE WAS ASSASSINATED APRIL 14, 1865.*

HE WAS BORN NEAR HODGENVILLE, KY.

IN 1863, *LINCOLN DEDICATED THE CEMETERY AT GETTYSBURG WITH HIS FAMOUS "GETTYSBURG ADDRESS," ONE OF THE MOST MOVING EXPRESSIONS OF THE DEMOCRATIC SPIRIT EVER GIVEN.*

DURING HIS ADMINISTRATION, *THE CIVIL WAR TOOK PLACE, THE FIRST FEDERAL PAPER MONEY WAS ISSUED, FREE MAIL DELIVERY WAS ESTABLISHED, A PROCLAMATION WAS ISSUED FREEING THE SLAVES AND THE FIRST MILITARY DRAFT IN THE U.S.A. WAS STARTED.*

KERN

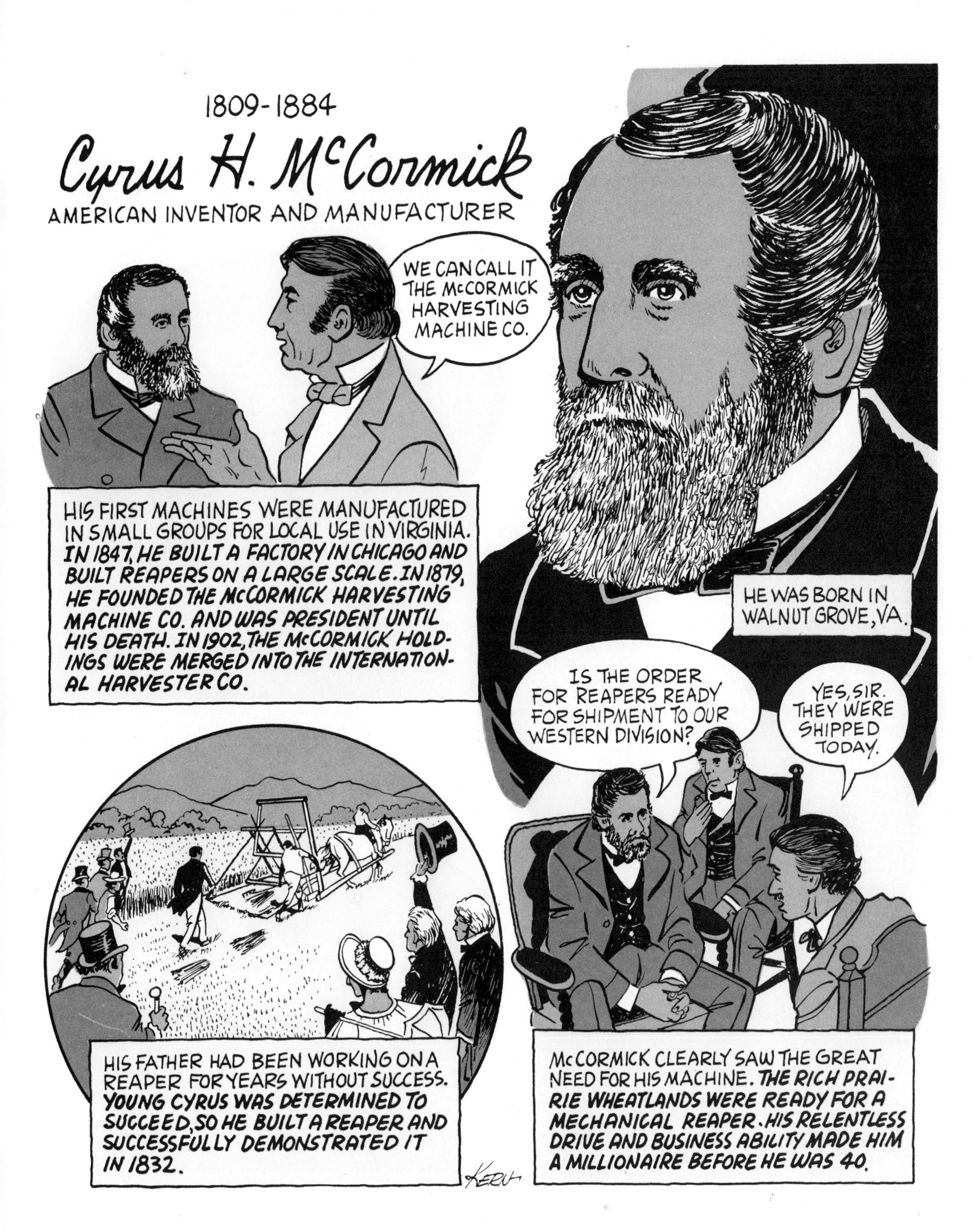
1809-1884
Cyrus H. McCormick
AMERICAN INVENTOR AND MANUFACTURER
WE CAN CALL IT THE McCORMICK HARVESTING MACHINE CO.
HIS FIRST MACHINES WERE MANUFACTURED IN SMALL GROUPS FOR LOCAL USE IN VIRGINIA. IN 1847, HE BUILT A FACTORY IN CHICAGO AND BUILT REAPERS ON A LARGE SCALE. IN 1879, HE FOUNDED THE McCORMICK HARVESTING MACHINE CO. AND WAS PRESIDENT UNTIL HIS DEATH. IN 1902, THE McCORMICK HOLDINGS WERE MERGED INTO THE INTERNATIONAL HARVESTER CO.
HE WAS BORN IN WALNUT GROVE, VA.
IS THE ORDER FOR REAPERS READY FOR SHIPMENT TO OUR WESTERN DIVISION?
YES, SIR. THEY WERE SHIPPED TODAY.
HIS FATHER HAD BEEN WORKING ON A REAPER FOR YEARS WITHOUT SUCCESS. YOUNG CYRUS WAS DETERMINED TO SUCCEED, SO HE BUILT A REAPER AND SUCCESSFULLY DEMONSTRATED IT IN 1832.
McCORMICK CLEARLY SAW THE GREAT NEED FOR HIS MACHINE. THE RICH PRAIRIE WHEATLANDS WERE READY FOR A MECHANICAL REAPER. HIS RELENTLESS DRIVE AND BUSINESS ABILITY MADE HIM A MILLIONAIRE BEFORE HE WAS 40.
KERN

1810-1888

Asa Gray

AMERICAN BOTANIST

WHILE STUDYING MEDICINE IN NEW YORK CITY, GRAY BECAME INTERESTED IN BOTANY AND SPENT MUCH OF HIS TIME ROAMING THROUGH THE COUNTRYSIDE IN SEARCH OF PLANTS. **GRAY TAUGHT SCIENCE AND WAS A CURATOR AT THE NEW YORK LYCEUM OF NATURAL HISTORY, BEFORE HE WAS APPOINTED PROFESSOR OF NATURAL HISTORY AT THE UNIVERSITY OF MICHIGAN. IN 1842 HE BECAME PROFESSOR OF NATURAL HISTORY AT HARVARD WHERE HE STAYED UNTIL HIS DEATH.**

I'LL SAY THIS FOR HIM, HE REALLY KNOWS WHAT HE IS DOING.

HIS BOOK, "MANUAL OF THE BOTANY OF THE NORTHERN UNITED STATES" (1848), **INCREASED THE KNOWLEDGE OF PLANTS FOUND IN THE NORTHEASTERN U.S. GRAY WAS THE LEADING AUTHORITY OF HIS TIME ON PLANT LIFE IN THE U.S.**

HE WAS BORN AT SAUQUOIT, N.Y.

IN 1857, DARWIN WROTE TO GRAY, OUTLINING FOR THE FIRST TIME HIS THEORY OF EVOLUTION. **GRAY SUPPORTED DARWIN'S PRINCIPLES OF EVOLUTION AND VIGOROUSLY DEFENDED THEM AGAINST THE ATTACKS BY LOUIS AGASSIZ.**

KERN

1810-1891

Phineas T. Barnum

AMERICA'S FAMOUS SHOWMAN

JUST CALL ME THE PRINCE OF HUMBUG AND HOKUM.

HE WAS BORN IN BETHEL, CONN.

BARNUM'S CAREER IN THE AMUSEMENT FIELD BEGAN IN NEW YORK CITY IN 1834 WHEN HE EXHIBITED AN AGED NEGRESS SAID TO HAVE BEEN THE ***NURSE FOR GEORGE WASHINGTON.*** ***IN 1841 HE BOUGHT SCUDDER'S AMERICAN MUSEUM IN NEW YORK CITY. THE CHIEF ATTRACTION WAS A DWARF KNOWN AS GENERAL TOM THUMB. IN 1871, HE LAUNCHED HIS GREATEST UNDERTAKING AS A SHOWMAN, A MOBILE CIRCUS WHICH WAS PUBLICIZED AS "THE GREATEST SHOW ON EARTH." TEN YRS. LATER, JAMES A. BAILEY AND BARNUM MERGED TO FORM "THE BARNUM AND BAILEY CIRCUS" WHICH BECAME WORLD FAMOUS.***

I'LL FEATURE YOU ALL OVER AMERICA.

IN 1850, BARNUM ARRANGED A VERY PROFITABLE ***AMERICAN CONCERT TOUR FOR JENNY LIND, THE FAMOUS SWEDISH SOPRANO. THE TOTAL CASH FOR THIS VENTURE WAS MORE THAN $700,000 FOR 95 CONCERTS.***

THE AMERICAN PEOPLE LIKE TO BE HUMBUGGED.

HE WAS THE AUTHOR OF SEVERAL BOOKS. THOSE OF NOTE WERE HIS ***"AUTOBIOGRAPHY," "THE HUMBUGS OF THE WORLD" AND "MONEY-GETTING."***

KERN

1811- 1872

Horace Greeley

NEWSPAPER PUBLISHER AND EDITOR

I SAY PARDON THEM ALL.
I DO NOT AGREE!

GREELEY WAS 15YRS. OLD WHEN HE BECAME AN APPRENTICE FOR A VERMONT NEWSPAPER. IN 1833, HE MOVED TO NEW YORK CITY WHERE HE HELPED FOUND A DAILY PAPER THAT RAN FOR ONLY THREE WEEKS. ***IN 1834, HE STARTED THE "NEW YORKER," A POPULAR WEEKLY LITERARY MAGAZINE. IN 1841, GREELEY FOUNDED THE "NEW YORK TRIBUNE," A PENNY DAILY, AND EDITED IT FOR 31YRS. HE WAS ONE OF THE FIRST EDITORS TO JOIN THE REPUBLICAN PARTY AND HELPED LINCOLN GET THE NOMINATION FOR PRESIDENT. AFTER THE CIVIL WAR, HE URGED GIVING PARDONS TO ALL MEMBERS OF THE CONFEDERACY.***

HE WAS BORN IN AMHERST, N.H.

PUT THIS EDITORIAL ON THE FRONT PAGE!

GREELEY WAS A LEADER IN THE ANTI-SLAVERY MOVEMENT. ***HIS EDITORIALS MOLDED PUBLIC OPINION FOR 20YRS. BEFORE THE CIVIL WAR.***

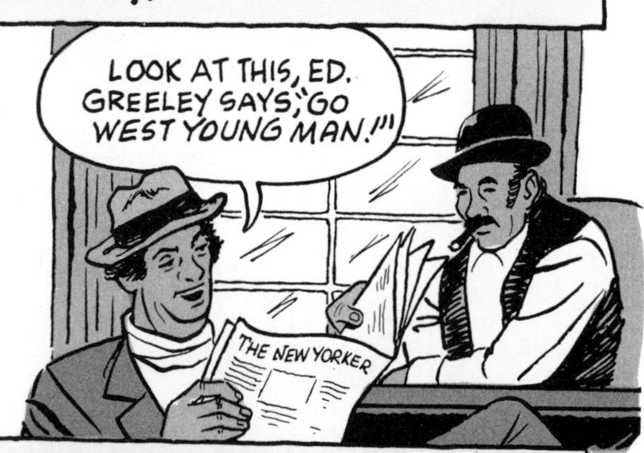

THE PHRASE ***"GO WEST YOUNG MAN" WAS ORIGINATED BY JOHN SOULE, AN INDIANA NEWSPAPERMAN. GREELEY POPULARIZED IT IN HIS "NEW YORKER MAGAZINE."***

KERN

1811 - 1896
Harriet Beecher Stowe
AMERICAN AUTHOR AND ABOLITIONIST
SHE WAS EDUCATED AT LITCHFIELD AND HARTFORD, CONN. IN 1832, HER FATHER, A MINISTER, MOVED HIS FAMILY TO CINCINNATI, OHIO. THREE YEARS LATER, SHE MARRIED A SEMINARY PROFESSOR. MRS. STOWE TRAVELED WITH HER HUSBAND INTO KENTUCKY WHERE SHE HEARD THE STORIES OF RUNAWAY SLAVES. IN 1852, SHE WROTE "UNCLE TOM'S CABIN" WHICH GAVE HER NATIONAL FAME. 500,000 COPIES WERE SOLD IN THE U.S. WITHIN 5 YEARS, AND THE BOOK WAS TRANSLATED INTO MORE THAN 20 FOREIGN LANGUAGES. THIS BOOK WAS RESPONSIBLE FOR AROUSING THE ANTISLAVERY SENTIMENT IN THE NORTH, AND MUST BE REGARDED AS A VERY IMPORTANT FACTOR IN HASTENING THE CIVIL WAR.
SHE WAS BORN IN LITCHFIELD, CONN.
I WOULD LIKE TO PUBLISH ALL OF YOUR BOOKS.
SHE SPENT A YEAR ABROAD AFTER SHE WROTE "UNCLE TOM'S CABIN." ON HER RETURN SHE AGAIN ATTACKED SLAVERY WITH HER BOOK "DRED, A TALE OF THE GREAT DISMAL SWAMP."
I ENJOY ALL OF YOUR BOOKS, ESPECIALLY "OLD TOWN FOLKS."
MRS. STOWE ALSO WROTE NOVELS DEALING WITH NEW ENGLAND IN THE LATE 1700'S. THESE INCLUDE "THE MINISTER'S WOOING," "OLD TOWN FOLKS" AND A COLLECTION OF STORIES, "OLD TOWN FIRESIDE STORIES."
KERN

1813 - 1861

Stephen A. Douglas

ONE OF AMERICA'S GREAT ORATORS AND POLITICAL LEADERS

DOUGLAS ALWAYS WANTED TO BE A LAWYER. HE WAS 20YRS. OLD WHEN ADMITTED TO THE BAR. ***HE WAS A STATE LEGISLATOR, A SUPREME COURT JUDGE OF ILLINOIS, A U.S. REPRESENTATIVE AND A U.S. SENATOR. DOUGLAS WAS AN OUTSTANDING SPOKESMAN FOR WESTWARD EXPANSION AND THE ANNEXATION OF TEXAS, AND SUPPORTED THE WAR WITH MEXICO. THE SLAVERY CONTROVERSY WAS THE GREAT ISSUE AT HIS TIME. DOUGLAS WAS NOT OPPOSED TO SLAVERY. HE BELIEVED THE PEOPLE OF THE TERRITORIES SHOULD DECIDE WHETHER OR NOT SLAVERY SHOULD BE PERMITTED WITHIN THEIR BORDERS AND HE THOUGHT THE PROBLEM COULD BE RESOLVED BY PEACEFUL MEANS. HE WAS RESPONSIBLE FOR THE PASSAGE OF THE FAMOUS KANSAS-NEBRASKA BILL OF 1854.***

HE WAS BORN IN BRANDON, VT.

I SAY, A HOUSE DIVIDED AGAINST ITSELF CANNOT STAND.
MY ARGUMENT IS, LET POPULAR SOVEREIGNTY DECIDE EXPANSION OF SLAVERY.

HE HAD A LARGE HEAD AND BROAD SHOULDERS AND WAS NICKNAMED ***"THE LITTLE GIANT."*** DOUGLAS WON RESPECT IN THE SENATE FOR HIS ***EXCEPTIONAL ABILITIES.***

DOUGLAS AND LINCOLN OPPOSED EACH OTHER IN THE 1858 ILLINOIS SENATE RACE. ***THEIR SLAVERY DEBATES ATTRACTED NATIONAL ATTENTION. DOUGLAS WON THE SENATE SEAT, BUT LOST HIS BID FOR THE PRESIDENCY TO LINCOLN IN 1860, RECEIVING 12 ELECTORAL VOTES TO 180 FOR LINCOLN.***

KERN

1813 - 1887

Henry Ward Beecher

CONGREGATIONAL MINISTER AND ABOLITIONIST

SLAVERY IS AGAINST GOD'S LAW.

BEECHER STUDIED THEOLOGY UNDER HIS FATHER, LYMAN BEECHER, AND BECAME KNOWN AS A ***PULPIT ORATOR***. ***HE DELIVERED VIGOROUS SERMONS ATTACKING SLAVERY. FROM 1837-47 HE PREACHED IN INDIANAPOLIS, THEN WENT TO THE PLYMOUTH CONGREGATIONAL CHURCH IN BROOKLYN WHERE HE REMAINED UNTIL HIS DEATH. BEECHER'S ADDRESSES WERE DRAMATIC AND WITTY. HE CHOSE ORIGINAL SUBJECTS FOR HIS SERMONS WHICH OPPOSED ANYTHING HE CONSIDERED AN INJUSTICE TO MAN.***

HE WAS BORN IN LITCHFIELD, CONN.

FOLLOW THE TEACHINGS OF JESUS!

BEECHER WAS ONE OF THE ***MOST ELOQUENT PREACHERS OF HIS TIME. HE WROTE A NOVEL AND PATRIOTIC ADDRESSES. HIS "LIFE OF JESUS THE CHRIST" WAS COMPLETED BY HIS SONS AFTER HIS DEATH.***

HE EDITED A POLITICO-RELIGIOUS JOURNAL CALLED THE "***INDEPENDENT***" FROM 1861-64 AND THE "***CHRISTIAN UNION***" FROM 1870-81.

KERN

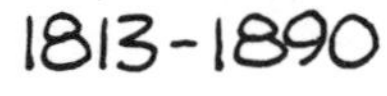

John C. Frémont

AMERICAN EXPLORER AND ARMY OFFICER

FRÉMONT WAS EDUCATED AT THE COLLEGE OF CHARLESTON, S.C. HE WAS COMMISSIONED A SECOND LIEUTENANT IN THE TOPOGRAPHICAL ENGINEERS, U.S. ARMY. ***HE MADE IMPORTANT SURVEYS TO THE WIND RIVER CHAIN OF THE ROCKIES IN 1842. KIT CARSON, THE FAMOUS SCOUT, SERVED AS HIS GUIDE. IN 1843, HE SURVEYED THE OREGON TRAIL TO THE MOUTH OF THE COLUMBIA RIVER ON THE PACIFIC COAST. FRÉMONT AND HIS ENTIRE EXPEDITION MADE A WINTER CROSSING OF THE SIERRA NEVADA MTS. AND SETTLED IN CALIFORNIA WHERE HE ORGANIZED DISCONTENTED AMERICANS TO REVOLT AGAINST MEXICO.***

HE WAS BORN IN SAVANNAH, GA.

HE'S OUR MAN, RIGHT, ED?

SORRY, GENTLEMEN, I MUST WITHDRAW.

IN 1856, ***HE WAS THE FIRST REPUBLICAN CANDIDATE FOR PRESIDENT OF THE U.S.*** BUT, LOST TO PRES. BUCHANAN. IN 1864, FRÉMONT WAS A PRESIDENTIAL NOMINEE SELECTED BY THE RADICAL REPUBLICAN GROUP BUT WITHDREW IN FAVOR OF LINCOLN.

YES, SIR?

DISPATCH THIS MESSAGE TO PRESIDENT HAYES.

FROM 1878-83 HE SERVED AS ***TERRITORIAL GOVERNOR OF ARIZONA.***

KERN

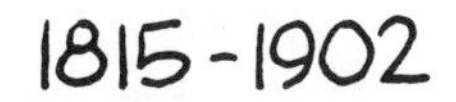

1815-1902

Elizabeth C. Stanton

SOCIAL REFORMER AND A LEADER IN THE WOMEN'S RIGHTS MOVEMENT

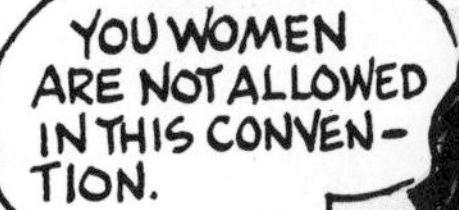

YOU WOMEN ARE NOT ALLOWED IN THIS CONVEN-TION.

SHE GRADUATED FROM THE FEMALE SEMINARY IN TROY, N.Y. IN 1840, SHE ATTENDED THE WORLD ANTISLAVERY CONVENTION IN LONDON WITH HER HUSBAND, ***BUT WAS REFUSED ADMISSION BE-CAUSE OF HER SEX. IN 1848, SHE JOINED LUCRETIA MOTT, ANOTHER REJECTED DELEGATE, IN CALLING THE FIRST WOMEN'S RIGHTS CONVENTION, HELD AT SENECA FALLS, N.Y. THE RESULT WAS THE FIRST FORMAL DEMAND FOR THE EXTENSION OF SUFFRAGE TO WOMEN. SHE WAS ACTIVE IN THE TEMPERANCE AND ABOLITION MOVEMENTS, BUT HER MAIN CRU-SADE WAS FOR WOMEN'S RIGHTS.***

SHE WAS BORN IN JOHNSTOWN, N.Y.

I NEED ALL THE HELP I CAN GET IN THIS GREAT MOVEMENT.

SHE WAS PRESIDENT OF THE NATIONAL WOMEN'S SUFFRAGE ASSOCIATION, HOLD-ING THIS POSITION UNTIL 1893. MRS. STANTON WAS COEDITOR OF "REVOLU-TION," THE VOICE OF THE FEMINIST MOVEMENT.

I WOULD LIKE TO GET THE YOUNG VIEW OF THIS BOOK.

SHE WAS ONE OF THE JOINT AUTHORS OF "***A HISTORY OF WOMAN SUFFRAGE.***"

KERN

THOREAU GRADUATED FROM HARVARD, TAUGHT SCHOOL AND TUTORED. HE LIVED WITH RALPH WALDO EMERSON, THE ESSAYIST AND PHILOSOPHER, FOR TWO YEARS. **IN 1845, HE WENT TO WALDEN POND ON THE OUTSKIRTS OF CONCORD AND LIVED IN A CRUDE HUT. THOREAU KEPT A JOURNAL CALLED "WALDEN," AN EXCELLENT REPORT ON AN EXPERIMENT IN LIVING. HE WANTED TO PROVE TO HIMSELF THAT MAN COULD ESCAPE THE EVILS OF COMMERCIALISM. HE WAS A POWERFUL SOCIAL CRITIC. THOREAU HAD A GREAT GIFT FOR STYLE IN HIS WRITING. HE WROTE WITH FRESHNESS AND GREAT CARE.**

HE WAS BORN IN CONCORD, MASS.

DOWN! DOWN! DOWN! DOWN! DOWN!

UP-UP-UP-UP-UP!

HIS BOOKS HAD GREAT INFLUENCE THROUGHOUT THE WORLD. **"WALDEN" WAS ADOPTED AS THE HANDBOOK OF THE BRITISH LABOR PARTY. THOREAU'S "CIVIL DISOBEDIENCE" HAS BEEN THE BASIS FOR PEACEFUL REVOLTS ALL OVER THE WORLD.**

THOREAU SUPPORTED HIMSELF BY DOING ODD JOBS. **MOST OF HIS TIME WAS SPENT IN THE STUDY OF NATURE AND MEDITATING ON PHILOSOPHICAL PROBLEMS.**

KERN

1817-1895

Frederick Douglass

NEGRO ORATOR, WRITER AND LEADER OF THE ANTISLAVERY MOVEMENT

AS A BOY, DOUGLASS SAW THE CRUEL TREATMENT OF HIS PEOPLE. IN 1838, HE ESCAPED TO MASSACHUSETTS AND BECAME ONE OF THE **GREATEST NEGRO ORATORS SPEAKING FOR THE ANTISLAVERY SOCIETY. HIS NAME BECAME A SYMBOL OF FREEDOM AMONG THE SLAVES OF THE SOUTH. AFTER LECTURING FOR 2 YEARS IN THE BRITISH ISLES ON THE U.S. SLAVERY QUESTION, HE RETURNED HOME, BOUGHT HIS FREEDOM, AND FOUNDED THE "NORTH STAR", AN ABOLITIONIST NEWSPAPER. DOUGLASS CAMPAIGNED FOR ABRAHAM LINCOLN DURING THE PRESIDENTIAL ELECTION OF 1860. DOUGLASS WAS MINISTER TO HAITI FROM 1889-91.**

THANK YOU FOR COMING, FREDERICK.
THANK YOU FOR YOUR KINDNESS, MR. PRESIDENT.

DOUGLASS CALLED ON PRES. LINCOLN SEVERAL TIMES TO DISCUSS THE SLAVERY PROBLEM. **AFTER THE WAR, HE FOUGHT FOR THE PASSAGE OF THE 13th, 14th AND 15th AMENDMENTS TO THE CONSTITUTION.**

YOU'RE DOING A FINE JOB, GENTLEMEN.

DURING THE CIVIL WAR DOUGLASS **ORGANIZED TWO NEGRO REGIMENTS IN MASSACHUSETTS.**

KERN

1819 - 1867

Elias Howe

INVENTOR OF THE FIRST PRACTICAL SEWING MACHINE

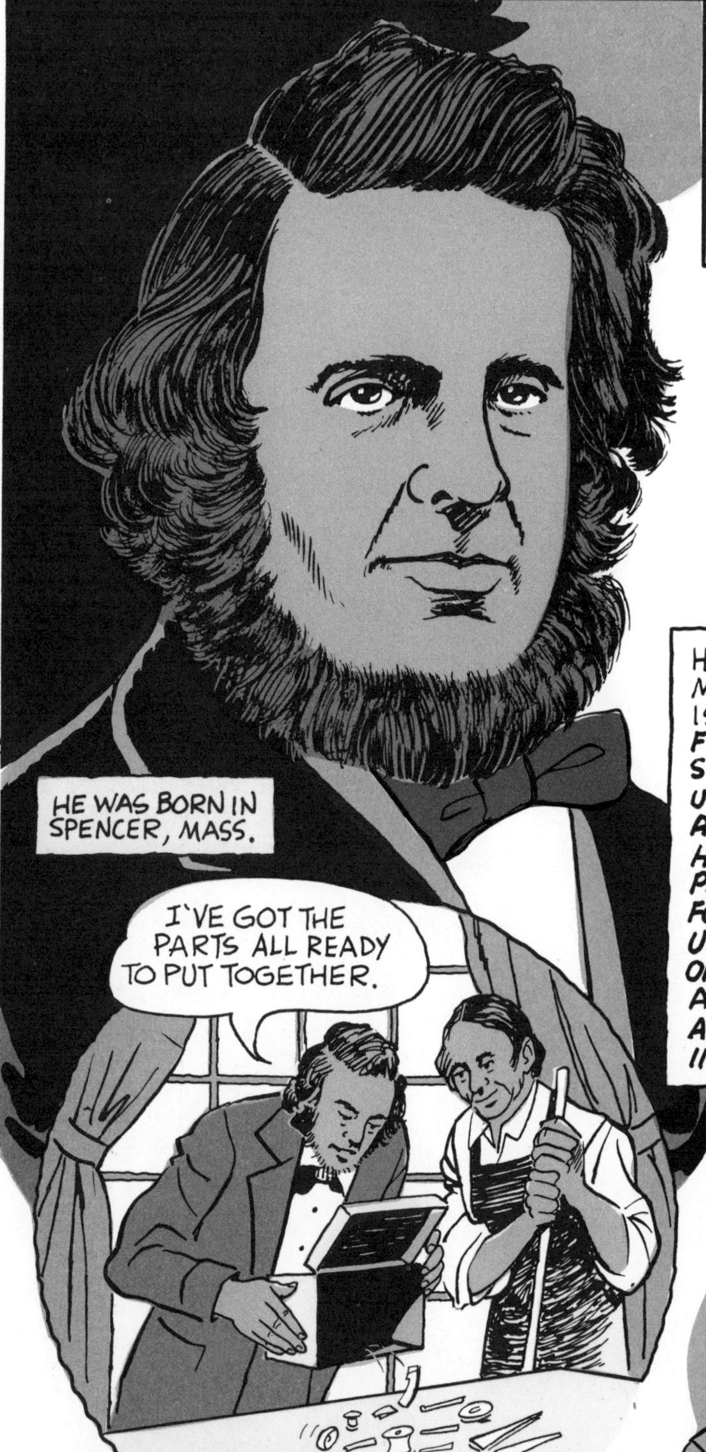

I'VE GOT THE PARTS ALL READY TO PUT TOGETHER.

WHILE WORKING IN A WATCHMAKING SHOP, HE OVERHEARD A REMARK THAT A ***GREAT FORTUNE AWAITED THE MAN WHO COULD INVENT A SEWING MACHINE AND STARTED WORKING ON ONE.***

I THINK I'VE GOT IT!

HOWE WAS 17 YRS. OLD WHEN HE WENT TO LOWELL, MASS., WHERE HE WORKED, FIRST AS A MACHINIST, THEN IN A SHOP MAKING WATCHES. ***HE FINISHED HIS INVENTION IN 1845. HIS LOCK-STITCH MACHINE SEWED 250 STITCHES A MINUTE. HOWE WAS GRANTED A PATENT IN 1846. AFTER BUILDING ONLY 4 MACHINES IN THE U.S., HE WENT TO GREAT BRITAIN WHERE HE SOLD HIS PATENT RIGHTS TO A CORSET MANUFACTURER FOR $1,250. IN 1849, HOWE RETURNED TO THE U.S. TO FIND THAT SEVERAL MEN HAD INFRINGED ON HIS PATENTS. HE WENT TO COURT TO CLAIM ROYALTIES. FINALLY IN 1854, HE WON HIS SUITS AND RECEIVED A LARGE FORTUNE FOR HIS INVENTION.***

YOU GOT YOUR PATENT AT THE RIGHT TIME, ELIAS.

MANY PAST INVENTORS CONTRIBUTED TO THE SUCCESS OF THE FIRST PRACTICAL SEWING MACHINE, ***BUT HOWE'S PATENTS WERE THE FIRST IN THE U.S.***

1819 - 1890

Christopher L. Sholes

AMERICAN JOURNALIST AND INVENTOR OF THE FIRST TYPEWRITER

SHOLES MADE 25 DIFFERENT MACHINES IN HIS MILWAUKEE MACHINE SHOP. ***HE WAS ASSISTED BY CARLOS GLIDDEN AND SAMUEL SOULE. THE THREE MEN ALSO INVENTED A PAGE NUMBERING MACHINE IN 1866.***

HE WAS BORN IN MOORESBURG, PA.

HE PATENTED THE TYPEWRITER IN 1868, AND ***SOLD THE RIGHTS TO REMINGTON IN 1873 FOR $12,000.***

THE TYPEWRITER CAUSED A SENSATION AT THE CENTENNIAL WORLD'S FAIR IN PHILADELPHIA IN 1876. ***PEOPLE PAID 25¢ FOR A SMALL PIECE OF PAPER WITH TYPEWRITING ON IT!***

WELL, WOULD YOU LOOK AT THAT!
SHOLES WAS A NEWSPAPER EDITOR AS WELL AS A WISCONSIN LEGISLATOR.
MARK TWAIN, THE FAMOUS AUTHOR, CALLED HIS NEW TYPEWRITER THE "LITERARY PIANO".
KERN

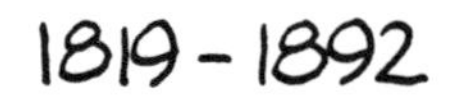

Cyrus W. Field

AMERICAN MERCHANT AND FINANCIER

FIELD IS RECOGNIZED AS THE PROMOTER OF THE FIRST SUCCESSFUL TELEGRAPH CABLE ACROSS THE ATLANTIC. MONEY FROM THE BRITISH AND AMERICAN GOVERNMENTS MADE POSSIBLE 4 ATTEMPTS TO LAY THE CABLE. FINALLY IN JULY 1866, THE FIRST FULLY SUCCESSFUL CABLE WAS LAID. LATER ON, FIELD CENTERED HIS INTERESTS ON RAILROADS AND NEWSPAPERS. HE GAINED CONTROL OF THE NEW YORK ELEVATED RAILROAD AND WAS ITS PRESIDENT FROM 1877-80. HE BOUGHT TWO NEW YORK NEWSPAPERS AND CONSOLIDATED THEM INTO THE "MAIL AND EXPRESS."

HE WAS BORN IN STOCKBRIDGE, MASS.

I PRESENT THIS MEDAL TO YOU WITH THE THANKS OF THE U.S. CONGRESS.

THE U.S. CONGRESS GAVE HIM A GOLD MEDAL IN RECOGNITION FOR HIS ACHIEVEMENT. HE ALSO HAD HONORS CONFERRED ON HIM FROM OTHER COUNTRIES.

THIS IS THE RESULT OF YEARS OF HARD WORK.

FIELD MADE A FORTUNE AS THE HEAD OF THE PAPER MERCHANDISING FIRM OF CYRUS W. FIELD AND CO.

KERN

1819-1892

Walt Whitman

ONE OF AMERICA'S GREAT POETS

I HAVE GREAT RESPECT FOR YOU YOUNG SOLDIERS WHO FOUGHT FOR YOUR COUNTRY.

WHITMAN WAS A TYPESETTER, SCHOOLTEACHER, NEWSPAPERMAN AND BUILDER AND SELLER OF HOUSES. *HE OPPOSED SLAVERY WITH A PASSION AND WROTE MANY ARTICLES AGAINST IT. DURING THE CIVIL WAR HE SERVED AS A VOLUNTEER MILITARY NURSE IN ARMY HOSPITALS. FROM HIS EXPERIENCES HE WROTE "SPECIMEN DAYS" AND "DRUM TAPS," WHICH APPEARED IN HIS "LEAVES OF GRASS" COLLECTION. WHITMAN'S PERSONAL EXPERIENCES IN THE WAR STRENGTHENED HIS DEVOTION TO THE UNION AND TO THE YOUTH OF AMERICA. CALLED "THE GOOD GRAY POET," HE PROFOUNDLY INFLUENCED BOTH POETIC FORM AND CONTENT.*

HE WAS BORN AT WEST HILLS ON LONG ISLAND, N.Y.

WE HAVE A COUNTRY TO BE PROUD OF!

HIS POEMS PRAISE *AMERICA AND DEMOCRACY.* HE SAID, *"THE CHIEF REASON FOR THE BEING OF THE UNITED STATES OF AMERICA IS TO BRING ABOUT THE COMMON GOOD WILL OF ALL MANKIND, THE SOLIDARITY OF THE WORLD."*

WHITMAN'S "LEAVES OF GRASS," HIS FIRST COLLECTION OF POEMS, *WAS PUBLISHED IN NINE DIFFERENT EDITIONS BETWEEN 1856-92. INCLUDED WERE SUCH NOTABLE POEMS AS "PIONEER O PIONEERS," "PASSAGE TO INDIA" AND "CAPTAIN, MY CAPTAIN," THE WELL KNOWN POEM ON THE DEATH OF ABRAHAM LINCOLN.*

AMERICAN WRITER, POET, LECTURER AND SOCIAL REFORMER

HERE IS A HARD-HITTING EDITORIAL.

COMMONWEALTH

SHE WAS BORN IN NEW YORK CITY.

AT AN EARLY AGE, SHE WROTE POETRY FOR MAGAZINES. IN 1843, SHE MARRIED SAMUEL GRIDLEY HOWE, AMERICAN REFORMER AND PHILANTHROPIST, AND MOVED TO BOSTON WHERE SHE HELPED HER HUSBAND WITH HIS ANTISLAVERY ACTIVITIES, EDITING AN ABOLITIONIST NEWSPAPER CALLED THE "COMMONWEALTH." FROM 1868 ON, SHE WAS ASSOCIATED WITH THE MOVEMENT FOR WOMEN'S EMANCIPATION, AND WAS THE FOUNDER AND PRESIDENT FOR MANY YEARS OF THE NEW ENGLAND WOMAN SUFFRAGE ASSOCIATION AND THE ASSOCIATION FOR THE ADVANCEMENT OF WOMEN. IN 1872, SHE FOUNDED THE WORLD PEACE ASSOCIATION AND LECTURED THROUGHOUT THE COUNTRY FOR THESE CAUSES.

WE WANT TO THANK YOU FOR GIVING US YOUR FINE POEMS TO READ.

IN FEB. 1862, SHE WROTE HER BEST KNOWN POEM, "THE BATTLE HYMN OF THE REPUBLIC," WHICH BECAME THE MAJOR WAR SONG OF THE UNION TROOPS.

MRS HOWE WROTE AND LECTURED ON MANY SUBJECTS. AMONG HER WORKS ARE THE COLLECTION OF POEMS FROM "SUNSET RIDGE," "POEMS OLD AND NEW," AND BIOGRAPHICAL WORKS, "LIFE OF MARGARET FULLER" AND "SKETCHES OF REPRESENTATIVE WOMEN OF NEW ENGLAND."

William W. Mayo
1819-1911
HE WAS BORN IN MANCHESTER, ENGLAND.

PHYSICIANS, FOUNDERS OF THE WORLD-RENOWNED MAYO CLINIC

William J. Mayo
1861-1939
HE WAS BORN IN LESUEUR, MINNESOTA.

Charles H. Mayo
1865-1939
HE WAS BORN IN ROCHESTER, MINNESOTA.
WILLIAM W. MAYO CAME TO THE U.S. IN 1845 TO PRACTICE HIS PROFESSION AS A CHEMIST IN NEW YORK CITY. IN 1854 HE GRADUATED IN MEDICINE FROM THE UNIVERSITY OF MISSOURI. HE MOVED HIS FAMILY TO LESUEUR, MINN., IN 1855. IN 1863 HE MOVED TO ROCHESTER, MINN. WILLIAM J. MAYO AND CHARLES H. MAYO WERE ASSOCIATED WITH THEIR FATHER IN HIS PRACTICE IN ROCHESTER. THE TWO BROTHERS STARTED A CLINIC IN 1889 AT ST. MARY'S HOSPITAL IN ROCHESTER. THEY ESTABLISHED THE MAYO FOUNDATION FOR MEDICAL EDUCATION AND RESEARCH IN 1915.
ON AUG. 21, 1833, A TORNADO DESTROYED A LARGE PART OF ROCHESTER. THE VICTIMS WERE CARED FOR BY DR. MAYO (SENIOR) IN A TEMPORARY HOSPITAL. THE SISTERS OF ST. FRANCIS OFFERED TO BUILD A PERMANENT HOSPITAL IF DR. MAYO WOULD ASSIST. HE AGREED, AND A WORLD-FAMOUS MEDICAL CENTER WAS QUIETLY BORN.

KERN
THIS 22-STORY "OLD BUILDING" WAS COMPLETED IN 1929. THE CLINIC TREATS PATIENTS FROM ALL PARTS OF THE WORLD.

1820-1906

Susan B. Anthony

AMERICAN REFORMER AND LEADER IN THE WOMAN SUFFRAGE MOVEMENT

SHE TAUGHT SCHOOL FOR 15 YRS., WAS ACTIVE IN THE ANTISLAVERY AND TEMPERANCE MOVEMENTS, AND WAS A FIRM BELIEVER IN COEDUCATION. **SHE TRAVELED THROUGH 60 NEW YORK STATE COUNTIES IN HER CRUSADE TO GET THE RIGHT TO VOTE FOR WOMEN. IN 1868, SHE FOUNDED AND PUBLISHED "THE REVOLUTION," A WOMAN'S RIGHTS NEWSPAPER. IN 1872, SHE VOTED IN THE ELECTION, AND WAS ARRESTED AND THROWN IN JAIL. HER TRIAL ATTRACTED NATIONAL ATTENTION. SUSAN ANTHONY WAS ONE OF A FEW WOMEN TO BE IMMORTALIZED IN MARBLE IN THE U.S. CAPITOL ROTUNDA. IN 1950, SHE WAS ELECTED TO THE HALL OF FAME HONORING GREAT AMERICANS.**

SHE WAS ONE OF 4 WOMEN TO BE HONORED **ON A 3¢ STAMP IN 1936. OTHERS WERE MARTHA WASHINGTON, POCAHONTAS AND WHISTLER'S MOTHER.**

IT WAS THROUGH HER EFFORTS THAT MARRIED WOMEN IN NEW YORK STATE WERE GIVEN THE GUARDIANSHIP OF THEIR CHILDREN AND THE CONTROL OF THEIR OWN EARNINGS.

KERN

1821-1912

Clara Barton

FOUNDER OF THE AMERICAN RED CROSS

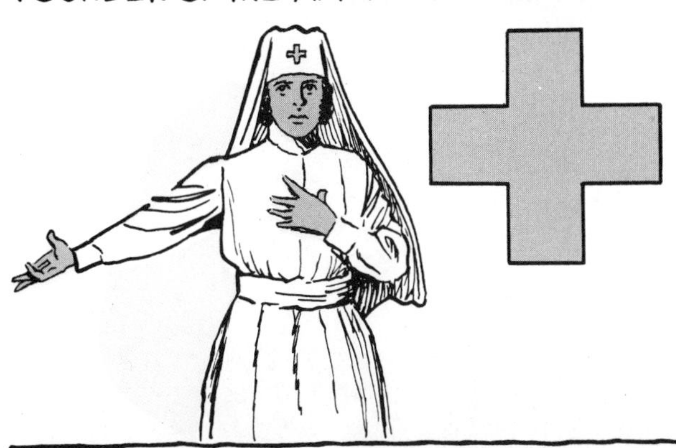

DURING HER EARLY LIFE, SHE WAS A SUCCESSFUL TEACHER. IN 1854, SHE WENT TO WASHINGTON, D.C., WHERE SHE CLERKED IN THE PATENT OFFICE, ***THE FIRST WOMAN EVER TO HOLD SUCH A POSITION. DURING THE CIVIL WAR SHE CARRIED SUPPLIES TO SOLDIERS AND CARED FOR WOUNDED MEN ON THE BATTLEFIELD. AFTER THE WAR SHE ORIGINATED A SYSTEMATIC SEARCH FOR MISSING SOLDIERS. SHE AND HER STAFF MARKED MORE THAN 12,000 GRAVES IN THE ANDERSONVILLE, GA., NATIONAL CEMETERY. IT WAS THROUGH HER EFFORTS THAT THE AMERICAN RED CROSS WAS FOUNDED IN 1881. SHE WAS THE FIRST PRESIDENT UNTIL 1904. CLARA BARTON DEVOTED HER LIFE TO THE GOOD OF HUMANITY.***

SHE HEADED RELIEF WORK IN THE YELLOW FEVER EPIDEMIC IN FLORIDA (1887), IN THE JOHNSTOWN FLOOD (1889), THE SPANISH-AMERICAN WAR (1889) AND THE GALVESTON FLOOD OF 1900.

SHE WAS BORN IN OXFORD, MASS.

KERN

HER DEEDS ON THE BATTLEFIELD DURING THE CIVIL WAR ***ATTRACTED NATIONAL ATTENTION. SHE WAS CALLED "ANGEL OF THE BATTLEFIELD."***

1822-1885

Ulysses S. Grant

COMMANDER-IN-CHIEF OF THE UNION ARMIES AT THE CLOSE OF THE CIVIL WAR AND ***EIGHTEENTH*** PRESIDENT OF THE UNITED STATES (1869-77)

GENTLEMEN, MEET MY NEW COMMANDER-IN-CHIEF.

IN 1843, GRANT GRADUATED FROM WEST POINT AND FOUGHT IN THE MEXICAN WAR. RESIGNING FROM THE ARMY IN 1854, HE TRIED BUSINESS BUT FAILED COMPLETELY. ***HE WAS ALMOST 40 YRS. OLD WHEN HE OFFERED HIS SERVICES AT THE START OF THE CIVIL WAR. IN AUG. 1861, LINCOLN MADE HIM A BRIGADIER GENERAL. SUDDENLY THIS STORE CLERK WAS A NATIONAL HERO AS HE WON VICTORY UPON VICTORY. TOWARDS THE END OF THE WAR, LINCOLN APPOINTED HIM COMMANDER OF ALL THE UNION ARMIES. HE WON MANY FRIENDS IN THE NORTH AND SOUTH WHEN HE ALLOWED LEE'S MEN TO KEEP THEIR HORSES "FOR THE SPRING PLOWING." GRANT WAS AN HONEST PRESIDENT WHO DID A GOOD JOB DURING ONE OF AMERICA'S MOST DIFFICULT PERIODS.***

HE WAS BORN IN POINT PLEASANT, OHIO.

COLORADO-1876

DURING HIS PRESIDENCY, ***THE FIRST TRANSCONTINENTAL RAILROAD WAS COMPLETED, THE 15th AMENDMENT WAS ADOPTED, CUSTER MADE HIS LAST STAND, COLORADO JOINED THE UNION, THE TELEPHONE WAS INVENTED, THE NATIONAL BASEBALL LEAGUE WAS ORGANIZED AND ONE-CENT POST CARDS WERE ISSUED.***

THE PEOPLE HAVE RESPONDED TO YOUR NEED!

IN 1884, GRANT INVESTED ALL HIS MONEY IN A BANKING FIRM WHICH FAILED. ***HIS MEMOIRS, PUBLISHED BY MARK TWAIN, EARNED $500,000 FOR GRANT AND HIS FAMILY.***

1822-1893

Rutherford B. Hayes

LAWYER, GENERAL, GOVERNOR AND **NINETEENTH** PRESIDENT OF THE UNITED STATES (1877-81)

GENERAL, YOU ARE NOW A CONGRESSMAN.

HAYES WAS VALEDICTORIAN OF HIS GRADUATING CLASS IN 1842, WENT TO HARVARD LAW SCHOOL AND WAS ADMITTED TO THE OHIO BAR. ***HE SERVED WITH THE UNION FORCES IN THE CIVIL WAR AS A COLONEL AND LATER A BRIGADIER GENERAL. WHILE STILL IN THE ARMY HE WAS NOMINATED AND ELECTED TO CONGRESS. HAYES REFUSED TO LEAVE THE FIELD OF BATTLE TO CAMPAIGN. IN 1867, HE WAS ELECTED GOV. OF OHIO AND SERVED FOR THREE TERMS. HIS OUTSTANDING RECORD OF HONESTY, GOVERNMENT ECONOMY, AND IMPROVED CIVIL SERVICE LEGISLATION LED TO HIS ELECTION TO THE PRESIDENCY IN 1877. HAYES RETIRED FROM POLITICS IN 1881, DEVOTING HIS LIFE TO EDUCATION AND RELIGION.***

HE WAS BORN IN DELAWARE, OHIO.

WE CAN NOW HAVE A PERMANENT RECORD OF YOUR VOICE.

WE HAVE DECIDED ON YOU, MR. PRESIDENT.

THE HAYES-TILDEN PRESIDENTIAL ELECTION WAS SO CLOSE THAT A SPECIAL COMMITTEE HAD TO DECIDE WHO WON. ***THEY CHOSE HAYES 3 DAYS BEFORE THE INAUGURATION.***

DURING HIS PRESIDENCY, THE LAST FEDERAL TROOPS WERE WITHDRAWN FROM SOUTHERN STATES, THE FIRST GREAT RAILROAD STRIKE TOOK PLACE, THE FIRST PHONOGRAPH WAS INVENTED AND ELECTRICITY WAS FIRST USED FOR LIGHTING STREETS.

KERN

1822-1903

Frederick L. Olmsted

LANDSCAPE ARCHITECT AND AUTHOR

I HAVE TRIED TO PRESERVE THE NATURAL TERRAIN.

AFTER GRADUATING FROM YALE UNIVERSITY, HE TRAVELED THROUGHOUT EUROPE AND THE U.S., STUDYING LANDSCAPE GARDENING AND AGRICULTURAL METHODS. ***HE PLANNED AND DESIGNED BROOKLYN'S PROSPECT PARK, NEW YORK'S MORNINGSIDE PARK, WASHINGTON AND JACKSON PARK IN CHICAGO AND THE CAPITOL GROUNDS IN WASHINGTON, D.C. HE WAS ONE OF THE FIRST LANDSCAPE ARCHITECTS IN AMERICA TO PRESERVE THE NATURAL FEATURES OF THE TERRAIN IN HIS PLANNING. SOME OF HIS BOOKS INCLUDE "WALKS AND TALKS OF AN AMERICAN FARMER IN ENGLAND" AND "THE COTTON KINGDOM."***

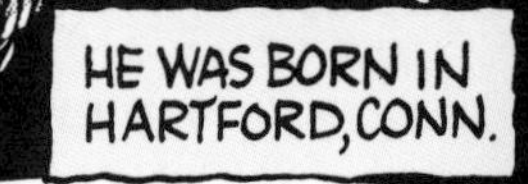

HE WAS BORN IN HARTFORD, CONN.

FUNCTION AND BEAUTY ARE COMBINED IN THIS DESIGN.

YOU HAVE CREATED A RURAL ATMOSPHERE.

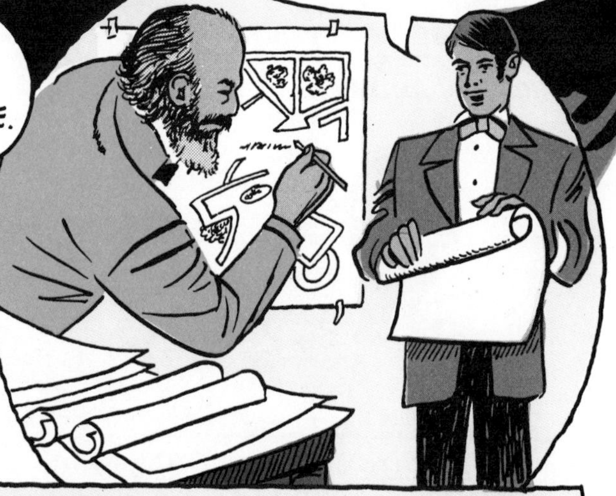

THAT'S AN ORIGINAL SIGNATURE YOU HAVE, FREDERICK.

HE DESIGNED THE GROUNDS FOR THE ***1893 CHICAGO WORLD'S FAIR AND THE CAMPUS GROUNDS AT STANFORD AND THE UNIVERSITY OF CALIFORNIA.***

IN 1858, HE WAS THE ***FIRST MAN TO USE THE TERM LANDSCAPE ARCHITECT WHEN HE SIGNED HIS NAME TO THE PLANS FOR NEW YORK'S CENTRAL PARK.***

KERN

1823-1893

Francis Parkman

FAMOUS AMERICAN HISTORIAN

WHILE IN HARVARD HE BECAME INTERESTED IN THE STORIES OF THE INDIANS AND THEIR CONFLICTS WITH THE EARLY SETTLERS. ***AFTER HE GRADUATED IN 1846, HE MADE HIS FAMOUS OREGON TRAIL JOURNEY, LIVING FOR MONTHS WITH THE INDIANS, GAINING INVALUABLE KNOWLEDGE OF THE WILDLIFE OF THE WOODS. THE HARDSHIPS WHICH HE ENDURED PERMANENTLY INJURED HIS HEALTH AND LEFT HIM NEARLY BLIND. IN 1849, HE PUBLISHED "CALIFORNIA AND OREGON TRAIL". SO HE COULD SUPPORT HIS FAMILY WHILE HE WROTE, HE BECAME A HORTICULTURIST. SOME OF HIS WORKS WERE "THE JESUITS IN NORTH AMERICA" AND "LASALLE AND THE DISCOVERY OF THE GREAT WEST."***

HE WAS BORN IN BOSTON, MASS.
THESE TWO GREAT POWERS FOUGHT FURIOUSLY FOR COMPLETE CONTROL.
YOU PUT IT ALL TOGETHER VERY WELL.

THE FIRST BOOK HE WROTE, ***"THE CONSPIRACY OF PONTIAC," WAS ONE OF THE MOST THOROUGH STUDIES EVER MADE. HE HAD TO GO TO EUROPE 5 TIMES FOR MATERIAL.***

HIS GREAT BOOK, ***"FRANCE AND ENGLAND IN THE NEW WORLD," GAVE THE COMPLETE HISTORY OF THE STRUGGLE BETWEEN FRANCE AND GREAT BRITAIN FOR THE CONTROL OF NORTH AMERICA. PARKMAN BEGAN WITH THE END OF THE PERIOD AND WORKED BACKWARD.***

1823-1896

Mathew B. Brady

AMERICAN PHOTOGRAPHER KNOWN FOR HIS PICTORIAL HISTORY OF THE CIVIL WAR

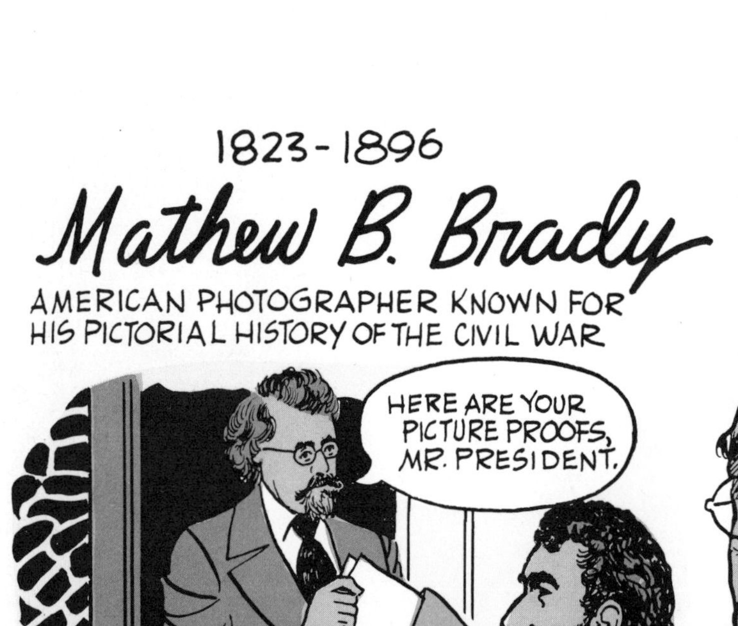
HERE ARE YOUR PICTURE PROOFS, MR. PRESIDENT.

DURING HIS YOUTH, BRADY LEARNED THE ART OF MAKING WATCH CASES AND STUDIED PAINTING AND DAGUERREOTYPY. **HIS PORTRAIT GALLERY IN NEW YORK WAS AN IMMEDIATE SUCCESS. BY 1855, BRADY CHANGED FROM DAGUERREOTYPES TO PHOTOGRAPH PLATES. HIS PHOTOS WON PRIZES IN THE LONDON AND NEW YORK WORLD'S FAIRS. HE PHOTOGRAPHED EVERY PRESIDENT FROM JOHN Q. ADAMS TO WILLIAM McKINLEY EXCEPT WM. HENRY HARRISON. HIS PHOTO OF ABRAHAM LINCOLN APPEARS ON TODAY'S $5 BILL.**

HE WAS BORN IN WARREN CO., N.Y.

BRADY SPENT HIS ENTIRE FORTUNE PHOTOGRAPHING THE CIVIL WAR. **HE WAS FORCED INTO BANKRUPTCY. THE GOVERNMENT BOUGHT HIS PLATES FOR ONLY $25,000.**

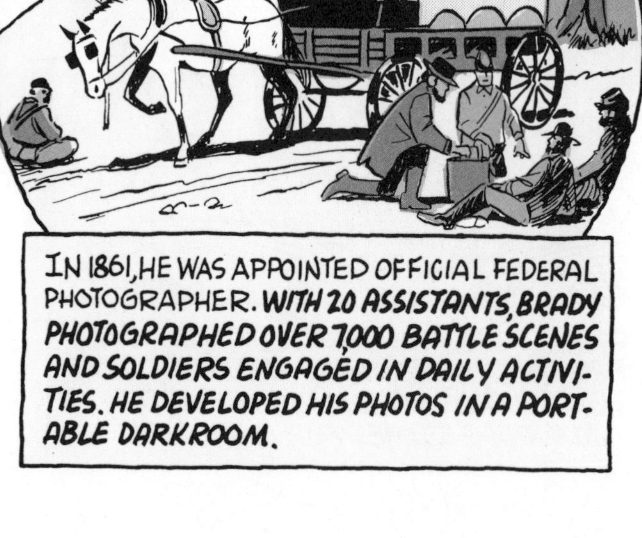

IN 1861, HE WAS APPOINTED OFFICIAL FEDERAL PHOTOGRAPHER. **WITH 20 ASSISTANTS, BRADY PHOTOGRAPHED OVER 7,000 BATTLE SCENES AND SOLDIERS ENGAGED IN DAILY ACTIVITIES. HE DEVELOPED HIS PHOTOS IN A PORTABLE DARKROOM.**

1823-1899
Joseph Medill
CRUSADING AMERICAN EDITOR AND PUBLISHER
FOR PRESIDENT
HE CAME TO OHIO IN 1832, WAS ADMITTED TO THE BAR IN 1846 AND PRACTICED IN NEW PHILADELPHIA. MEDILL ENTERED THE PUBLISHING FIELD IN 1849 WHEN HE FOUNDED A FREE-SOIL PAPER. IN 1855, HE BOUGHT THE CHICAGO "TRIBUNE" WITH TWO PARTNERS AND MADE IT ONE OF THE NATION'S MOST SUCCESSFUL NEWSPAPERS. HE HELPED FOUND THE REPUBLICAN PARTY AND STAUNCHLY SUPPORTED LINCOLN IN HIS PRESIDENTIAL CAMPAIGN.
HE WAS BORN NEAR ST. JOHN, NEW BRUNSWICK, CANADA.
THESE INIQUITIES IN GOVERNMENT MUST STOP!
I WILL SERVE TO THE BEST OF MY ABILITY, MR. PRESIDENT.
HE SERVED AT THE ILLINOIS CONSTITUTIONAL CONVENTION OF 1869, WAS ON THE CIVIL SERVICE COMMISSION UNDER PRES. GRANT AND WAS MAYOR OF CHICAGO (1872-74).
MEDILL WAS A CRUSADING EDITOR WHO FOUGHT VIGOROUSLY FOR GOVERNMENT REFORM. HE CONTROLLED THE "TRIBUNE" AS PUBLISHER FROM 1874 UNTIL HIS DEATH.
KERN

1823 - 1913

Harriet Tubman

AMERICAN ABOLITIONIST AND ESCAPED SLAVE

FROM HERE ON WE MUST BE VERY QUIET!

SHE WAS BORN A SLAVE AND DID HEAVY LABOR IN THE FIELDS UNTIL SHE ESCAPED TO FREE NORTHERN TERRITORY IN 1849. ***WITH SHEER DETERMINATION SHE FINALLY ARRIVED IN PHILADELPHIA. HARRIET TUBMAN HELPED HER BROTHER, SISTER AND PARENTS ESCAPE TO THE NORTH. SHE GUIDED MORE THAN 300 SLAVES TO FREEDOM OVER THE UNDERGROUND RAILROAD WHERE SHE WAS A CONDUCTOR. HER PEOPLE CALLED HER "MOSES" BECAUSE SHE LED THEM OUT OF BONDAGE. SHE PUT HER TRUST IN GOD'S GUIDANCE IN HER DARING JOURNEYS IN AND OUT OF THE SOUTH.***

SHE WAS BORN IN DORCHESTER CO., MARYLAND.

I AM APPEALING FOR YOUR HELP!

SHE RAISED FUNDS TO START A HOME FOR ***ELDERLY NEGROES AFTER THE WAR.***

WHEN THE CIVIL WAR STARTED, SHE WORKED FOR THE UNION ARMY AS A ***COOK, A SPY AND SCOUT.***

1824 - 1863

Thomas "Stonewall" Jackson

CONFEDERATE GENERAL

ORPHANED AT AN EARLY AGE, JACKSON RECEIVED HIS EDUCATION IN A COUNTRY SCHOOL. AT 18 HE WAS ADMITTED TO WEST POINT. GRADUATING IN 1846, HE JOINED THE FIGHTING IN MEXICO WHERE HE DISTINGUISHED HIMSELF IN THE BATTLES OF VERA CRUZ AND CONTRERAS. FROM 1851 UNTIL THE BEGINNING OF CIVIL WAR, JACKSON TAUGHT AT THE VIRGINIA MILITARY INSTITUTE AT LEXINGTON, VA. ***HIS CHRISTIAN FAITH INFLUENCED HIS WHOLE LIFE. HE PRAYED BEFORE AND AFTER EACH BATTLE. HE WAS PROMOTED TO THE RANK OF MAJOR GENERAL AFTER THE BATTLE OF BULL RUN. DURING THE SUMMER OF 1962 JACKSON WON FAME IN THE SHENANDOAH VALLEY BY HIS REMARKABLE TACTICAL MANEUVERS AGAINST 3 UNION ARMIES WHO COULDN'T TRAP HIM. HE HELPED GEN. ROBERT E. LEE DEFEAT GEN. McCLELLAN IN THE 7 DAYS' BATTLE AT RICHMOND.***

HE WAS BORN AT CLARKSBURG, VA.

WHILE LEADING HIS FORCES AGAINST GEN. HOOKER, ***HE WAS ACCIDENTALLY SHOT BY HIS OWN MEN. JACKSON HAS BEEN CALLED THE BEST OFFICER GEN. LEE HAD. WHEN JACKSON DIED, LEE COULDN'T FIND AN ADEQUATE REPLACEMENT.***

JACKSON AND HIS MEN STOOD THEIR GROUND SO FIRMLY DURING THE ***FIRST BATTLE OF BULL RUN THAT HE WAS KNOWN AS "STONEWALL" AND HIS MEN AS "STONEWALL'S BRIGADE."***

KERN

1824 - 1893

Leland Stanford

AMERICAN CAPITALIST, GOVERNOR, RAILROAD BUILDER AND U.S. SENATOR

CONGRATULATIONS, MR. GOVERNOR.

HE STUDIED LAW AND PRACTICED IN WISCONSIN AND IN 1852 JOINED HIS BROTHERS IN CALIFORNIA. ***ALWAYS INTERESTED IN POLITICS, HE WON THE GOVERNORSHIP OF CALIFORNIA IN THE 1861 ELECTION. IN 1863, HE JOINED A GROUP THAT BUILT THE CENTRAL PACIFIC AND SOUTHERN PACIFIC RAILROADS AND SERVED AS PRESIDENT. IN 1885, STANFORD WAS ELECTED U.S. SENATOR FROM CALIFORNIA WHERE HE SERVED UNTIL HIS DEATH.***

HE WAS BORN IN WATERVLIET, N.Y.

CALIFORNIA MUST STAND FIRM FOR THE UNION!
STANFORD HELPED KEEP CALIFORNIA LOYAL TO THE UNION DURING THE CIVIL WAR.

I MAKE THIS ANNOUNCEMENT IN THE MEMORY OF OUR DEAR SON.

IN 1885, HE FOUNDED LELAND STANFORD JUNIOR UNIVERSITY, PALO ALTO, CAL. WITH ***AN ENDOWMENT OF $65,000,000 IN MEMORY OF HIS SON. IN 1906, THE UNIVERSITY WAS PARTLY DESTROYED BY THE GREAT EARTHQUAKE, BUT WAS LATER RESTORED.***

KERN

1826-1864
Stephen C. Foster
ONE OF AMERICA'S BEST-LOVED SONGWRITERS
HE HAD VERY LITTLE MUSICAL TRAINING BUT HIS GIFT OF MELODY ENABLED HIM TO COMPOSE THE WORDS AND MUSIC TO MORE THAN 200 SONGS. FROM 1845 HIS SONGS FOR THE BLACKFACE MINSTRELS WON FAME THROUGHOUT THE COUNTRY. SOME OF HIS BEST KNOWN SONGS ARE "OLD FOLKS AT HOME," "MY OLD KENTUCKY HOME," "OLD BLACK JOE," "BEAUTIFUL DREAMER" AND "JEANIE WITH THE LIGHT BROWN HAIR". MANY OF HIS SONGS TELL OF THE LIFE OF THE NEGRO ON THE SOUTHERN PLANTATIONS BEFORE THE CIVIL WAR. THEY ARE DEEPLY MOVING IN THEIR SINCERITY AND SIMPLICITY. HE DIED IN POVERTY IN NEW YORK.
HE WAS BORN IN LAWRENCEVILLE, PA.
HEY, MR. FOSTER, I SURE LIKE THAT "OH SUSANNA" SONG!
THAT MAKES ME HAPPY, MIKE!
BEAUTIFUL DREAMER!
FOSTER FREED AMERICAN MUSIC FROM DEPENDENCE ON EUROPEAN MUSICAL TRADITIONS.
KERN
IN 1848, HE WROTE "OH SUSANNA," WHICH BROUGHT HIM FAME BUT ALMOST NO MONEY.

1829-1906

Carl Schurz

EDITOR, SOLDIER AND POLITICAL LEADER, WHO HAS BEEN CALLED THE GREATEST *AMERICAN CITIZEN OF GERMAN BIRTH*

I UNDERSTAND YOUR MERIT SYSTEM IS WORKING VERY WELL, CARL.

I'M HOPING FOR THE BEST, MR. PRESIDENT.

IN 1852, SCHURZ CAME TO THE UNITED STATES AND SETTLED IN MADISON, WIS. ***DURING THE CIVIL WAR, HE SERVED AS A BRIGADIER GENERAL. AFTER THE WAR, HE ESTABLISHED A GERMAN-LANGUAGE NEWSPAPER IN ST. LOUIS, MO., WHICH BECAME A VERY POWERFUL INFLUENCE IN THE WEST. IN 1869, HE WAS ELECTED U.S. SENATOR FROM MISSOURI AND SERVED WITH DISTINCTION. IN 1877, PRES. HAYES APPOINTED HIM SECRETARY OF THE INTERIOR. HE FOUGHT FOR FAIR TREATMENT FOR THE INDIANS, AND INSTALLED A CIVIL SERVICE MERIT SYSTEM IN HIS DEPT.***

THIS SCHURZ GUY WRITES A FINE EDITORIAL.

AFTER 1881, SCHURZ WAS EDITOR OF THE ***"NEW YORK EVENING POST" AND CHIEF EDITORIAL WRITER FOR "HARPERS WEEKLY." HIS BOOKS INCLUDE "LIFE OF HENRY CLAY" AND "ABRAHAM LINCOLN."***

HE WAS BORN IN LIBLAR, GERMANY.

WE ARE HAPPY TO HAVE YOU JOIN US, MR. SCHURZ.
THANK YOU, SIR!

HE WAS A LEADER IN THE ANTISLAVERY FIGHT. ***AS A REWARD FOR CAMPAIGNING FOR LINCOLN, HE WAS APPOINTED MINISTER TO SPAIN. SCHURZ WAS ONE OF THE MOST PROMINENT ORATORS OF HIS TIME.***

KERN

1830-1886

Chester A. Arthur

LAWYER, GENERAL, VICE-PRESIDENT AND ***TWENTY-FIRST***
PRESIDENT OF THE UNITED STATES (1881-85)

I SEE YOU ARE READY TO GO TO WORK, CHESTER.

HE WAS EDUCATED AT UNION COLLEGE, NEW YORK, AND ADMITTED TO THE BAR IN 1853. ***DURING THE CIVIL WAR, HE SERVED AS AN INSPECTOR GENERAL. PRES. GRANT APPOINTED HIM COLLECTOR OF THE PORT OF NEW YORK, BUT IN 1878, PRES. HAYES REMOVED HIM IN THE INTEREST OF PARTY HARMONY. HE WAS NOMINATED FOR VICE-PRESIDENT WITH GARFIELD AND BECAME PRESIDENT AT HIS DEATH. MARK TWAIN SAID, "IT WOULD BE HARD TO BETTER PRES. ARTHUR'S ADMINISTRATION."***

HE WAS BORN IN FAIRFIELD, VT.

WE THANK YOU, MR. ARTHUR, FOR YOUR HELP TO MY PEOPLE.

IN 1885, HE ACHIEVED PROMINENCE WHEN HE WON A CASE ESTABLISHING ***THE RIGHT FOR NEGROES TO RIDE ANY NEW YORK STREETCAR.***

PACIFIC TIME
MOUNTAIN TIME
CENTRAL TIME
EASTERN TIME

DURING HIS TERM AS PRESIDENT, ***STANDARD TIME WAS ADOPTED, THE AMERICAN FEDERATION OF LABOR WAS ORGANIZED, THE LINOTYPE WAS INVENTED, THE CIVIL SERVICE ACT WAS PASSED AND THE WASHINGTON MONUMENT WAS DEDICATED.***

KERN

1830-1886

Emily Dickinson

ONE OF THE MOST IMPORTANT POETS IN THE U.S.

BUT I DON'T WANT THEM PUBLISHED.

SHE WENT TO AMHERST ACADEMY FOR 3YRS. AND TO MOUNT HOLYOKE SEMINARY FOR 1YR. ***AFTER A ROMANTIC DISAPPOINTMENT, SHE LIVED IN HER FAMILY HOME DURING HER ENTIRE LIFE-TIME, WRITING EXQUISITE BITS OF VERSE FOR HERSELF FOR YEARS. HER PERSONAL EMOTIONAL PROBLEM MADE HER A GREAT LYRICAL POET OF LOVE, DEATH AND IMMORTALITY. DURING HER LIFETIME, LESS THAN 10 OF HER POEMS WERE PRINTED ANONYMOUSLY AND MOST OF THEM WERE PUBLISHED AGAINST HER WISHES.***

SHE WAS BORN IN AMHERST, MASS.
I'M NOBODY! WHO ARE YOU? ARE YOU NOBODY TOO?

LAVINIA, YOUR SISTER'S POEMS ARE BEAUTIFUL!

AFTER HER DEATH, HER SISTER TURNED OVER ALL OF EMILY'S ***POEMS TO A PUBLISHER WHICH TODAY ARE CRITICALLY APPLAUDED THROUGHOUT THE WORLD.***

KERN

LOOKING FROM HER UPSTAIRS WINDOW INTO THE GARDEN, SHE WROTE, ***"I'M NOBODY! WHO ARE YOU? ARE YOU NOBODY TOO?" SHE DIED A NOBODY, BUT TODAY HER POETRY AND PROSE CAN BE HEARD ON RECORDS AND HER POEMS ARE TAUGHT IN SCHOOLS FROM ELEMENTARY TO UNIVERSITY LEVEL.***

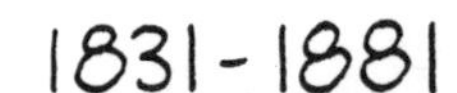

James A. Garfield

TEACHER, SOLDIER CONGRESSMAN, SENATOR AND ***TWENTIETH*** PRESIDENT OF THE UNITED STATES (MAR. 4, - SEPT. 19, 1881)

THIS NEW PARTY NEEDS OUR HELP NOW!

GARFIELD WAS 17 WHEN HE WORKED AS A CANAL BOAT TOWBOY, ***BECAME A COLLEGE PRESIDENT AT 26, WAS THE YOUNGEST GENERAL IN THE UNION ARMY AT 30, SPENT 17 YRS. IN CONGRESS WHERE HE BECAME ONE OF THE FINEST ORATORS OF HIS DAY AND LEADER OF THE REPUBLICAN PARTY. GARFIELD BECAME AN AUTHORITY ON CONSTITUTIONAL RIGHTS AND ON EDUCATIONAL, TARIFF AND FINANCIAL QUESTIONS. DURING HIS PRESIDENCY THE AMERICAN RED CROSS WAS ORGANIZED BY CLARA BARTON AND TUSKEGEE INSTITUTE WAS OPENED BY BOOKER T. WASHINGTON.***

HE WAS BORN IN ORANGE, OHIO.

I AM A STALWART. ARTHUR IS NOW PRESIDENT!

ON JULY 2, 1881, ***HE WAS SHOT BY A DISGRUNTLED OFFICE SEEKER. GARFIELD LAY FOR 80 DAYS WITH A BULLET THROUGH HIS SPINE BEFORE HE DIED. HE SERVED ONLY 200 DAYS AS PRESIDENT.***

HAVE YOU HAD ENOUGH?

AT AGE 18 HE TAUGHT SCHOOL FOR $48 A MONTH. ***THE LOCAL BULLY HAD DRIVEN THE LAST TEACHER AWAY SO GARFIELD HAD TO DEFEAT HIM TO QUALIFY FOR THE JOB.***

KERN

1833-1893

Edwin Booth

FIRST GREAT AMERICAN ACTOR

HE WAS 16 YRS. OLD WHEN HE DEBUTED ON THE STAGE IN "RICHARD III." HE TRAVELED TO CALIFORNIA AND AUSTRALIA AND IN 1856 RETURNED TO THE U.S. ***HE PRODUCED "HAMLET" IN NEW YORK WHICH RAN FOR 100 CONSECUTIVE NIGHTS. HE SPENT OVER ONE MILLION DOLLARS ERECTING THE BOOTH THEATRE IN NEW YORK WHICH WAS THE SCENE OF MANY TRIUMPHS, BUT THE PANIC OF 1873 FORCED HIM INTO BANKRUPTCY. FOR THE REST OF HIS LIFE HE WAS A ROVING ACTOR IN THE U.S. AND EUROPE. HIS FAVORITE ROLES WERE SHYLOCK, HAMLET, ROMEO AND OTHELLO. HE APPEARED LAST AS HAMLET IN 1891.***

EDWIN, YOU'VE DONE WONDERS FOR OUR PROFESSION.

HE WAS THE FOUNDER AND FIRST PRESIDENT OF THE PLAYERS CLUB IN NEW YORK CITY.

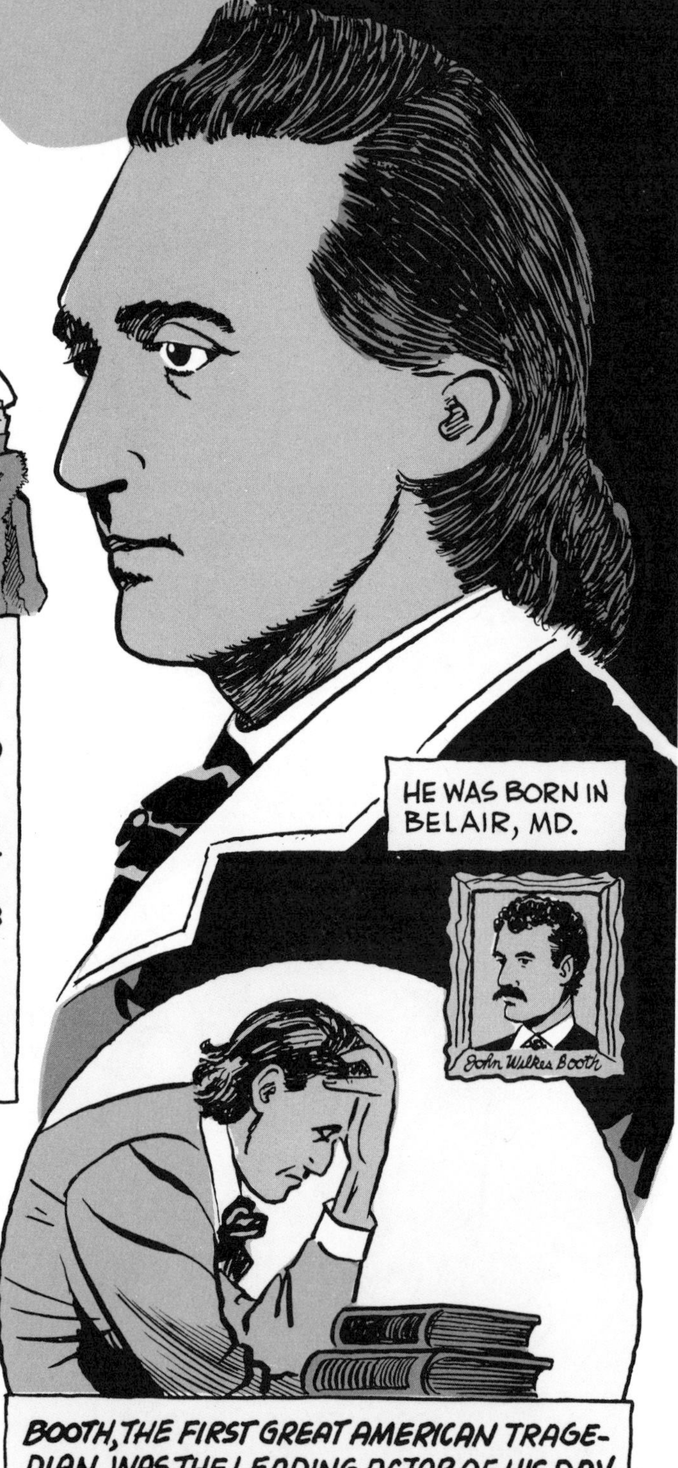

BOOTH, THE FIRST GREAT AMERICAN TRAGEDIAN, WAS THE LEADING ACTOR OF HIS DAY. SON OF A FAMOUS ACTOR, JUNIUS BRUTUS, AND BROTHER OF JOHN WILKES BOOTH, EDWIN'S CAREER WAS INTERRUPTED AFTER HIS BROTHER SHOT LINCOLN.

KERN

1833-1901

Benjamin Harrison

LAWYER, GENERAL, SENATOR AND **TWENTY-THIRD** PRESIDENT OF THE UNITED STATES (1889-93)

I NEED YOUR HELP TO PASS THESE NEEDED BILLS.
I'LL DO ALL I CAN TO HELP YOU, BEN.

HARRISON, THE GRANDSON OF WM. HENRY HARRISON, OUR 9th PRESIDENT, SPENT A ROUGH LIFE ON THE FRONTIER, TRUDGING MILES THROUGH THE SNOW TO ATTEND SCHOOL. LATER HE STUDIED LAW AND WAS ADMITTED TO THE BAR WHEN HE WAS 20, PRACTICING IN INDIANAPOLIS, INDIANA. DURING THE CIVIL WAR, HE DISTINGUISHED HIMSELF AS A COLONEL. HE WAS A COURAGEOUS LEADER. ***AFTER THE WAR, HE WAS A SUCCESSFUL LAWYER, SERVING AS A U.S. SENATOR FROM 1881-87 WHERE HE FOUGHT FOR CIVIL SERVICE REFORM, A STRONG NAVY AND VETERANS' PENSIONS. DUE TO THE POPULARITY OF HIS FAMOUS GRANDFATHER HE WAS NOMINATED FOR THE PRESIDENCY AND WON. HE WAS NEVER A POPULAR LEADER, BUT WAS A MAN OF HIGH INTELLIGENCE, ABILITY AND PERSONAL HONESTY.***

HE WAS BORN AT NORTH BEND, OHIO.
THE FIRST 4 AMERICAN BATTLESHIPS
WASHINGTON - 1889
MONTANA - 1889
NORTH DAKOTA - "
SOUTH DAKOTA - "
IDAHO - 1890
WYOMING - 1890

I HOPE WE HAVE THIS CHANCE AGAIN.

HIS LAST IMPORTANT ACT AS PRESIDENT WAS AN ATTEMPT TO ANNEX HAWAII, AT THE ***REQUEST OF THE HAWAIIAN GOVERNMENT, BUT THE SENATE FAILED TO ACT.***

DURING HIS ADMINISTRATION, ***WASHINGTON, MONTANA, IDAHO, NORTH DAKOTA, SOUTH DAKOTA AND WYOMING JOINED THE UNION. THE FIRST PAN-AMERICAN CONFERENCE TOOK PLACE, THE FIRST 4 AMERICAN BATTLESHIPS WERE BUILT AND OKLAHOMA WAS OPENED TO SETTLEMENT.***

KERN

1834(?)-1890

Chief Sitting Bull

FAMOUS MEDICINE MAN AND LEADER OF THE HUNKPAPA SIOUX INDIANS

HE WAS BORN IN WHAT IS NOW SOUTH DAKOTA.

SITTING BULL WAS ADMIRED BY HIS PEOPLE FOR HIS GENEROSITY, GOOD MANNERS AND HIS FAITHFULNESS TO INDIAN TRADITIONS. ***MANY ERRONEOUSLY THINK THAT HE LED THE INDIANS AT THE BATTLE OF THE LITTLE BIG HORN IN 1876 WHERE CUSTER LOST HIS LIFE, BUT SITTING BULL, ALONG WITH CRAZY HORSE, MADE THE PREPARATIONS FOR THE BATTLE. AFTER THIS BATTLE SITTING BULL AND HIS FOLLOWERS ESCAPED TO CANADA. IN 1881, HE RETURNED TO THE U.S. AND WAS CONFINED AT FORT RANDALL IN SOUTH DAKOTA. AFTER 2 YRS. HE WENT TO LIVE ON THE STANDING ROCK RESERVATION IN SOUTH DAKOTA.***

AS A BOY SITTING BULL WAS KNOWN AS ***"JUMPING BADGER". AFTER SHOWING GREAT BRAVERY IN A FIGHT AGAINST THE CROW INDIANS, HE WAS HONORED BY RECEIVING HIS FATHER'S NAME.***

WHILE ON THE RESERVATION HE HELPED START THE ***"GHOST DANCE." THE GOVERNMENT, THINKING HE WAS GOING TO RENEW THE INDIAN WARS, SENT INDIAN POLICEMEN TO ARREST SITTING BULL. DURING THE STRUGGLE HE AND HIS SON WERE KILLED.***

1834-1902

John Wesley Powell

AMERICAN GEOLOGIST, ETHNOLOGIST AND EXPLORER

HE WAS EDUCATED AT ILLINOIS AND OBERLIN COLLEGES. POWELL SERVED IN THE UNION ARMY DURING THE CIVIL WAR, LOSING AN ARM AT THE BATTLE OF SHILOH. AFTER THE WAR HE WAS A PROFESSOR OF GEOLOGY AT ILLINOIS WESLEYAN COLLEGE AND LATER AT ILLINOIS NORMAL UNIVERSITY. IN 1869, ***WITH A GROUP OF STUDENTS, HE LED THE FIRST EXPEDITION DOWN THE COLORADO RIVER, WHERE HE MADE AN INTENSIVE STUDY OF THE REGION AND GATHERED VALUABLE ETHNOLOGICAL AND ANTHROPOLOGICAL INFORMATION CONCERNING THE AMERICAN INDIANS. IN 1879 HE ORGANIZED THE BUREAU OF ETHNOLOGY FOR THE SMITHSONIAN INSTITUTE. WITH VISION BEYOND HIS TIMES, HE RECOMMENDED RECLAMATION OF THE ARID LANDS AND CAREFUL USE OF RESOURCES.***

HE WAS BORN IN MOUNT MORRIS, N.Y.
WE HOPE YOU WILL HONOR US BY ACCEPTING THE DIRECTORSHIP.

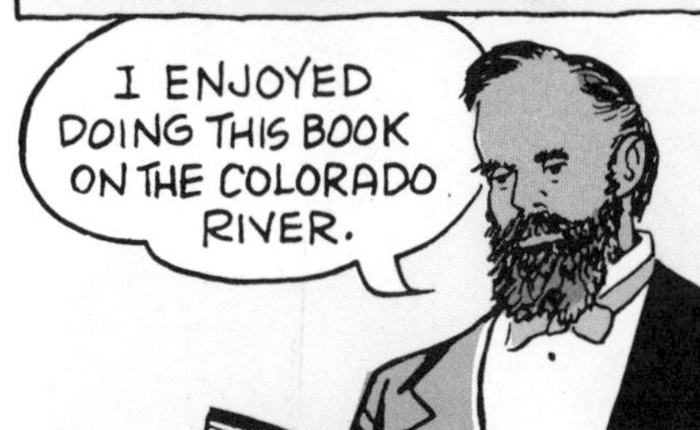

I ENJOYED DOING THIS BOOK ON THE COLORADO RIVER.

HIS BOOKS INCLUDE ***"EXPLORATIONS OF THE COLORADO RIVER OF THE WEST," "INTRODUCTION TO THE STUDY OF INDIAN LANGUAGES"*** AND ***"REPORT ON THE LANDS OF THE ARID REGION OF THE UNITED STATES."***

KERN

POWELL'S CANYON EXPLOITS MADE HIM FAMOUS. THE U.S. CONGRESS VOTED FINANCIAL AID AND ESTABLISHED A 10YR. SURVEY OF THE REGION WHICH EVENTUALLY ***DEVELOPED INTO THE U.S. GEOLOGICAL SURVEY. HE BECAME THE DIRECTOR IN 1881.***

1834 - 1906

Marshall Field

AMERICAN BUSINESSMAN

AFTER GETTING HIS EDUCATION IN A PUBLIC SCHOOL AND AN ACADEMY NEAR CONWAY, MASS., FIELD FOUND WORK AS A CLERK IN A DRY-GOODS STORE IN CHICAGO. ***IN 1861, HE WAS PROMOTED TO GENERAL MANAGER. A YEAR LATER HE WAS MADE A PARTNER. IN 1865, THE STORE WAS CALLED FIELD, PALMER AND LEITER. THE TWO PARTNERS RETIRED IN 1881. PIONEERING IN MODERN RETAILING, HE SET UP A NEW FIRM AND CALLED IT MARSHALL FIELD AND CO. AS HIS FORTUNE GREW FIELD BECAME A PHILANTHROPIST. HIS GIFTS INCLUDE AN $8,000,000 GRANT TO BUILD THE CHICAGO NATURAL HISTORY MUSEUM AND VALUABLE LAND FOR THE UNIVERSITY OF CHICAGO CAMPUS.***

HE WAS BORN NEAR CONWAY, MASS.
YOU DESERVE SINCERE CONGRATULATIONS FOR YOUR FINE WORK!

I WOULD SAY YOU HAVE REACHED YOUR GOAL.

FIELD ESTABLISHED BRANCHES IN NEW YORK, ENGLAND, GERMANY, SWITZERLAND, FRANCE AND JAPAN.

KERN

IN 25 YRS. FIELD EXPANDED HIS BUSINESS TO BECOME THE ***LARGEST RETAIL DRY-GOODS ENTERPRISE IN THE WORLD WITH ANNUAL SALES OF MORE THAN $60,000,000.***

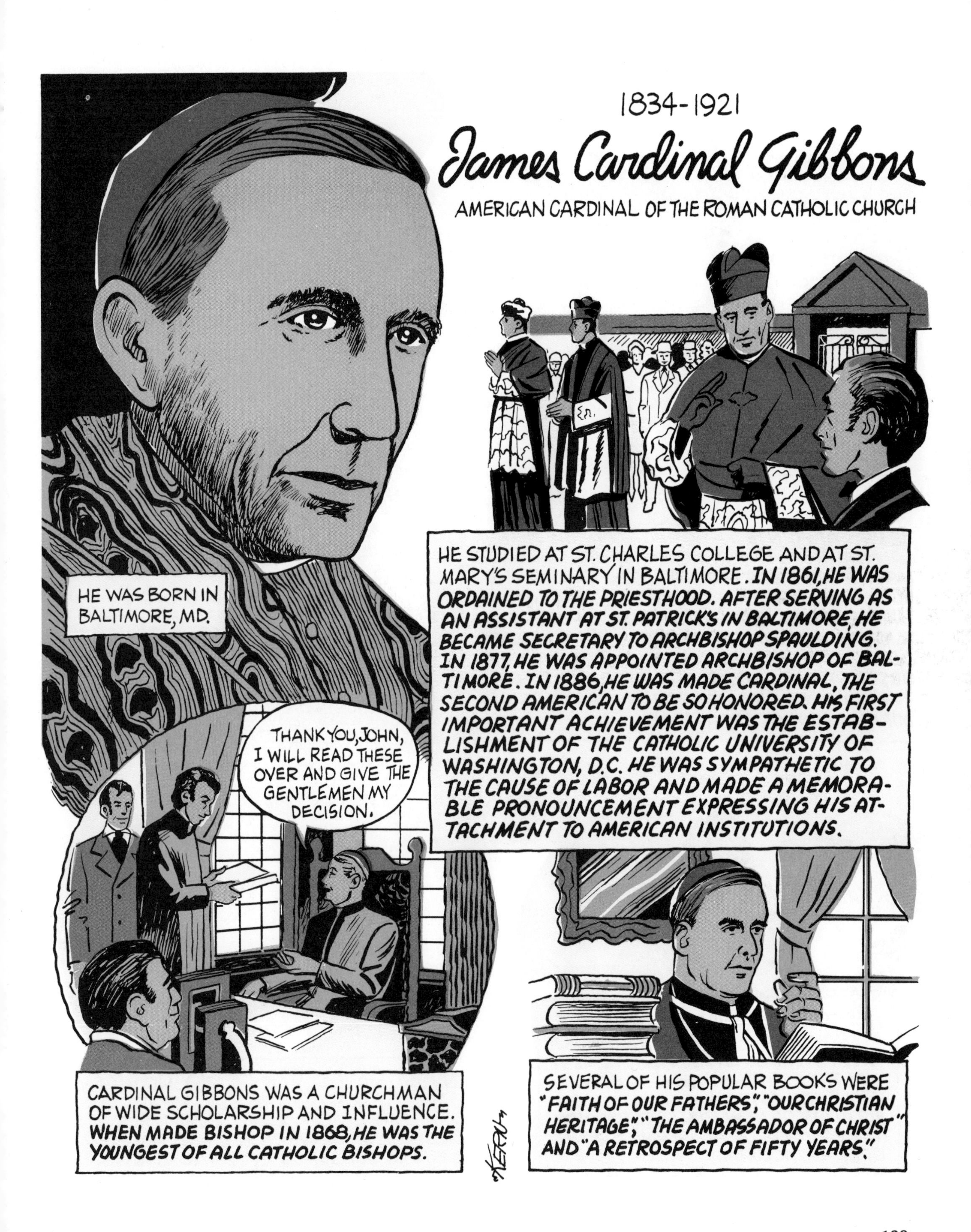
1834-1921
James Cardinal Gibbons
AMERICAN CARDINAL OF THE ROMAN CATHOLIC CHURCH
HE WAS BORN IN BALTIMORE, MD.
HE STUDIED AT ST. CHARLES COLLEGE AND AT ST. MARY'S SEMINARY IN BALTIMORE. IN 1861, HE WAS ORDAINED TO THE PRIESTHOOD. AFTER SERVING AS AN ASSISTANT AT ST. PATRICK'S IN BALTIMORE, HE BECAME SECRETARY TO ARCHBISHOP SPAULDING. IN 1877, HE WAS APPOINTED ARCHBISHOP OF BALTIMORE. IN 1886, HE WAS MADE CARDINAL, THE SECOND AMERICAN TO BE SO HONORED. HIS FIRST IMPORTANT ACHIEVEMENT WAS THE ESTABLISHMENT OF THE CATHOLIC UNIVERSITY OF WASHINGTON, D.C. HE WAS SYMPATHETIC TO THE CAUSE OF LABOR AND MADE A MEMORABLE PRONOUNCEMENT EXPRESSING HIS ATTACHMENT TO AMERICAN INSTITUTIONS.
THANK YOU, JOHN, I WILL READ THESE OVER AND GIVE THE GENTLEMEN MY DECISION.
CARDINAL GIBBONS WAS A CHURCHMAN OF WIDE SCHOLARSHIP AND INFLUENCE. WHEN MADE BISHOP IN 1868, HE WAS THE YOUNGEST OF ALL CATHOLIC BISHOPS.
SEVERAL OF HIS POPULAR BOOKS WERE "FAITH OF OUR FATHERS," "OUR CHRISTIAN HERITAGE," "THE AMBASSADOR OF CHRIST" AND "A RETROSPECT OF FIFTY YEARS."
KERN

1835-1909

Simon Newcomb

ASTRONOMER-MATHEMATICIAN

THESE COMPUTATIONS ARE CORRECT.

IN 1853, HE CAME FROM CANADA TO THE U.S. WHERE HE TAUGHT SCHOOL IN MARYLAND. **HE WAS APPOINTED A COMPUTER IN THE AMERICAN NAUTICAL ALMANAC OFFICE AT CAMBRIDGE, MASS. WHILE THERE HE WENT TO THE LAWRENCE SCIENTIFIC SCHOOL AT HARVARD, GRADUATING IN 1858. FROM 1861-97 HE WAS PROFESSOR OF MATHEMATICS IN THE U.S. NAVY. HE HAD GREAT INFLUENCE IN THE DEVELOPMENT OF THE NAVAL OBSERVATORY. AFTER HIS RETIREMENT FROM THE NAVY HE WAS AWARDED THE RANK OF ADMIRAL BY CONGRESS IN 1906.**

HE WAS BORN IN WALLACE, NOVA SCOTIA, CANADA.

PARALLAX IS THE DIFFERENCE IN DIRECTION OF AN OBJECT WHEN SEEN FROM TWO POSITIONS WHICH ARE NOT IN A DIRECT LINE WITH EACH OTHER AND THE OBJECT.

THIS GIVES US A CLEARER PICTURE OF PLANET POSITION.

NEWCOMB WAS ONE OF THE FOREMOST ASTRONOMER-MATHEMATICIANS OF HIS DAY. HIS GREATEST ACHIEVEMENT WAS THE ESTABLISHMENT OF CONSTANTS OF ASTRONOMY AND THE COMPUTATION OF NEW TABLES TO PREDICT THE POSITION OF THE PLANETS WITH GREATER ACCURACY.

HE INVESTIGATED MANY ASTRONOMICAL SUBJECTS, SUCH AS THE SOLAR PARALLAX AND THE SPEED OF LIGHT. **ALMANACS ALL OVER THE WORLD WERE REVISED FOLLOWING HIS SUCCESSFUL INVESTIGATIONS.**

KERN

1835-1910
Samuel L. Clemens
ONE OF AMERICA'S GREAT WRITERS, HUMORISTS AND STORY TELLERS
MARK TWAIN GREW UP DURING THE HEIGHT OF THE RIVER TRAFFIC ON THE MISSISSIPPI. AS A YOUNG BOY HE WROTE HUMOROUS SKETCHES AND VERSE FOR HIS BROTHER'S NEWSPAPER. IN 1857 HE BECAME AN APPRENTICE RIVER PILOT. HIS EXPERIENCES WERE RECORDED IN HIS LATER BOOKS. IN 1862, TWAIN WAS A REPORTER IN VIRGINIA CITY, NEVADA. THIS WAS THE BEGINNING OF HIS LITERARY CAREER. "HUCKLEBERRY FINN," "TOM SAWYER" AND "LIFE ON THE MISSISSIPPI" WERE WRITTEN AFTER THE CIVIL WAR WHEN PEOPLE CLAMORED FOR CALM AND THE EASY-GOING LIFE OF BY-GONE DAYS.
HE WAS BORN IN FLORIDA, MO.
WHERE ON EARTH DID YOU FIND THAT MONSTROUS HAT?
THE NAME'S MARK TWAIN.
TWAIN HAD A DOMINATING PERSONALITY WITH GREAT WIT AND CHARM. HE WAS POPULAR AT PARTIES IN AMERICA AND EUROPE, ALTHOUGH HE WAS LIKELY TO DO OR SAY SOMETHING VERY SHOCKING AT ANYTIME.
MARK TWAIN WAS THE PEN NAME FOR SAMUEL LANGHORNE CLEMENS. HE TOOK THE NAME AFTER THE DEATH OF A RIVER BOAT PILOT WHO WROTE FOR A NEW ORLEANS NEWSPAPER. "MARK TWAIN" WAS THE PILOT'S CALL TO INDICATE THAT THE WATER WAS TWO FATHOMS DEEP.
KERN

1835-1919

Andrew Carnegie

AMERICAN STEEL MANUFACTURER AND PHILANTHROPIST

HE WAS BORN IN DUNFERMLINE, SCOTLAND.
I WANT TO HELP PEOPLE WHO NEED HELP.

YOU NOW HAVE COMPLETE CONTROL.

IN 1848, HE CAME TO THE U.S. AND WORKED AS A WEAVER'S ASSISTANT IN A COTTON MILL EARNING $1.20 A WEEK, THEN AS A TELEGRAPH OPERATOR EARNING $25 A MONTH. ***CARNEGIE'S STOCK IN THE WOODRUFF SLEEPING CAR CO. AND HIS OIL INVESTMENTS LAID THE FOUNDATION FOR HIS FORTUNE. IN 1868, CARNEGIE INTRODUCED THE BESSEMER PROCESS FOR MAKING STEEL IN THE U.S. IN 1888, HE WAS THE MAIN OWNER OF THE HOMESTEAD STEEL WORKS AND HAD CONTROLLING INTEREST IN 7 OTHER LARGE STEEL PLANTS. HIS INTERESTS WERE THEN CONSOLIDATED INTO THE CARNEGIE STEEL CO. IN 1901, IT WAS MERGED INTO THE U.S. STEEL CORP.***

READ THIS ARTICLE AND SEE WHAT I MEAN.

CARNEGIE'S GIFTS DURING HIS LIFETIME WERE GREATER THAN THOSE OF ANY OTHER AMERICAN. ***HE GAVE AWAY $350,000,000 FOR THE BETTERMENT OF MANKIND. IT WAS LARGELY BECAUSE OF HIS FINANCIAL HELP THAT THOUSANDS OF COMMUNITIES HAVE PUBLIC LIBRARIES.***

HE PUBLISHED AN ARTICLE CALLED "***THE GOSPEL OF WEALTH,***" OUTLINING HIS IDEAS ON HOW LARGE FORTUNES SHOULD BE USED FOR THE BETTERMENT OF SOCIETY.

KERN

1836 - 1910

Winslow Homer

GREAT AMERICAN PAINTER AND ILLUSTRATOR

DID YOU KNOW THAT HOMER HATED HIS FIRST JOB AND QUIT, VOWING NEVER TO WORK AGAIN FOR WAGES FOR ANY MAN?

HOMER LIVED IN BOSTON UNTIL HE WAS 23YRS. OLD. HE JOINED THE STAFF OF "***HARPER'S WEEKLY***" AND DID ILLUSTRATION WORK WHILE STUDYING AT THE ***NATIONAL ACADEMY OF DESIGN IN NEW YORK CITY. HOMER'S EARLY PAINTINGS SHOWED EVERYDAY LIFE IN NEW ENGLAND AND VIRGINIA. AFTER THE WAR HE WENT TO EUROPE WHERE HE EXHIBITED HIS PAINTINGS WITH GREAT SUCCESS. HE LATER MOVED TO THE MAINE COAST WHERE HE PAINTED THE SEA AND FISHERFOLKS FOR WHICH HE BECAME FAMOUS. HIS "TORNADO BAHAMAS" IS A DRAMATIC WATERCOLOR HANGING IN THE METROPOLITAN MUSEUM IN NEW YORK CITY.***

HE WAS BORN IN BOSTON, MASS.

"ON A LEE SHORE" IS ALSO ONE OF HIS FINEST OILS.

SOME OF HIS GREAT SEA PAINTINGS WERE "***EIGHT BELLS,***" "***WEST WIND***" AND "***MENDING THE NETS.***"

KERN

HOMER SERVED AS A WAR CORRESPONDENT WITH THE UNION ARMY DURING THE CIVIL WAR. ***MANY SKETCHES OF BATTLEFIELD SCENES WERE LATER USED FOR HIS POPULAR WAR PICTURES.***

1837- 1899

Dwight L. Moody

AMERICAN EVANGELIST

I WOULD LIKE TO JOIN YOUR FINE ORGANIZATION.

IN 1865, MOODY LEFT HIS JOB AS A SHOE SALESMAN IN BOSTON, WENT TO CHICAGO AND ENGAGED IN ***MISSIONARY WORK***. HIS SUNDAY SCHOOL DEVELOPED INTO THE CHICAGO AVE. CHURCH WHERE HE BECAME A LAY PASTOR. ***IN 1870, IRA SANKEY, SINGER AND COMPOSER OF HYMNS, JOINED HIM. MOODY FOUNDED AN INTERDENOMINATIONAL CHURCH AND THE MOODY PRESS IN CHICAGO. HE ALSO FOUNDED A PRIVATE HIGH SCHOOL FOR GIRLS AND ANOTHER FOR BOYS NEAR NORTHFIELD, MASS.***

HE WAS BORN IN NORTHFIELD, MASS.
I WANT TO MAKE THIS THE FINEST SCHOOL IN THE COUNTRY FOR THE TRAINING OF CHRISTIAN WORKERS.

2,530,000 PEOPLE HEARD YOU AND IRA DURING YOUR 1873-75 CAMPAIGN IN GREAT BRITAIN.

MOODY CONDUCTED GREAT EVANGELISTIC CAMPAIGNS IN THE U.S. AND GREAT BRITAIN, WHICH LED TO ALMOST UNPRECEDENTED RELIGIOUS AWAKENING.

IN 1886, HE FOUNDED THE ***MOODY BIBLE INSTITUTE, A SCHOOL FOR TRAINING WORKERS IN CHRISTIAN SERVICE.*** THIS SCHOOL OFFERS A PROGRAM ON A COLLEGE LEVEL, REACHING A LARGE AUDIENCE THROUGH ITS RADIO STATION, AND DISTRIBUTES FREE CHRISTIAN LITERATURE WORLDWIDE.

KERN

1837-1908

Grover Cleveland

LAWYER, GOVERNOR AND **TWENTY-SECOND** AND **TWENTY-FOURTH** PRESIDENT OF THE UNITED STATES (1885-89 AND 1893-97)

IF ANYTHING HAPPENS TO ME, YOU, AS VICE-PRESIDENT, WILL TAKE OVER. FOLLOWING IN SUCCESSION WILL BE THE SEC. OF STATE, SEC. OF THE TREASURY AND THEN THE SEC. OF WAR.
U.S. PRESIDENT

HE WAS BORN IN CALDWELL, NEW JERSEY.

I WILL NOT TOLERATE CORRUPTION AND EXTRAVAGANCE IN MY ADMINISTRATION!

AS A YOUNG MAN HE CLERKED IN A GROCERY STORE, THEN STUDIED LAW AND WAS ADMITTED TO THE BAR AT AGE 22. ***HE WAS AN ASSISTANT ATTORNEY, A SHERIFF AND MAYOR, BEFORE HE BECAME GOV. OF NEW YORK WHERE HE SERVED FOR 1 YEAR BEFORE BEING ELECTED PRESIDENT IN 1885. CLEVELAND WAS THE ONLY PRESIDENT TO SERVE ONE TERM, LOSE AN ELECTION AND THEN WIN FOR A SECOND TERM. A CONSERVATIVE, HONEST AND FRUGAL ADMINISTRATOR, HE FOUGHT EXTRAVAGANCE AND CORRUPTION.*** CLEVELAND WAS 49 WHEN HE MARRIED 21-YR.-OLD FRANCES FOLSOM, THE YOUNGEST FIRST LADY IN U.S. HISTORY. AFTER HIS 2ND TERM CLEVELAND RETIRED TO PRINCETON, N.J., WRITING AND LECTURING.

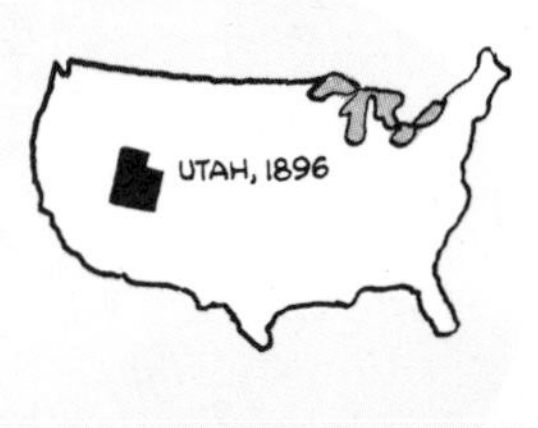

DURING HIS FIRST ADMINISTRATION, THE ***PRESIDENTIAL SUCCESSION BILL WAS PASSED. THE STATUE OF LIBERTY WAS DEDICATED AND THE INTERSTATE COMMERCE ACT WAS PASSED.***

DURING CLEVELAND'S SECOND TERM, UTAH JOINED THE UNION, THE FIRST CLUTCH-DRIVEN AUTOMOBILE WAS INVENTED, THE WORLD'S COLUMBIAN EXPOSITION OPENED IN CHICAGO AND THE PULLMAN STRIKE TOOK PLACE.

KERN

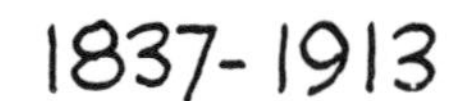

J. Pierpont Morgan

GREAT AMERICAN FINANCIER, ART COLLECTOR AND PHILANTHROPIST

WE THANK YOU, JOHN, FOR YOUR GREAT GENEROSITY.

HE WAS BORN IN HARTFORD, CONN.

ONE OF AMERICA'S GREATEST FINANCIERS STARTED OUT WORKING FOR HIS FATHER IN LONDON. AT 23 HE CAME TO NEW YORK AS AN AGENT FOR HIS FATHER'S FIRM. ***AT 32 HE GAINED CONTROL OF THE ALBANY AND SUSQUEHANNA RAILROADS. HE THEN ESTABLISHED THE FIRM OF DREXEL MORGAN AND CO. IN 1895, IT BECAME THE J. P. MORGAN AND CO. AFFILIATED WITH THE FIRMS IN LONDON AND PARIS, THESE BECAME THE MOST INFLUENTIAL BANKING FIRMS IN THE WORLD. MORGAN FINANCED THE RAILROAD BUILDERS, THE INTERNATIONAL HARVESTER CO. AND HELPED ORGANIZE THE U.S. STEEL CO. HE GAVE HUGE SUMS TO THE HARVARD MEDICAL SCHOOL AND FINANCED THE CATHEDRAL OF ST. JOHN THE DIVINE IN NEW YORK. HE FOUNDED THE LYING-IN HOSPITAL IN NEW YORK.***

THE COUNTRY NEEDS YOUR HELP, JOHN.

I'LL DO MY BEST, MR. PRESIDENT.

AFTER THE PANIC OF 1893, PRES. CLEVELAND CALLED ON MORGAN TO ***RELIEVE THE PRESSURE ON THE U.S. TREASURY. DURING THE PANIC OF 1907 HE HELPED STABILIZE THE FINANCIAL CONDITION OF THE COUNTRY.***

KERN

MORGAN WAS THE LEADING PRIVATE ART COLLECTOR OF HIS TIME. ***HE HELPED FOUND THE METROPOLITAN MUSEUM OF ART IN NEW YORK. HE WAS ALSO KNOWN AS A GREAT YACHTSMAN, WINNING THE INTERNATIONAL CUP 4 TIMES.***

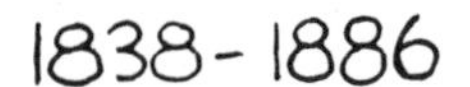

Henry H. Richardson

ROMANESQUE-REVIVAL ARCHITECT

THIS IS A MANSARD ROOF CROWNED BY IRON CASTINGS.
VERY INGENIOUS, HENRY.

HE WAS EDUCATED AT HARVARD UNIVERSITY AND THE ÈCOLE DES BEAUX-ARTS IN PARIS. IN 1866 HE JOINED A FIRM IN NEW YORK CITY. HIS DESIGNS OF SMALL LIBRARIES, RAILROAD STATIONS AND BROWN-STAINED SHINGLED HOUSES PROGRESSED TOWARD AN AUTHENTIC *AMERICAN STYLE, WHICH GREATLY INFLUENCED LATER ARCHITECTS SUCH AS LOUIS SULLIVAN, JOHN ROOT AND FRANK LLOYD WRIGHT. RICHARDSON WAS THE MOST IMPORTANT ARCHITECT OF HIS GENERATION IN THE U.S. HE WAS THE FIRST AMERICAN ARCHITECT TO HAVE AN INTERNATIONAL REPUTATION.*

HE WAS BORN IN ST. JAMES PARISH, LOUISIANA.

HIS FIRST GREAT WORK WAS *TRINITY CHURCH IN BOSTON, MASS. ITS PICTURESQUE TOWERS AND HEAVY ROUND ARCHES LED TO A "ROMANESQUE REVIVAL" STYLE IN THE 1880'S.*

HERE ARE THE PLANS FOR YOUR NEW BUILDING, MR. FIELD.
VERY GOOD, HENRY.

DURING THE LAST 5 YRS. OF HIS LIFE HE DEVELOPED A MORE *FUNCTIONAL STYLE. HIS MARSHALL FIELD BUILDING IN CHICAGO (1885) BEST SHOWS THIS TENDENCY.*

KERN

1838-1905

John Milton Hay

AMERICAN STATESMAN AND AUTHOR

HAY WAS EDUCATED AT BROWN UNIVERSITY, STUDIED LAW IN ABRAHAM LINCOLN'S OFFICE AND WAS ADMITTED TO THE ILLINOIS BAR AT 23. ***PRES. LINCOLN MADE HIM ONE OF HIS PRIVATE SECRETARIES. DURING THE CIVIL WAR, HE SERVED AS A COLONEL. IN 1865, HE WAS APPOINTED SEC. OF THE U.S. LEGATION TO PARIS, VIENNA AND MADRID. IN 1868, HE CAME BACK TO THE U.S. AND DEVOTED HIMSELF TO WRITING FOR THE NEXT 20 YRS. IN 1897, PRES. McKINLEY APPOINTED HIM AMBASSADOR TO GREAT BRITAIN AND IN 1898 HE WAS APPOINTED SEC. OF STATE. HE SERVED IN THE CABINETS OF PRESIDENTS McKINLEY AND THEODORE ROOSEVELT UNTIL HIS DEATH. HAY WAS RESPONSIBLE FOR FORMING MUCH OF THE FOREIGN POLICY OF THE UNITED STATES OF HIS TIME. HE IS BEST REMEMBERED FOR HIS OPEN-DOOR POLICY IN CHINA.***

HAY WAS AN EDITORIAL WRITER FOR THE NEW YORK "TRIBUNE" FOR 5 YRS. ONE OF HIS MOST CELEBRATED WORKS, IN COLLABORATION WITH JOHN NICOLAY, WAS ***"ABRAHAM LINCOLN, A HISTORY," 10 VOLS.***

HE DIRECTED PEACE NEGOTIATIONS AFTER THE SPANISH-AMERICAN WAR, PROTECTED AMERICAN INTERESTS IN CHINA DURING ***THE BOXER REBELLION, AND OPENED THE WAY TO AMERICAN CONSTRUCTION AND MANAGEMENT OF THE PANAMA CANAL.***

KERN

1838 - 1914

John Muir

AUTHOR, EXPLORER AND NATURALIST

MUIR WAS 11 YRS. OLD WHEN HE MOVED TO WISCONSIN WITH HIS PARENTS. HE GREW UP ON A FARM AND DEVELOPED A LOVE FOR NATURE. AT 22 HE GRADUATED FROM THE UNIVERSITY OF WISCONSIN. HE TRAMPED THROUGH LARGE AREAS OF THE U.S., EUROPE, ASIA, AFRICA AND THE ARCTIC. **FOR 6 YRS. HE ROAMED IN THE YOSEMITE VALLEY, AND WAS THE FIRST MAN TO EXPLAIN THE GLACIAL ORIGIN OF YOSEMITE VALLEY. IN 1879, HE DISCOVERED A GLACIER IN ALASKA WHICH IS NAMED FOR HIM. HE FOUNDED THE SIERRA CLUB. HIS WRITINGS INCLUDE "TRAVELS IN ALASKA," "THE MOUNTAINS OF CALIFORNIA" AND "A THOUSAND MILE WALK TO THE GULF."**

HE WAS BORN IN DUNBAR, SCOTLAND.

WE MUST DO EVERYTHING POSSIBLE TO PRESERVE OUR FORESTS, MR. PRESIDENT.

A REDWOOD FOREST IN THE CALIFORNIA COASTAL RANGE NEAR SAN FRANCISCO WAS NAMED "**MUIR WOODS**" IN 1908 TO HONOR HIS CONTRIBUTION TO **FOREST CONSERVATION**.

KNOWN AS "**THE FATHER OF OUR NATIONAL PARK SYSTEM**", **MUIR WAS A GREAT CAMPAIGNER FOR CONSERVATION IN THE U.S. HE PERSUADED PRES. THEODORE ROOSEVELT TO PUT ASIDE 148,000,000 ACRES OF LAND FOR FOREST RESERVES.**

1838-1918

Archbishop John Ireland

ELOQUENT ROMAN CATHOLIC CHURCHMAN

YOU CAN QUOTE ME. "I UPHOLD AMERICAN IDEALS AND DEFEND THE RIGHTS OF THE WORKING PEOPLE."

HE WAS EDUCATED IN FRANCE AND MOVED TO THE U.S WITH HIS FAMILY WHEN HE WAS A YOUNG BOY. ***IN 1861, IRELAND WAS ORDAINED. IN 1875, HE BECAME COADJUTOR TO THE BISHOP AND SUCCEEDED TO THE SEE OF ST. PAUL, MINN., IN 1884, AND WAS MADE AN ARCHBISHOP IN 1888. IRELAND DEFENDED THE RIGHTS OF THE WORKING PEOPLE. HE WAS RESPONSIBLE FOR THE BUILDING OF THE CATHEDRAL OF ST. PAUL AND THE ST. PAUL SEMINARY. AS AN AUTHOR HE WROTE "THE CHURCH IN MODERN SOCIETY."***

HE WAS BORN IN IRELAND.

IRELAND ACTIVELY PROMOTED IMMIGRATION TO AMERICA. ***HE WAS KNOWN AS THE "CONSECRATED BLIZZARD" FOR HIS ENERGETIC ACTIVITY IN CHURCH AND CIVIL AFFAIRS.***

HE WAS A GREAT TEMPERANCE LEADER AND ORGANIZED THE FIRST TOTAL ***ABSTINENCE SOCIETY IN MINNESOTA. HIS GREAT ELOQUENCE AND ABILITY MADE HIM ONE OF AMERICA'S GREAT CHURCH LEADERS.***

KERN

1839-1937

John D. Rockefeller

AMERICAN FINANCIER AND PHILANTHROPIST

HE WAS BORN IN RICHFORD, N.Y.
THERE YOU ARE, YOUNG MAN. PUT IT IN THE BANK.
THANK YOU, SIR.
HE BECAME FAMOUS IN HIS LATER YEARS WHEN HE GAVE **SHINY NEW DIMES AS MEMENTOS TO STRANGERS HE MET.**
KERN

WE SHOULD START BRANCHING OUT.

HE WAS THE SON OF A PEDDLER WHEN HE MOVED TO CLEVELAND, OHIO, WITH HIS FAMILY. AT 16 HE CLERKED IN A PRODUCE FIRM, SAVED ENOUGH MONEY AND WITH A PARTNER FORMED A GRAIN COMMISSION BUSINESS. ***AT 23 HE ENTERED THE OIL BUSINESS, REORGANIZING IT TO RUN EFFICIENTLY. IN 15 YRS. HE WAS PRODUCING OIL FOR THE CONSUMER UNDER ONE CO. STANDARD OIL WAS ORGANIZED BY ROCKEFELLER IN 1870 AND BY 1872 HE OWNED ALL THE MAIN REFINERIES IN THE U.S., BUILDING TANK CARS TO SET UP A DISTRIBUTION SYSTEM. THE COURTS DISSOLVED THE STANDARD OIL TRUST IN 1872 AND BY 1911 A NEW DECISION BROKE THE COMPANY INTO SEPARATE CORPORATIONS. HE RETIRED FROM ACTIVE MANAGEMENT OF BUSINESS IN 1895 WITH A PERSONAL FORTUNE OF $1 BILLION.***

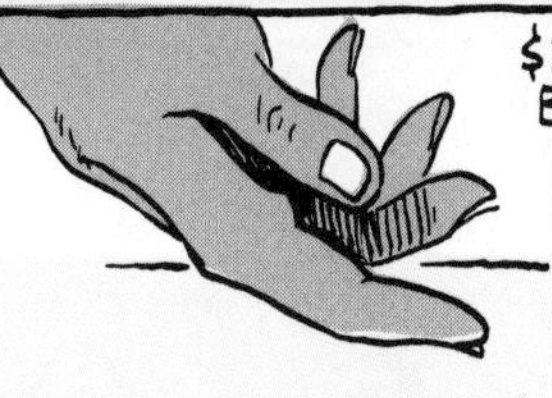

BEFORE HE DIED HE GAVE AWAY $500 MILLION TO FOUNDATIONS AND ORGANIZATIONS. BEST KNOWN WERE THE ROCKEFELLER FOUNDATION, THE INSTITUTE OF MEDICAL RESEARCH, AND THE LAURA SPELMAN MEMORIAL IN MEMORY OF HIS WIFE. HE PROMOTED CHILD WELFARE AND THE STUDY OF SOCIAL SCIENCES THROUGHOUT THE WORLD.

1840-1902
Thomas Nast
AMERICAN POLITICAL CARTOONIST
THESE TWO CARTOONS WILL TAKE CARE OF MR. GREELEY!
NAST CAME TO NEW YORK WITH HIS MOTHER WHEN HE WAS 6YRS. OLD. HE STUDIED AT THE NATIONAL ACADEMY OF DESIGN. AT 15 HE WAS A DRAFTSMAN FOR AN ILLUSTRATED WEEKLY AND SKETCHED WARFARE SCENES IN ITALY FOR NEW YORK, LONDON AND PARIS NEWSPAPERS. IN 1861, HE WAS A STAFF ARTIST FOR "HARPER'S WEEKLY" WHERE HE INFLUENCED PUBLIC OPINION IN FAVOR OF THE NORTH. NAST WAS AN EXCELLENT DRAFTSMAN AND DESIGNER. HIS BLACK AND WHITE DRAWINGS WERE EXHIBITED IN MANY MUSEUMS AND GALLERIES. HIS DRAMATIC CARTOONS DURING THE PRESIDENTIAL CAMPAIGN OF 1872 HELPED DEFEAT HORACE GREELEY. NAST IS CREDITED WITH STARTING THE SANTA CLAUS IDEA IN A SERIES OF SKETCHES WHICH APPEARED IN "HARPER'S WEEKLY."
HE WAS BORN AT LANDAU, BAVARIA.
THE TAMMANY TIGER, SYMBOL OF THE CORRUPT TAMMANY POLITICAL MACHINE IN NEW YORK CITY.
REPUBLICAN LAMB INQUIRE WITHIN - DEMOCRATIC TIGER
ANOTHER SUCH VICTORY AND I AM UNDONE.
NAST'S REPUBLICAN ELEPHANT FIRST APPEARED IN 1874.
HE INVENTED THE ELEPHANT FOR THE REPUBLICAN PARTY AND POPULARIZED THE DONKEY FOR THE DEMOCRATS.
KERN
NAST'S CARICATURES OF THE TAMMANY TIGER HELPED BREAK UP THE NOTORIOUS TWEED RING, A CORRUPT POLITICAL MACHINE IN NEW YORK.

1840(?)-1904
Chief Joseph
NEZ PERCÉ INDIAN CHIEF
I HAVE IT IN MY HEART. I AM TIRED OF FIGHTING.
CHIEF JOSEPH IS BEST KNOWN FOR HIS MILITARY RETREAT OF 1877 THROUGH IDAHO, WASHINGTON AND MONTANA. HIS TRIBE REFUSED TO RECOGNIZE LAND CESSIONS MADE IN 1863 AND CHIEF JOSEPH REALIZED HE COULDN'T FACE THE STRONG U.S. FORCES SO HE MADE A BRILLIANT RETREAT WHILE FIGHTING OFF THE U.S. TROOPS. HE LED HIS PEOPLE MORE THAN A THOUSAND MILES, BUT WAS FINALLY FORCED TO SURRENDER, WHEN HE AND HIS PEOPLE WERE 50 MILES FROM THE CANADIAN BORDER. CHIEF JOSEPH'S IMPASSIONED LAMENT AT HIS FAILURE TO SAVE HIS PEOPLE CONSTITUTES ONE OF THE FINEST PIECES OF RHETORIC IN INDIAN HISTORY: "I WILL FIGHT NO MORE FOREVER...."
HE WAS BORN IN OREGON.
THERE WILL BE NO SCALPING IN ANY OF OUR BATTLES.
AFTER COMPLETING HIS FAMOUS RETREAT, HE LIVED AT COLVILLE RESERVATION, WASHINGTON.
KERN
IN FIGHTING, HE NOT ONLY SHOWED RARE MILITARY GENIUS BUT ALSO GREAT HUMANITY.

1841 - 1935

Oliver W. Holmes, Jr.

AMERICAN LAWYER KNOWN AS THE GREATEST JUSTICE OF THE SUPREME COURT SINCE JOHN MARSHALL

I BELIEVE LAWS SHOULD BE MADE TO FIT THE CHANGING NEEDS OF THE PEOPLE AND THAT THEY SHOULD NOT BE CONSIDERED A FIXED SET OF RULES.

SON OF THE FAMOUS AUTHOR, HE GRADUATED FROM HARVARD LAW SCHOOL WHEN HE WAS 20, AND GOT HIS LAW DEGREE 5 YRS. LATER. HE SERVED IN THE UNION ARMY FOR 3 YRS. AS A LIEUTENANT COLONEL. IN 1867, HE WAS ADMITTED TO THE BAR AND PRACTICED IN BOSTON. HE BECAME A PROFESSOR OF LAW AT HARVARD, THEN ACCEPTED AN APPOINTMENT AS ASSOCIATE JUSTICE OF THE MASSACHUSETTS SUPREME COURT WHERE HE SERVED UNTIL 1899 WHEN ***HE BECAME CHIEF JUSTICE. IN 1902, PRES. THEODORE ROOSEVELT APPOINTED HIM TO THE U.S. SUPREME COURT UNTIL HE RETIRED IN 1932. HE BECAME KNOWN FOR HIS LIBERAL INTERPRETATION OF THE CONSTITUTION. AS A MEMBER OF THE SUPREME COURT HOLMES WAS DISTINGUISHED FOR HIS GREAT LEGAL LEARNING, SOUND JUDGEMENT, HUMOR AND POWER OF EXPRESSION.***

HE WAS BORN IN BOSTON, MASS.

MR. PRESIDENT! GET YOUR BIG HEAD DOWN!!

DURING THE CIVIL WAR, HE GUIDED PRES. LINCOLN THROUGH THE BATTLE LINE NEAR WASHINGTON. ***HE REPRIMANDED THE PRES. FOR EXPOSING HIMSELF TO ENEMY FIRE.***

THE LIFE OF THE LAW IS NOT LOGIC BUT EXPERIENCE.
KERN

HE WAS KNOWN AS THE ***"GREAT DISSENTER"*** BECAUSE HE PROTESTED STRONGLY AGAINST THE ***14th. AMENDMENT.***

1842-1910

William James

DISTINGUISHED AMERICAN PSYCHOLOGIST AND PHILOSOPHER

I CONSIDER RELIGION AND PHILOSOPHY REWARDING SUBJECTS FOR STUDY.

JAMES STUDIED AT LAWRENCE SCIENTIFIC SCHOOL AND LATER RECEIVED HIS DEGREE IN MEDICINE FROM HARVARD WHERE HE TAUGHT FOR 35YRS. ***HE DID MUCH TO RAISE PSYCHOLOGY TO A FULL-FLEDGED SCIENCE. IN 1890, HE PUBLISHED THE "PRINCIPLES OF PSYCHOLOGY." THIS BOOK ESTABLISHED HIM AS ONE OF THE MOST INFLUENTIAL THINKERS OF HIS DAY. HIS ESSAY, "THE WILL TO BELIEVE," STATED THAT "A PERSON HAS THE RIGHT TO BELIEVE THINGS THAT DO NOT HAVE SCIENTIFIC EVIDENCE."***

1843-1916

Henry James

DISTINGUISHED AMERICAN NOVELIST AND SHORT STORY WRITER

BROTHER TO WILLIAM JAMES, HENRY WAS EDUCATED IN NEW YORK, LONDON, PARIS AND GENEVA. JAMES GAVE UP THE STUDY OF LAW FOR A LITERARY CAREER. AS A YOUNG MAN HE CONTRIBUTED SHORT STORIES TO THE "ATLANTIC MONTHLY." ***HIS EARLY NOVELS DEALT WITH THE IMPACT OF EUROPEAN CULTURE ON AMERICANS TRAVELING OR LIVING ABROAD. HE WAS NOTED FOR HIS SKILLFUL HANDLING OF THE PSYCHOLOGICAL NOVEL. SOME OF HIS WORKS WERE "THE PORTRAIT OF A LADY" AND "THE TURN OF THE SCREW."***

MY NOVELS DEAL WITH THE INTERNATIONAL SOCIAL SCENE.

1843 - 1901

William McKinley

SOLDIER, CONGRESSMAN, GOVERNOR AND ***TWENTY-FIFTH*** PRESIDENT OF THE UNITED STATES (1897-01)

WE MUST HAVE A SOUND MONEY SYSTEM.

MC KINLEY WAS 9 YRS. OLD WHEN HE MOVED WITH HIS FAMILY TO POLAND, OHIO, AND ENROLLED IN A PRIVATE SCHOOL. HE THEN WENT TO ALLEGHENY COLLEGE IN MEADVILLE, PA., BUT DID NOT GRADUATE BECAUSE OF ILLNESS. DURING THE CIVIL WAR HE SERVED ON THE STAFF OF RUTHERFORD B. HAYES WHO LATER BECAME PRESIDENT. IN 1867, HE WAS ADMITTED TO THE BAR, THEN BECAME A CONGRESSMAN FROM OHIO 10 YRS. LATER. ***AS GOV. OF OHIO IN 1892, HE SUPPORTED THE GOLD STANDARD AND SOUND MONEY. IN 1896, MCKINLEY RAN FOR PRESIDENT. UNWILLING TO LEAVE HIS AILING WIFE, HE CONDUCTED "FRONT PORCH" SPEECHES FROM HIS HOME IN CANTON. HE RECEIVED 271 ELECTORAL VOTES TO BRYAN'S 176. DURING HIS ADMINISTRATION, HE EXPANDED AMERICAN OVERSEAS TERRITORIES INCLUDING PUERTO RICO, GUAM AND THE PHILIPPINE ISLANDS DURING AND AFTER THE SPANISH-AMERICAN WAR.***

HE WAS BORN IN NILES, OHIO.

DURING HIS PRESIDENCY, ***HAWAII WAS ANNEXED TO THE U.S., THE BATTLESHIP "MAINE" WAS BLOWN UP IN HAVANA HARBOR, THE AMERICAN BASEBALL LEAGUE WAS FOUNDED, THE ALASKAN GOLD RUSH WAS STARTED AND MAJOR WALTER REED CONQUERED YELLOW FEVER.***

WHILE SHAKING HANDS WITH WELL-WISHERS AT THE PAN-AMERICAN EXPOSITION IN BUFFALO, ***HE WAS SHOT BY A MAN WITH A GUN CONCEALED IN A HANDKERCHIEF. HE DIED 8 DAYS LATER, SEPT. 14, 1901. THEODORE ROOSEVELT SUCCEEDED HIM IN OFFICE.***

KERN

1843-1931

Stephen M. Babcock

AMERICAN AGRICULTURAL CHEMIST

BABCOCK GRADUATED FROM TUFTS COLLEGE AND LATER STUDIED AT THE UNIVERSITY OF GÖTTINGEN IN GERMANY. IN 1887, HE CAME TO THE UNIVERSITY OF WISCONSIN AS A PROFESSOR OF AGRICULTURAL CHEMISTRY WHERE HE STAYED FOR THE REST OF HIS LIFE. ***HE EXPERIMENTED WITH THE CHEMISTRY OF MILK, CHEESE AND OTHER DAIRY PRODUCTS. DR. BABCOCK WAS ONE OF THE GREAT CONTRIBUTORS TO THE DEVELOPMENT OF DAIRYING IN THE UNITED STATES.***

HE WAS BORN IN BRIDGEWATER, N.Y.

IN 1890, DR. BABCOCK FOUND A SIMPLE METHOD OF TESTING THE RICHNESS, OR BUTTERFAT CONTENT, IN MILK. ***HIS PROCESS HAS BEEN CALLED ONE OF THE WORLD'S MOST IMPORTANT DISCOVERIES. HE REFUSED TO PATENT HIS TESTS, THEREBY MAKING HIS DISCOVERIES FREE TO ALL THE WORLD.***

I THINK I HAVE FINALLY FOUND THE ANSWER, JOHN.

THE SIMPLE AND RELIABLE BABCOCK TEST MAKES IT POSSIBLE TO TEST MILK QUALITY. ***THIS TEST PROVIDED A TREMENDOUS TECHNICAL ADVANCE FOR FARMERS. HE CONDUCTED DAIRY FEEDING EXPERIMENTS THAT LED TO THE RECOGNITION OF VITAMIN A.***

KERN

1844-1916

Thomas Eakins

ONE OF AMERICA'S GREATEST PAINTERS

I NEED MORE DETAIL IN THE MAN'S FACE.

EAKINS BEGAN HIS ART TRAINING IN THE PENNSYLVANIA ACADEMY OF FINE ARTS, THEN STUDIED ANATOMY AT JEFFERSON MEDICAL COLLEGE IN PHILADELPHIA. THIS HELPED TO MAKE HIM A MASTER OF THE HUMAN FIGURE. ***TWO OF HIS BEST KNOWN COMPOSITIONS WERE "THE AGNEW CLINIC" AND "THE GROSS CLINIC." HE TAUGHT AT THE PENNSYLVANIA ACADEMY OF FINE ARTS AND THE ART STUDENTS LEAGUE. HE PAINTED PORTRAITS AND SCENES OF OUTDOOR LIFE AND SPORTING EVENTS. WITH PAINSTAKING DETAIL HE BROUGHT GREAT VITALITY AND DEEP HUMAN INSIGHT INTO HIS PAINTINGS. WHILE HE IS NOW CONSIDERED ONE OF AMERICA'S GREATEST PAINTERS, NEITHER FAME NOR FORTUNE WERE HIS DURING HIS LIFETIME.***

HIS "MAX SCHMITT IN A SINGLE SCULL" IS EXCELLENT.

EAKINS WAS ONE OF THE FOREMOST PAINTERS OF THE REALISTIC SCHOOL OF THE LATE 19th AND EARLY 20th CENTURIES. MANY OF HIS PAINTINGS HANG IN THE METROPOLITAN MUSEUM OF ART IN NEW YORK.

HE TRAVELED TO PARIS AND SPAIN WHERE ***HE STUDIED REALISM PAINTERS SUCH AS VELASQUEZ AND GOYA. THESE ARTISTS' PAINTINGS GREATLY INFLUENCED HIS STYLE.***

1845-1926
Mary Cassatt
AMERICAN IMPRESSIONIST PAINTER
SHE DRAWS VERY WELL.
SHE WAS BORN NEAR PITTS-BURGH, PA.
SHE STUDIED AT THE PHILADELPHIA ACADEMY OF ART, BUT SPENT MUCH OF HER TIME ABROAD VISI-TING ART GALLERIES IN ITALY AND SPAIN AND LATER SETTLED IN PARIS. HER WORK SHOWS THE INFLUENCE OF THE GREAT IMPRESSIONIST PAINTER EDGAR DEGAS, BUT IS EASILY AND REMARKABLY DISTINGUISHED BY FORTHRIGHT-NESS IN BOLD DRAFTSMANSHIP. SHE WAS SO OUTSTANDING IN HER WORK THAT DEGAS SAID, "I WOULD NOT HAVE ADMITTED THAT A WOMAN COULD DRAW AS WELL AS THAT." SHE SPENT MOST OF HER LIFE IN PARIS AND RECEIVED LITTLE RECOGNITION DURING HER LIFETIME FROM HER HOMELAND.
HER PRINTS ARE EXCEPTIONALLY BEAUTIFUL.
MARY CASSATT IS BEST KNOWN FOR HER MOTHER-AND-CHILD PAINTINGS. THESE ARE NOT SENTIMENTAL, BUT ARE WARM AND HUMAN, WITH SIMPLE LINES AND LUMINOUS COLOR-ING.
SHE IS RECOGNIZED FOR HER PAINTINGS AND PASTELS BUT HER INDIVIDUAL TALENT IS MORE REMARKABLE FOR HER PRINTS.
KERN

1845-1937

Elihu Root

CORPORATION LAWYER, STATESMAN AND CABINET OFFICER

YOUR IDEAS ARE SOUND, ELIHU.
WE SHOULD PUT THEM INTO EFFECT IMMEDIATELY.

ROOT ATTENDED HAMILTON COLLEGE AND STUDIED LAW AT NEW YORK UNIVERSITY. IN 1813 HE BECAME WELL-KNOWN FOR HIS DEFENSE OF "BOSS" TWEED WHO WAS CHARGED WITH POLITICAL CORRUPTION. ROOT WAS ONE OF THE ABLEST CORPORATION LAWYERS IN THE U.S. HIS CLIENTS GAVE HIM ENORMOUS FEES FOR HIS LEGAL WORK. ROOT SERVED BOTH MCKINLEY AND ROOSEVELT AS SEC. OF WAR. HE WAS ONE OF OUR NATION'S OUTSTANDING CABINET MEMBERS, SERVING WITH DISTINCTION. AS WAR SEC. HE CENTRALIZED AUTHORITY AND IMPROVED PROMOTIONS. HE HELPED FOUND THE ARMY WAR COLLEGE TO PROVIDE OFFICERS WITH FURTHER TRAINING. IN 1909 THE NEW YORK LEGISLATURE ELECTED HIM TO THE U.S. SENATE WHERE HE SERVED UNTIL 1915.

HE WAS BORN IN CLINTON, N.Y.

IF EVER TWO COUNTRIES SHOULD ALWAYS BE AT PEACE, IT IS CANADA AND THE UNITED STATES.

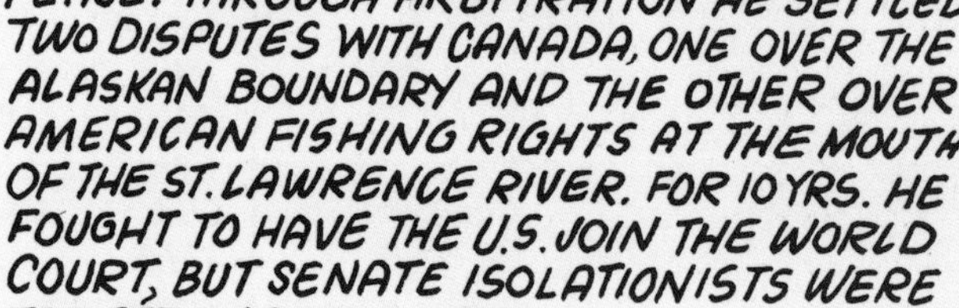

THIS CHART WILL GIVE YOU THE PICTURE.

AS CABINET OFFICER, HE IMPROVED ORGANIZATION OF THE ARMY AND STATE DEPT. THIS GREATLY CONTRIBUTED TO OUR EFFECTIVENESS IN THE FIRST WORLD WAR AND TO THE FORMATION OF A PROFESSIONAL DIPLOMATIC SERVICE.

ROOT WAS A TIRELESS WORKER FOR WORLD PEACE. THROUGH ARBITRATION HE SETTLED TWO DISPUTES WITH CANADA, ONE OVER THE ALASKAN BOUNDARY AND THE OTHER OVER AMERICAN FISHING RIGHTS AT THE MOUTH OF THE ST. LAWRENCE RIVER. FOR 10 YRS. HE FOUGHT TO HAVE THE U.S. JOIN THE WORLD COURT, BUT SENATE ISOLATIONISTS WERE TOO STRONG FOR HIM.

KERN

1846-1914

George Westinghouse

AMERICAN ENGINEER AND MANUFACTURER

THESE FIGURES SHOW THAT BUSINESS HAS PICKED UP DRAMATICALLY.

AS A YOUNG MAN, HE WORKED IN HIS FATHER'S FACTORY, WORKING WITH MACHINERY. HIS FIRST INVENTION WAS A RAILWAY FROG, A DEVICE WHICH MADE IT POSSIBLE FOR A TRAIN TO PASS FROM ONE TRACK TO THE OTHER. DURING THE CIVIL WAR, WESTINGHOUSE SERVED UNTIL 1864, THEN FOR 2 YRS. WAS AN ASSISTANT ENGINEER IN THE U.S. NAVY. ***IN 1869, HE PATENTED THE AIR BRAKE WHICH WAS AN IMMEDIATE SUCCESS AND HE ORGANIZED A COMPANY TO MANUFACTURE IT. THIS BRAKE WAS USED ON PASSENGER TRAINS AND SINCE BEEN ADOPTED FOR RAILWAY, RAPID-TRANSIT CARS, MOTOR TRUCKS AND BUSES. HE ALSO INTRODUCED ALTERNATING CURRENT FOR ELECTRIC LIGHTS, DEVELOPED AND MANUFACTURED STEAM TURBINES, AND WAS A PIONEER IN THE USE OF ELECTRIC POWER FOR RAILROADS.***

HERE'S THE ORDER FOR THE NIAGARA FALLS GENERATORS.

HE CERTAINLY DESERVES THIS HONOR.

DURING HIS LIFETIME WESTINGHOUSE ORGANIZED ***60 COMPANIES AND PATENTED ALMOST 400 INVENTIONS. IN 1955, HE WAS ELECTED TO THE HALL OF FAME.***

KERN

UNDER HIS DIRECTION, HIS COMPANY MANUFACTURED GENERATORS FOR THE POWER PLANTS AT ***NIAGARA FALLS AND FOR THE RAPID-TRANSIT SYSTEMS OF NEW YORK AND LONDON.***

1847-1911

Joseph Pulitzer

AMERICAN JOURNALIST AND PUBLISHER

WE'VE GOT TO GET THAT STORY!

PULITZER WAS 17 YRS. OLD WHEN HE CAME TO THE U.S. AND IMMEDIATELY JOINED THE UNION ARMY IN THE CIVIL WAR. IN 1865, HE JOINED THE ST. LOUIS "WESTLICHE POST" AS A REPORTER. BY 1871, HE WAS MANAGING EDITOR AND PART OWNER. HE SPENT A YR. AS A CORRESPONDENT FOR THE "*NEW YORK SUN*." IN 1879, PULITZER BOUGHT TWO ST. LOUIS NEWSPAPERS AND COMBINED THEM INTO THE "*POST-DISPATCH*". 4 YRS. LATER HE BOUGHT THE NEW YORK "*WORLD*" ***WHICH BECAME ONE OF THE OUTSTANDING NEWSPAPERS OF ITS DAY. HE WAS ELECTED TO CONGRESS FROM NEW YORK IN 1884 BUT RESIGNED IN 1886 BECAUSE OF ILL HEALTH. ALMOST TOTALLY BLIND, HE CARRIED ON HIS WORK UNTIL HIS DEATH.***

HE WAS BORN IN MAKO, HUNGARY.
MY PAPERS ARE BACKING YOU ONE HUNDRED PERCENT.
THANK YOU JOE.

YOU ARE THE FIRST TO RECEIVE THE PULITZER PRIZE.

HE ESTABLISHED THE PULITZER PRIZES TO ENCOURAGE AMERICAN LITERATURE AND ART. SINCE 1917 THESE PRIZES ARE AWARDED FOR OUTSTANDING ACHIEVEMENTS IN AMERICAN LETTERS AND JOURNALISM.

PULITZER WAS VERY INFLUENTIAL IN GETTING HORACE GREELEY NOMINATED AS THE REPUBLICAN CANDIDATE FOR THE PRESIDENCY IN 1872. ***WHEN HE DIED HE LEFT $2 MILLION TO COLUMBIA UNIVERSITY GRADUATE SCHOOL OF JOURNALISM, $500,000 TO THE NEW YORK PHILHARMONIC SOCIETY AND THE SAME AMOUNT TO THE METROPOLITAN MUSEUM OF ART.***

1847 - 1922

Alexander Graham Bell

AMERICAN SCIENTIST, INVENTOR OF THE TELEPHONE

YOU HEARD ME CALL?
I HEARD EVERY WORD YOU SAID!

HIS FATHER TAUGHT DEAF-MUTES TO SPEAK. ALEXANDER BECAME INTERESTED IN THE PROBLEMS OF SPEECH AND HEARING. AFTER SPENDING A YR. AT THE UNIVERSITY OF LONDON STUDYING THE SCIENCE OF HEARING, HE CAME TO THE U.S. IN 1871 AND WAS A PROFESSOR AT BOSTON UNIVERSITY WHERE HE DEVOTED HIMSELF TO TEACHING DEAF-MUTES. ***HE TRIED METHODS TO HELP THE DEAF TO HEAR VIBRATIONS OF SOUND. PREOCCUPIED WITH THE POSSIBILITIES OF A MACHINE THAT WOULD ELECTRICALLY TRANSMIT SPEECH, HE AND A FRIEND ACCIDENTALLY DISCOVERED HOW THIS COULD HAPPEN IN 1874. THE PRINCIPLE OF THE TELEPHONE WAS FOUND AND BELL WAS GRANTED A PATENT IN 1876.***

HE WAS BORN IN EDINBURGH, SCOTLAND.

BELL OPENED THE NEW YORK - CHICAGO LONG DISTANCE LINE IN 1892.

MANY INVENTORS WERE WORKING ON A WAY TO SEND HUMAN SPEECH BY WIRE, BUT BELL WAS THE FIRST TO FIND THE RIGHT WAY.

BELL LIVED FOR ALMOST 50 YRS. AFTER HIS INVENTION OF THE TELEPHONE. HE DESIGNED AN ELECTRICAL PROBE AND TRIED IN VAIN TO LOCATE THE BULLET IN PRES. GARFIELD'S BODY WHO HAD BEEN SHOT BY AN ASSASSIN. ***BELL RECEIVED MANY HONORARY DEGREES FROM UNIVERSITIES AS A LEADING AUTHORITY ON THE EDUCATION OF THE DEAF.***

KERN

1847-1931
Thomas Alva Edison
ONE OF AMERICA'S GREATEST INVENTORS

EDISON HAD 3 MONTHS OF FORMAL SCHOOLING BUT HE ***CHANGED THE LIVES OF MILLIONS OF PEOPLE WITH HIS ELECTRIC LIGHT AND THE PHONOGRAPH.*** WHEN HE WAS 12 YRS. OLD, HE WAS SELLING PAPERS, PEANUTS AND SANDWICHES ON TRAINS. DURING THE CIVIL WAR, HE ROAMED FROM CITY TO CITY AS A TELEGRAPH OPERATOR. ***IN 1876, HE ESTABLISHED HIS OWN LABORATORY. THE NEXT YEAR HE INVENTED THE PHONOGRAPH AND 2 YRS. LATER THE INCANDESCENT ELECTRIC LIGHT BULB. EDISON IMPROVED THE INVENTIONS OF OTHER PEOPLE, SUCH AS THE TELEPHONE, TYPEWRITER, MOTION PICTURE, ELECTRIC GENERATOR AND ELECTRIC-POWERED TRAINS.***

HE WAS BORN AT MILAN, OHIO.

TO YOU, MR. EDISON, FOR ALL YOU HAVE DONE FOR YOUR COUNTRY AND ALL MANKIND.

THIS IS ONE OF THE PLEASURES OF THIS OFFICE.

FRANCE AND GREAT BRITAIN BESTOWED MANY HONORS ON HIM. IN 1928, ***HE RECEIVED THE CONGRESSIONAL GOLD MEDAL "FOR DEVELOPMENT AND APPLICATION OF INVENTIONS THAT HAVE REVOLUTIONIZED CIVILIZATION IN THE LAST CENTURY."***

KERN

EDISON PATENTED MORE THAN ***1,100 INVENTIONS IN 60 YRS. IN JULY 1956, PRES. EISENHOWER SIGNED A PROCLAMATION MAKING HIS WEST ORANGE, NEW JERSEY, LABORATORY A NATIONAL MONUMENT.***

1849-1926

Luther Burbank

FAMOUS AMERICAN HORTICULTURIST AND PLANT BREEDER

THESE PLANTS WILL WORK FOR MAN.

AS A BOY HE WAS ALWAYS INTERESTED IN NATURE. HE STUDIED AT THE ACADEMY IN LANCASTER, WORKED IN A FACTORY, AND WHEN 21 YRS. OLD, HE BOUGHT A 17-ACRE PLOT OF LAND TO BEGIN BREEDING PLANTS. HE PRODUCED A POTATO WHICH ***MADE MILLIONS FOR ITS GROWERS. IN 1875, HE MOVED TO CALIFORNIA, AND BY 1893 HAD ESTABLISHED HIS GREAT EXPERIMENTAL FARM AT SEBASTOPOL, CAL. HE ACHIEVED RESULTS BY CROSSING AND SELECTION. BURBANK DEVOTED HIS LIFE TO CREATING NEW TREES, FRUITS, FLOWERS, VEGETABLES, GRAINS AND GRASSES. HE IS THE WORLD'S BEST-KNOWN PLANT ORIGINATOR. HE AUTHORED "NEW CREATIONS," "HOW PLANTS ARE TRAINED TO WORK FOR MAN" AND "THE HARVEST OF THE YEARS."***

HE WAS BORN IN LANCASTER, MASS.

THIS IS A START, JOHN.

BURBANK ORIGINATED MANY BERRIES OF COMMERCIAL VALUE. ***HIS PLUM AND PRUNE EXPERIMENTS COMPLETELY CHANGED THE GROWING OF THESE FRUITS IN CALIFORNIA.***

MY TEACHER SAYS WE CAN THANK LUTHER BURBANK FOR MANY OF THE FOODS WE EAT.

AT THE TIME OF HIS DEATH ***BURBANK HAD 3000 EXPERIMENTS UNDER WAY AND WAS GROWING 5,000 DISTINCT BOTANICAL SPECIMENS. MANY OF THE FOODS WE EAT EVERY DAY ARE A RESULT OF HIS REMARKABLE WORK.***

KERN

1850-1924

Samuel Gompers

LABOR LEADER, CO-FOUNDER OF AFL

LET'S LEAVE THE GOVERNMENT OUT OF OUR NEGOTIATIONS!

HE WAS 13 YRS. OLD WHEN HE MOVED TO THE U.S.A. AT 14 HE BECAME THE FIRST REGISTERED MEMBER OF THE CIGARMAKERS INTERNATIONAL UNION. HE MADE THIS ORGANIZATION ONE OF THE MOST SUCCESSFUL TRADE UNIONS. ***WHEN THE AMERICAN FEDERATION WAS FOUNDED IN 1886, GOMPERS INSISTED THAT UNIONS SHOULD BARGAIN WITH THE EMPLOYERS AND AVOID BECOMING INVOLVED WITH GOVERNMENT AND POLITICAL PARTIES. HE CAMPAIGNED VIGOROUSLY TO GET RID OF THE LABOR INJUNCTION ISSUED BY COURTS TO CURB STRIKES. HE SUPPORTED LABOR LAWS REGULATING CONDITIONS AND HOURS OF WORK FOR WOMEN AND MINORS. GOMPERS DEVOTED HIS LIFE TO THE FEDERATION AND DIED A POOR MAN. HE WROTE "AMERICAN LABOR AND THE WAR" AND "SEVENTY YEARS OF LIFE AND LABOR."***

HE WAS BORN IN LONDON, ENGLAND.

I'M DEPENDING ON YOU, SAM, TO DO A GOOD JOB.

I'LL DO MY BEST, MR. PRESIDENT.

DURING WORLD WAR I, PRES. WILSON APPOINTED HIM A COMMISSION MEMBER OF NATIONAL DEFENSE AT THE VERSAILLES PEACE CONFERENCE IN 1919. ***HE WAS THE CHAIRMAN OF THE COMMISSION OF INTERNATIONAL LABOR LEGISLATION.***

WE MUST PROTECT THE WORKING MAN.

GOMPERS SERVED AS FIRST PRESIDENT OF THE AMERICAN FEDERATION OF LABOR FOR ***37 YRS. HE WAS THE GUIDING INFLUENCE IN SHAPING THE A F L AND THE DEPT. OF LABOR.***

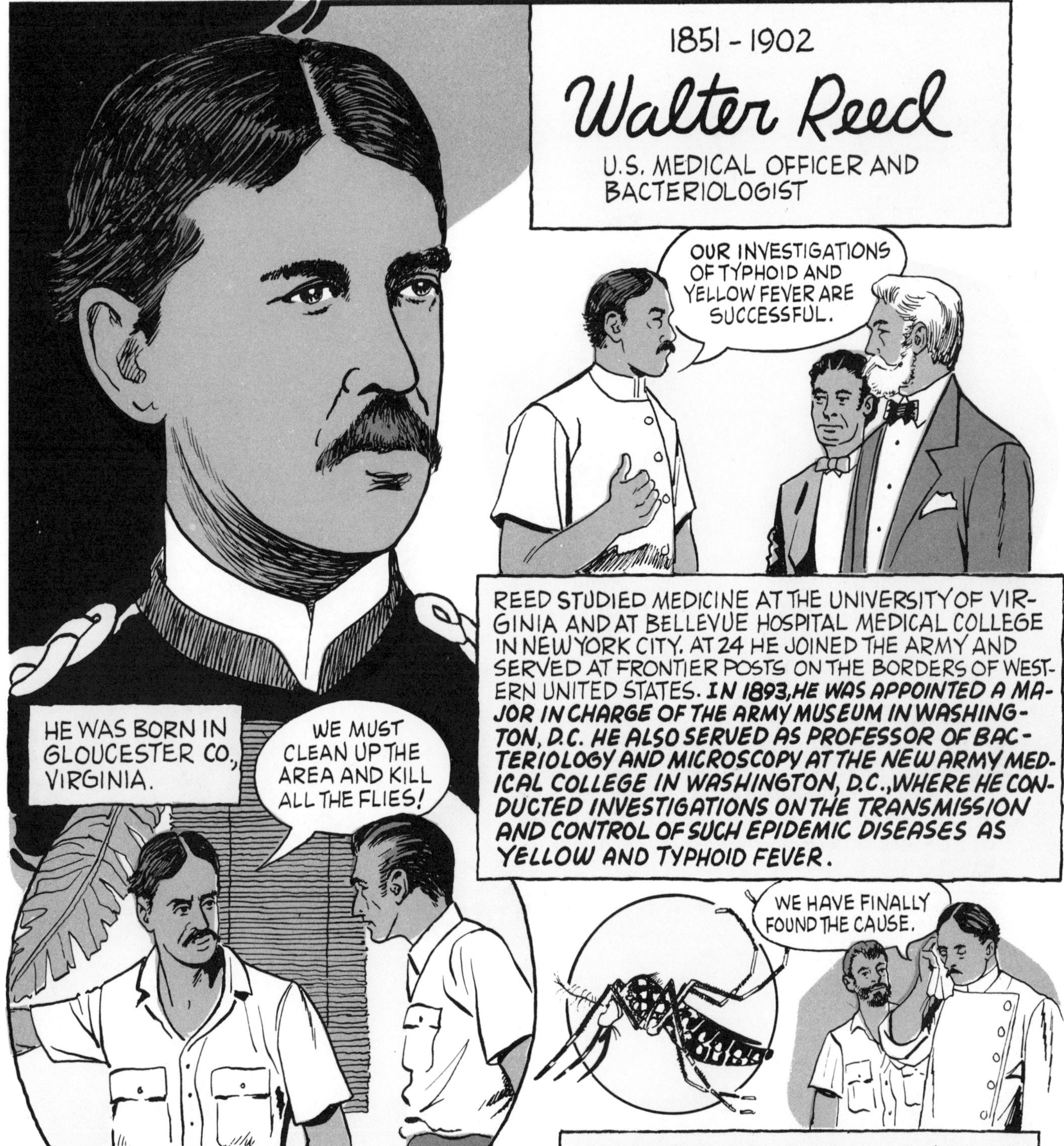
1851 - 1902
Walter Reed
U.S. MEDICAL OFFICER AND BACTERIOLOGIST
OUR INVESTIGATIONS OF TYPHOID AND YELLOW FEVER ARE SUCCESSFUL.
REED STUDIED MEDICINE AT THE UNIVERSITY OF VIRGINIA AND AT BELLEVUE HOSPITAL MEDICAL COLLEGE IN NEW YORK CITY. AT 24 HE JOINED THE ARMY AND SERVED AT FRONTIER POSTS ON THE BORDERS OF WESTERN UNITED STATES. IN 1893, HE WAS APPOINTED A MAJOR IN CHARGE OF THE ARMY MUSEUM IN WASHINGTON, D.C. HE ALSO SERVED AS PROFESSOR OF BACTERIOLOGY AND MICROSCOPY AT THE NEW ARMY MEDICAL COLLEGE IN WASHINGTON, D.C., WHERE HE CONDUCTED INVESTIGATIONS ON THE TRANSMISSION AND CONTROL OF SUCH EPIDEMIC DISEASES AS YELLOW AND TYPHOID FEVER.
HE WAS BORN IN GLOUCESTER CO., VIRGINIA.
WE MUST CLEAN UP THE AREA AND KILL ALL THE FLIES!
WE HAVE FINALLY FOUND THE CAUSE.
DURING THE SPANISH-AMERICAN WAR HE HEADED A COMMISSION TO STUDY THE SPREAD OF TYPHOID FEVER IN ARMY CAMPS. HIS EXPERIMENTS SHOWED THAT FLIES WERE THE CARRIERS OF THE INFECTION AND THAT UNCLEANLINESS HELPED SPREAD THE DISEASE.
KERN
HIS GREATEST CONTRIBUTION CAME IN 1900, AS THE DIRECTOR OF A COMMISSION TO INVESTIGATE THE CAUSE AND TRANSMISSION OF YELLOW FEVER AMONG AMERICAN TROOPS IN CUBA. HIS EXPERIMENTS ESTABLISHED THAT THE BITE OF A MOSQUITO TRANSMITS YELLOW FEVER AND SHOWED HOW IT COULD BE CONTROLLED.

1854-1932

George Eastman

AMERICAN INVENTOR, MANUFACTURER AND PHILANTHROPIST

IT'S CALLED A "KODAK." YOU PRESS THE BUTTON -- WE DO THE REST.

EASTMAN MADE IT POSSIBLE FOR MILLIONS OF PEOPLE TO ENJOY THE INEXPENSIVE HOBBY OF PHOTOGRAPHY. ***IN 1884, HE PATENTED THE FIRST PRACTICAL FILM IN ROLL FORM, AND DESIGNED A ROLL HOLDER FOR WINDING IT. BY 1888, HIS FIRST PERFECTED "KODAK" CAMERA WAS BUILT. IN 1892, THE EASTMAN KODAK CO. WAS ESTABLISHED IN ROCHESTER, N.Y., MANUFACTURING PHOTOGRAPHY EQUIPMENT ON A MASS PRODUCTION BASIS. EASTMAN MADE GIFTS TOTALING MORE THAN $100,000,000 TO THE MASSACHUSETTS INSTITUTE OF TECHNOLOGY, THE UNIVERSITY OF ROCHESTER AND THE EASTMAN SCHOOL OF MUSIC.***

I PREDICT A GREAT FUTURE FOR THIS FILM.

EASTMAN DEVELOPED FLEXIBLE TRANSPARENT FILM WHICH PROVED ***VITAL IN THE DEVELOPMENT OF THE MOTION PICTURE INDUSTRY.***

THE GEORGE EASTMAN HOUSE IN ROCHESTER, N.Y., BECAME A MUSEUM OF PHOTOGRAPHY IN 1948, EXHIBITING ANTIQUE CAMERAS AND HISTORIC PHOTOGRAPHS.

KERN

1854-1932
John Philip Sousa
AMERICA'S MOST FAMOUS COMPOSER OF BAND MUSIC, KNOWN AS THE "MARCH KING"
HERE HE COMES, DAD. THE GREAT SOUSA!
SOUSA WAS AN ORCHESTRA CONDUCTOR AT 17. HE WAS 26 WHEN HE WAS THE LEADER OF THE U.S. MARINE BAND. HE HELD THIS POSITION FOR 12 YRS. SOUSA THEN FORMED HIS OWN BAND, MAKING FOUR TOURS TO EUROPE AND LATER A WORLD TOUR. DURING THE SPANISH-AMERICAN WAR HE SERVED AS MUSICAL DIRECTOR FOR THE UNITED STATES ARMY. SOUSA WAS KNOWN AS THE "MARCH KING" BECAUSE OF HIS LIVELY AND TUNEFUL MARCHES. HE WROTE "THE STARS AND STRIPES FOREVER", "SEMPER FIDELIS," "EL CAPITAN," "WASHINGTON POST MARCH," "HANDS ACROSS THE SEA" AND "HIGH SCHOOL CADETS."
HE WAS BORN IN WASHINGTON, D.C.
MY SINCERE CONGRATULATIONS TO YOU, JOHN.
KING EDWARD VII OF BRITAIN PRESENTED HIM WITH THE ORDER OF VICTORIA, NAMED FOR THE KING'S MOTHER.
HE WROTE OVER 100 MARCHING SONGS, 5 NOVELS AND SEVERAL COMIC OPERAS. HE LEFT HIS HUGE BAND MUSIC COLLECTION TO THE UNIVERSITY OF ILLINOIS CONCERT BAND.
KERN

1855-1925

Robert M. La Follette, Sr.

PROGRESSIVE POLITICAL LEADER

THE WILL OF THE PEOPLE SHALL BE THE LAW OF THE LAND.

LA FOLLETTE GRADUATED FROM THE UNIVERSITY OF WISCONSIN AND WAS ADMITTED TO THE BAR IN 1880. HE SERVED AS A CONGRESSMAN, GOVERNOR AND U.S. SENATOR. **"FIGHTING BOB" WAS A NICKNAME GIVEN HIM FOR HIS VIGOROUS POLITICAL BATTLES. HE WAS THE VOICE OF THE COMMON MAN, ASKING FOR JUSTICE AND EQUALIZATION IN GOVERNMENT. IN THE SENATE HE WORKED FOR REFORM LEGISLATION, VOTED AGAINST AMERICA'S ENTRY INTO WORLD WAR I AND OPPOSED JOINING THE LEAGUE OF NATIONS.**

HE WAS BORN IN PRIMOSE, WIS.

YOUR RECORD HAS BEEN OUTSTANDING BOB!

LA FOLLETTE WAS ONE OF THE MOST IMPORTANT FIGURES IN WISCONSIN POLITICS FOR 25 YRS. LEADER OF THE PROGRESSIVE REPUBLICANS, CALLED THE "INSURGENTS," HE WAS A CANDIDATE **FOR THE PRESIDENCY 4 TIMES BUT FAILED EACH TIME TO GET THE NOMINATION.**

HE WAS RESPONSIBLE FOR **MORE CONSTRUCTIVE LEGISLATION THAN ANY MAN OF HIS GENERATION. IN 1957, HE WAS ELECTED TO THE SENATE HALL OF FAME.**

KERN

1856- 1915

Booker T. Washington

OUTSTANDING EDUCATOR, REFORMER, WRITER AND FOUNDER OF TUSKEGEE INSTITUTE

GENTLEMEN, WITH YOUR HELP WE CAN MAKE TUSKEGEE A GREAT SCHOOL FOR OUR PEOPLE.

HE WAS BORN A SLAVE AND WORKED IN THE SALTWORKS AND COAL MINES OF WEST VIRGINIA, ATTENDING SCHOOL AT NIGHT. ***HE WAS 16 YRS. OLD WHEN HE WALKED 500 MILES FROM HIS HOME TO HAMPTON INSTITUTE TO ATTEND SCHOOL. HE GRADUATED IN 1875. AFTER TEACHING AT HAMPTON INSTITUTE HE WAS CHOSEN TO ORGANIZE A SIMILAR SCHOOL FOR NEGROES AT TUSKEGEE, ALABAMA. HIS SCHOOL OPENED IN AN OLD CHURCH WITH 30 STUDENTS AND GREW INTO THE FAMOUS TUSKEGEE INSTITUTE, SUCCESSFULLY COMBINING THE INDUSTRIAL TRADES AND PROFESSIONS AS WELL AS ACADEMIC SUBJECTS. HE WAS AN OUTSTANDING SPEAKER AND ADDRESSED AUDIENCES THROUGHOUT THE WORLD ON PROBLEMS OF THE NEGRO.***

HE WAS BORN IN HALESFORD, VA.

I SHALL NEVER PERMIT MYSELF TO STOOP SO LOW AS TO HATE ANY MAN.

"UP FROM SLAVERY" WAS ONE OF HIS MOST FAMOUS BOOKS.
UP FROM SLAVERY

SOME OF HIS BOOKS WERE ***"THE FUTURE OF THE AMERICAN NEGRO," "UP FROM SLAVERY," "WORKING WITH THE HANDS" AND "TUSKEGEE AND ITS PEOPLE." HE ORGANIZED RURAL EXTENSION WORK AMONG NEGROES AND STARTED A NATIONAL NEGRO BUSINESS LEAGUE.***

HIS ***"ATLANTA COMPROMISE"*** SPEECH AT THE 1895 COTTON STATES EXPOSITION IN ATLANTA SPOTLIGHTED HIM AS ***SPOKESMAN FOR NEGRO PEOPLE. BECAUSE OF HIS EMPHASIS ON WORK AND SELF HELP RATHER THAN AGITATION, HE BECAME A GO-BETWEEN FOR WHITES AND BLACKS. HIS FAILURE TO SPEAK OUT FOR NEGRO "RIGHTS" AND "EQUALITY" BROUGHT CRITICISM FROM SOME OTHER BLACK LEADERS.***

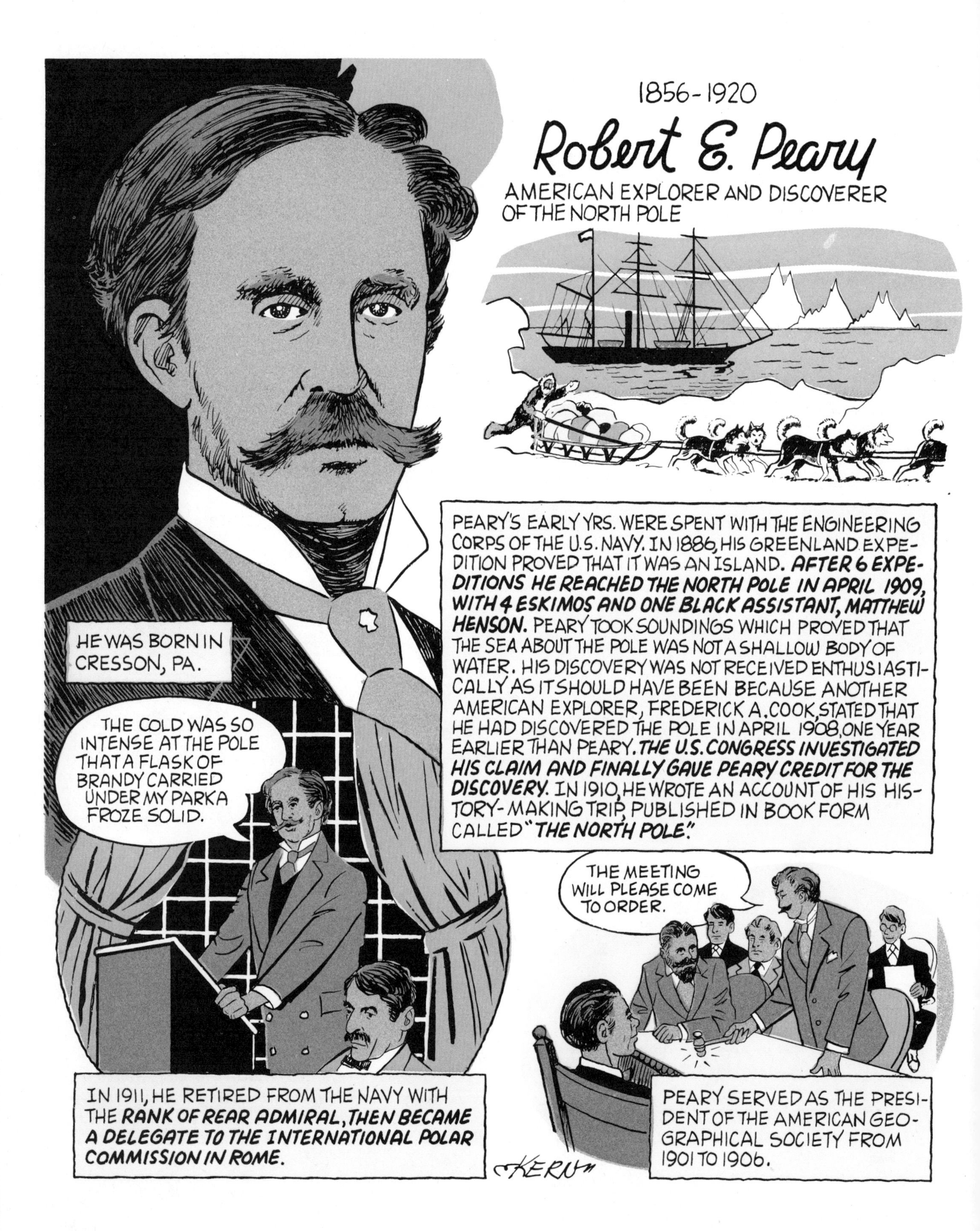
1856-1920
Robert E. Peary
AMERICAN EXPLORER AND DISCOVERER OF THE NORTH POLE
PEARY'S EARLY YRS. WERE SPENT WITH THE ENGINEERING CORPS OF THE U.S. NAVY. IN 1886, HIS GREENLAND EXPEDITION PROVED THAT IT WAS AN ISLAND. AFTER 6 EXPEDITIONS HE REACHED THE NORTH POLE IN APRIL 1909, WITH 4 ESKIMOS AND ONE BLACK ASSISTANT, MATTHEW HENSON. PEARY TOOK SOUNDINGS WHICH PROVED THAT THE SEA ABOUT THE POLE WAS NOT A SHALLOW BODY OF WATER. HIS DISCOVERY WAS NOT RECEIVED ENTHUSIASTICALLY AS IT SHOULD HAVE BEEN BECAUSE ANOTHER AMERICAN EXPLORER, FREDERICK A. COOK, STATED THAT HE HAD DISCOVERED THE POLE IN APRIL 1908, ONE YEAR EARLIER THAN PEARY. THE U.S. CONGRESS INVESTIGATED HIS CLAIM AND FINALLY GAVE PEARY CREDIT FOR THE DISCOVERY. IN 1910, HE WROTE AN ACCOUNT OF HIS HISTORY-MAKING TRIP, PUBLISHED IN BOOK FORM CALLED "THE NORTH POLE."
HE WAS BORN IN CRESSON, PA.
THE COLD WAS SO INTENSE AT THE POLE THAT A FLASK OF BRANDY CARRIED UNDER MY PARKA FROZE SOLID.
THE MEETING WILL PLEASE COME TO ORDER.
IN 1911, HE RETIRED FROM THE NAVY WITH THE RANK OF REAR ADMIRAL, THEN BECAME A DELEGATE TO THE INTERNATIONAL POLAR COMMISSION IN ROME.
PEARY SERVED AS THE PRESIDENT OF THE AMERICAN GEOGRAPHICAL SOCIETY FROM 1901 TO 1906.
KERN

1856 - 1924

Louis H. Sullivan

INFLUENTIAL EARLY MODERN ARCHITECT

CHICAGO SHOULD BE PROUD OF THIS BUILDING.

IN 1872, SULLIVAN STUDIED FOR A YEAR AT MASSACHUSETTS INSTITUTE OF TECHNOLOGY. IN 1873, HE MOVED TO PHILADELPHIA WHERE HE WORKED IN THE OFFICE OF ARCHITECT WM. LA BARA JENNYS. IN 1874, HE WENT TO PARIS FOR FURTHER STUDY. HE RETURNED IN 1876 AND SETTLED IN CHICAGO WHERE HE HAD VARIOUS ARCHITECT JOBS. ***IN 1900, SULLIVAN OPENED HIS OWN OFFICE AND BECAME THE LEADING FIGURE IN THE CHICAGO SCHOOL OF ARCHITECTURE. HE WAS ONE OF THE GREAT FORERUNNERS OF MODERN ARCHITECTURE, NOTABLY IN HIS DEVELOPMENT OF NEW FORMS FOR SKYSCRAPERS AND OTHER TYPES OF STEEL FRAMED STRUCTURES. HIS MASTERPIECE WAS THE CARSON PIRIE SCOTT BUILDING IN CHICAGO.*** HE DESIGNED SKYSCRAPERS IN ST. LOUIS, BUFFALO AND CHICAGO. ***FRANK LLOYD WRIGHT WAS ONE OF HIS STUDENTS.***

HE WAS BORN IN BOSTON, MASS.

TODAY WE ARE HONORING POSTHUMOUSLY, ONE OF AMERICA'S GREAT ARCHITECTS.

HIS THEORY OF FUNCTIONAL ARCHITECTURE WAS NOT WIDELY ACCEPTED WHILE HE WAS LIVING. ***SINCE HIS DEATH THE WORLD HAS RECOGNIZED HIM AS A GREAT PIONEER IN ARCHITECTURE. 19 YRS. AFTER HIS DEATH, HE WAS RECOGNIZED BY THE AMERICAN INSTITUTE OF ARCHITECTURE WITH A GOLD MEDAL.***

WE SHOULD STRIVE FOR ORIGINAL DESIGNS.

SULLIVAN WROTE ARTICLES CALLING FOR A ***NEW ARCHITECTURAL STYLE TO EXPRESS THE TIMES. HE FOUGHT BORROWING DESIGNS FROM THE PAST. DELICATE ORNAMENTATION WAS A HALLMARK OF HIS STYLE.***

KERN

1856-1924

Woodrow Wilson

LAWYER, PROFESSOR, UNIVERSITY PRESIDENT, GOVERNOR AND ***TWENTY-EIGHTH*** PRESIDENT OF THE UNITED STATES (1913-21)

IT IS A FEARFUL THING TO LEAD THIS GREAT PEACEFUL PEOPLE INTO WAR, INTO THE MOST TERRIBLE AND DISASTROUS OF ALL WARS, CIVILIZATION ITSELF SEEMING TO BE IN THE BALANCE.

WILSON GRADUATED FROM PRINCETON IN 1879, PRACTICED LAW IN ATLANTA, GEORGIA, IN 1882, AND RECEIVED A PH.D. FROM HOPKINS UNIVERSITY. HE TAUGHT HISTORY AND POLITICAL ECONOMY AT BRYN MAWR COLLEGE AND WESLEYAN UNIVERSITY. *IN 1902 HE WAS ELECTED PRESIDENT OF PRINCETON, SERVING UNTIL 1910. WILSON WON AS GOVERNOR OF NEW JERSEY WITH THE LARGEST MAJORITY ANY DEMOCRAT HAD EVER HAD IN THAT STATE. NOMINATED FOR PRESIDENT AT THE 1912 DEMOCRATIC CONVENTION, HE WON THE ELECTION EASILY. HE SOUGHT TO BASE FOREIGN POLICY ON FIRM MORAL PRINCIPLES, RATHER THAN "DOLLAR DIPLOMACY." WILSON WAS REELECTED IN 1916 ON THE SLOGAN "HE KEPT US OUT OF WAR." BUT ON APR. 2, 1917, HE APPEARED BEFORE CONGRESS, ASKING WAR TO MAKE "THE WORLD SAFE FOR DEMOCRACY." CONGRESS DECLARED WAR ON GERMANY APR. 6, 1917.*

HE WAS BORN IN STAUNTON, VA.

SORRY, MR. PRESIDENT, THE SENATE WILL NOT ACCEPT YOUR TREATY.

AFTER WORLD WAR I ***WILSON PROPOSED 14 POINTS AS THE BASIS OF PEACE. THE SENATE REFUSED TO RATIFY THE TREATY OF VERSAILLES WHICH HE BROUGHT BACK FROM FRANCE IN JULY 1919. HE RECEIVED THE NOBEL PEACE PRIZE IN 1920 BUT WAS A BROKEN, DISAPPOINTED MAN.***

DURING HIS ADMINISTRATION ***THE 17th, 18th AND 19th AMENDMENTS TO THE CONSTITUTION WERE ADOPTED, THE U.S. ENTERED AND WON WORLD WAR I, THE LEAGUE OF NATIONS AND THE FEDERAL RESERVE SYSTEM WERE ESTABLISHED, AND THE VIRGIN ISLANDS WERE PURCHASED FROM DENMARK.***

KERN

Daniel Guggenheim

INDUSTRIALIST AND PHILANTHROPIST

INDUSTRIAL DEVELOPMENT IS THE KEYSTONE TO THE GROWTH OF THE U.S.

DANIEL HAD ONLY ONE YEAR OF HIGH SCHOOL. THE FAMILY STARTED IN A LACE AND EMBROIDERY BUSINESS BEFORE SWITCHING TO METALS. YOUNG DANIEL FOLLOWED HIS FATHER AS HEAD OF THE FAMILY COPPER INTERESTS. ***HIS PLANNING MADE POSSIBLE THE COMBINATION ON A LARGE SCALE OF COPPER MINING, SMELTING AND REFINING. CHAIRMAN OF THE BOARD OF THE AMERICAN SMELTING CO. FROM 1901 TO 1919, HE EXTENDED THE ACTIVITIES OF THE FIRM TO TAKE OVER GOLD MINES IN ALASKA, TIN AND NITRATE MINES IN SOUTH AMERICA, AND RUBBER PLANTATIONS IN AFRICA. HE INTRODUCED MASS PRODUCTION METHODS IN MINING AND METALLURGY.***

HE WAS BORN IN PHILADELPHIA, PA.

WE WANT TO HELP MANKIND AND THIS IS OUR WAY OF DOING IT.

IN 1924 HE ESTABLISHED THE DANIEL AND FLORENCE GUGGENHEIM FOUNDATION TO ***PROMOTE THE WELL-BEING OF MANKIND THROUGHOUT THE WORLD.***

THE AIRPLANE IS THE FUTURE OF THE WORLD.

IN 1925 HE MADE POSSIBLE THE SCHOOL OF ***AERONAUTICS AT NEW YORK UNIVERSITY, AND IN 1926 THE DANIEL GUGGENHEIM FOUNDATION FOR THE PROMOTION OF AERONAUTICS.***

KERN

1857-1929

Thorstein Veblen

SOCIAL SCIENTIST AND SOCIAL CRITIC

IT'S UP TO YOU SCIENTISTS AND ENGINEERS TO PLAN THE NEW ECONOMIC SOCIETY.

HE WAS EDUCATED AT CARLETON COLLEGE (MINN.) AND JOHNS HOPKINS AND YALE UNIVERSITIES. FROM 1892 TO 1906 HE TAUGHT POLITICAL ECONOMY AT THE UNIVERSITY OF CHICAGO AND ECONOMICS AT LELAND STANFORD UNTIL 1909. FROM 1918 TO 1927 HE WAS A TEACHER AT THE SCHOOL OF SOCIAL RESEARCH, NEW YORK CITY. ***VEBLEN ANALYZED THE PSYCHOLOGICAL BASES OF SOCIAL INSTITUTIONS, WHICH HELPED FOUND INSTITUTIONAL ECONOMICS. HE SUGGESTED THAT PRODUCTION AND DISTRIBUTION BE CONTROLLED BY ENGINEERS, FORESHADOWING OUR PRESENT "TECHNOCRACY."*** HE WAS WITHOUT A DOUBT THE MOST ORIGINAL AND CREATIVE THINKER IN THE HISTORY OF AMERICAN ECONOMIC THOUGHT.

HE WAS BORN IN CATO, WISCONSIN.

THIS BOOK IS A PROTEST AGAINST THE FALSE VALUES AND SOCIAL WASTE OF THE UPPER CLASSES.

THE THEORY OF THE LEISURE CLASS

FROM 1896 TO 1905 HE WAS MANAGING EDITOR OF THE "***JOURNAL OF POLITICAL ECONOMY.***" HE PUBLISHED "***THE THEORY OF THE LEISURE CLASS***" AND "***THE THEORY OF BUSINESS ENTERPRISE.***"

THIS IS MY PREDICTION OF THE FUTURE OF OUR CAPITALIST SYSTEM.

VEBLEN'S "***THEORY OF BUSINESS ENTERPRISE,***" PUBLISHED IN 1904, CRITICIZES THE CAPITALIST SYSTEM AND PREDICTS ***THAT IT WILL DRIFT INTO EITHER FASCISM OR SOCIALISM.***

KERN

1857-1930

William H. Taft

LAWYER, JUDGE, PROFESSOR, SEC. OF WAR, **TWENTY-SEVENTH** PRESIDENT OF THE UNITED STATES (1909-13) AND CHIEF JUSTICE OF THE SUPREME COURT

I HAD HOPED YOU WOULD ACCEPT MY APPOINTMENT.

IN 1878, TAFT GRADUATED SECOND IN HIS CLASS FROM YALE UNIVERSITY AND WAS ADMITTED TO THE BAR IN 1800. **OVER THE YEARS HE BECAME ONE OF THE MOST PROMINENT AND RESPECTED MEN IN THE COUNTRY. EACH SUCCEEDING PRESIDENT CALLED ON HIM TO SERVE WITH THEM. ONE OF TAFT'S GREATEST ACHIEVEMENTS WAS HIS APPOINTMENT BY PRES. McKINLEY TO SERVE AS CIVIL GOVERNOR OF THE PHILIPPINES. TAFT BUILT ROADS, SCHOOLS, POST OFFICES AND BANKS. HE ORGANIZED THE GOVERNMENT AND SET UP A JUDICIAL SYSTEM. HE REJECTED TWO APPOINTMENTS BY PRES. THEODORE ROOSEVELT TO SERVE ON THE SUPREME COURT, BECAUSE HE FELT HIS JOB IN THE PHILIPPINES WAS NOT FINISHED. TAFT EASILY DEFEATED THE DEMOCRATIC CANDIDATE WILLIAM J. BRYAN IN THE ELECTION OF 1908.**

THE NATION STILL NEEDS YOU, BILL.
THANK YOU, MR. PRESIDENT. THIS IS AN AMBITION REALIZED.
KERN

IN 1921, PRES. HARDING APPOINTED HIM **CHIEF JUSTICE OF THE U.S. SUPREME COURT. THIS WAS HIS GREATEST AMBITION. HE WAS THE ONLY FORMER PRESIDENT TO BE APPOINTED TO THIS POST.**

DURING HIS ADMINISTRATION THE *16th* **AMENDMENT TO THE CONSTITUTION WAS ADOPTED, ARIZONA AND NEW MEXICO JOINED THE UNION, THE ROOSEVELT DAM WAS COMPLETED, PEARY REACHED THE NORTH POLE, AMUNDSEN REACHED THE SOUTH POLE AND THE PARCEL POST SERVICE BEGAN.**

1857-1938

Clarence S. Darrow

FAMOUS CRIMINAL LAWYER AND REFORMER

NO CLIENT OF MINE HAS EVER SUFFERED THE DEATH PENALTY.

DARROW WAS ADMITTED TO THE BAR IN 1878 AND PRACTICED LAW IN CHICAGO UNTIL HIS RETIREMENT IN 1927. HE ACTED AS THE DEFENSE COUNSEL IN MANY OF THE MOST WIDELY PUBLICIZED CASES OF HIS TIME. ***HE GAINED NATIONAL ATTENTION WHEN HE DEFENDED EUGENE V. DEBS IN THE AMERICAN RAILWAY UNION CASE IN 1894. DARROW WAS THE LEGAL CHAMPION FOR THE UNDERPRIVILEGED AND OPPRESSED. HE OPPOSED CAPITAL PUNISHMENT. IN 1924 HE DEFENDED LOEB AND LEOPOLD ON TRIAL FOR MURDER BY PROVIDING PSYCHIATRIC EVIDENCE OF TEMPORARY INSANITY AND WON COMMUTATION OF DEATH SENTENCES.***

HE WAS BORN IN KINSMAN, OHIO.

WHEN I'M PICKING A JURY, I LIKE TO SEE A FELLOW IN THE BOX WHO'S BEEN COON-HUNTING WITH ME.

ON OF HIS BEST KNOWN TRIALS WAS THE JOHN T. SCOPES CASE (1925) IN WHICH ***HE UPHELD THE RIGHT TO TEACH EVOLUTION IN TENNESSEE SCHOOLS. HE WAS OPPOSED BY, AND LOST TO, WILLIAM JENNINGS BRYAN.***

I WAS ALWAYS GLAD WHEN I SAW AN IRISHMAN ENTER THE JURY BOX. I KNEW HE WOULD BE EMOTIONAL, KINDLY AND FORGIVING.

AFTER HIS RETIREMENT HE LECTURED AND DEBATED OPPONENTS ON SOCIAL ISSUES. DARROW'S BOOKS WERE ***"CRIME, ITS CAUSE AND TREATMENT," "RESIST NOT EVIL" AND "EYE FOR AN EYE."***

1858-1919

Theodore Roosevelt

CONSERVATIONIST, SOLDIER, GOVERNOR, VICE-PRESIDENT AND ***TWENTY-SIXTH*** PRESIDENT OF THE UNITED STATES (1901-09)

COME GENTLEMEN, LET US HAVE PEACE.

AFTER GRADUATING FROM HARVARD, ROOSEVELT QUICKLY BUILT UP A REPUTATION AS A FIGHTER FOR CIVIL SERVICE REFORMS. ***DURING THE SPANISH-AMERICAN WAR HE LED HIS "ROUGH RIDERS" TO VICTORY IN THE FAMOUS CHARGE UP SAN JUAN HILL IN CUBA. IN 1898 HE WAS ELECTED GOV. OF NEW YORK. IN 1900 HE WAS THE CANDIDATE FOR VICE-PRESIDENT WITH McKINLEY. ROOSEVELT BECAME PRESIDENT IN 1901, AFTER McKINLEY'S ASSASSINATION. KNOWN TO MILLIONS AS "TEDDY," HE BROUGHT ABOUT REFORMS TO REGULATE BIG BUSINESS AND BECAME KNOWN AS A "TRUSTBUSTER". HE WON THE FIRST NOBEL PEACE PRIZE AWARDED TO AN AMERICAN FOR ARBITRATING A PEACE TREATY BETWEEN RUSSIA AND JAPAN. ONE OF HIS MOTTOS IN FOREIGN POLICY WAS "SPEAK SOFTLY AND CARRY A BIG STICK."***

HE WAS BORN IN NEW YORK CITY.

NICE SHOT, DAD.

DURING HIS ADMINISTRATION ***THE DEPTS. OF COMMERCE AND LABOR WERE ESTABLISHED, THE CONSTRUCTION OF THE PANAMA CANAL BEGAN, OKLAHOMA JOINED THE UNION, AND THE U.S. FOREST SERVICE WAS CREATED.***

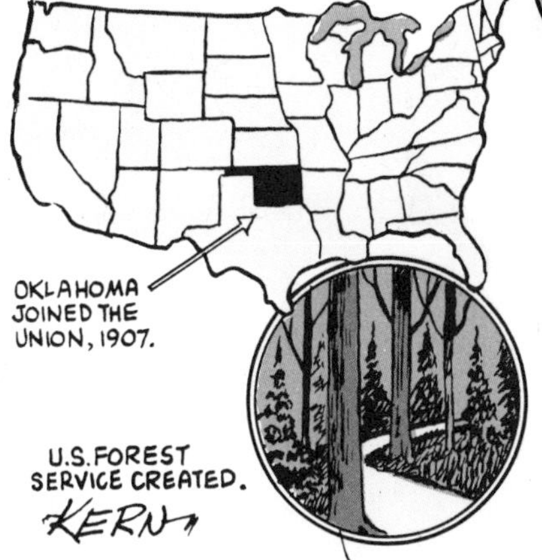

OKLAHOMA JOINED THE UNION, 1907.
U.S. FOREST SERVICE CREATED.
KERN

ROOSEVELT WAS A PUNY CHILD SUFFERING FROM ASTHMA AND POOR EYESIGHT. ***WHILE STILL YOUNG, HE WENT WEST, BUILT UP HIS HEALTH, AND BECAME A GREAT CONSERVATIONIST. AS PRESIDENT HE HUNTED BIG GAME IN AFRICA, CLIMBED THE MATTERHORN AND EXPLORED SOUTH AMERICAN RIVERS.***

1858-1928

George W. Goethals

ARMY OFFICER AND ENGINEER WHO DIRECTED THE COMPLETION OF THE PANAMA CANAL

A GRADUATE FROM WEST POINT IN 1880, GOETHALS WAS APPOINTED A SECOND LIEUTENANT IN THE U.S. ARMY ENGINEERING CORPS. EARLY IN HIS ENGINEERING CAREER **HE SUPERVISED THE CONSTRUCTION OF THE CANAL LOCKS AND DAMS OF THE MUSCLE SHOALS PROJECT ON THE TENNESSEE RIVER. IN 1907 PRES. ROOSEVELT APPOINTED HIM CHIEF OF THE ARMY ENGINEERS IN THE CONSTRUCTION OF THE PANAMA CANAL. THROUGH GOETHALS' BRILLIANT HANDLING OF THE PROBLEMS OF SUPPLY, ORGANIZATION, SANITATION AND HEALTH, THE CANAL WAS READY FOR USE AHEAD OF SCHEDULE. IN 1914 HE RETIRED FROM THE ARMY TO BECOME THE FIRST CIVILIAN GOVERNOR OF THE PANAMA CANAL ZONE. HE RESIGNED IN 1916.**

TELL YOUR MEN TO MOVE THOSE SUPPLIES AND FAST, COLONEL.

HE WAS BORN IN BROOKLYN, N.Y.

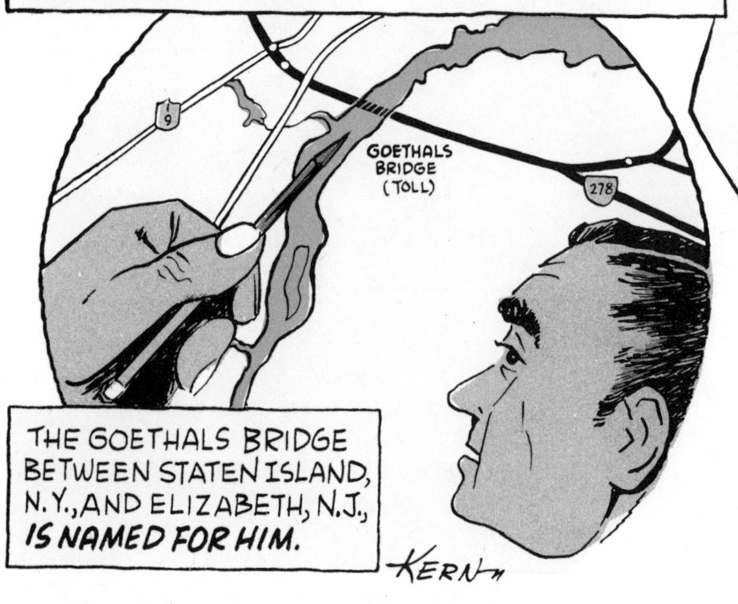

THE GOETHALS BRIDGE BETWEEN STATEN ISLAND, N.Y., AND ELIZABETH, N.J., **IS NAMED FOR HIM.**

DURING WORLD WAR I HE WAS ON ACTIVE DUTY AS QUARTERMASTER GENERAL AND DIRECTOR OF **PURCHASE, STORAGE AND TRAFFIC. HE WAS RECOGNIZED AS ONE OF THE GREATEST SUPPLY MEN PRODUCED DURING THE WAR.**

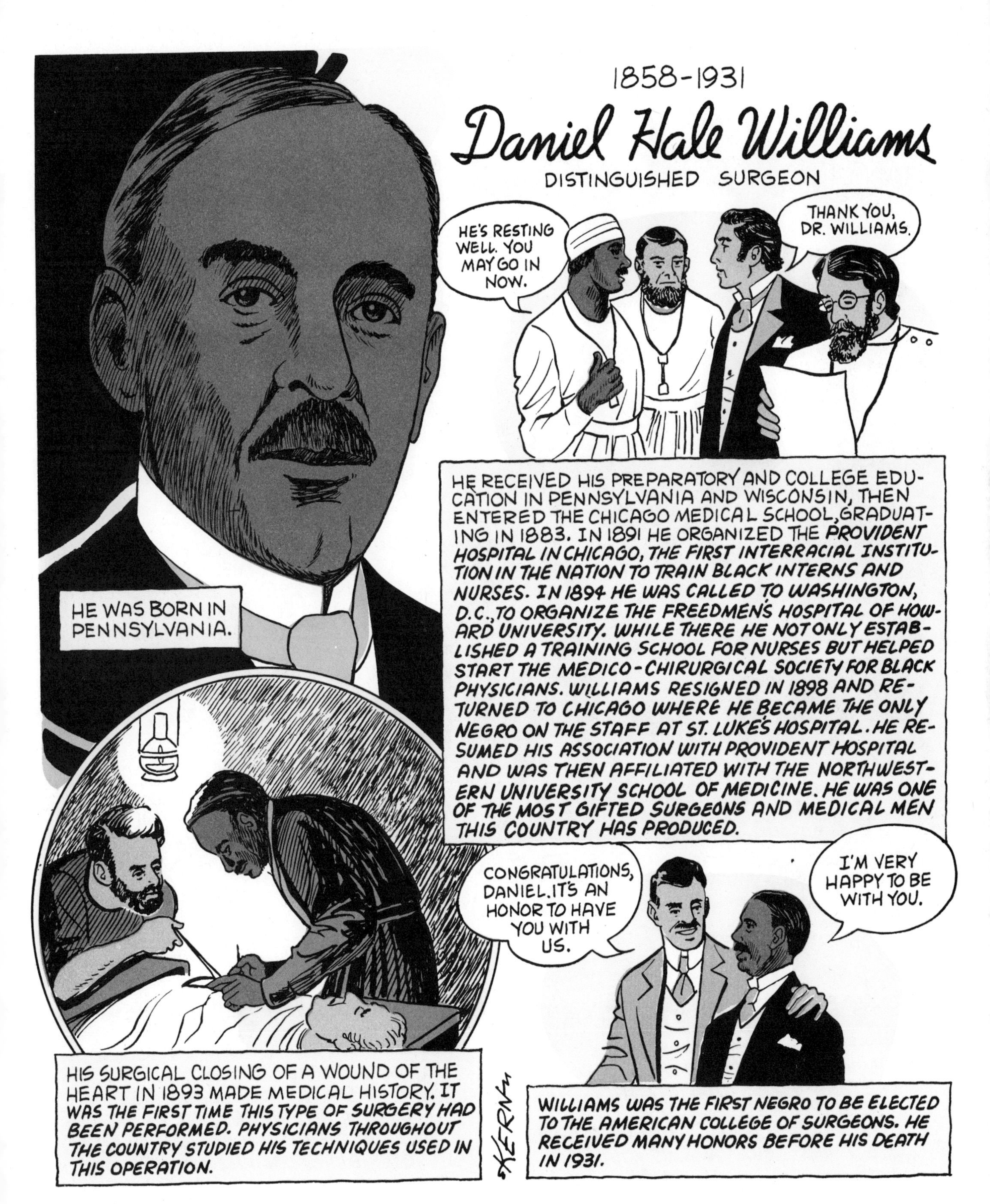
1858-1931
Daniel Hale Williams
DISTINGUISHED SURGEON
HE'S RESTING WELL. YOU MAY GO IN NOW.
THANK YOU, DR. WILLIAMS.
HE WAS BORN IN PENNSYLVANIA.
HE RECEIVED HIS PREPARATORY AND COLLEGE EDUCATION IN PENNSYLVANIA AND WISCONSIN, THEN ENTERED THE CHICAGO MEDICAL SCHOOL, GRADUATING IN 1883. IN 1891 HE ORGANIZED THE PROVIDENT HOSPITAL IN CHICAGO, THE FIRST INTERRACIAL INSTITUTION IN THE NATION TO TRAIN BLACK INTERNS AND NURSES. IN 1894 HE WAS CALLED TO WASHINGTON, D.C., TO ORGANIZE THE FREEDMEN'S HOSPITAL OF HOWARD UNIVERSITY. WHILE THERE HE NOT ONLY ESTABLISHED A TRAINING SCHOOL FOR NURSES BUT HELPED START THE MEDICO-CHIRURGICAL SOCIETY FOR BLACK PHYSICIANS. WILLIAMS RESIGNED IN 1898 AND RETURNED TO CHICAGO WHERE HE BECAME THE ONLY NEGRO ON THE STAFF AT ST. LUKE'S HOSPITAL. HE RESUMED HIS ASSOCIATION WITH PROVIDENT HOSPITAL AND WAS THEN AFFILIATED WITH THE NORTHWESTERN UNIVERSITY SCHOOL OF MEDICINE. HE WAS ONE OF THE MOST GIFTED SURGEONS AND MEDICAL MEN THIS COUNTRY HAS PRODUCED.
CONGRATULATIONS, DANIEL. IT'S AN HONOR TO HAVE YOU WITH US.
I'M VERY HAPPY TO BE WITH YOU.
HIS SURGICAL CLOSING OF A WOUND OF THE HEART IN 1893 MADE MEDICAL HISTORY. IT WAS THE FIRST TIME THIS TYPE OF SURGERY HAD BEEN PERFORMED. PHYSICIANS THROUGHOUT THE COUNTRY STUDIED HIS TECHNIQUES USED IN THIS OPERATION.
KERN
WILLIAMS WAS THE FIRST NEGRO TO BE ELECTED TO THE AMERICAN COLLEGE OF SURGEONS. HE RECEIVED MANY HONORS BEFORE HIS DEATH IN 1931.

1858 - 1939
Charles A. Eastman
AMERICAN INDIAN PHYSICIAN AND WRITER
HE WAS BORN IN REDWOOD FALLS, MINNESOTA.
IN 1887 EASTMAN GRADUATED FROM DARTMOUTH AND RECEIVED HIS MEDICAL DEGREE FROM BOSTON UNIVERSITY IN 1890. HE SPENT THE NEXT 3YRS. AS A DOCTOR AT PINE RIDGE AGENCY IN SOUTH DAKOTA. EASTMAN WAS THE FIRST INDIAN TO HOLD SUCH A POSITION. HE HAD A PRIVATE PRACTICE FOR A SHORT TIME, THEN BECAME VERY ACTIVE IN YMCA AND BOY SCOUT WORK. ONE OF HIS GREATEST CONTRIBUTIONS WAS CREATING BETTER UNDERSTANDING BETWEEN THE INDIANS AND THE WHITES.
NORTH DAKOTA
SOUTH DAKOTA
NEBRASKA
MINNESOTA
HIS BOOKS, "INDIAN BOYHOOD," "FROM THE DEEP WOODS TO CIVILIZATION" AND "THE SOUL OF THE INDIAN," GIVE US A TRUE PICTURE OF THE LIFE OF HIS PEOPLE. EASTMAN'S SIOUX NAME WAS OHIYESA.
KERN
HE WAS THE U.S. GOVERNMENT DOCTOR AND ATTORNEY FOR THE SIOUX IN MINNESOTA, NORTH DAKOTA, SOUTH DAKOTA AND NEBRASKA. HE SET DOWN THE ALPHABET FOR HIS LANGUAGE AND COMPILED A DICTIONARY.

1859 - 1952

John Dewey

PHILOSOPHER, PSYCHOLOGIST AND EDUCATOR

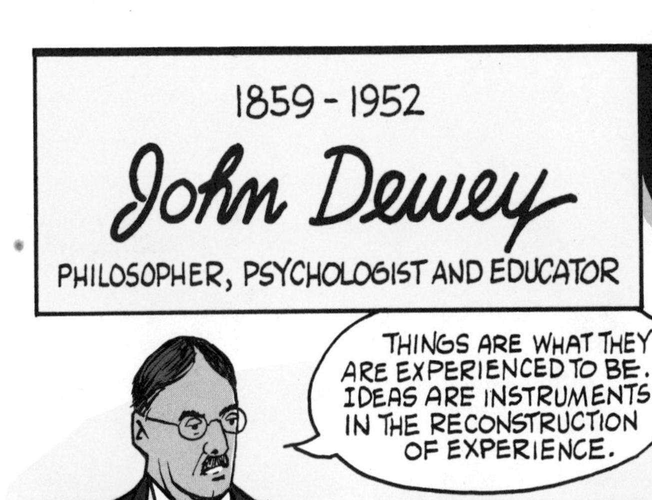

THINGS ARE WHAT THEY ARE EXPERIENCED TO BE. IDEAS ARE INSTRUMENTS IN THE RECONSTRUCTION OF EXPERIENCE.

DEWEY GRADUATED FROM THE UNIVERSITY OF VERMONT IN 1879. IN 1884 HE RECEIVED HIS PH.D. FROM JOHNS HOPKINS UNIVERSITY. ***HE WAS A PROFESSOR OF PHILOSOPHY AT THE UNIVERSITY OF MINNESOTA FOR 1 YR. AND THEN AT THE UNIVERSITY OF MICHIGAN FOR 5 YRS. HE SERVED AS THE HEAD OF THE DEPT. OF PHILOSOPHY AND EDUCATION AT THE UNIVERSITY OF CHICAGO. FROM 1904 UNTIL HE RETIRED IN 1930 HE WAS PROFESSOR OF PHILOSOPHY AT COLUMBIA UNIVERSITY. DEWEY'S PHILOSOPHY, SOMETIMES CALLED "INSTRUMENTALISM," WAS PRACTICAL, SIMILAR TO WILLIAM JAMES WHO BELIEVED THAT AN IDEA MUST BE JUDGED BY HOW IT WORKS.***

HE WAS BORN IN BURLINGTON, VT.

IF AN IDEA DOES WHAT IT INTENDS AS A PLAN OF ACTION, IT IS TRUE, IF IT FAILS, IT IS FALSE.

THIS PLAN IS KNOWN AS PROGRESSIVE EDUCATION.

AFTER WORLD WAR I HE SPENT 2 YRS. LECTURING AT THE UNIVERSITY OF PEKING. ***IN 1924 HE PREPARED A PLAN FOR THE REORGANIZATION OF THE NATIONAL SCHOOLS FOR THE GOVERNMENT OF TURKEY.***

WHILE AT THE UNIVERSITY OF CHICAGO, DEWEY TESTED HIS ***EDUCATIONAL PRINCIPLES IN A SERIES OF EXPERIMENTS AT THE UNIVERSITY HIGH SCHOOL. THESE EXPERIMENTS EMPHASIZED LEARNING THROUGH EXPERIMENTATION AND HAD GREAT INFLUENCE ON THE PROGRESSIVE EDUCATION MOVEMENT AND EDUCATIONAL PRACTICES IN AMERICA.***

KERN

1860-1925

William J. Bryan

ORATOR, STATESMAN AND EDITOR

I ADVOCATE FREE SILVER TO PROVIDE FOR A MORE BAL-ANCED ECONOMY.

AFTER GRADUATING FROM THE COLLEGE OF LAW IN CHICAGO HE PRACTICED IN JACKSONVILLE FOR 4 YRS., THEN MOVED TO LINCOLN, NEB., WHERE HE BECAME A LEADING ATTORNEY. ***FROM 1891 TO 1895 HE SERVED IN THE U.S. CONGRESS, WHERE HE FOUGHT FOR THE FREE COINAGE OF SILVER AT A FIXED RATE WITH GOLD. IN 1896, AS A DELEGATE TO THE DEMOCRATIC NATIONAL CONVENTION AT CHICAGO, HE WROTE THE FREE-SILVER PLANK OF THE PLATFORM. HE DELIVERED THE FAMOUS SPEECH WHICH SAID "YOU SHALL NOT CRUCIFY MANKIND UPON A CROSS OF GOLD." THIS SPEECH WON HIM THE NOMINATION FOR PRESIDENT. BRYAN, "THE PEERLESS LEADER" OF THE DEMOCRATIC PARTY, WAS DEFEATED FOR THE PRESIDENCY THREE TIMES, TWICE BY McKINLEY AND ONCE BY TAFT.***

HE WAS BORN IN SALEM, ILL.

SCOPES, YOU HAVE DEFIED STATE LAW. YOUR TEACHINGS ARE CONTRARY TO THE BIBLE.

WELCOME TO MY CABINET, BILL.
KERN

WOODROW WILSON APPOINTED BRYAN SEC. OF STATE. ***HE NEGOTIATED 30 TREATIES OF ARBITRATION WITH FOREIGN COUNTRIES. HE RESIGNED IN 1915, DISAPPROVING WILSON'S POLICIES AFTER THE SINKING OF THE "LUSITANIA."***

BRYAN LED THE PROSECUTION OF JOHN SCOPES WHO WAS ARRESTED FOR TEACHING ***EVOLUTION IN THE TENN. PUBLIC SCHOOLS. CLARENCE DARROW, THE FAMOUS LAWYER, DEFENDED SCOPES, BUT BRYAN WON. SCOPES WAS FINED $100. THE CONVICTION WAS LATER REVERSED ON A TECHNICALITY, BUT BRYAN DID NOT LIVE TO SEE THE REVERSAL.***

1860 - 1935

Jane Addams

SOCIAL WORKER AND HUMANITARIAN

IN ANSWER TO YOUR QUESTION, HULL HOUSE IS FOR EVERYONE REGARDLESS OF RACE, COLOR OR CREED.

SHE WAS BORN IN CEDARVILLE, ILL.

SHE WAS EDUCATED AT ROCKFORD FEMALE SEMINARY, THE PHILADELPHIA MEDICAL COLLEGE AND IN EUROPE. ***IN 1889 SHE ESTABLISHED THE HULL HOUSE IN CHICAGO, ONE OF THE FIRST SOCIAL SETTLEMENT HOUSES IN THE UNITED STATES. THERE SHE INTRODUCED A GREAT VARIETY OF PROGRAMS FROM DAY NURSING TO COLLEGE COURSES FOR PEOPLE OF EVERY NATION AND RACE. SHE WAS A FIRM BELIEVER IN THE NEED FOR RESEARCH INTO THE CAUSE OF CRIME AND POVERTY AND THE NEED FOR TRAINED SOCIAL WORKERS. MISS ADDAMS LECTURED ON PUBLIC HEALTH, UNEMPLOYMENT RELIEF AND SOCIAL INSURANCE. SHE WAS A LEADER IN THE FIGHT TO GIVE WOMEN THE VOTE. FROM 1915-1929 SHE WAS PRESIDENT OF THE WOMEN'S INTERNATIONAL LEAGUE FOR PEACE AND FREEDOM.***

CONGRATULATIONS TO YOU BOTH.

THESE WOMEN WILL BE WORKING AN 8-HOUR DAY FROM NOW ON.

SHE SHARED THE 1931 ***NOBEL PEACE PRIZE WITH THE NOTED AMERICAN EDUCATOR, NICHOLAS MURRAY BUTLER. SOME OF HER BOOKS WERE "THE SPIRIT OF YOUTH AND THE CITY STREETS" AND "NEWER IDEALS OF PEACE."***

SHE WAS CLOSELY ASSOCIATED WITH SUCH IMPORTANT REFORMS AS THE ***FIRST 8-HOUR LAW FOR WORKING WOMEN, THE FIRST STATE CHILD-LABOR LAW, HOUSING REFORM AND THE FIRST JUVENILE COURT.***

1860-1943

George Washington Carver

WORLD-FAMOUS SCIENTIST

THESE EXPERIMENTS ARE SO IMPORTANT TO THE SOUTH.

CARVER WAS BORN OF SLAVE PARENTS. WHEN HE WAS 2 MO. OLD HE AND HIS MOTHER WERE KIDNAPPED BY NIGHT RAIDERS. HIS MASTER BOUGHT HIM BACK IN EXCHANGE FOR A RACE HORSE VALUED AT $300. **HE WORKED HIS WAY THROUGH SCHOOL, GRADUATING FROM IOWA STATE COLLEGE OF AGRICULTURE AND MECHANICAL ARTS. HE THEN JOINED THE FACULTY AND STAYED UNTIL 1896. BOOKER T. WASHINGTON INVITED HIM TO TUSKEGEE INSTITUTE, WHERE HE STAYED THE REST OF HIS LIFE. HE WON INTERNATIONAL FAME AS AN AGRICULTURAL CHEMIST. HE WORKED TO REVOLUTIONIZE THE AGRICULTURE OF THE SOUTH. CARVER DERIVED OVER 300 PRODUCTS FROM THE PEANUT AND OVER 100 FROM THE SWEET POTATO. HE GAVE HIS ENTIRE LIFE SAVINGS OF $33,000 TO THE GEORGE WASHINGTON CARVER FOUNDATION, ESTABLISHED AT TUSKEGEE INSTITUTE IN 1940.**

HE WAS BORN NEAR DIAMOND GROVE, MO.

THESE PLANTS WILL REVOLUTIONIZE THE AGRICULTURE OF THE SOUTH.

DR. CARVER, YOU ARE A GREAT AMERICAN. WE ARE PROUD OF YOU!

HE CONVINCED THE FARMERS OF ALABAMA THEY COULD GROW **PEANUTS, PECANS AND SWEET POTATOES IN PLACE OF COTTON. SINCE THEN THE PEANUT CROP ALONE HAS BROUGHT THE SOUTH $60 MILLION IN ONE YEAR.**

AMONG THE MANY HONORS HE RECEIVED WERE **THE SPRINGARN MEDAL IN 1923 AND THE ROOSEVELT MEDAL FOR DISTINGUISHED SERVICE TO SCIENCE IN 1939. IN 1916 HE WAS ELECTED A FELLOW IN THE ROYAL SOCIETY OF ARTS IN LONDON.**

KERN

1860-1948

John J. Pershing

COMMANDER OF AMERICAN FORCES IN EUROPE DURING WORLD WAR I

WE MUST PRESERVE THE UNITY OF THE AMERICAN ARMY IN COMBAT. WE MUST FIGHT INDEPENDENTLY, FOR OUR ARMY IS TRAINED FOR FAST DRIVING WARFARE!

IN 1886 PERSHING GRADUATED FROM THE U.S MILITARY ACADEMY. HE TAUGHT MILITARY TACTICS AT WEST POINT, THEN WENT ON ACTIVE DUTY DURING THE SPANISH-AMERICAN WAR. FROM 1899-1903 HE WAS STATIONED IN THE PHILIPPINES. ***WHEN THE U.S. ENTERED WORLD WAR I HE WAS APPOINTED COMMANDER-IN-CHIEF OF THE AMERICAN FORCES HE SUCCEEDED IN KEEPING THE AMERICAN ARMY AS A UNIFIED FIGHTING FORCE DESPITE THE PRESSURE TO DIVIDE IT AMONG THE ALLIED FORCES. HIS CONTRIBUTION TO THE ALLIED VICTORY WAS WIDELY ACCLAIMED. IN OCT. 1917 HE WAS PROMOTED TO THE RANK OF FULL GENERAL AND IN SEPT. 1919 HE RECEIVED THE TITLE "GENERAL OF THE ARMIES OF THE UNITED STATES."***

HE WAS BORN IN LINN COUNTY, MO.

I HAVE SUCCEEDED IN COMBINING IN ONE ORGANIZATION THE REGULAR ARMY, THE NATIONAL GUARD AND THE PERMANENT RESERVES.

PERSHING SERVED AS THE CHIEF OF STAFF OF THE U.S. ARMIES FROM 1921-24, THEN RETIRED TO WRITE HIS MEMOIRS. HIS "***EXPERIENCES IN THE WORLD WAR***" ***WON THE PULITZER PRIZE FOR HISTORY IN 1932.***

KERN

IN 1915 THE LOSS OF HIS WIFE AND THREE DAUGHTERS IN A FIRE AT ARMY QUARTERS IN SAN FRANCISCO ***AROUSED THE SYMPATHY OF THE ENTIRE NATION. ONLY HIS SON, WARREN, WAS SAVED. PERSHING WAS IN EL PASO, TEX., WHEN THE TRAGEDY STRUCK.***

1861-1932

Frederick J. Turner

AMERICAN EDUCATOR AND HISTORIAN

I BELIEVE THAT WESTERN ENVIRONMENT GAVE SHAPE TO THE AMERICAN CHARACTER AND TRANSFIGURED THE COUNTRY'S INSTITUTIONS.

HE GRADUATED FROM THE UNIVERSITY OF WIS. IN 1884. HE LEFT THE STATE TO GET HIS PH.D. AT JOHNS HOPKINS UNIVERSITY, BUT RETURNED IN 1889 TO TEACH AT HIS ALMA MATER FOR 21 YRS. IN 1910 HE WENT TO HARVARD AS A HISTORY PROFESSOR. ***HIS BOOK, "THE SIGNIFICANCE OF THE FRONTIER IN AMERICAN HISTORY," GREW OUT OF A PAPER HE GAVE AT THE AM. HISTORICAL SOCIETY CONFERENCE AT CHICAGO IN 1893. THIS BOOK COMPLETELY CHANGED THE UNDERSTANDING AND WRITING OF AMERICAN HISTORY. HE DOMINATED THE WRITING OF HISTORY FOR MORE THAN 30 YRS. TURNER BELIEVED THAT THE FRONTIER WAS THE CRADLE OF AMERICAN DEMOCRACY, AND STATED THAT THE WEST WAS ONE OF THE INFLUENCES MOLDING THE NATION'S CIVILIZATION.***

TURNER'S CONTRIBUTIONS TO HISTORIOGRAPHY ARE STILL DISCUSSED TODAY.

TURNER, A MASTERFUL TEACHER AND TIRELESS RESEARCHER, WAS AWARDED THE ***PULITZER PRIZE FOR HISTORY IN 1933.***

HE WAS BORN IN PORTAGE, WIS.

YOU HAVE DOMINATED THE WRITING OF HISTORY FOR MORE THAN 30 YRS.

HE WAS A PIONEER IN INTERDISCIPLINARY TECHNIQUES USING THE MATERIALS AND METHODS OF THE ***GEOGRAPHER, THE ECONOMIST AND SOCIOLOGIST IN HISTORY. HE SAID, "HISTORY IS THE BIOGRAPHY OF SOCIETY IN ALL ITS DEPARTMENTS."***

KERN

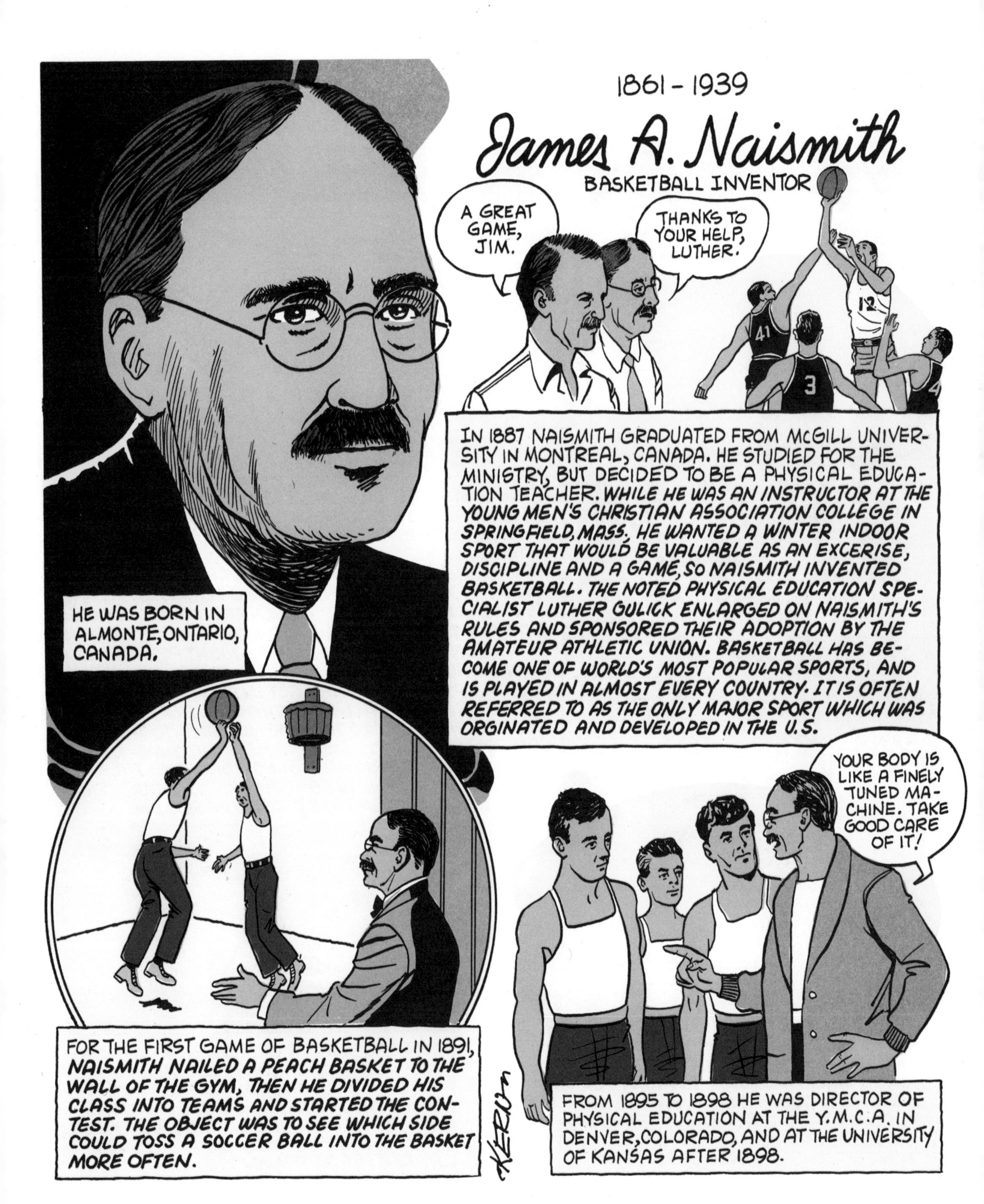
1861 - 1939
James A. Naismith
BASKETBALL INVENTOR
A GREAT GAME, JIM.
THANKS TO YOUR HELP, LUTHER.
IN 1887 NAISMITH GRADUATED FROM McGILL UNIVERSITY IN MONTREAL, CANADA. HE STUDIED FOR THE MINISTRY, BUT DECIDED TO BE A PHYSICAL EDUCATION TEACHER. WHILE HE WAS AN INSTRUCTOR AT THE YOUNG MEN'S CHRISTIAN ASSOCIATION COLLEGE IN SPRINGFIELD, MASS. HE WANTED A WINTER INDOOR SPORT THAT WOULD BE VALUABLE AS AN EXCERISE, DISCIPLINE AND A GAME, SO NAISMITH INVENTED BASKETBALL. THE NOTED PHYSICAL EDUCATION SPECIALIST LUTHER GULICK ENLARGED ON NAISMITH'S RULES AND SPONSORED THEIR ADOPTION BY THE AMATEUR ATHLETIC UNION. BASKETBALL HAS BECOME ONE OF WORLD'S MOST POPULAR SPORTS, AND IS PLAYED IN ALMOST EVERY COUNTRY. IT IS OFTEN REFERRED TO AS THE ONLY MAJOR SPORT WHICH WAS ORGINATED AND DEVELOPED IN THE U.S.
HE WAS BORN IN ALMONTE, ONTARIO, CANADA.
YOUR BODY IS LIKE A FINELY TUNED MACHINE. TAKE GOOD CARE OF IT!
FOR THE FIRST GAME OF BASKETBALL IN 1891, NAISMITH NAILED A PEACH BASKET TO THE WALL OF THE GYM, THEN HE DIVIDED HIS CLASS INTO TEAMS AND STARTED THE CONTEST. THE OBJECT WAS TO SEE WHICH SIDE COULD TOSS A SOCCER BALL INTO THE BASKET MORE OFTEN.
FROM 1895 TO 1898 HE WAS DIRECTOR OF PHYSICAL EDUCATION AT THE Y.M.C.A. IN DENVER, COLORADO, AND AT THE UNIVERSITY OF KANSAS AFTER 1898.
KERN

1861-1944

George W. Norris

PROGRESSIVE, INDEPENDENT STATESMAN

THE DEVELOPMENT OF THIS GREAT VALLEY IS IMPERATIVE!

NORRIS STUDIED LAW AT VALPARAISO UNIVERSITY. IN 1885 HE MOVED TO BEAVER CITY, NEBRASKA, WHERE HE OPENED A LAW OFFICE. FROM 1895 TO 1902 HE WAS JUDGE OF THE 14TH NEBRASKA COURT. ***HE WAS ELECTED TO THE U.S. HOUSE OF REPRESENTATIVES IN 1902, WHERE HE SERVED FOR 10YRS. IN 1912 HE WAS ELECTED TO THE U.S. SENATE. NORRIS OPPOSED ENTRY OF THE U.S. INTO WORLD WAR I AND THE LEAGUE OF NATIONS. HE BELIEVED AND FOUGHT FOR PUBLIC OWNERSHIP OF PUBLIC UTILITIES. HE LED A CAMPAIGN FOR THE PASSAGE OF THE ACT IN 1933 WHICH CREATED THE TENNESSEE VALLEY AUTHORITY. NORRIS ALSO HELPED PASS THE 20TH AMENDMENT TO THE U.S. CONSTITUTION. THIS SHORTENED THE TIME BETWEEN CONGRESSIONAL ELECTIONS AND THE FIRST MEETING OF THE NEW CONGRESS TO REDUCE THE INFLUENCE OF DEFEATED CONGRESSMEN.***

A BEAST IS LOOSE IN THE WORLD. WE MUST HELP SUBDUE IT!

NORRIS SPENT ***40YRS. IN CONGRESS. HE IGNORED PARTY POLITICS TO FIGHT FOR WHATEVER HE THOUGHT WAS RIGHT.*** HE SUPPORTED AID TO BRITAIN IN THE EARLY YEARS OF WORLD WAR II. IN 1942 HE RAN FOR REELECTION AS AN INDEPENDENT BUT WAS DEFEATED.

KERN

NORRIS DAM ON THE CLINCH RIVER IS 265 FT. HIGH AND 1,860 FT. LONG.

IN RECOGNITION OF HIS EFFORTS FOR THE PASSAGE OF THE TENNESSEE VALLEY AUTHORITY BILL, ***ONE OF THE FIRST GREAT DAMS ON THE TENNESSEE RIVER WAS NAMED IN HIS HONOR. HIS AUTOBIOGRAPHY, "FIGHTING LIBERAL," WAS PUBLISHED AFTER HIS DEATH, IN 1945.***

1862-1948

Charles Evans Hughes

DISTINGUISHED STATESMAN AND JURIST

I AM GOING TO SET UP A PUBLIC SERVICE COMMISSION AND FIGHT FOR DIRECT PRIMARY ELECTIONS.

HUGHES STUDIED AT THE COLUMBIA UNIVERSITY SCHOOL OF LAW. IN 1884 HE WAS ADMITTED TO THE BAR AND BEGAN PRACTICE IN NEW YORK CITY. IN 1905 HE WAS SPECIAL ATTORNEY FOR THE NEW YORK LEGISLATURE ***INVESTIGATING LIFE INSURANCE COMPANIES IN NEW YORK STATE. THE RESULT WAS A COMPLETE REORGANIZATION OF LAWS GOVERNING INSURANCE COMPANIES. THIS INVESTIGATION RESULTED IN HIS BEING ELECTED GOVERNOR OF NEW YORK AND REELECTED IN 1908. WHILE GOVERNOR HE INSTITUTED MANY POLITICAL REFORMS, AND ELIMINATED A GREAT DEAL OF POLITICAL CORRUPTION IN BOTH MAJOR PARTIES. HE RESIGNED IN 1910 TO BECOME ASSOCIATE JUSTICE OF THE U.S. SUPREME COURT, SERVING UNTIL 1916. HUGHES LED THE AMERICAN DELEGATION TO THE PAN-AMERICAN CONFERENCE AND THEN ACCEPTED A SEAT ON THE WORLD COURT IN 1928.***

HE WAS BORN IN GLEN FALLS, N.Y.

MR. PRESIDENT, I AM CONSIDERED A CONSERVATIVE BUT AS CHIEF JUSTICE I WILL SUPPORT YOUR "NEW DEAL" LIBERAL PROPOSALS.

HUGHES SERVED AS ***CHIEF JUSTICE OF THE U.S. SUPREME COURT FROM 1930-41. HE IS CONSIDERED ONE OF OUR GREATEST CHIEF JUSTICES. HE THEN RESIGNED AND SPENT HIS REMAINING YRS. IN WASHINGTON, D.C.***

I WOULD BE HONORED IF YOU WOULD BE MY SECRETARY OF STATE.
THANK YOU, MR. PRESIDENT, I ACCEPT.

IN 1916 HE WAS DRAFTED BY THE REPUBLICANS TO RUN FOR ***THE U.S. PRESIDENCY. WOODROW WILSON WON BY A SLIM MARGIN. IN 1921 PRES. HARDING APPOINTED HIM SEC. OF STATE. HE HELD THIS OFFICE UNTIL 1925.***

KERN

1862–1956

Connie Mack

BASEBALL PLAYER, MANAGER AND CLUB OWNER

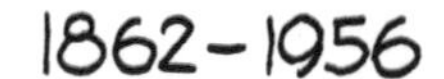

CONNIE MACK (BORN CORNELIUS ALEXANDER McGILLICUDDY) STARTED HIS BASEBALL CAREER IN 1884 AS A CATCHER IN THE SOUTHERN NEW ENGLAND LEAGUE. FROM 1886 TO 1899 MACK PLAYED WITH THE WASHINGTON AND PITTSBURGH TEAMS, DURING THIS TIME HE MANAGED THE PITTSBURGH TEAM FOR 3 YRS. *STARTING IN 1901, HE SERVED AS OWNER-MANAGER OF THE PHILADELPHIA ATHLETICS UNTIL HE RETIRED IN 1950. UNDER HIS SUPERB LEADERSHIP AND THROUGH HIS PARENTAL HANDLING OF PROBLEM BALL PLAYERS, THE ATHLETICS MADE ONE OF THE MOST REMARKABLE RECORDS IN BASEBALL HISTORY. HIS TEAM WON 9 AM. LEAGUE CHAMPIONSHIPS AND 5 WORLD SERIES. MANY EXPERTS SAY HIS 1911 ATHLETICS, WITH 2ND BASEMAN EDDIE COLLINS AND THE $100,000 INFIELD, WAS THE GREATEST TEAM IN THE HISTORY OF THE GAME. OTHERS RATE HIS 1929 TEAM THE BEST.*

HE WAS BORN IN EAST BROOKFIELD, MASSACHUSETTS.

LOOKING AT A PHOTO OF HIMSELF WHEN HE WAS 26 YRS. OLD. *HE HAD BEEN PLAYING PROFESSIONAL BASEBALL FOR 3 YRS.*

HE SPENT MORE THAN 60 YRS. IN BASEBALL. *HIS PRESENCE ON THE BENCH DIRECTING HIS PLAYERS WITH A WAVE OF HIS SCORECARD WAS ONE OF BASEBALL'S MOST FAMILIAR SIGHTS FOR 50 YEARS.*

MACK WAS APPOINTED TO THE BASEBALL HALL OF FAME IN 1937. HE AUTHORED "MY 66 YEARS IN THE BIG LEAGUES."

KERN

1863-1947
Henry Ford
AUTOMOBILE MANUFACTURER
THINK IT WILL WORK, HENRY?
HE WAS BORN ON A FARM NEAR GREENFIELD, MICHIGAN.
AT 16 HE WAS A MACHINIST IN DETROIT. HE BEGAN EXPERIMENTING WITH ENGINES AND COMPLETED HIS FIRST GASOLINE ENGINE IN 1893. HE ORGANIZED THE FORD MOTOR CO. IN 1903. PIONEER OF THE ASSEMBLY-LINE METHOD, HE DEVELOPED AND MASS-PRODUCED THE "MODEL T" AUTOMOBILE AND SOLD IT AT A PRICE THE AVERAGE MAN COULD AFFORD. FROM 1908-27 HE SOLD MORE THAN 15,000,000 "MODEL T'S." HALF THE AUTOMOBILES MADE BETWEEN 1917 AND 1927 WERE FORDS. HE SHARED PROFITS WITH HIS EMPLOYEES, INTRODUCED AN 8-HR. DAY AND SET THE MINIMUM WAGE AT $5 A DAY. FORD DEVELOPED THE V-8 ENGINE IN 1932, A FEATURE LATER ADOPTED BY OTHER AUTOMOBILE MAKERS.
I CAN BUILD ONE BOMBER AN HOUR!
MY MUSEUM EXHIBITS MAN'S PROGRESS IN THE FIELDS OF SCIENCE, INVENTION, HANDICRAFT, TRANSPORTATION, MANUFACTURING AND AGRICULTURE.
WHEN THE U.S. ENTERED WORLD WAR II, HE ANNOUNCED THAT HE WOULD BUILD A PLANT WHICH COULD PRODUCE ONE BOMBER AN HOUR. HE BUILT THE WILLOW RUN, MICH., PLANT, THE LARGEST AIRCRAFT ASSEMBLY PLANT IN THE WORLD, AND PRODUCED B-24 LIBERATORS UNTIL THE END OF THE WAR.
KERN
FORD ESTABLISHED GREENFIELD VILLAGE IN DEARBORN, MICH., A GROUP OF AMERICAN HISTORICAL BUILDINGS AND LANDMARKS. HE ALSO FOUNDED THE EDISON INSTITUTE SCHOOL AND THE HENRY FORD MUSEUM IN DEARBORN. STOCK AND LARGE SUMS OF MONEY WERE GIVEN TO THE FORD FOUNDATION.

1864-1946
Alfred Stieglitz
AMERICAN PHOTOGRAPHER, EDITOR, ART COLLECTOR AND ART GALLERY DIRECTOR
STIEGLITZ HAD A KEEN EYE FOR BEAUTY.
HE WAS BORN IN HOBOKEN, N.J.
STIEGLITZ WAS EDUCATED AT THE COLLEGE OF THE CITY OF NEW YORK AND THE UNIVERSITY OF BERLIN. HE SETTLED IN NEW YORK AND WORKED AS A PHOTO-ENGRAVER FOR 3 YRS. FROM 1893-96 HE WAS EDITOR OF "AMERICAN AMATEUR PHOTOGRAPHER." HE WAS THE FOUNDER, WITH EDWARD STEICHEN, OF THE PHOTO-SECESSION, AN ORGANIZATION TO PROMOTE PHOTOGRAPHY AS AN ART FORM. FROM 1905-46 HE OPERATED A GALLERY IN NEW YORK WHERE HE EXHIBITED THE PAINTINGS OF GEORGIA O'KEEFFE, JOHN MARIN AND OTHERS. AS AN ART DEALER HE IS CREDITED WITH FIRST BRINGING MODERNISM TO AMERICAN ART. STIEGLITZ WAS INSTRUMENTAL IN CREATING PUBLIC ACCEPTANCE OF DEVELOPMENTS IN ART AND PHOTOGRAPHY.
I TRIED A DIFFERENT METHOD OF PHOTOGRAPHING YOUR WIFE. HOW DO LIKE IT?
GREAT!
WE OWE MUCH TO STIEGLITZ FOR THIS SPLENDID DISPLAY.
HE WAS WORLD FAMOUS FOR HIS PHOTOGRAPHS, PARTICULARLY FOR HIS UNUSUAL PORTRAITS. HE WROTE MANY ARTICLES ON PHOTOGRAPHY FOR TECHNICAL AND ART MAGAZINES.
STIEGLITZ WAS THE FIRST IN THE UNITED STATES TO PUT FRENCH POST-IMPRESSIONIST PAINTINGS ON EXHIBIT.
KERN

1865-1923

Warren G. Harding

NEWSPAPERMAN, U.S. SENATOR AND ***TWENTY-NINTH*** PRESIDENT OF THE UNITED STATES (1921-23)

THIS IS A FINE HARD-HITTING EDITORIAL.
THE MARION STAR

HARDING ATTENDED RURAL SCHOOL, THEN WENT TO OHIO CENTRAL COLLEGE, GRADUATING IN 1882. HE WAS 18 YRS. OLD WHEN HE MOVED TO MARION, OHIO, WITH HIS FAMILY AND WORKED FOR THE LOCAL "DEMOCRATIC MIRROR" FOR $1.00 A WEEK. ***HARDING AND A FRIEND BOUGHT THE "MARION STAR" FOR $300 AND MADE IT INTO A SUCCESSFUL DAILY PAPER. PERSUADED TO ENTER POLITICS, HE SERVED AS A STATE SENATOR, LIEUTENANT GOVERNOR, AND IN 1914 WAS ELECTED TO THE U.S. SENATE. IN 1920 HE WAS NOMINATED BY A SMALL GROUP OF SENATORS WHO MANEUVERED TO NOMINATE HIM ON THE 10th. BALLOT. THE AMERICAN PEOPLE ELECTED HARDING AND COOLIDGE BY AN OVERWHELMING MAJORITY.***

HE WAS BORN IN CORSICA, OHIO.

YOU BETRAYED ME, ALBERT, WHEN I GAVE YOU AUTHORITY OVER OIL LEASES.

THIS SORT OF THING IS BAD FOR OUR COUNTRY.
OIL SCANDAL SEC. FALL INVOLVED

DURING HIS TERM IN OFFICE ***THE TEAPOT DOME OIL SCANDAL OCCURRED, THE U.S. SIGNED A PEACE TREATY WITH GERMANY, AUSTRIA AND HUNGARY, THE NATIONAL BUDGET SYSTEM WAS ESTABLISHED, THE LINCOLN MEMORIAL WAS DEDICATED AND THE WASHINGTON ARMS LIMITATION CONFERENCE TOOK PLACE.***

IN 1923 CORRUPTION ROCKED HIS ADMINISTRATION INVOLVING MANY OF HIS APPOINTEES. ***THE WORST SCANDAL INVOLVED ALBERT B. FALL, SEC. OF INTERIOR, WHO HAD ACCEPTED LARGE SUMS OF MONEY FROM PRIVATE FIRMS INVOLVING GOV. OIL LEASES. HARDING DIED SUDDENLY JULY 28, 1923, BEFORE THE SENATE INVESTIGATING COMMITTEE COULD GATHER MATERIAL WHICH MIGHT HAVE RESULTED IN HIS IMPEACHMENT.***

KERN

1865 - 1923

Charles P. Steinmetz

GERMAN-AMERICAN MATHEMATICIAN AND
ELECTRICAL ENGINEER

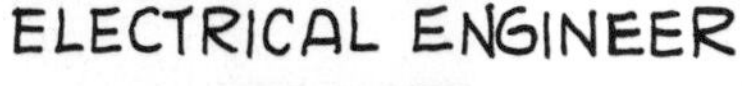

THE FREQUENCY OF ALTERNATING CURRENT IS THE NUMBER OF CYCLES IN A SECOND.

HE WAS BORN IN BRESLAU, GERMANY.

IN 1888 STEINMETZ FLED FROM GERMANY JUST BEFORE RECEIVING HIS PH.D. FROM BRESLAU UNIVERSITY, BECAUSE HE WAS THREATENED WITH ARREST FOR STUDENT SOCIAL ACTIVITY. IN 1889 HE CAME TO THE U.S. AND TAUGHT ELECTRICITY AT UNION COLLEGE IN SCHENECTADY, N.Y. ***HE WAS OFFERED A JOB WITH THE NEWLY FOUNDED GENERAL ELECTRIC CO. WHERE HE SPENT HIS ENTIRE CAREER DOING RESEARCH. FROM HIS LABORATORY, WHERE HE LIVED AND WORKED FOR SOME YEARS, CAME MANY INVENTIONS AND EXPERIMENTAL DISCOVERIES. STEINMETZ WAS ACTIVELY CONCERNED WITH SOCIAL PROBLEMS. HE BELIEVED THAT PRIVATE OWNERSHIP WOULD EVENTUALLY YIELD TO GOVERNMENT OWNERSHIP UNDER PRIVATE MANAGEMENT.***

HERE'S YOUR PROBLEM, TOM.

A-C CAN BE SENT LONG DISTANCES WITH MUCH LESS LOSS OF POWER THAN DIRECT CURRENT.

HE IS BEST KNOWN FOR HIS RESEARCH IN THE FIELD OF ELECTRICITY. HIS EXPERIMENTS CONTRIBUTED GREATLY TO THE USE OF ELECTRICITY AS AN INDUSTRIAL SOURCE OF POWER AND LIGHT. HE BUILT A GENERATOR FOR PRODUCING LIGHTNING ARTIFICIALLY.

KERN

STEINMETZ WAS BROUGHT UP IN POVERTY, POLITICAL MISFORTUNE AND A PHYSICAL DEFORMITY WHICH MADE HIM A CRIPPLE FOR LIFE. ***ALL OF THESE THINGS DID NOT PREVENT HIM FROM BECOMING A SCIENTIFIC GENIUS!***

1865 - 1946

Gifford Pinchot

STATESMAN AND CONSERVATIONIST

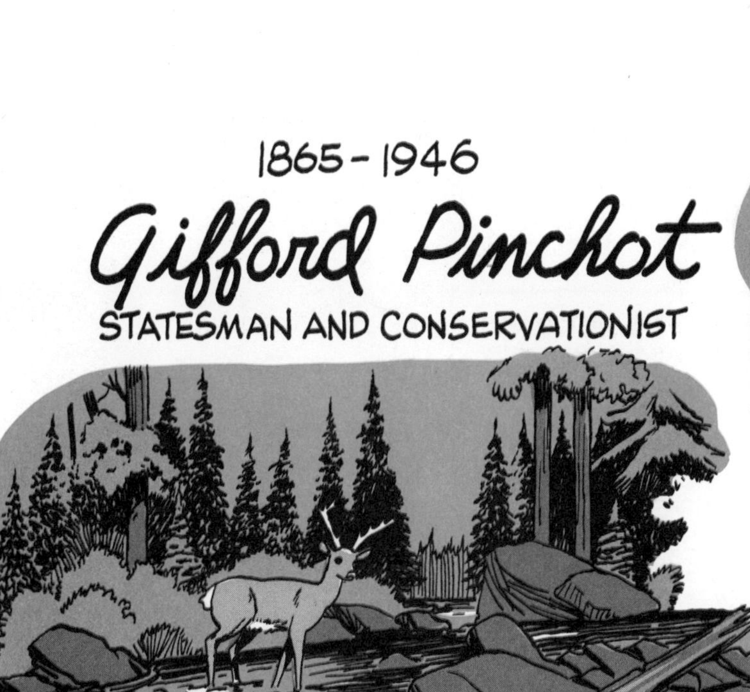

HE GRADUATED FROM YALE UNIVERSITY AND STUDIED FORESTRY IN MANY EUROPEAN COUNTRIES. IN 1890, ***HE BEGAN THE FIRST SYSTEMATIC FORESTRY WORK IN THE U.S. AT BILTMORE, N.C. FROM 1898 - 1910 PINCHOT SERVED AS CHIEF OF THE DIVISION OF FORESTRY OF THE U.S. DEPT. OF AGRICULTURE. HE WAS ELECTED PRESIDENT OF THE NATIONAL CONSERVATION COMMITTEE. HE FOUNDED THE PINCHOT SCHOOL OF FORESTRY AT YALE UNIVERSITY, WHERE HE TAUGHT FOR MANY YEARS. DURING WORLD WAR I HE WAS A MEMBER OF THE U.S. FOOD ADMINISTRATION. PINCHOT WAS ONE OF THE FIRST PERSONS TO ADVOCATE PLANNED CONSERVATION OF AMERICA'S FORESTS.***

HE WAS BORN IN SIMSBURY, CONN.

YOU WERE VERY UNFAIR TO MY SEC. OF INTERIOR!

SORRY, MR. PRESIDENT, I STILL THINK I AM RIGHT.

WE MUST SETTLE. THE PEOPLE NEED COAL.

FROM 1923-27 HE WAS GOVERNOR OF PENNSYLVANIA, THEN AGAIN FROM 1931-35. ***PINCHOT WAS FRIENDLY TO LABOR AND HELPED SETTLE THE GREAT COAL STRIKE OF 1923.***

KERN

WHILE CHIEF OF FORESTRY UNDER PRES. TAFT, PINCHOT FILED CHARGES AGAINST THE SEC. OF INTERIOR, ACCUSING HIM OF ABANDONING THE CONSERVATION POLICIES INSTITUTED DURING THE PRESIDENCY OF THEODORE ROOSEVELT. ***PRES. TAFT UPHELD HIS SEC. OF INTERIOR AND DISMISSED PINCHOT FOR INSUBORDINATION.***

1867-1912
Wilbur Wright

THEY BUILT THEIR FIRST POWER-DRIVEN HEAVIER-THAN-AIR MACHINE AND FLEW IT AT KITTY HAWK N.C., DEC. 17, 1903. ORVILLE PILOTED THE PLANE. ***HE FLEW 120 FT. WILBUR FLEW IT 852 FT. AND STAYED IN THE AIR 59 SECONDS, AT A SPEED OF ABOUT 6.8 MILES AN HOUR.***

BOTH BOYS WENT TO HIGH SCHOOL, WILBUR AT RICHMOND, IND. AND ORVILLE AT DAYTON. EACH FAILED TO GET THEIR DIPLOMAS AS THEY DIDN'T BOTHER TO GO TO COMMENCEMENT EXCERCISES. IN 1893 THE BROTHERS STARTED THE WRIGHT CYCLE CO., MAKING THEIR LIVING SELLING AND REPAIRING BICYCLES. THEIR INTERESTS TURNED TO FLYING AND AFTER A SERIES OF EXPERIMENTS THEY FINALLY CAME UP WITH A STABILIZING MECHANISM THAT SOLVED THE PROBLEMS OF CONTROLLING BALANCE IN FLIGHT.

AMERICAN INVENTORS WHO BUILT THE FIRST SUCCESSFUL AIRPLANE

1871-1948
Orville Wright

IN 1909 THEY DESIGNED A BIPLANE WHICH WAS ACCEPTED BY THE WAR DEPT. ***WILBUR AND ORVILLE RECEIVED MANY HONORS, INCLUDING AN AWARD FROM THE U.S. CONGRESS AND THE LANGLEY MEDAL OF THE SMITHSONIAN INSTITUTE IN 1910. THEIR ORIGINAL PLANE IS IN THE NAT'L MUSEUM IN WASHINGTON, D.C.***

1868-1944

William Allen White

AMERICAN JOURNALIST AND AUTHOR

WHITE WENT TO EMPORIA COLLEGE AND THE UNIVERSITY OF KANSAS. AT 22 HE LEFT COLLEGE AND WORKED ON NEWSPAPERS THROUGHOUT KANSAS. IN 1895 HE RETURNED TO EMPORIA AND BECAME ***EDITOR AND OWNER OF THE "GAZETTE." HIS EDITORIAL, "WHAT'S THE MATTER WITH KANSAS?" MADE HIM NATIONALLY FAMOUS. THIS ARTICLE WAS USED BY THE REPUBLICAN PARTY IN THE CAMPAIGN TO ELECT WILLIAM McKINLEY PRESIDENT OF THE UNITED STATES. WHITE'S EDITORIALS PLAYED AN IMPORTANT PART IN THE POLITICAL AFFAIRS OF OUR NATION, AS WELL AS PORTRAYING LIFE IN A MIDWESTERN TOWN WITH DEEP VISION AND A BROAD HUMAN OUTLOOK.***

HE WAS BORN IN EMPORIA, KAN.
THIS WHITE CAN SURE WRITE EDITORIALS.
EMPORIA GAZETTE

WE MUST BE PREPARED FOR ANY EVENTUALITY.

IN 1940 HE ORGANIZED THE COMMITTEE TO DEFEND AMERICA BY AIDING THE ALLIES, WHICH GREATLY INFLUENCED THE PREPAREDNESS MEASURES OF THE GOVERNMENT ***PRIOR TO THE JAPANESE ATTACK ON PEARL HARBOR.***

HE WAS KNOWN AS ***"THE SAGE OF EMPORIA." HIS SMALL TOWN WEEKLY NEWSPAPER, "THE EMPORIA GAZETTE," BECAME ONE OF THE MOST FAMOUS PAPERS IN THE WORLD. IN 1923 HE WON THE PULITZER PRIZE FOR HIS EDITORIALS AND IN 1947 HE WAS AWARDED A POSTHUMOUS PULITZER PRIZE FOR HIS AUTOBIOGRAPHY.***

KERN

1869-1959

Frank Lloyd Wright

ONE OF AMERICA'S MOST IMAGINATIVE AND INFLUENTIAL ARCHITECTS

THIS COUNTRY IS READY FOR NEW ARCHITECTURAL DESIGNS.

AFTER STUDYING CIVIL ENGINEERING AT THE UNIVERSITY OF WISCONSIN, HE WORKED IN THE ARCHITECTURAL FIRM OF ADLER AND SULLIVAN IN CHICAGO IN 1888. **HE OPENED HIS OWN OFFICE IN 1894. HE DESIGNED NEARLY 800 BUILDINGS DURING HIS CAREER. HE WAS THE FIRST TO BREAK AWAY FROM THE VICTORIAN STYLE OF ARCHITECTURE AND DEVELOP A STYLE WHICH WAS FUNCTIONAL. ONE OF WRIGHT'S BEST KNOWN WORKS IS THE IMPERIAL HOTEL IN TOKYO, JAPAN (1916-22). THIS ENGINEERING TRIUMPH CAME THROUGH UNHARMED IN THE 1923 EARTHQUAKE WHICH DESTROYED MOST OF TOKYO. ONCE IN COURT HE ADMITTED HE WAS THE WORLD'S GREATEST ARCHITECT. "I WAS UNDER OATH," HE EXPLAINED LATER.**

HE WAS BORN IN RICHLAND CENTER, WISCONSIN.

KAUFMAN HOUSE

OTHER FAMOUS BUILDINGS DESIGNED BY WRIGHT INCLUDE TWO BUILDINGS FOR **THE JOHNSON WAX CO. AT RACINE, WIS., AND THE GUGGENHEIM MUSEUM IN NEW YORK CITY.**

KERN

HIS "PRAIRIE HOUSE" DESIGNS BEFORE WORLD WAR I BEGAN A MIDWESTERN TREND IN RESIDENTIAL ARCHITECTURE, **PROVIDING OPEN SPACE AND ALLOWING MORE NATURAL LIGHT. CHICAGO'S ROBIE HOUSE IS THE MOST FAMOUS OF THESE. IN 1936 HE DESIGNED THE BEAUTIFUL KAUFMAN HOUSE NEAR PITTSBURGH, PA. THIS DESIGN WAS KNOWN AS FAR-OUT ARCHITECTURE.**

1872 - 1933

Calvin Coolidge

GOVERNOR, VICE-PRESIDENT AND **THIRTIETH** PRESIDENT OF THE UNITED STATES (1923-29)

HE WAS BORN IN PLYMOUTH NOTCH, VERMONT.
DURING HIS ADMINISTRATION **THE SOLDIERS BONUS BILL WAS PASSED, THE U.S. MARINES LANDED IN NICARAGUA TO PROTECT AMERICAN INTERESTS, LINDBERGH MADE HIS SOLO FLIGHT FROM NEW YORK TO PARIS, AND TRANSATLANTIC RADIO TELEPHONE SERVICE BEGAN.**

I AM GOING TO SAY THIS JUST ONCE. CUT GOVERNMENT SPENDING TO THE BONE!

IN 1895 COOLIDGE GRADUATED "CUM LAUDE" FROM AMHERST COLLEGE. IN 1897 HE WAS ADMITTED TO THE MASSACHUSETTS BAR. HE BECAME ACTIVE IN THE REPUBLICAN PARTY, AND DESPITE HIS RESERVE CONTINUED TO WIN MANY POLITICAL ELECTIONS, BECOMING GOVERNOR OF MASSACHUSETTS AND VICE-PRESIDENT WITH WARREN G. HARDING. **COOLIDGE BECAME THE FIRST VICE-PRESIDENT TO ATTEND CABINET MEETINGS. WHEN HARDING SUDDENLY DIED, COOLIDGE BECAME PRESIDENT AND WAS SWORN IN BY HIS FATHER WHO WAS A NOTARY PUBLIC. "SILENT CAL," AS HE WAS KNOWN, BROUGHT FRUGALITY TO GOVERNMENT AND REDUCED THE NATIONAL DEBT BY MORE THAN A BILLION DOLLARS A YR. IN 1924 HE WAS NOMINATED BY THE REPUBLICANS AND WON BY A BIG MARGIN.**

THERE YOU ARE, GENTLEMEN.

AT A NEWS CONFERENCE IN 1927 COOLIDGE HANDED EACH NEWSMAN A NOTE SAYING, **"I DO NOT CHOOSE TO RUN FOR PRESIDENT IN 1928." HE DIDN'T EVEN COME TO THE 1928 CONVENTION AND RETIRED IN 1929.**

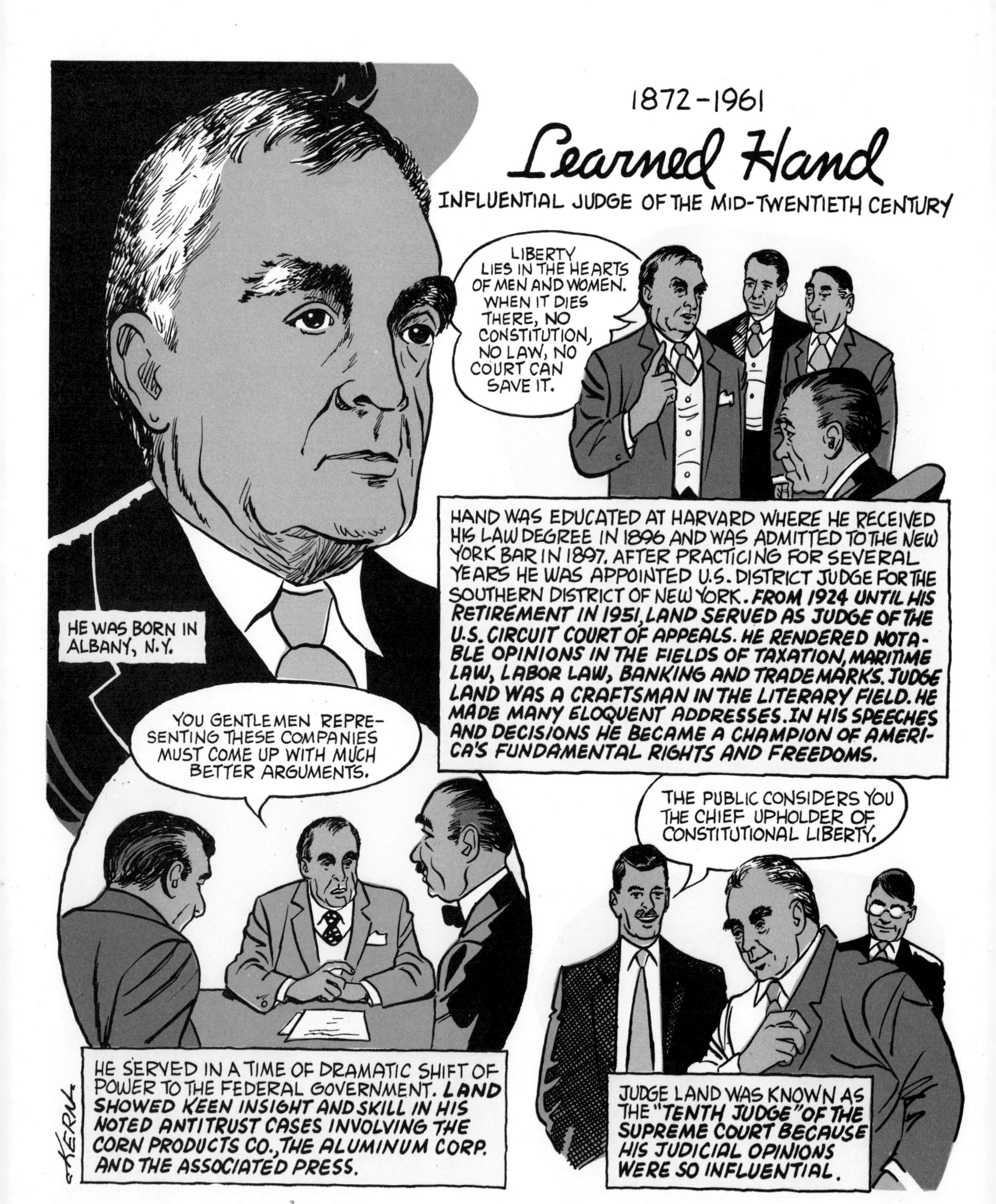
1872-1961
Learned Hand
INFLUENTIAL JUDGE OF THE MID-TWENTIETH CENTURY
LIBERTY LIES IN THE HEARTS OF MEN AND WOMEN. WHEN IT DIES THERE, NO CONSTITUTION, NO LAW, NO COURT CAN SAVE IT.
HE WAS BORN IN ALBANY, N.Y.
HAND WAS EDUCATED AT HARVARD WHERE HE RECEIVED HIS LAW DEGREE IN 1896 AND WAS ADMITTED TO THE NEW YORK BAR IN 1897. AFTER PRACTICING FOR SEVERAL YEARS HE WAS APPOINTED U.S. DISTRICT JUDGE FOR THE SOUTHERN DISTRICT OF NEW YORK. FROM 1924 UNTIL HIS RETIREMENT IN 1951, LAND SERVED AS JUDGE OF THE U.S. CIRCUIT COURT OF APPEALS. HE RENDERED NOTABLE OPINIONS IN THE FIELDS OF TAXATION, MARITIME LAW, LABOR LAW, BANKING AND TRADEMARKS. JUDGE LAND WAS A CRAFTSMAN IN THE LITERARY FIELD. HE MADE MANY ELOQUENT ADDRESSES. IN HIS SPEECHES AND DECISIONS HE BECAME A CHAMPION OF AMERICA'S FUNDAMENTAL RIGHTS AND FREEDOMS.
YOU GENTLEMEN REPRESENTING THESE COMPANIES MUST COME UP WITH MUCH BETTER ARGUMENTS.
THE PUBLIC CONSIDERS YOU THE CHIEF UPHOLDER OF CONSTITUTIONAL LIBERTY.
HE SERVED IN A TIME OF DRAMATIC SHIFT OF POWER TO THE FEDERAL GOVERNMENT. LAND SHOWED KEEN INSIGHT AND SKILL IN HIS NOTED ANTITRUST CASES INVOLVING THE CORN PRODUCTS CO., THE ALUMINUM CORP. AND THE ASSOCIATED PRESS.
JUDGE LAND WAS KNOWN AS THE "TENTH JUDGE" OF THE SUPREME COURT BECAUSE HIS JUDICIAL OPINIONS WERE SO INFLUENTIAL.
KERN

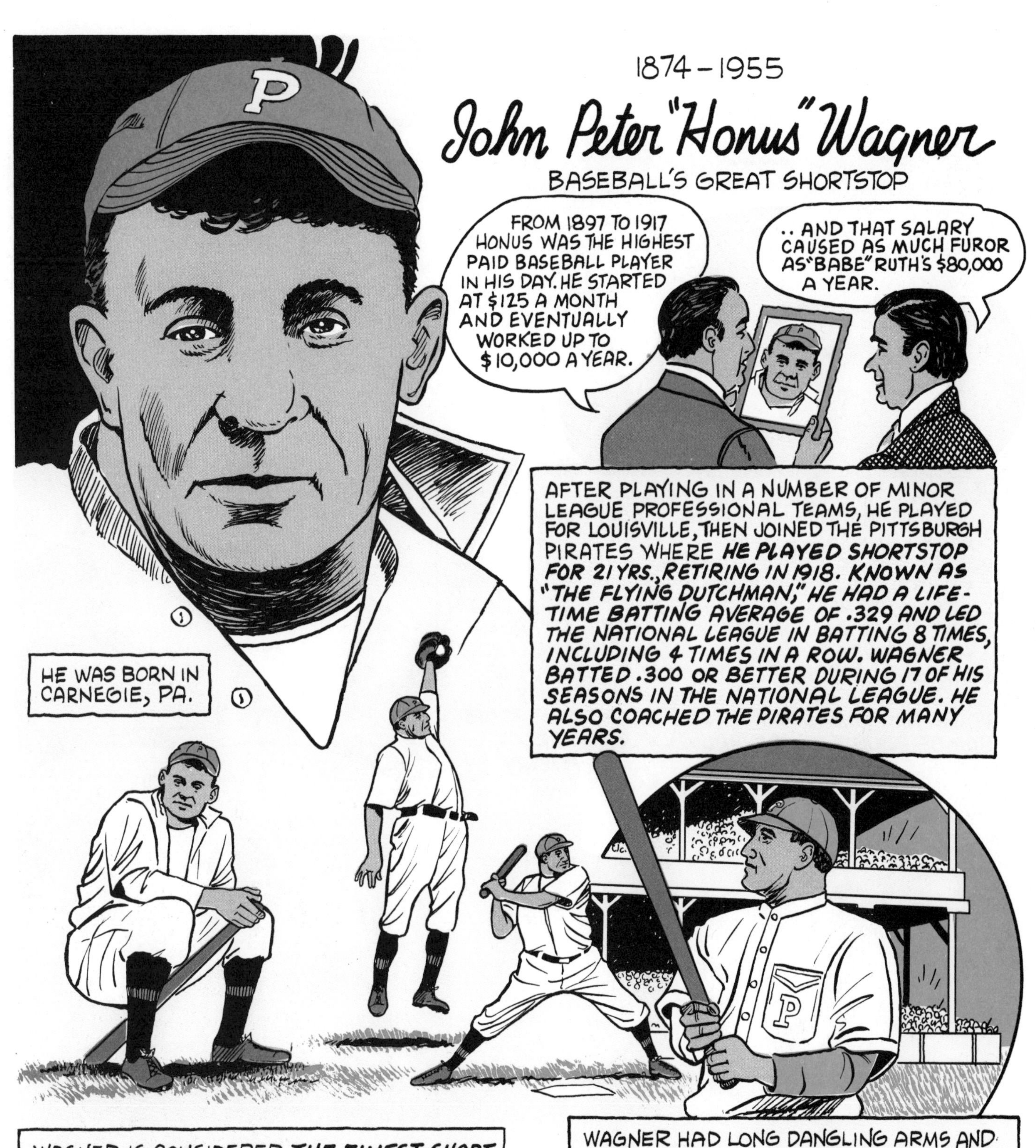
1874-1955
John Peter "Honus" Wagner
BASEBALL'S GREAT SHORTSTOP
FROM 1897 TO 1917 HONUS WAS THE HIGHEST PAID BASEBALL PLAYER IN HIS DAY. HE STARTED AT $125 A MONTH AND EVENTUALLY WORKED UP TO $10,000 A YEAR.
.. AND THAT SALARY CAUSED AS MUCH FUROR AS "BABE" RUTH'S $80,000 A YEAR.
AFTER PLAYING IN A NUMBER OF MINOR LEAGUE PROFESSIONAL TEAMS, HE PLAYED FOR LOUISVILLE, THEN JOINED THE PITTSBURGH PIRATES WHERE HE PLAYED SHORTSTOP FOR 21 YRS., RETIRING IN 1918. KNOWN AS "THE FLYING DUTCHMAN," HE HAD A LIFE-TIME BATTING AVERAGE OF .329 AND LED THE NATIONAL LEAGUE IN BATTING 8 TIMES, INCLUDING 4 TIMES IN A ROW. WAGNER BATTED .300 OR BETTER DURING 17 OF HIS SEASONS IN THE NATIONAL LEAGUE. HE ALSO COACHED THE PIRATES FOR MANY YEARS.
HE WAS BORN IN CARNEGIE, PA.
WAGNER IS CONSIDERED THE FINEST SHORT-STOP IN BASEBALL HISTORY AND PROBABLY WAS THE GREATEST ALL-AROUND PLAYER. HE STOLE 61 BASES IN 1907 AND LED THE LEAGUE IN STOLEN BASES 5 TIMES. HE WAS UNSURPASSED AS A FIELDER.
KERN
WAGNER HAD LONG DANGLING ARMS AND HUGE HANDS. HIS LEGS WERE BOWED BUT NO ONE COULD GET A BASEBALL THROUGH THEM. DURING HIS CAREER HE PLAYED IN 2,785 GAMES. HE WAS ELECTED TO THE NATIONAL BASEBALL HALL OF FAME IN 1936.

1874 - 1963

Robert Lee Frost

ONE OF AMERICA'S FOREMOST POETS

THE LAND WAS OURS BEFORE WE WERE THE LAND'S. SHE WAS OUR LAND MORE THAN A HUNDRED YEARS BEFORE WE WERE HER PEOPLE.

FROST WENT TO DARTMOUTH COLLEGE AND HARVARD UNIVERSITY BUT DIDN'T EARN HIS DEGREE. HE WROTE POETRY AS A YOUNG BOY, BUT NOTHING WAS PUBLISHED UNTIL HE WAS 39. IN 1913-14 "A BOY'S WILL" AND "NORTH OF BOSTON" WERE PUBLISHED IN LONDON. THEY CONTAIN TWO FAMOUS POEMS, "MENDING WALL" AND "THE DEATH OF THE HIRED MAN." HE RETURNED TO THE U.S. FROM ENGLAND AND FOUND HE HAD BECOME FAMOUS. FROST BECAME A LECTURER AT AMHERST COLLEGE, THE UNIVERSITY OF MICHIGAN AND THE UNIVERSITY OF VERMONT. FROM 1939 TO 1941 HE SERVED AS A PROFESSOR OF POETRY AT HARVARD UNIVERSITY. FROST TRAVELED TO MANY CITIES READING HIS POETRY. IN 1961 HE READ "THE GIFT OUTRIGHT" AT JOHN F. KENNEDY'S INAUGURATION.

HE WAS BORN IN SAN FRANCISCO, CALIFORNIA.

CONGRATULATIONS! YOUR PROSE READS LIKE POETRY.

I AM AN OPTIMIST BUT FIRST I ACCEPT HARD FACTS AND SEE HUMAN LIFE AS DIFFICULT.

FROST WON THE PULITZER PRIZE FOR POETRY FOUR TIMES: "NEW HAMPSHIRE" IN 1924, "COLLECTED POEMS" IN 1931, "A FURTHER RANGE" IN 1937, AND "A WITNESS TREE" IN 1943. OTHER WORKS ARE "THE ROAD NOT TAKEN," "BIRCHES" AND "STOPPING BY WOODS ON A SNOWY EVENING."

KERN

IN 1950 THE CONGRESS OF THE U.S. VOTED HIM AN AWARD FOR HIS CONTRIBUTIONS TO AMERICAN THOUGHT AND WISDOM AND HIS WORD PICTURES OF THE AMERICAN PEOPLE. HIS POETRY CONTAINS GREAT INSIGHT AND SLY HUMOR.

1874 - 1964

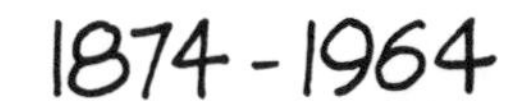

Herbert Hoover

ENGINEER, SEC. OF COMMERCE AND *THIRTY-FIRST* PRESIDENT OF THE UNITED STATES (1929-33)

I NEED YOUR HELP, HERBERT.
I AM ALWAYS HAPPY TO SERVE.

HE WAS BORN IN WEST BRANCH, IOWA.

HOOVER GRADUATED FROM STANFORD UNIVERSITY WITH A DEGREE IN ENGINEERING. HE WAS A MANAGER OF GOLD MINING OPERATIONS IN AUSTRALIA, SUPERVISOR OF ENGINEERING PROJECTS IN MANY COUNTRIES, INCLUDING CHINA AND AUSTRALIA, CHAIRMAN OF THE COMMISSION FOR RELIEF IN BELGIUM AND U.S. FOOD ADMINISTRATOR. ***IN 1921 PRES. HARDING APPOINTED HIM SEC. OF COMMERCE. THIS POST PREPARED HIM TO FACE BROADER PROBLEMS OF THE ECONOMIC DEPRESSION HE HAD TO COPE WITH DURING HIS PRESIDENCY. AFTER HE LEFT THE PRESIDENCY, HOOVER WAS APPOINTED BY PRES. TRUMAN TO HEAD VARIOUS GOVERNMENT COMMISSIONS. PRES. EISENHOWER APPOINTED HIM TO HEAD A COMMISSION TO REORGANIZE THE FEDERAL GOVERNMENT. PRES. HOOVER WAS AN EXCELLENT EXECUTIVE, A GREAT HUMANITARIAN AND A SKILLFUL BUSINESSMAN. HE SPENT HIS LAST YEARS WRITING BOOKS AND LECTURING.***

LET'S HAVE A HOLIDAY FROM REPARATIONS AND WAR DEBTS FOR ONE YEAR.

WHILE HOOVER WAS PRESIDENT ***THE 20th AMENDMENT TO THE CONSTITUTION WAS ADOPTED, THE FEDERAL FARM BOARD WAS ESTABLISHED, THE MORATORIUM ON WAR DEBTS WAS DECLARED, MANCHURIA WAS INVADED BY JAPAN, AND THE RECONSTRUCTION FINANCE CORP. WAS SET UP.***

THIS DEPRESSION IS TEMPORARY. PROSPERITY IS "JUST AROUND THE CORNER."

KERN

MANY PEOPLE THINK THAT HOOVER WAS A GREAT PRESIDENT WHO IS UNFAIRLY JUDGED BECAUSE ***THE GREAT DEPRESSION OCCURRED DURING HIS ADMINISTRATION.***

1875-1948
D. W. Griffith
PIONEER AMERICAN MOTION PICTURE DIRECTOR AND PRODUCER
"THE BIRTH OF A NATION" WAS AN EPIC OF THE CIVIL WAR.
GRIFFITH ATTENDED THE UNIVERSITY OF KENTUCKY, THEN BECAME AN ACTOR AND MANAGER OF COMPANIES PRODUCING ROAD SHOWS. IN 1913 HE BECAME AN INDEPENDENT PRODUCER. HIS 1915 PRODUCTION OF "THE BIRTH OF A NATION" WAS THE FIRST FULL LENGTH FEATURE MOTION PICTURE AND IS A CINEMATIC MASTERPIECE. GRIFFITH'S FILMS ESTABLISHED HIM AS A LEADING PRODUCER OF HIS TIME. HE IS CREDITED WITH THE DEVELOPMENT OF MANY UNIQUE METHODS OF CINEMATOGRAPHY. HIS PICTURES CONTAINED POWERFUL DRAMATIC SITUATIONS AND VIVID CHARACTERS, PRODUCED WITH NEW TECHNICAL DEVICES.
HE WAS BORN IN LA GRANGE, KY.
I FEEL THAT THIS WILL BE A LASTING ASSOCIATION.
IN 1919, GRIFFITH, ALONG WITH DOUGLAS FAIRBANKS, MARY PICKFORD AND CHARLES CHAPLIN, FORMED THE UNITED ARTISTS CORP. TO PRODUCE FEATURE PICTURES. THE BEST OF HIS TALKING PICTURES WAS "ABRAHAM LINCOLN," MADE IN 1930.
GET A CLOSE-UP, JIM.
GRIFFITH IS CREDITED WITH ORIGINATING SUCH DEVICES FOR MOTION PICTURES AS THE FLASHBACK, THE CLOSE-UP AND THE FADE-OUT.
KERN

1875–1955

Mary McLeod Bethune

DISTINGUISHED AMERICAN EDUCATOR AND HUMANITARIAN

IF I HAVE A LEGACY TO LEAVE TO MY PEOPLE, IT IS MY PHILOSOPHY OF LIVING AND SERVING.

SHE WAS BORN IN MAYESVILLE, S.C.

SHE WAS THE 15 th OF 17 CHILDREN BORN TO PARENTS WHO HAD BEEN SLAVES. WHEN SHE WAS NINE, MISSIONARIES OPENED A FREE SCHOOL TEN MILES FROM HER HOME. MARY WALKED TO SCHOOL EACH DAY, THEN TRIED TO TEACH HER FAMILY THE THINGS SHE HAD LEARNED. ***WITH THE HELP OF WHITE FRIENDS SHE ATTENDED SCOTIA SEMINARY AT CONCORD, N.C., AND THEN ACCEPTED A SCHOLARSHIP TO STUDY AT THE MOODY INSTITUTE IN CHICAGO. IN 1935 SHE FOUNDED THE NATIONAL COUNCIL OF NEGRO WOMEN. DURING WORLD WAR II SHE SERVED AS DIRECTOR OF NEGRO AFFAIRS OF THE NATIONAL YOUTH ADMINISTRATION UNDER PRES. FRANKLIN D. ROOSEVELT. MRS. BETHUNE, WHO WAS CALLED THE FIRST LADY OF THE NEGRO RACE, WAS AWARDED THE SPRINGARN MEDAL IN 1935 FOR HER OUTSTANDING CONTRIBUTIONS TOWARDS IMPROVEMENT OF EDUCATIONAL AND OCCUPATIONAL OPPORTUNITIES.***

60,000 WOMEN WORKED FOR 13 YRS. TO RAISE MONEY FOR THIS STATUE, WHICH COST $500,000. *SHE IS SHOWN HERE HANDING HER LAST WILL AND TESTAMENT TO THE TWO CHILDREN.*

IN COLLEGE MRS. BETHUNE STRESSED BLACK HERITAGE. SHE TAUGHT US TO CELEBRATE OUR OWN HEROINES AND HEROES.

THIS MEMORIAL TO MARY McLEOD BETHUNE IN LINCOLN PARK, WASHINGTON, D.C., COMMEMORATES HER SERVICES TO HER PEOPLE AND THE NATION. ***THIS IS THE FIRST MEMORIAL TO A BLACK AMERICAN OR TO A WOMAN TO BE ERECTED IN A PUBLIC PARK IN OUR NATION'S CAPITAL.***

KERN

IN 1904 SHE FOUNDED THE BETHUNE-COOKMAN COLLEGE AT DAYTONA BEACH, FLORIDA, ***WITH 5 PUPILS AND ONLY $1.50. SHE SERVED AS PRESIDENT UNTIL 1942.***

1876 – 1958

Charles F. Kettering

AMERICAN INVENTOR AND ENGINEER

HE WAS BORN NEAR LOUDONVILLE, OHIO.

THE SLOAN-KETTERING INSTITUTE IS A DEFINITE BENEFIT TO ALL MANKIND.

KETTERING WAS EDUCATED IN WOOSTER COLLEGE AND OHIO STATE UNIVERSITY. BAD EYESIGHT INTERFERED WITH HIS EDUCATION, SO IT WAS 1903 BEFORE HE FINISHED AT OHIO STATE UNIVERSITY. ***HE THEN WORKED AS AN INVENTOR FOR THE NATIONAL CASH REGISTER CO. IN DAYTON, OHIO. WHILE THERE HE INVENTED SEVERAL ACCOUNTING MACHINES. HE RESIGNED TO WORK ON AN AUTOMOBILE IGNITION SYSTEM. THE RESULT WAS THE FIRST ELECTRIC STARTER, WHICH WAS INSTALLED IN A CADILLAC IN FEB. 1911. KETTERING THEN ORGANIZED THE CHARLES F. KETTERING LABORATORIES. IN 1916 THIS CO. WAS MADE PART OF THE GENERAL MOTORS CORP. IN 1947 HE RESIGNED AS VICE-PRESIDENT IN CHARGE OF RESEARCH AT GENERAL MOTORS TO BECOME THEIR RESEARCH CONSULTANT. KETTERING WAS CO-SPONSOR OF THE SLOAN-KETTERING INSTITUTE FOR CANCER RESEARCH FOUNDED IN 1948.***

WITHOUT THIS DEVICE THE ENGINE WOULD TURN THE STARTER TOO FAST AND RUIN IT.

BESIDES DEVELOPING THE ***SELF STARTER. HE DEVELOPED THE DELCO FARM LIGHT SYSTEM, ODORLESS, NONTOXIC AND NONFLAMMABLE REFRIGERANTS, ETHYL GASOLINE, QUICK-DRYING LACQUER, A TWO-CYCLE DIESEL ENGINE FOR TRAINS AND A HIGH COMPRESSION AUTOMOBILE ENGINE.***

WE ARE WORKING ON MANY NEW IDEAS TO DEFEAT THE ENEMY.

KETTERING WAS A MILITARY ADVISOR AND ***CHAIRMAN OF THE NATIONAL INVENTORS COUNCIL DURING WORLD WAR II.***

KERN

HE WAS BORN IN PHILADELPHIA, PA.

JOHN AND ELAINE BARRIE IN "MY DEAR CHILDREN."

JOHN, "THE GREAT PROFILE", WAS THE YOUNGEST BROTHER OF LIONEL AND ETHEL. ***HE PLAYED MANY ROLES ON STAGE, SCREEN AND RADIO. HIS PLAYS INCLUDE "RICHARD III" AND "HAMLET." AMONG HIS MOTION PICTURE SUCCESSES WERE "DON JUAN," "BEAU BRUMMELL" AND "MARIE ANTOINETTE." IN HIS LATER YEARS (1940) HE TURNED TO COMEDY, APPEARING IN THE PLAY "MY DEAR CHILDREN" AND ON RADIO PROGRAMS.***

HE WAS BORN IN LONDON, ENGLAND.

John Barrymore

1882 - 1942

Lionel Barrymore

1878 - 1954

THE BROTHER OF JOHN AND ETHEL, ***LIONEL MADE HIS DEBUT IN THE THEATER IN 1893. HE WON FAME ON THE STAGE, RADIO AND IN MOTION PICTURES. HIS ANNUAL PERFORMANCE AS SCROOGE IN "A CHRISTMAS CAROL" MADE HIM A VERY POPULAR RADIO PERFORMER. HE WAS WELL KNOWN FOR HIS MANY MOTION PICTURES: "A FREE SOUL", "DAVID COPPERFIELD" AND THE "DR. KILDARE" SERIES. LIONEL WAS A DIRECTOR, ARTIST AND COMPOSER. IN HIS LATER YRS. HE WAS CONFINED TO A WHEELCHAIR.***

AS SHE APPEARED IN "ROMEO AND JULIET."

Ethel Barrymore

1879 - 1959

AN OUTSTANDING ACTRESS OF THE AMERICAN STAGE, SISTER TO JOHN AND LIONEL, ***ETHEL STARRED IN MANY PLAYS INCLUDING "A DOLL'S HOUSE," "ROMEO AND JULIET," "THE SECOND MRS. TANQUERAY" AND "THE CORN IS GREEN." SOME OF HER MOTION PICTURE CREDITS WERE "RASPUTIN AND THE EMPRESS" AND "NONE BUT THE LONELY HEART."***

SHE WAS BORN IN PHILADELPHIA, PA.

KERN

1878-1967

Carl Sandburg

AMERICAN POET AND BIOGRAPHER

HERE'S A POEM BY SANDBURG, THE COMMON MAN'S POET.

SANDBURG, THE SON OF A SWEDISH BLACKSMITH, LEFT SCHOOL WHEN HE WAS 13 YRS. OLD. AFTER SERVING IN THE SPANISH-AMERICAN WAR, HE ENTERED LOMBARD COLLEGE IN GALESBURG, WHERE HE STARTED TO WRITE POETRY. **AFTER WORKING WITH THE SOCIALIST PARTY IN MILWAUKEE, HE WENT TO CHICAGO AS AN EDITORIAL WRITER FOR THE "DAILY NEWS." WRITING POETRY IN HIS SPARE TIME, HE SOON FOUND AN AUDIENCE FOR HIS POEMS WHICH WERE PUBLISHED IN "A MAGAZINE OF VERSE." SANDBURG'S WRITINGS WERE ABOUT FARMS, PRAIRIES AND THE HOPES AND SUFFERINGS OF THE COMMON PEOPLE-- THE "DIVINE AVERAGE." HE WAS ALSO WELL KNOWN AS A SINGER AND COLLECTOR OF FOLK SONGS.**

YOUR LINCOLN BIOGRAPHY IS CONSIDERED ONE OF THE BEST OF THIS GENERATION.

THE GREATEST BIOGRAPHY OF THIS GENERATION WAS SANDBURG'S "**ABRAHAM LINCOLN**," WHICH TOOK 20 YRS. TO RESEARCH AND WRITE.

KERN

HE WON THE PULITZER PRIZE **FOR HISTORY IN 1940 FOR "ABRAHAM LINCOLN, THE WAR YEARS." IN 1951 HE AGAIN WON THE PULITZER PRIZE, THIS TIME FOR HIS "COLLECTED POEMS."** SOME OF HIS OTHER FAMOUS BOOKS AND POEMS ARE "**ROOTABAGA STORIES**," "**CHICAGO**," "**CORNHUSKERS**," AND "**SLABS OF THE SUNBURNT WEST.**"

1879 - 1935

Will Rogers

AMERICAN HUMORIST, ACTOR AND AUTHOR

HE WENT TO KEMPER MILITARY ACADEMY IN BOONVILLE, MO., FOR 2 YRS. IN 1898 HE LEFT SCHOOL, BECAME A COWBOY IN THE TEXAS PANHANDLE, AND THEN WENT TO ARGENTINA AND SOUTH AFRICA WHERE HE JOINED ***"TEXAS JACK'S WILD WEST CIRCUS." IN 1905 ROGERS MADE HIS FIRST STAGE APPEARANCE IN NEW YORK, AND FINALLY REACHED FAME IN 1916 WHEN HE APPEARED WITH THE ZIEGFELD FOLLIES. IN 1918 HE ACTED IN MOVIES AND IN 1934 APPEARED IN EUGENE O'NEILL'S STAGE PLAY, "AH, WILDERNESS." ROGERS, A TALENTED WRITER, WROTE NEWS COMMENTS WHICH WERE SYNDICATED BY MORE THAN 350 DAILY NEWSPAPERS. IN 1926 HE WAS PRES. COOLIDGE'S "AMBASSADOR OF GOODWILL" IN EUROPE. IN 1927 HE WROTE "LETTERS OF A SELF-MADE DIPLOMAT TO HIS PRESIDENT."***

HE WAS BORN NEAR OOLOGAH, OKLA.

WE SHOULDN'T ELECT A PRESIDENT, WE SHOULD ELECT A MAGICIAN.

ROGERS AND THE CELEBRATED AVIATOR, WILEY POST, WERE FLYING TO THE ORIENT ***WHEN THEIR PLANE CRASHED AUG. 15, 1935. BOTH WERE KILLED.*** A BRONZE STATUE WAS PLACED IN STATUARY HALL IN THE U.S. CAPITOL, IN ***MEMORY OF WILL ROGERS.***

A NOTED HOMESPUN PHILOSOPHER, HE WAS ALSO REGARDED AS ONE OF THE GREATEST ROPERS OF ALL TIME. ***HE BECAME FAMOUS FOR HIS HOMELY WITTICISMS WHILE PERFORMING.***

I NEVER MET A MAN I DIDN'T LIKE . . .
WILL ROGERS
1879 - 1935

KERN

1879-1955
Albert Einstein
OUTSTANDING GERMAN-AMERICAN PHYSICIST, CALLED THE "FATHER OF THE ATOMIC AGE"
WHEN PACKETS OF LIGHT ENERGY STRIKE METAL THEY FORCE IT TO RELEASE ELECTRONS.
HE WAS BORN IN ULM, GERMANY.
EINSTEIN STUDIED PHYSICS AND MATHEMATICS AT THE SWISS POLYTECHNIC INSTITUTE IN ZURICH, SWITZERLAND, GRADUATING IN 1900. DURING HIS FREE TIME WHILE WORKING FOR THE SWISS PATENT OFFICE IN BERN, HE DID SCIENTIFIC INVESTIGATIONS. ONE RESULT OF HIS WORK WAS THE PHOTO ELECTRIC CELL OR "ELECTRIC EYE" WHICH MADE POSSIBLE MOTION PICTURES AND TELEVISION. IN 1921 HE RECEIVED THE NOBEL PRIZE IN PHYSICS FOR THIS ACHIEVEMENT. HE WORKED OUT THE FAMOUS EQUATION E=MC² (MASS AND ENERGY ARE DIRECTLY RELATED). THIS FORMULA WAS USED TO WORK OUT SOME OF THE BASIC PROBLEMS OF ATOMIC ENERGY. EINSTEIN'S "THE ELECTRODYNAMICS OF MOVING BODIES" EXPLAINED THE SPECIAL THEORY OF RELATIVITY, WHICH REVOLUTIONIZED SCIENTIFIC THOUGHT WITH NEW CONCEPTIONS OF TIME, SPACE, MOTION, MASS AND GRAVITATION. HE LAID THE BASIS FOR SPLITTING THE ATOM.
WE FOLLOWED YOUR THEORY AND IT WILL WORK!
THANK YOU FOR OFFERING ME THE PRESIDENCY OF ISRAEL. I AM NOT FIT FOR SUCH A POSITION.
IN 1933 EINSTEIN CAME TO THE U.S. AND WAS ASSOCIATED WITH PRINCETON'S INSTITUTE OF ADVANCED STUDIES. HIS THEORY ON RELATIVITY MADE NUCLEAR FISSION POSSIBLE, WHICH LED TO THE FIRST ATOMIC BOMB IN 1945.
HE RECEIVED WORLDWIDE RECOGNITION FOR HIS CONTRIBUTION TO MODERN PHYSICS. EINSTEIN HAD AN INTENSE CONCERN FOR HUMANITY. HE DESPISED REGIMENTATION AND MILITARISM IN ANY FORM, ADVOCATING INSTEAD INTELLECTUAL FREEDOM AND PACIFISM.
KERN

1880-1956

Henry L. Mencken

AMERICAN AUTHOR, EDITOR AND CRITIC

THAT WAS AN EXCELLENT COLUMN ON THE PRESIDENT.

MENCKEN STUDIED ENGINEERING AT THE BALTIMORE POLYTECHNIC INSTITUTE. HE BEGAN HIS JOURNALISTIC CAREER AS A REPORTER ON THE BALTIMORE "MORNING HERALD." MOST OF HIS LIFE WAS SPENT AS A REPORTER, EDITOR AND COLUMNIST FOR THE BALTIMORE "SUN" AND LITERARY CRITIC AND COEDITOR FOR "SMART SET" MAGAZINE. WITH DRAMA CRITIC GEORGE JEAN NATHAN MENCKEN FOUNDED THE "AMERICAN MERCURY," A MAGAZINE OF SATIRE AND COMMENT ON POLITICS, AMERICAN LIFE AND CUSTOMS. MENCKEN WAS EDITOR UNTIL 1933. HE GREATLY INFLUENCED AMERICAN WRITING IN THE 1920'S. "BOOBOISIE" WAS THE NAME HE GAVE THE AMERICAN MIDDLE CLASS WHICH WAS A SPECIAL TARGET OF HIS CRITICISM. HE GREATLY ADMIRED LITERARY WORKS THAT SATIRIZED LIFE IN AMERICA.

HE WAS BORN IN BALTIMORE, MD.

NICE WORK, TED. YOU MIGHT REDO THE SECOND PARAGRAPH.

HE HAD GREAT RESPECT FOR AND ENCOURAGED REALISTIC WRITERS LIKE **SINCLAIR LEWIS, EUGENE O'NEILL, SHERWOOD ANDERSON, F. SCOTT FITZGERALD AND THEODORE DREISER.**

I DO NOT APPROVE OF MANY AMERICAN CUSTOMS BUT I HAVE GREAT LOVE FOR THE AMERICAN LANGUAGE.

IN 1918 MENCKEN PUBLISHED "**THE AMERICAN LANGUAGE," A LONG STUDY ON THE HISTORY OF AMERICAN SPEECH. THE BOOK GAINED WORLDWIDE RECOGNITION AND WAS REVISED AND ENLARGED THREE TIMES.**

1880-1959

George C. Marshall

AMERICAN SOLDIER, STATESMAN, SEC. OF STATE AND SEC. OF DEFENSE

WITH YOUR HELP, EISENHOWER AND MAC ARTHUR, AMERICA WILL SUCCEED IN THIS WAR.

MARSHALL ENTERED VIRGINIA MILITARY INSTITUTE BECAUSE THE LOCAL CONGRESSMAN WOULD NOT APPOINT HIM TO WEST POINT. HE GRADUATED IN 1901, AND RECEIVED HIS COMMISSION AS A 2nd LIEUTENANT IN 1902. WHILE AT V.M.I. MARSHALL WAS ALL-SOUTHERN FOOTBALL TACKLE AND SENIOR FIRST CAPTAIN OF THE CADET CORPS. HE SERVED IN THE PHILIPPINES, THEN IN THE U.S. FROM 1903 TO 1913. DURING WORLD WAR I MARSHALL PLANNED AND DIRECTED THE TRANSFER OF A FULLY EQUIPPED FORCE OF 500,000 MEN AND 2,700 GUNS TO THE ARGONNE FRONT IN LESS THAN 2 WEEKS. THIS HAS BEEN CALLED ONE OF THE WAR'S GREATEST ACCOMPLISHMENTS. DURING WORLD WAR II HE WAS RESPONSIBLE FOR TRAINING AND ARMING 8,250,000 MEN INTO ONE OF THE GREATEST FIGHTING FORCES IN HISTORY.

CONGRATULATIONS, GEORGE, FOR THE NEW HONOR AS PRESIDENT OF THE AMERICAN RED CROSS.

THIS WAR WAS THE MOST TERRIBLE TRAGEDY OF THE HUMAN RACE!

IN 1947, WHILE SEC. OF STATE, HE SUGGESTED THE "MARSHALL PLAN" WHICH CALLED FOR BILLIONS OF DOLLARS TO BE SPENT BY THE U.S. TO REBUILD WAR-TORN EUROPE. IN 1953 HE RECEIVED THE NOBEL PEACE PRIZE FOR CARRYING OUT THE PLAN, THE ONLY CAREER SOLDIER TO BE SO HONORED.

©KERN

MARSHALL WAS CHIEF OF STAFF OF THE U.S. ARMY DURING WORLD WAR II. LATER HE SERVED AS SEC. OF STATE AND SEC. OF DEFENSE UNDER PRESIDENT TRUMAN. HE WAS THE FIRST PROFESSIONAL SOLDIER TO SERVE AS SEC. OF STATE.

1880-1964
Douglas MacArthur
GENERAL OF WORLD WAR II AND KOREAN ACTION
MAC ARTHUR BROADCASTS SURRENDER CEREMONIES ABOARD THE BATTLESHIP MISSOURI.
HE GRADUATED FROM THE U.S. MILITARY ACADEMY IN 1903 ON TOP OF HIS CLASS. HE SERVED IN THE PHILIPPINES AND VARIOUS U.S. POSTS UNTIL 1914. DURING WORLD WAR I HE WAS A COLONEL WITH THE FAMOUS "RAINBOW" DIVISION. IN 1918 HE WAS PROMOTED TO BRIGADIER GENERAL; IN 1930, ARMY CHIEF OF STAFF (THE YOUNGEST IN U.S. HISTORY); IN 1941 COMMANDER OF ALL U.S. ARMY FORCES; IN 1942, COMMANDER OF THE ALLIED FORCES IN THE SOUTHWEST PACIFIC. HE OPENED A 3 YR. SUCCESSFUL OFFENSIVE AGAINST THE JAPANESE. IN DEC. 1944, HE BECAME 5-STAR GENERAL AND IN APR. 1945 HE TOOK CHARGE OF ALL AMERICAN ARMY FORCES IN THE PACIFIC. WHEN THE JAPANESE SURRENDERED AUG. 14, 1945, PRES. TRUMAN NAMED MACARTHUR SUPREME COMMANDER FOR THE ALLIED POWERS TO RECEIVE THE SURRENDER.
HE WAS BORN IN LITTLE ROCK, ARK.
CONGRATULATIONS, GENERAL.
I WILL ESTABLISH REFORMS IN GOVERNMENT, EDUCATION AND INDUSTRY WHICH WILL TRANSFORM JAPAN INTO A DEMOCRACY.
IN 1950, AFTER THE OUTBREAK IN HOSTILITIES IN KOREA, HE WAS CHOSEN TO COMMAND THE U.N. FORCES TO FIGHT THE COMMUNISTS. PRES. TRUMAN RELIEVED HIM OF HIS COMMAND BECAUSE HE DID NOT AGREE WITH U.N. POLICIES.
KERN
MAC ARTHUR BRILLIANTLY ADMINISTERED THE OCCUPATION AND REORGANIZATION OF JAPAN. HE IS BEST KNOWN FOR HIS ORGANIZATIONAL AND STRATEGICAL SKILLS.

1880 - 1968

Helen Keller

AMERICAN DEAF AND BLIND AUTHOR AND LECTURER

SHE WAS 19 MONTHS OLD WHEN A SERIOUS ILLNESS DESTROYED HER SIGHT AND HEARING. **UNABLE TO LEARN TO SPEAK, SHE WAS COMPLETELY SHUT OFF FROM THE WORLD. WHEN SHE WAS 7, ANNE SULLIVAN CAME FROM BOSTON TO TEACH HER. SHE WAS ABLE TO MAKE CONTACT WITH HELEN THROUGH THE SENSE OF TOUCH. SHE CREATED AN ALPHABET BY WHICH SHE SPELLED OUT WORDS ON HELEN'S HAND. SLOWLY HELEN WAS ABLE TO CONNECT WORDS WITH OBJECTS. WITHIN 3 YRS. SHE KNEW THE ALPHABET AND COULD READ AND WRITE IN BRAILLE. BY THE TIME SHE WAS 16 SHE COULD SPEAK WELL ENOUGH TO GO TO RADCLIFFE COLLEGE WHERE SHE GRADUATED IN 1904 WITH HONORS. ANNE SULLIVAN STAYED WITH HER THROUGH ALL THESE YRS., INTERPRETING ALL THE LECTURES AND CLASS DISCUSSIONS TO HER. AFTER COLLEGE HELEN DECIDED TO SPEND HER LIFE PROMOTING BETTER CARE FOR THE BLIND. MUCH OF THE MONEY SHE EARNED LECTURING AND WRITING WENT TO CHARITIES FOR THE BLIND.**

WHEN ANNE SULLIVAN DIED IN 1936, POLLY THOMPSON, WHO HAD BEEN HELEN'S SECRETARY, REPLACED HER. **DURING WORLD WAR II HELEN WORKED WITH WAR-BLINDED SOLDIERS.**

SHE WAS BORN IN TUSCUMBIA, ALA.

HELEN WROTE MANY BOOKS AND ARTICLES. HER "**THE STORY OF MY LIFE**" **WAS DEDICATED TO HER LIFELONG FRIEND, DR. ALEXANDER GRAHAM BELL,**" WHO TAUGHT THE DEAF TO SPEAK AND ENABLED THE LISTENING EAR TO HEAR SPEECH." **THE PULITZER-PRIZE WINNING "THE MIRACLE WORKER" IS ABOUT HER LIFE.**

1880 - 1969

John L. Lewis

LABOR LEADER, CO-FOUNDER OF CIO

WE NEED GOOD MEN FOR OUR ORGANIZATIONAL WORK.

· LEWIS WAS 12 YRS. OLD WHEN HE WENT TO WORK AS A MINER. HE THEN TRAVELED ABOUT THE COUNTRY FOR 12 YRS. UNTIL HE MET AND IMPRESSED SAMUEL GOMPERS, PRES. OF THE AMERICAN FEDERATION OF LABOR, WHO GAVE HIM A JOB AS LEGISLATIVE REPRESENTATIVE OF THE UNITED MINE WORKERS. ***FROM 1911 TO 1917 LEWIS WAS AN ORGANIZER FOR THE A.F.L. THEN THE UNITED MINE WORKERS ELECTED HIM VICE-PRESIDENT, AND IN 1920 MADE HIM PRESIDENT. LEWIS FAVORED ORGANIZING WORKERS IN BASIC INDUSTRIES RATHER THAN BY TRADES. IN 1947 HE WAS FINED $10,000 AND THE UNION $3,500,000 FOR HIS DEFIANCE OF A RESTRAINING ORDER ISSUED UNDER THE TAFT-HARTLEY ACT, DIRECTING THE MINERS TO END A STRIKE WHICH CONSTITUTED A THREAT TO PUBLIC WELFARE. HE DIRECTED THE MINERS TO RETURN TO WORK, BUT HE BECAME A BITTER FOE OF THE TAFT-HARTLEY ACT.***

HE WAS BORN IN LUCAS, IOWA.
WE DEMAND THAT CONGRESS DO SOMETHING ABOUT THE LAGGING ECONOMY.

I HAVE THE BACKING OF THE U.M.W. TO PUT MY IDEAS TO WORK.

LEWIS WAS RESPONSIBLE FOR THE REMARKABLE RISE IN THE STANDARD OF LIVING OF MINERS AFTER WORLD WAR I. ***HE BROUGHT ABOUT IMPROVED SAFETY STANDARDS, PENSIONS AND VACATION PAY.***

RECOGNIZED AS ONE OF THE MOST POWERFUL OF AMERICAN LABOR LEADERS, ***LEWIS HAD A STORMY AND CONTROVERSIAL CAREER. HIS CONTROL OVER THE U.M.W. GAVE HIM AN IMPORTANT POSITION IN NATIONAL LABOR RELATIONS AND INFLUENCE OVER THE AMERICAN ECONOMY.***

1881 - 1965

Branch Rickey

NOTED BASEBALL EXECUTIVE

YOU WILL BE INSULTED AND MISTREATED ON THE FIELD, BUT YOU MUST TURN THE OTHER CHEEK. YOU MUST NOT FIGHT BACK!

RICKEY CREATED THE **FIRST MINOR LEAGUE "FARM" TRAINING SYSTEM FOR A MAJOR LEAGUE TEAM WHILE HE WAS GENERAL MANAGER OF THE ST. LOUIS CARDINALS (1919-42), AND DEVELOPED THEM INTO. ONE OF BASEBALL'S MOST POWERFUL DYNASTIES.** IN 1946, WHILE GENERAL MANAGER OF THE BROOKLYN DODGERS, HE SIGNED **JACKIE ROBINSON TO PLAY WITH THE DODGER'S MINOR LEAGUE AT MONTREAL, CANADA. THEN IN 1947 HE SELECTED JACKIE TO BE THE FIRST BLACK IN ORGANIZED MAJOR LEAGUE BASEBALL.**

HE WAS BORN IN STOCKDALE, OHIO.

HE BATTED .311 AND HELPED THE DODGERS **WIN 6 NATIONAL LEAGUE PENNANTS AND THE 1955 WORLD SERIES.**

1919-1972

Jackie Robinson

BLACK BASEBALL PLAYER

JACKIE GREW UP IN CAL. AND ATTENDED UCLA IN LOS ANGELES. **HE WAS THE FIRST UCLA ATHLETE TO WIN 4 LETTERS IN A SINGLE YEAR. HE PLAYED PRO FOOTBALL AND NEGRO LEAGUE PRO BASEBALL. IN 1947 HE JOINED THE BROOKLYN DODGERS AS A SHORTSTOP, BECOMING THE FIRST BLACK PLAYER IN MAJOR LEAGUE BASEBALL. AT FIRST JACKIE HAD TO ENDURE RESENTMENT AND CRUEL REMARKS FROM TEAMMATES, OPPONENTS AND SPECTATORS. EVENTUALLY HE TALKED BACK AND ASSERTED HIS RIGHTS. HE STAYED FOR 10 YEARS.**

IN 1962 HE WAS VOTED INTO THE BASEBALL HALL OF FAME. **ROBINSON FOUGHT CONTINUALLY FOR EQUALITY FOR HIS PEOPLE.**

HE WAS BORN IN CAIRO, GEORGIA.

©KERN

1882–1945

Robert H. Goddard

AMERICAN SCIENTIST, FATHER OF MODERN ROCKETS AND SPACE FLIGHT

IT GIVES ME GREAT PLEASURE TO GIVE YOU THIS CHECK FOR ONE MILLION DOLLARS.

IN HIS MIDTEENS HE BECAME DEDICATED TO ADVANCING THE SCIENCE OF **ROCKETRY AND SPACE TRAVEL. HE WORKED ON THIS WITHOUT LETTING UP ALL HIS LIFE DESPITE RECURRING ILLNESS. GODDARD ATTENDED WORCESTER POLYTECHNICAL INSTITUTE AND CLARK UNIVERSITY. IN 1920 HE PREDICTED THE USE OF ROCKETS TO EXPLORE HIGH ALTITUDES. IN 1926 HE SUCCESSFULLY LAUNCHED THE WORLD'S FIRST LIQUID FUEL ROCKET NEAR WORCESTER. IN 1930 HE FIRED A ROCKET TO A HEIGHT OF 2,000 FT. AT A SPEED OF 500 MI. AN HR. IN 1935, NEAR ROSWELL, NEW MEXICO, HE FIRED THE FIRST ROCKET WHICH WENT FASTER THAN SOUND. DURING WORLD WAR II HE DIRECTED RESEARCH IN JET PROPULSION FOR THE NAVY.**

HE WAS BORN IN WORCESTER, MASS.

THIS LIQUID-FUEL ROCKET IS STABILIZED BY THIS GYRO STEERING APPARATUS.

THERE IT GOES!

GODDARD HAD ABOUT **150 PATENTS TO HIS CREDIT. IN 1960 THE U.S. GOV'T PAID ONE MILLION DOLLARS TO HIS HEIRS IN RECOGNITION OF ITS INFRINGEMENTS ON HIS PATENTED ROCKET INVENTIONS.**

THE EXPERIMENTS HE MADE WITH LIQUID FUEL ROCKETS **MADE INTERCONTINENTAL MISSILES POSSIBLE. HE WAS THE FIRST TO PROVE THAT A ROCKET WORKS IN A VACUUM BETTER THAN IN THE ATMOSPHERE AND HE WAS THE FIRST TO SUGGEST A WAY TO SHOOT A ROCKET AWAY FROM THE EARTH.**

1882 - 1945

Franklin D. Roosevelt

ASSISTANT SEC. OF THE NAVY, GOVERNOR OF NEW YORK AND **THIRTY-SECOND** PRESIDENT OF THE UNITED STATES (1933-45)

I PLEDGE TO LIFT THIS COUNTRY OUT OF THE DEPRESSION AND SET UP ECONOMIC SAFEGUARDS TO PREVENT FUTURE DEPRESSIONS IN THE UNITED STATES.
HE WAS BORN IN HYDE PARK, N.Y.
MY FRIENDS!
AID TO MOTHERS AND CHILDREN, HANDICAPPED, UNEMPLOYED AND AGED.

ROOSEVELT ATTENDED GROTON SCHOOL IN MASS., HARVARD UNIVERSITY AND COLUMBIA UNIVERSITY LAW SCHOOL. HE PASSED THE BAR EXAMINATION IN 1907, BUT SHOWED LITTLE INTEREST IN THE LEGAL PROFESSION. ***HIS POLITICAL CAREER BEGAN AS A STATE SENATOR FROM NEW YORK. IN 1913 WILSON APPOINTED HIM ASS'T SEC. OF THE NAVY WHERE HE DID AN OUTSTANDING JOB. IN 1921 ROOSEVELT WAS CRIPPLED BY AN ATTACK OF POLIO, WHICH LEFT HIM WITHOUT THE USE OF HIS LEGS. THIS HANDICAP DID NOT KEEP HIM FROM BECOMING GOV. OF NEW YORK AND THEN PRESIDENT OF THE U.S. ROOSEVELT ORIGINATED "THE NEW DEAL", AN EMERGENCY APPROACH TO THE GREAT DEPRESSION. HE GUIDED THE U.S. THROUGH WORLD WAR II, BUT DIDN'T LIVE TO SEE FINAL VICTORY. THE PEOPLE OF THE U.S. HONORED HIM BY ELECTING HIM PRESIDENT FOUR TIMES.***

THESE ARE THE PRINCIPLES FOR WHICH THE FREE NATIONS ARE FIGHTING.

ROOSEVELT WILL ALWAYS BE REMEMBERED FOR HIS INSPIRING "***FOUR FREEDOMS***" SPEECH DELIVERED IN 1941. "***FREEDOM OF SPEECH,***" "***FREEDOM OF WORSHIP***" "***FREEDOM FROM WANT***" AND "***FREEDOM FROM FEAR***" WERE AN INSPIRATION TO ALL THE WORLD DURING SOME OF ***HISTORY'S DARKEST WAR YEARS.***

KERN

WHILE PRESIDENT, THE ***TWENTY-FIRST AMENDMENT TO THE CONSTITUTION WAS ADOPTED, THE PUBLIC WORKS PROGRAM BEGUN, THE SOCIAL SECURITY ACT WAS PASSED AND THE FAMOUS "FIRESIDE CHATS" BECAME AN AMERICAN INSTITUTION. THE JAPANESE ATTACK ON PEARL HARBOR PLUNGED THE U.S. INTO WORLD WAR II IN 1941.***

1882-1965

Felix Frankfurter

DISTINGUISHED JURIST AND EDUCATOR

I DON'T KNOW WHAT I WOULD DO WITHOUT YOU, FELIX.

FRANKFURTER CAME TO THE U.S. WHEN HE WAS 12 YRS. OLD. HE GRADUATED FROM THE COLLEGE OF THE CITY OF NEW YORK AND HARVARD LAW SCHOOL. **HE WAS A PROFESSOR OF LAW AT HARVARD FOR 25 YRS (1914-39). HE WAS A STAUNCH SUPPORTER OF PRES. FRANKLIN ROOSEVELT AND BECAME ONE OF HIS CLOSEST ADVISORS, CONTRIBUTING TO THE DRAFTING OF MUCH NEW DEAL LEGISLATION. IN 1939 ROOSEVELT APPOINTED HIM ASSOCIATE JUSTICE OF THE SUPREME COURT. HE SERVED FROM 1939 UNTIL HIS RETIREMENT IN 1962. WHILE ON THE COURT HIS LEGAL OPINIONS SHOW HIS DISLIKE OF JUDICIAL LAWMAKING. HE BELIEVED LAWS SHOULD BE MADE ONLY BY THE ELECTED REPRESENTATIVES OF THE PEOPLE.**

HE WAS BORN IN VIENNA, AUSTRIA.
YOUR CONTRIBUTIONS TO OUR COUNTRY HAVE BEEN OUTSTANDING.

NOW THAT THE WAR IS OVER I WANT YOU TO GO TO THE VERSAILLES PEACE CONFERENCE.

DURING WORLD WAR I HE HELD SEVERAL IMPORTANT POSTS IN WASHINGTON, D.C. **IN 1919 HE WENT TO THE VERSAILLES PEACE CONFERENCE AS LEGAL AIDE TO PRES. WILSON. FRANKFURTER WAS ONE OF THE FOUNDERS OF THE AMERICAN CIVIL LIBERTIES UNION.**

HE WON WIDE ACCLAIM AS A **GREAT TEACHER AND POET.** ARCHIBALD MACLEISH SAID **FRANKFURTER "HAD MORE INFLUENCE ON MORE LIVES THAN ANY OTHER MAN OF HIS GENERATION."**

1884-1962

Eleanor Roosevelt

AMERICAN WRITER AND HUMANITARIAN

THESE PEOPLE DESERVE THE SAME THINGS THAT YOU AND I HAVE.

MRS. ROOSEVELT WAS THE WIFE OF FRANKLIN D. ROOSEVELT, THIRTY-SECOND PRESIDENT OF THE U.S. **A DISTINGUISHED PUBLIC FIGURE IN HER OWN RIGHT, SHE NO DOUBT WAS THE MOST ACTIVE FIRST LADY IN PUBLIC AFFAIRS IN AMERICAN HISTORY. SHE WON FAME THROUGHOUT THE WORLD FOR HER HUMANITARIAN WORK. DURING WORLD WAR II SHE TRAVELED TO LATIN AMERICA, EUROPE AND OTHER PARTS OF THE WORLD. MRS. ROOSEVELT WORKED WITH YOUNG PEOPLE AND THE UNDERPRIVILEGED AND FOUGHT LONG AND HARD FOR EQUAL RIGHTS FOR MINORITY GROUPS. DURING F.D.R'S LONG PRESIDENCY, SHE SERVED AS A CHANNEL OF DIRECT COMMUNICATION BETWEEN THESE GROUPS AND THE WHITE HOUSE.**

SHE WAS BORN IN NEW YORK CITY.
AS THE WIFE OF ONE OF OUR GREAT PRESIDENTS, I ASK YOU TO SERVE.
THANK YOU, MR. PRESIDENT. WOMEN SHOULD BE AMONG THE DELEGATES, NO MATTER WHAT THE SUBJECT UNDER DISCUSSION.

THROUGH THE YEARS MEN HAVE MADE WARS. IT IS ONLY FAIR TO SUGGEST THAT WOMEN CAN HELP TO MAKE A LASTING PEACE.

SHE BECAME WELL KNOWN AS A LECTURER AND RADIO SPEAKER. HER BOOKS INCLUDE "**THIS IS MY STORY**," "**THIS I REMEMBER**" AND "**ON MY OWN**." SHE ALSO WROTE A SYNDICATED DAILY NEWSPAPER COLUMN CALLED "**MY DAY**." **SHE HELPED FOUND AMERICANS FOR DEMOCRATIC ACTION.**

KERN

PRESIDENT TRUMAN APPOINTED HER A DELEGATE TO THE **UNITED NATIONS GENERAL ASSEMBLY. SHE SERVED FROM 1945 TO 1951. IN 1946 SHE THE CHAIRMAN OF THE UN'S HUMAN RIGHTS COMMISSION AND HELPED DRAFT THE UNIVERSAL DECLARATION OF HUMAN RIGHTS. IN 1961 SHE AGAIN BECAME A DELEGATE TO THE GEN. ASSEMBLY.**

1884-1972

Harry S. Truman

SOLDIER, JUDGE, SENATOR, VICE-PRESIDENT AND **THIRTY-THIRD** PRESIDENT OF THE UNITED STATES (1945-53)

MY DOCTRINE WILL FIGHT COMMUNISM.

TRUMAN MOVED WITH HIS PARENTS TO INDEPENDENCE, MO., WHERE HE ATTENDED SCHOOL. HE SPENT MUCH OF HIS TIME STUDYING HIS FAVORITE SUBJECT, AMERICAN HISTORY. HE WORKED FOR THE SANTA FE RAILROAD AND THE ***KANSAS CITY "STAR"*** AND CLERKED IN KANSAS CITY BANKS. ***HE DISTINGUISHED HIMSELF DURING WORLD WAR I AS AN ARTILLERY OFFICER. AS A SENATOR HE HELPED SAVE MILLIONS BY CUTTING DOWN WASTE AND CORRUPTION IN THE HANDLING OF DEFENSE CONTRACTS. AT THE 1944 DEMOCRATIC CONVENTION TRUMAN WAS ROOSEVELT'S RUNNING MATE. 83 DAYS LATER F.D.R. WAS DEAD AND TRUMAN WAS SWORN IN AS PRESIDENT. HE WAS A COURAGEOUS AND AGGRESSIVE PRESIDENT. HE WAS RESPONSIBLE FOR THE TOUGH "TRUMAN DOCTRINE" WHICH GUARANTEED U.S. AID TO NATIONS RESISTING COMMUNISM. HE APPROVED THE "MARSHALL PLAN" FOR REBUILDING WAR-TORN EUROPE AND HE SENT U.S. TROOPS AND PLANES TO DEFEND SOUTH KOREA.***

HE WAS BORN IN LAMAR, MO.

THIS WAS A VERY DIFFICULT DECISION TO MAKE.

SECRETARY OF DEFENSE

DURING HIS ADMINISTRATION, WORLD WAR II ENDED WITH THE SURRENDER OF GERMANY AND JAPAN, THE UNITED NATIONS WAS ORGANIZED, THE TWENTY-SECOND AMENDMENT TO THE CONSTITUTION WAS ADOPTED, THE FIRST ATOMIC BOMB WAS EXPLODED AT ALAMOGORDO, N. M., AND THE ARMY, NAVY AND AIR FORCE WERE UNIFIED UNDER A SEC. OF DEFENSE.

KERN

AFTER GERMANY SURRENDERED MAY 8, 1945, THE U.S. HAD PERFECTED THE **ATOM BOMB**. ***TRUMAN MADE THE DECISION TO DROP THE BOMB ON HIROSHIMA AUG. 6, 1945, AND ON NAGASAKI AUG. 9. JAPAN SURRENDERED AUG. 14. THIS ACT SAVED MANY THOUSANDS OF AMERICAN LIVES.***

1885–1951

Sinclair Lewis

NOBEL-PRIZE NOVELIST AND SOCIAL CRITIC

DID YOU READ WHAT LEWIS SAID ABOUT US?

LEWIS ATTENDED YALE UNIVERSITY, GRADUATING IN 1908. HE HELD A NUMBER OF JOBS THROUGHOUT THE U.S. BEFORE FINALLY SETTLING WITH A PUBLISHING CO. IN NEW YORK. IN 1913 HE FINISHED HIS FIRST NOVEL, "**OUR MR. WRENN.**" THIS WAS FOLLOWED BY 4 MORE NOVELS, NONE SUCCESSFUL. ***IN 1920 WHILE LIVING IN WASHINGTON, D.C., HE FINISHED HIS FIRST MAJOR NOVEL, "MAIN STREET." TREMENDOUSLY SUCCESSFUL, IT WAS CALLED THE LITERARY SENSATION OF THE 1920'S. LEWIS WROTE "BABBITT" (1922), "ARROWSMITH" (1925), "ELMER GANTRY" (1927) AND "DODSWORTH" (1929). HIS BOOKS AROUSED MORE DISCUSSION THAN ANY OTHER WRITER OF HIS TIME. HE SATIRIZED TYPICAL AMERICANS, ANGERING THOSE WHO READ HIS NOVELS. HIS POPULAR "MAIN STREET" RIDICULES THE NARROW-MINDEDNESS OF LIFE IN A SMALL MIDWEST TOWN. SAUK CENTER, HIS BIRTHPLACE, IS BELIEVED TO BE THE LOCALE FOR "MAIN STREET."***

SOME OF HIS OTHER NOVELS WERE "***ANN VICKERS,***" "***IT CAN'T HAPPEN HERE***" AND "***CASS TIMBERLANE.***"

YOU ARE A CREDIT TO AMERICA. THE NOBEL PRIZE IS THE WORLD'S RECOGNITION OF OUTSTANDING ACHIEVEMENT.

HE WON THE PULITZER PRIZE FOR "ARROWSMITH" ***BUT REFUSED IT. IN 1930 HE ACCEPTED THE NOBEL PRIZE FOR "BABBITT." LEWIS WAS THE FIRST AMERICAN WRITER TO RECEIVE THIS AWARD.***

1885-1952
Karen Horney
GERMAN-AMERICAN PSYCHIATRIST AND PSYCHOANALYST
SHE WAS BORN IN HAMBURG, GERMANY.
AS MRS. HORNEY TOLD YOU, DEAR, YOU MUST LEARN TO MAKE YOUR OWN DECISIONS!
SHE WAS EDUCATED AT THE UNIVERSITY OF FREIBURG. FROM 1920 TO 1932 SHE TAUGHT AT THE INSTITUTE FOR PSYCHOANALYSIS IN BERLIN. SHE CAME TO THE U.S. AND SERVED AS ASSOCIATE DIRECTOR OF THE CHICAGO INSTITUTE FOR PSYCHOANALYSIS FOR 2 YRS., THEN TAUGHT AT THE NEW YORK PSYCHOANALYSIS INSTITUTE UNTIL 1941 WHEN SHE WAS APPOINTED DEAN OF THE AMERICAN INSTITUTE FOR PSYCHOANALYSIS. SHE FOUNDED A SCHOOL OF PSYCHOANALYSIS WHICH DIFFERED FROM FREUD'S. IT WAS BASED ON THE BELIEF THAT NEUROSES ARE THE PRIME RESULT OF EMOTIONAL CONFLICTS WHICH ARISE FROM DISTURBANCES IN PERSONAL RELATIONSHIPS.
YOU ARE WITHDRAWING FROM ALL YOUR FRIENDS, DAD.
THESE ARE GREAT BOOKS, KAREN.
I TRIED TO ALERT MY READERS TO THE IMPORTANCE OF THERAPY.
KAREN HORNEY CLAIMED THERE ARE TWO KINDS OF NEUROSES. SITUATION NEUROSES, ACCORDING TO HER THEORY, ARISE FROM ANXIETY. CHARACTER NEUROSES ARE BASIC HOSTILITIES TO THE ENVIRONMENT RESULTING FROM THE LACK OF LOVE AND AFFECTION IN CHILDHOOD.
KERN
SOME OF HER WRITINGS ARE "THE NEUROTIC PERSONALITY OF OUR TIME," "NEW WAYS IN PSYCHOANALYSIS," "SELF ANALYSIS," "OUR INNER CONFLICTS" AND "NEUROSIS AND HUMAN GROWTH."

1885-1966

Chester W. Nimitz

COMMANDER-IN-CHIEF OF THE UNITED STATES PACIFIC FLEET IN THE WAR AGAINST JAPAN

NIMITZ GRADUATED FROM THE U.S. NAVAL ACADEMY IN 1905. DURING WORLD WAR I HE WAS CHIEF OF STAFF TO THE COMMANDER OF THE U.S. SUBMARINE FLEET IN THE ATLANTIC. ADVANCING THROUGH THE RANKS HE WAS MADE A ***REAR ADMIRAL AND CHIEF OF THE BUREAU OF PERSONNEL IN WASH., D.C. IN DEC. 1941 NIMITZ ARRIVED IN PEARL HARBOR TO TAKE COMMAND OF A FLEET THAT HAD BEEN CRIPPLED IN THE JAPANESE ATTACK ON DEC. 7. A SOFT-SPOKEN, MILD-MANNERED MAN, NIMITZ, THROUGH HIS BOLD TACTICS, PLANNED STRATEGY AND BRILLIANT USE OF FORCES, WON VICTORIES AT GUADALCANAL, MIDWAY, IWO JIMA AND LEYTE GULF, DRIVING THE JAPANESE BACK TO THEIR HOMELAND. IN 1944 NIMITZ WAS PROMOTED TO A FLEET ADMIRAL. AFTER THE WAR HE SUCCEEDED ADMIRAL ERNEST KING AS CHIEF OF NAVAL OPERATIONS.***

HE WAS BORN IN FREDERICKSBURG, TEXAS.

THE PURPOSE OF THIS U.N. COMMISSION IS TO BE SURE ALL DISPUTES ARE SETTLED.

KERN

WHEN JAPAN SURRENDERED, ***NIMITZ SIGNED FOR THE UNITED STATES IN TOKYO BAY.***

HE LEFT ACTIVE DUTY IN 1947 AND BECAME SPECIAL ASSISTANT TO THE SEC. OF THE NAVY. ***IN 1949, HE HEADED THE UNITED NATIONS MEDIATION COMMISSION IN THE DISPUTE OVER KASHMIR. IN 1951, HE WAS THE HEAD OF THE U.S. INTERNAL SECURITY COMMISSION.***

1886-1961

Tyrus Raymond "Ty" Cobb

GREAT ALL-AROUND BASEBALL PLAYER

KNOWN AS THE *"GEORGIA PEACH,"* COBB WAS PLAYING BASEBALL BEFORE HE WAS 19. *FOR 25 YRS. IN THE MAJOR LEAGUES, HE WAS A SENSATIONAL BATTER, A BRILLIANT FIELDER AND A GREAT RUNNER. HE JOINED THE DETROIT TIGERS IN 1905 AND BROKE MORE RECORDS THAN ANY OTHER PLAYER IN BASEBALL HISTORY. PROBABLY NO ONE WILL EVER EQUAL THEM. COBB'S LIFETIME BATTING AVERAGE WAS .367, HE MADE 4,191 BASE HITS, SCORED 2,244 RUNS, PLAYED IN 3,033 GAMES, STOLE 892 BASES (96 IN ONE SEASON) AND WAS AT BAT 11,429 TIMES! HE PLAYED 24 SEASONS IN THE AM. LEAGUE, 22 WITH DETROIT AND 2 WITH THE PHILADELPHIA ATHLETICS. FROM 1920 TO 1926 COBB MANAGED THE DETROIT TIGERS, THEN RETIRED AFTER 2 SEASONS WITH THE ATHLETICS. IN HIS TIME EVERY SPORTS WRITER GAVE HIM THE TITLE "THE GREATEST PLAYER IN THE HISTORY OF BASEBALL."*

HE WAS BORN IN NARROWS, GA.

ONE OF AMERICA'S TRULY GREAT ATHLETES.

WHEN THE BASEBALL HALL OF FAME SHRINE WAS ENGRAVED IN 1936, *TY COBB HEADED THE LIST.*

TY COBB
HE WAS A KIND AND GENEROUS MAN!

HE DIED A WEALTHY MAN, LEAVING GIFTS *FOR COLLEGE SCHOLARSHIPS TO WORTHY BOYS. HE ENLARGED AND ENDOWED THE HOSPITAL IN HIS HOMETOWN.*

KERN

HE WAS BORN IN SOUTH NORWALK, CONN.

1886-1972

Edward C. Kendall

AMERICAN BIOCHEMIST, AWARDED THE LASKER AWARD IN 1949 AND THE NOBEL PRIZE IN 1950 FOR HIS WORK IN THE CHEMISTRY OF CORTISONE

OUR PROJECT IS A COMPLETE SUCCESS.

KENDALL RECEIVED BACHELOR OF SCIENCE, MASTER OF SCIENCE AND A DOCTORATE IN CHEMISTRY DEGREES FROM COLUMBIA UNIVERSITY. ***FROM 1914 TO 1951 HE WAS WITH THE MAYO CLINIC IN ROCHESTER, MINN., FIRST AS HEAD OF BIOCHEMISTRY IN THE GRADUATE SCHOOL AND THEN IN 1921, PROFESSOR OF PHYSIOLOGICAL CHEMISTRY. FROM HIS RESEARCH HE WAS ABLE TO ISOLATE AND THEN SYNTHESIZE THE HORMONE CORTISONE.***

1896-1965

Philip S. Hench

AMERICAN PHYSICIAN, CO-WINNER OF THE LASKER AWARD IN 1949, AND CO-WINNER OF THE NOBEL PRIZE IN 1950 FOR HIS CLINICAL OBSERVATIONS ABOUT CORTISONE TREATMENTS FOR ARTHRITIC PATIENTS

THEY SEEM TO BE REACTING.
WE'LL GIVE THEM ONE MORE DAY!
KERN

HE WAS BORN IN PITTSBURGH, PA.

HENCH WAS HEAD OF THE SECTION FOR RHEUMATIC DISEASES AND ***INSTRUCTOR IN MEDICINE AT THE MAYO FOUNDATION GRADUATE SCHOOL (1926-57). IN 1957 HE WAS RELEASED FROM HIS DUTIES TO LECTURE AND WRITE ON MEDICAL PROJECTS.***

1887-1948

Aldo Leopold

PROFESSIONAL FORESTER, PIONEER CONSERVATIONIST, PROFESSOR OF GAME MANAGEMENT AND WRITER

LEOPOLD, THE MASTER ECOLOGIST, GRADUATED FROM YALE UNIVERSITY. FROM 1909 TO 1924 HE WORKED FOR THE U.S. FOREST SERVICE, WHERE HE ADVANCED AS CHIEF IN THE REGIONAL OFFICE IN ALBUQUERQUE, N. MEX. IN 1924 HE WAS CHOSEN ASSOCIATE DIRECTOR OF FOREST PRODUCTS LABORATORY AT MADISON, WIS. ***HIS GAME MANAGEMENT POLICY WAS A CLASSIC IN ITS FIELD. IN 1933 HE WAS APPOINTED A PROFESSOR IN GAME MANAGEMENT AT THE UNIVERSITY OF WISCONSIN, THE FIRST OF ITS TYPE IN THE COUNTRY. HE STAYED WITH THE UNIVERSITY UNTIL HIS DEATH. LEOPOLD'S BOOK, "SAND COUNTY ALMANAC," IS A DETAILED RECORD OF THE COUNTRY AND THE CREATURES THAT HE OBSERVED WITH HIS FAMILY DURING WEEKENDS AND HOLIDAYS.***

HE SPENT HIS LIFE IN FORESTRY AND WILDLIFE MANAGEMENT. ***LEOPOLD DIED FIGHTING A FOREST FIRE, TRYING TO SAVE THE WISCONSIN ACRES HE LOVED.***

HE WAS BORN IN BURLINGTON, IOWA.
WILDERNESS AREA

LEOPOLD HAD GREAT INFLUENCE ON PROFESSIONAL CONSERVATIONISTS. ***HE DEVELOPED THE IDEA OF WILDERNESS AREAS WITHIN NATIONAL PARKS IN AMERICA. HE WAS RESPONSIBLE FOR ESTABLISHING THE FIRST SOIL CONSERVATION AREA IN THE U.S. AND WAS A STRONG SUPPORTER OF DEER-HERD MANAGEMENT.***

1887 - 1964

Alvin C. York

WORLD WAR I HERO

HE WAS BORN IN PALL MALL, TENN.
THANK YOU. THIS GIFT IS GREATLY APPRECIATED.

YORK GREW UP ON A MOUNTAIN FARM AND DEVELOPED AMAZING MARKSMANSHIP WITH A RIFLE AND PISTOL. HE WAS A RELIGIOUS MAN AND ENLISTED IN THE ARMY IN 1917 AFTER HIS APPEAL AS A CONSCIENTIOUS OBJECTOR WAS TURNED DOWN. ***HE WENT TO FRANCE AS A CORPORAL WITH THE 82nd DIVISION'S 328th INFANTRY REGIMENT. HE FOUGHT IN THE ARGONNE-MEUSE OFFENSIVE IN NORTHEASTERN FRANCE. HIS PLATOON SUFFERED HEAVY CASUALTIES FROM A GERMAN MACHINE-GUN NEST. YORK LED SEVEN MEN AND CHARGED THE GERMANS. HE SINGLE-HANDEDLY KILLED 25, CAPTURED 132 AND TOOK 35 MACHINE GUNS. YORK WAS PROMOTED TO A SERGEANT AND WAS AWARDED THE CONGRESSIONAL MEDAL OF HONOR. GENERAL PERSHING CALLED HIM THE "GREATEST CIVILIAN SOLDIER OF THE WAR." HIS FINAL YEARS, HOWEVER, WERE FILLED WITH ILLNESS AND POVERTY.***

YOU ARE A CREDIT TO YOUR GREAT COUNTRY.

AFTER THE WAR SGT. YORK SETTLED ON A FARM IN TENN. DONATED BY THE STATE. AT HIS REQUEST MONEY DONATED TO HIM BY HIS ADMIRERS WAS USED TO FOUND THE YORK FOUNDATION TO PROMOTE THE EDUCATION OF MOUNTAIN CHILDREN. ***HIS HEROIC DEED WAS RECORDED IN HIS AUTOBIOGRAPHY, "SERGEANT YORK- HIS OWN LIFE STORY." ROYALTIES FROM HIS BOOK AND FILM WERE GIVEN TO THE FOUNDATION.***

MARSHAL FERDINAND FOCH, THE GREAT FRENCH COMMANDER, CALLED YORK'S FEAT "***THE GREATEST THING ACCOMPLISHED BY ANY PRIVATE SOLDIER OF ALL THE ARMIES OF EUROPE.***"

KERN

1888-1931

Knute Rockne

GREAT COLLEGE FOOTBALL COACH

NOTRE DAME'S LEGENDARY FOUR HORSEMEN OF 1924

HE WAS BORN IN VOSS, NORWAY.
REMEMBER, MEN, RIGHT LIVING AND RIGHT THINKING ARE THE KEYS TO VICTORY.

KNUTE WAS 5 WHEN HE CAME FROM NORWAY TO CHICAGO, ILLINOIS, IN 1893. HE ATTENDED SCHOOL THERE, THEN WENT TO NOTRE DAME, WHERE HE STUDIED CHEMISTRY AND PLAYED FOOTBALL, GRADUATING IN 1914. ***WHILE CAPTAIN OF THE FOOTBALL TEAM, ROCKNE REVOLUTIONIZED FOOTBALL STRATEGY BY STRESSING THE USE OF THE FORWARD PASS. HE WAS ONE OF THE MOST SUCCESSFUL COACHES IN THE HISTORY OF FOOTBALL. FROM 1914 TO 1918 ROCKNE WAS ASSISTANT FOOTBALL COACH AND A CHEMISTRY INSTRUCTOR AT NOTRE DAME. IN 1918 HE WAS SELECTED AS HEAD COACH, WHERE HE REMAINED UNTIL HIS DEATH. AMONG THE PLAYERS HE COACHED WERE THE IMMORTAL GEORGE GIPP AND THE 1924 BACKFIELD KNOWN AS THE "FOUR HORSEMEN." ROCKNE WAS KILLED IN A PLANE CRASH IN KANSAS.***

HIS FAME LIVES ON AS AN INSPIRATION TO THE YOUTH OF AMERICA.

IN 13 YRS., AS HEAD COACH AT NOTRE DAME, HIS TEAM ***WON 105 GAMES, LOST 12, TIED 5 AND SCORED 2,847 POINTS TO THEIR OPPONENTS' 667.***

KERN

ROCKNE WON NATIONAL RECOGNITION FOR HIS INSISTENCE ON ***GOOD SPORTSMANSHIP AND FOR HIS CLEVER FOOTBALL STRATEGY. HIS "ROCKNE SYSTEM" OF OFFENSIVE FOOTBALL MADE THE FORWARD PASS A FAST DECEPTIVE PLAY.***

Eugene O'Neill

NOBEL-PRIZE PLAYWRIGHT

SON OF A NOTED ACTOR, JAMES O'NEILL, HE WENT TO PRINCETON, THEN STUDIED PLAYWRITING AT HARVARD. HE HAD A VARIETY OF JOBS BEFORE HE STARTED WRITING PLAYS-- SAILOR, ACTOR, REPORTER. ***IN 1916 HE BECAME ASSOCIATED WITH THE PROVINCETOWN THEATER, MASS., AND WAS DIRECTOR OF THE PROVINCE TOWN PLAYHOUSE UNTIL 1927. O'NEILL'S PLAYS COVERED A RANGE OF SUBJECTS. HIS EARLIER PLAYS WERE TRAGIC THEMES AND REALISTIC. HIS LATER PLAYS WERE MYSTICAL, WHERE CHARACTERS BECAME SYMBOLS TO REPRESENT IDEAS. O'NEILL ALSO WROTE "THE LONG VOYAGE HOME," "MARCO MILLIONS," "AH, WILDERNESS!" (A COMEDY) AND "THE ICEMAN COMETH." THE LAST PLAY HE WROTE, "A TOUCH OF THE POET," WAS FIRST SHOWN IN STOCKHOLM, SWEDEN, IN 1957.***

THEATRE

REMARKABLE PLAY.

ALL OF YOUR PLAYS ARE SURE WINNERS, MR. O'NEILL.

ONE OF AMERICA'S MOST FORCEFUL PLAYWRIGHTS, ***HIS WIDE RANGE OF WRITING TECHNIQUES GREATLY INFLUENCED THE AMERICAN THEATER.***

KERN

FOUR OF O'NEILL'S PLAYS WON PULITZER PRIZES: ***"BEYOND THE HORIZON," "ANNA CHRISTIE," "STRANGE INTERLUDE" AND "LONG DAY'S JOURNEY INTO NIGHT." O'NEILL WON THE 1936 NOBEL PRIZE FOR LITERATURE.***

1888 - 1953

Jim Thorpe

AMERICAN ATHLETE

THORPE, A SAC AND FOX INDIAN, WENT TO HASKELL INSTITUTE AT LAWRENCE, KANSAS, AND THE CARLISLE INDIAN SCHOOL AT CARLISLE, PA. HE BECAME AN OUTSTANDING ATHLETE, STARRING IN FOOTBALL, BASEBALL AND TRACK. ***HIS BRILLIANT PLAYING ON THE FOOTBALL FIELD PUT HIM ON THE 1911 AND 1912 ALL-AMERICAN TEAMS. DURING THE 1912 OLYMPICS AT STOCKHOLM HE WAS THE FIRST PERSON TO WIN BOTH THE PENTATHLON AND DECATHLON EVENTS. AFTER HE LEFT CARLISLE IN 1913, HE PLAYED MAJOR LEAGUE BASEBALL WITH THE NEW YORK GIANTS, CINCINNATI REDS AND THE BOSTON BRAVES. THORPE ALSO PLAYED PROFESSIONAL FOOTBALL FOR THE CANTON BULLDOGS AND THE NEW YORK GIANTS. RETIRING IN 1929, HE WAS THE FIRST PRESIDENT OF THE AMERICAN PROFESSIONAL FOOTBALL ASSOCIATION, WHICH LATER BECAME THE NATIONAL FOOTBALL LEAGUE.***

HE WAS BORN NEAR PRAGUE, OKLAHOMA.

CONGRATULATIONS, JIM THORPE.

WHEN KING GUSTAF V OF SWEDEN PINNED THE OLYMPIC GOLD MEDAL ON HIM IN 1912, HE SAID, "***SIR, YOU ARE THE GREATEST ATHLETE IN THE WORLD.*" IN JAN. 1913, THE AMATEUR ATHLETIC UNION FOUND OUT THAT THORPE HAD PLAYED PROFESSIONAL BASEBALL. HE HAD TO RETURN ALL OF HIS OLYMPIC MEDALS AND TROPHIES.**

THANKS FOR THE HONOR.

HE PLAYED BIT PARTS IN WESTERN MOVIES, LECTURED ON INDIAN AFFAIRS AND SPORTS, AND WAS THE SUBJECT OF A FILM BIOGRAPHY, "JIM THORPE: ALL-AMERICAN." ***IN 1950 THE ASSOCIATED PRESS POLL NAMED HIM THE GREATEST FOOTBALL PLAYER AND ALL-ROUND ATHLETE OF THE 20th CENTURY.***

KERN

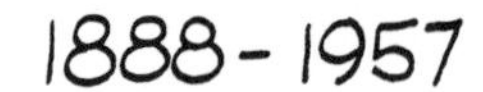

Richard E. Byrd

AMERICAN EXPLORER, NAVAL OFFICER AND AVIATOR

BYRD WENT TO THE VIRGINIA MILITARY INSTITUTE, THE UNIVERSITY OF VIRGINIA, AND THE U.S. NAVAL ACADEMY, GRADUATING FROM THE ACADEMY IN 1912. DURING WORLD WAR I HE WAS A LT. COMMANDER IN CHARGE OF THE U.S. NAVY AIR STATIONS IN NOVA SCOTIA. ***IN 1928 HE ORGANIZED A SCIENTIFIC EXPEDITION TO THE ANTARCTIC.*** 32 SCIENTISTS WENT WITH HIM. ***HE ESTABLISHED A BASE WHICH HE CALLED "LITTLE AMERICA." FROM THERE HE FLEW OVER THE SOUTH POLE IN NOV. 1929. IN RECOGNITION OF HIS ACCOMPLISHMENTS, CONGRESS MADE HIM A REAR ADMIRAL. ON HIS SECOND EXPEDITION (1933-35) HE CONDUCTED A SCIENTIFIC SURVEY OF THE ANTARCTIC CONTINENT. BYRD LED OTHER EXPEDITIONS IN 1939, 1947 AND 1955. IN WORLD WAR II HE SERVED WITH THE NAVY AS A CONFIDENTIAL ADVISOR IN REGARDS TO NAVAL AIR STATIONS IN THE PACIFIC. ALTHOUGH BYRD FAILED TO MAKE THE ANTARCTIC AMERICAN TERRITORY, HE WAS SUCCESSFUL IN OPENING THE POLAR FRONTIERS.***

HE WAS BORN IN WINCHESTER, VA.

AMERICA THANKS YOU FOR YOUR GREAT WORK.

HE WAS THE FIRST MAN TO FLY OVER BOTH THE NORTH AND SOUTH POLES. PRES. COOLIDGE PRESENTED HIM WITH A GOLD MEDAL "FOR VALOR IN EXPLORATION." MORE THAN ANY OTHER INDIVIDUAL, HE WAS RESPONSIBLE FOR OPENING ANTARCTICA TO THE WORLD OF SCIENCE.

HE RECEIVED MANY DECORATIONS INCLUDING ***THE CONGRESSIONAL MEDAL OF HONOR. SOME OF HIS BOOKS ARE "ALONE," "SKYWARD" AND "DISCOVERY."***

KERN

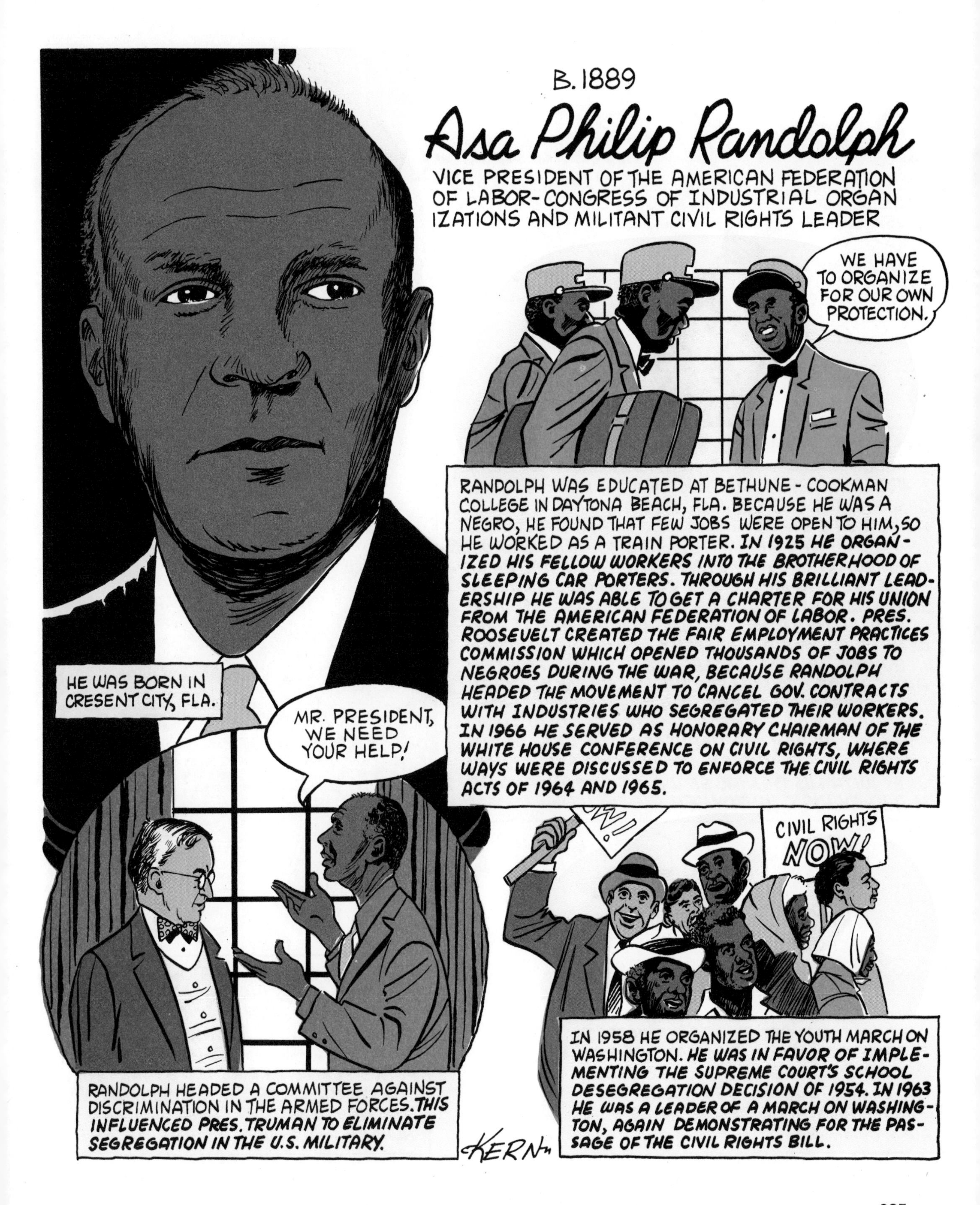
B. 1889
Asa Philip Randolph
VICE PRESIDENT OF THE AMERICAN FEDERATION OF LABOR-CONGRESS OF INDUSTRIAL ORGANIZATIONS AND MILITANT CIVIL RIGHTS LEADER
WE HAVE TO ORGANIZE FOR OUR OWN PROTECTION.
RANDOLPH WAS EDUCATED AT BETHUNE - COOKMAN COLLEGE IN DAYTONA BEACH, FLA. BECAUSE HE WAS A NEGRO, HE FOUND THAT FEW JOBS WERE OPEN TO HIM, SO HE WORKED AS A TRAIN PORTER. IN 1925 HE ORGANIZED HIS FELLOW WORKERS INTO THE BROTHERHOOD OF SLEEPING CAR PORTERS. THROUGH HIS BRILLIANT LEADERSHIP HE WAS ABLE TO GET A CHARTER FOR HIS UNION FROM THE AMERICAN FEDERATION OF LABOR. PRES. ROOSEVELT CREATED THE FAIR EMPLOYMENT PRACTICES COMMISSION WHICH OPENED THOUSANDS OF JOBS TO NEGROES DURING THE WAR, BECAUSE RANDOLPH HEADED THE MOVEMENT TO CANCEL GOV. CONTRACTS WITH INDUSTRIES WHO SEGREGATED THEIR WORKERS. IN 1966 HE SERVED AS HONORARY CHAIRMAN OF THE WHITE HOUSE CONFERENCE ON CIVIL RIGHTS, WHERE WAYS WERE DISCUSSED TO ENFORCE THE CIVIL RIGHTS ACTS OF 1964 AND 1965.
HE WAS BORN IN CRESENT CITY, FLA.
MR. PRESIDENT, WE NEED YOUR HELP!
CIVIL RIGHTS NOW!
RANDOLPH HEADED A COMMITTEE AGAINST DISCRIMINATION IN THE ARMED FORCES. THIS INFLUENCED PRES. TRUMAN TO ELIMINATE SEGREGATION IN THE U.S. MILITARY.
IN 1958 HE ORGANIZED THE YOUTH MARCH ON WASHINGTON. HE WAS IN FAVOR OF IMPLEMENTING THE SUPREME COURT'S SCHOOL DESEGREGATION DECISION OF 1954. IN 1963 HE WAS A LEADER OF A MARCH ON WASHINGTON, AGAIN DEMONSTRATING FOR THE PASSAGE OF THE CIVIL RIGHTS BILL.
KERN

1890-1969

Dwight D. Eisenhower

PROFESSIONAL SOLDIER, UNIVERSITY PRESIDENT AND **THIRTY-FOURTH** PRESIDENT OF THE UNITED STATES (1953-61)

"IKE" EISENHOWER ENTERED WEST POINT AFTER HIGH SCHOOL AND GRADUATED IN 1915. DURING WORLD WAR I HE SERVED AS AN INSTRUCTOR IN VARIOUS TRAINING CAMPS IN THE U.S. BETWEEN 1920 AND 1935 EISENHOWER WAS STATIONED IN THE PANAMA CANAL ZONE. *IN 1935 HE WAS APPOINTED AIDE TO GENERAL DOUGLAS MAC ARTHUR AND WENT WITH HIM TO THE PHILIPPINES. DURING WORLD WAR II EISENHOWER WAS THE SUPREME COMMANDER OF THE ALLIED ARMIES THAT DEFEATED GERMANY. AFTER THE WAR HE WAS PRESIDENT OF COLUMBIA UNIVERSITY AND WROTE "CRUSADE IN EUROPE," A BEST-SELLER. HE RESIGNED FROM THE ARMY IN 1952 TO RUN FOR THE PRESIDENCY UNDER THE REPUBLICAN TICKET. HE WON BY A LANDSLIDE, RECEIVING 442 ELECTORAL VOTES TO ADLAI STEVENSON'S 89. HE RAN FOR REELECTION IN 1956, AGAIN DEFEATING STEVENSON. HONEST AND COURAGEOUS, "IKE," WITH HIS GENIAL SMILE, WAS LOVED AND ADMIRED BY HIS COUNTRYMEN.*

HE WAS BORN IN DENISON, TEXAS.

EISENHOWER AND ULYSSES S. GRANT WERE THE *ONLY TWO WEST POINT GRADUATES TO BECOME PRESIDENT, ALSO THE ONLY TWO REPUBLICAN PRESIDENTS TO SERVE OUT TWO COMPLETE FOUR-YEAR TERMS. "IKE" WAS THE FIRST PRESIDENT TO HOLD A PILOT'S LICENSE.*

UNDER HIS ADMINISTRATION *THE MINIMUM WAGE WAS INCREASED, THE DEPT. OF HEALTH, EDUCATION AND WELFARE WAS CREATED, THE ST. LAWRENCE SEAWAY WAS COMPLETED, THE ATOMS-FOR-PEACE PLAN WAS ADOPTED BY THE U.N., THE WORLD'S FIRST ATOMIC SUBMARINE, THE "NAUTILUS," WAS LAUNCHED, AND ALASKA AND HAWAII BECAME STATES.*

KERN

1890-1973

"Eddie" Rickenbacker

ACE U.S. FIGHTER PILOT IN WORLD WAR I AND BOARD CHAIRMAN OF EASTERN AIRLINES

HE WAS BORN IN COLUMBUS, OHIO.

EDDIE'S FATHER DIED WHEN HE WAS 12, SO HE QUIT SCHOOL AND WORKED AT ODD JOBS. IN 1914 HE WAS RACING CARS AT 134 M.P.H., EARNING $40,000 A YEAR AND AN INTERNATIONAL REPUTATION. *IN 1917 EDDIE ENLISTED IN THE ARMY AS A CHAUFFEUR. HE WAS SOON TRANSFERRED TO FLYING SCHOOL AND WENT TO THE FRONT EARLY IN 1918. MANY OF HIS AERIAL BATTLES WERE WITH THE FAMOUS "FLYING CIRCUS" OF VON RICHTHOFEN, THE "RED BARON." FLYING WITHOUT A PARACHUTE IN A PRIMITIVE PLANE, EDDIE SHOT DOWN 21 GERMAN PLANES AND 5 OBSERVATION BALLOONS OVER FRANCE. HE RECEIVED THE DISTINGUISHED SERVICE CROSS AND THE CROIX DE GUERRE. AFTER WORLD WAR I RICKENBACKER OWNED THE INDIANAPOLIS SPEEDWAY FOR 18 YRS. HE WROTE "FIGHTING THE FLYING CIRCUS" AND "SEVEN CAME THROUGH."*

THE EMPLOYEES DO A GREAT AMOUNT OF THE WORK. LET'S TAKE CARE OF THEM NOW.

IN 1942, WHILE ON A CIVILIAN MORALE BOOSTING TOUR DURING WORLD WAR II, HIS PLANE WENT DOWN IN THE SOUTH PACIFIC. *8 MEN, WITH EDDIE IN COMMAND, DRIFTED FOR 24 DAYS ON RUBBER RAFTS BEFORE THEY WERE RESCUED. ONE MAN DIED.*

KERN

IN 1938 HE BECAME PRESIDENT OF EASTERN AIRLINES *AND LED THE CO. TO PROSPERITY. RICKENBACKER HAD GREAT REGARD FOR THE EMPLOYEES. HE INTRODUCED THE FIRST AIRLINE 40-HR. WEEK, PENSION FUND, GROUP INSURANCE AND STOCK-OPTION PLAN, AND PIONEERED IN HIRING WAR VETERANS.*

1891 - 1974

Earl Warren

CHIEF JUSTICE OF THE UNITED STATES SUPREME COURT (1953-69) AND GOVERNOR

EARL, THE JOB IS YOURS.
I AM DEEPLY HONORED, MR. PRESIDENT.

WARREN WENT TO THE UNIVERSITY OF CALIFORNIA AT BERKELEY, THEN TO ITS LAW SCHOOL. AFTER SERVING IN WORLD WAR I AS AN INFANTRY FIRST LIEUTENANT, WARREN WAS FIRST ALAMEDA COUNTY DISTRICT ATTORNEY, THEN STATE ATTORNEY GENERAL. HIS SUCCESS AS A PROSECUTOR PUSHED HIM INTO A POLITICAL CAREER. ***HE WAS ELECTED GOV. OF CALIFORNIA THREE TIMES, SERVING FROM 1943 TO 1953. HE WON BOTH THE DEMOCRATIC AND REPUBLICAN NOMINATIONS FOR GOV. IN 1946, THE FIRST MAN EVER TO DO THIS. IN 1948 WARREN WAS THE REPUBLICAN NOMINEE FOR VICE PRESIDENT. HE WAS UNSUCCESSFUL IN HIS TRY FOR THE REPUBLICAN NOMINATION FOR PRESIDENT IN 1948 AND 1952. PRES. EISENHOWER APPOINTED HIM CHIEF JUSTICE OF THE UNITED STATES SUPREME COURT IN 1953. HE HELD THIS JOB UNTIL 1969. WARREN WAS ONE OF THE MOST INFLUENTIAL AND CONTROVERSIAL JURISTS IN OUR HISTORY. THE GREAT ISSUES OF THE "WARREN COURT" INVOLVED CIVIL RIGHTS, SCHOOL DESEGREGATION, REAPPORTIONMENT AND CRIMINAL JUSTICE.***

HE WAS BORN IN LOS ANGELES, CAL.

ALL 50 STATES WILL REAPPORTION THEIR LEGISLATIVE DISTRICTS. LEGISLATORS REPRESENT PEOPLE, NOT TREES OR ACRES.

WARREN FOUGHT TO MAKE CONSTITUTIONAL RIGHTS MEANINGFUL FOR THE LOWEST AS WELL AS FOR THE HIGHEST OF MEN.

WHEN HE RETIRED AS CHIEF JUSTICE IN 1969, HE WAS A TEACHER, LECTURER AND AUTHOR. ***HIS BOOK, "A DEMOCRACY- IF YOU CAN KEEP IT," WAS PUBLISHED IN 1971.***

KERN

HE SERVED ON THE COMMISSION THAT CONCLUDED THAT ***LEE HARVEY OSWALD ACTED ALONE WHEN HE ASSASSINATED PRES. KENNEDY, NOV. 22, 1963. WARREN RANKS WITH JOHN MARSHALL AND ROGER TANEY AS ONE OF THE MOST IMPORTANT CHIEF JUSTICES IN OUR NATION'S HISTORY.***

1892 - 1971

Reinhold Niebuhr

THE GREATEST PROTESTANT THEOLOGIAN OF THE CENTURY

THE TRAGEDY OF MAN IS THAT HE CAN CONCEIVE SELF PERFECTION BUT HE CANNOT ACHIEVE IT.

NIEBUHR STUDIED AT ELMHURST (ILL.) COLLEGE AND EDEN THEOLOGICAL SEMINARY IN WEBSTER GROVES, MO., AND IN 1915 GRADUATED FROM YALE DIVINITY SCHOOL. HE BECAME THE PASTOR OF THE EVANGELICAL CHURCH IN DETROIT, MICH. HERE, HE WORKED FOR AND DEFENDED THE LABORER, CRITICIZING MANY INDUSTRIALISTS. IN 1928 HE JOINED UNION SEMINARY AS AN ASSISTANT PROFESSOR OF PHILOSOPHY OF RELIGION. ***BY 1939 NIEBUHR WAS A LEADING GOSPEL THEOLOGIAN. HE WAS HIGHLY RESPECTED BY PROTESTANT AND ROMAN CATHOLIC SCHOLARS WHO REGARDED HIM AS A GIANT IN THEOLOGY. NIEBUHR STRESSED "ORIGINAL SIN," WHICH HE EXPLAINED AS PRIDE, AS THE "UNIVERSALITY OF SELF-REGARD IN EVERYBODY'S MOTIVES WHETHER THEY ARE IDEALISTS OR REALISTS OR WHETHER THEY ARE BENEVOLENT OR NOT." HE ALSO BELIEVED THAT HISTORICAL DEVELOPMENT MEANS MORAL PROGRESS. HE BECAME DEAN OF UNION THEOLOGICAL SEMINARY IN NEW YORK CITY WHERE HE SERVED FROM 1950 TO 1960.***

HE WAS BORN IN WRIGHT CITY, MO.
MANKIND SHOULD NOT PASSIVELY ACCEPT EVIL, BUT SHOULD STRIVE FOR MORAL SOLUTIONS TO ALL PROBLEMS.

YOUR BOOK ON MORAL MAN REALLY BRINGS THE MESSAGE HOME.

NIEBUHR'S TEACHINGS AND WRITINGS INFLUENCED SUCH PUBLIC FIGURES AS ***DEAN ACHESON, GEORGE BUNDY, HANS J. MORGENTHAU AND ARTHUR M. SCHLESINGER, JR.***

KERN

SOME OF HIS BOOKS ARE ***"MORAL MAN AND IMMORAL SOCIETY," THE TWO-VOLUME "NATURE AND DESTINY OF MAN," "CHRISTIANITY AND POWER POLITICS" AND "DISCERNING THE SIGNS OF THE TIMES."***

1893 – 1964

Cole Porter

AMERICAN COMPOSER AND LYRICIST OF POPULAR MUSIC

THE SON OF WELL-TO-DO PARENTS, 10-YEAR-OLD COLE PORTER WROTE A SONG WHICH HIS MOTHER HAD PUBLISHED PRIVATELY. PORTER GRADUATED FROM YALE, THEN ENROLLED IN LAW AT HARVARD BUT TURNED FROM LAW TO MUSIC, STUDYING COMPOSITION AT HARVARD AND PARIS. IN 1916 HE HAD HIS FIRST SUCCESS AS COMPOSER OF THE SCORE FOR THE MUSICAL REVUE, "SEE AMERICA FIRST." DURING WORLD WAR I HE ENLISTED IN THE FRENCH FOREIGN LEGION AND LATER WAS TRANSFERRED TO THE FRENCH ARMY, SERVING UNTIL 1919. AFTER THE WAR HE RETURNED TO THE U.S. WHERE HIS WITTY LYRICS AND MELODIES MADE HIM ONE OF THE MOST NOTABLE FIGURES IN AMERICAN POPULAR MUSIC. PORTER'S FIRST MAJOR SUCCESS WAS "FIFTY MILLION FRENCHMEN," WRITTEN IN 1929. HE FELL WHILE HORSEBACK RIDING IN 1937. ALTHOUGH IN GREAT PAIN, WHILE AWAITING THE AMBULANCE HE WROTE THE LYRICS OF THE SONG "AT LONG LAST LOVE." HE WAS CRIPPLED FOR THE REST OF HIS LIFE AND THERE WAS SCARCELY A DAY THAT HE WAS FREE OF PAIN.

HE WAS BORN IN PERU, INDIANA.

LIKE THIS ONE?

HEY, THAT'S "NIGHT AND DAY!"

PORTER'S MUSICAL COMEDIES INCLUDE "ANYTHING GOES," "RED HOT AND BLUE," "LEAVE IT TO ME," "CAN CAN," "SILK STOCKINGS," AND "KISS ME KATE," CONSIDERED HIS FINEST AND MOST UNUSUAL MUSICAL, BASED ON SHAKESPEARE'S "THE TAMING OF THE SHREW."

SOME OF HIS WELL-KNOWN SONGS ARE "BEGIN THE BEGUINE," "NIGHT AND DAY," "YOU'RE THE TOP," "WHAT IS THIS THING CALLED LOVE" AND "SO IN LOVE AM I." HE COMPOSED THE MUSIC FOR THE MOTION PICTURES "BORN TO DANCE," "ROSALIE" AND "HIGH SOCIETY."

KERN

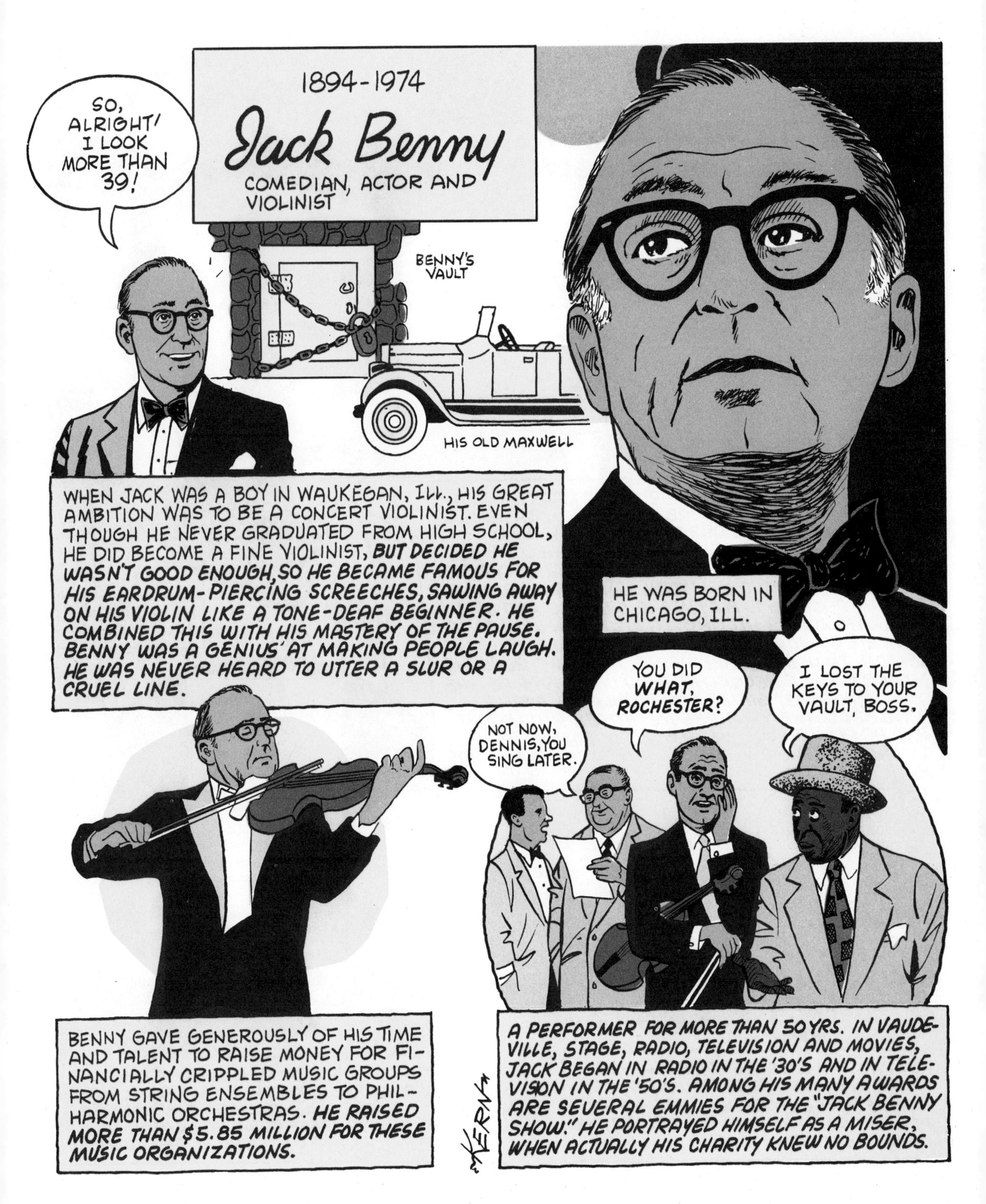
1894-1974
Jack Benny
COMEDIAN, ACTOR AND VIOLINIST
SO, ALRIGHT! I LOOK MORE THAN 39!
BENNY'S VAULT
HIS OLD MAXWELL
WHEN JACK WAS A BOY IN WAUKEGAN, ILL., HIS GREAT AMBITION WAS TO BE A CONCERT VIOLINIST. EVEN THOUGH HE NEVER GRADUATED FROM HIGH SCHOOL, HE DID BECOME A FINE VIOLINIST, BUT DECIDED HE WASN'T GOOD ENOUGH, SO HE BECAME FAMOUS FOR HIS EARDRUM-PIERCING SCREECHES, SAWING AWAY ON HIS VIOLIN LIKE A TONE-DEAF BEGINNER. HE COMBINED THIS WITH HIS MASTERY OF THE PAUSE. BENNY WAS A GENIUS AT MAKING PEOPLE LAUGH. HE WAS NEVER HEARD TO UTTER A SLUR OR A CRUEL LINE.
HE WAS BORN IN CHICAGO, ILL.
NOT NOW, DENNIS, YOU SING LATER.
YOU DID WHAT, ROCHESTER?
I LOST THE KEYS TO YOUR VAULT, BOSS.
BENNY GAVE GENEROUSLY OF HIS TIME AND TALENT TO RAISE MONEY FOR FINANCIALLY CRIPPLED MUSIC GROUPS FROM STRING ENSEMBLES TO PHILHARMONIC ORCHESTRAS. HE RAISED MORE THAN $5.85 MILLION FOR THESE MUSIC ORGANIZATIONS.
KERN
A PERFORMER FOR MORE THAN 50 YRS. IN VAUDEVILLE, STAGE, RADIO, TELEVISION AND MOVIES, JACK BEGAN IN RADIO IN THE '30'S AND IN TELEVISION IN THE '50'S. AMONG HIS MANY AWARDS ARE SEVERAL EMMIES FOR THE "JACK BENNY SHOW." HE PORTRAYED HIMSELF AS A MISER, WHEN ACTUALLY HIS CHARITY KNEW NO BOUNDS.

1895-1948

George Herman "Babe" Ruth

BASEBALL'S GREAT SLUGGER

RUTH WAS RAISED AS AN ORPHAN AT ST. MARY'S INDUSTRIAL SCHOOL IN BALTIMORE. HIS SKILL IN BASEBALL WAS RECOGNIZED BY ONE OF HIS TEACHERS WHO HELPED HIM START HIS CAREER. RUTH JOINED THE BOSTON RED SOX AS A LEFT-HANDED PITCHER IN 1914. THE SOX SOLD HIM TO THE NEW YORK YANKEES IN 1920. HE GAVE UP PITCHING TO PLAY IN THE OUTFIELD AND CONCENTRATE ON HIS HITTING. IN 1927 RUTH WON FAME WITH HIS 60 HOME RUNS DURING A SINGLE, 154-GAME SEASON. IN HIS LIFETIME HE HIT 714 HOME RUNS, THE MAJOR LEAGUE RECORD HE HELD UNTIL 1974. HE WAS ONE OF THE MOST GIFTED AND POPULAR PLAYERS IN BASEBALL. THE YANKEES RELEASED HIM IN 1934 AND HE PLAYED ONE YEAR WITH THE BOSTON BRAVES. IT WAS WITH THE BRAVES THAT HE HIT HIS 714th HOME RUN.

HE SET A RECORD FOR SCORELESS WORLD SERIES INNINGS.

RUTH WAS AN EXCELLENT LEFT-HANDED PITCHER. IN 163 GAMES HE WON 92, LOST 44. HIS PERCENTAGE WAS .676. HE WAS ALSO AN OUTSTANDING OUTFIELDER, ONE OF THE BEST OF HIS TIME.

HE PLAYED 2,503 GAMES. HIS LIFETIME BATTING AVERAGE WAS .342. RUTH WAS ELECTED TO THE BASEBALL HALL OF FAME IN 1936. WHEN THE YANKEES BUILT THEIR NEW STADIUM IT WAS NICKNAMED "THE HOUSE THAT RUTH BUILT."

KERN

1895 - 1972

J. Edgar Hoover

FIRST DIRECTOR OF THE FEDERAL BUREAU OF INVESTIGATION

WE'LL BUILD THIS BUREAU INTO ONE OF THE FINEST IN THE WORLD.

AFTER FINISHING HIGH SCHOOL, HOOVER STUDIED LAW AT GEORGE WASHINGTON UNIVERSITY. IN 1917 HE WAS ADMITTED TO THE BAR AND JOINED THE U.S. DEPT OF JUSTICE. *AFTER SERVING AS SPECIAL ASS'T TO THE ATTORNEY GENERAL, IN 1921 HE WAS NAMED ASS'T DIRECTOR OF THE INVESTIGATION SECTION OF THE JUSTICE DEPT. AT 29, HE WAS APPOINTED TO HEAD THE SMALL AND THEN INCOMPETENT FEDERAL BUREAU OF INVESTIGATION. HE MODERNIZED THE F.B.I. INTO ONE OF THE MOST EFFICIENT CRIME FIGHTING AGENCIES IN THE WORLD. HOOVER INTRODUCED A CENTRALIZED FINGERPRINT FILE, ESTABLISHED A NATIONAL CRIME LABORATORY, SET UP NEW STANDARDS FOR THE RECRUITING OF AGENTS, AND INTRODUCED SCIENTIFIC CRIME DETECTION METHODS. HE RAN A ONE-MAN SHOW. UNTIL HIS DEATH HE WAS THE ONLY DIRECTOR THE F.B.I. EVER HAD.*

DOWN WITH THE WAR!

NO - VIETNAM

GET OUT OF VIETNAM

HOOVER SERVED UNDER 8 PRESIDENTS AND 16 ATTORNEYS GENERAL, THROUGH THE *PROHIBITION ERA, THE GREAT DEPRESSION, THE 1920 GANG WARS, WORLD WAR II ESPIONAGE, CIVIL RIGHTS MARCHES, CAMPUS UNRESTS, AND ANTI-VIETNAM WAR PROTESTS OF THE 1960'S.*

YOU'RE UNDER ARREST.

DURING THE 1930'S, HOOVER'S INVESTIGATIONS AND *CAPTURES OF DANGEROUS CRIMINALS BROUGHT THE BUREAU INTO NATIONAL PROMINENCE FOR ITS DARING AND TOUGHNESS.*

1897-1962

William Faulkner

NOBEL-PRIZE NOVELIST

I SYMPATHIZE WITH YOU AND WILL DO ALL I CAN TO HELP YOUR CAUSE.
THANK YOU!

FAULKNER SERVED WITH THE ROYAL CANADIAN AIR AIR FORCE AND WAS WOUNDED IN AERIAL COMBAT. ON HIS RETURN TO THE U.S. HE TOOK SOME COURSES AT THE UNIVERSITY OF MISSISSIPPI AND WORKED AT ODD JOBS. ***HIS FIRST NOVEL, "SOLDIER'S PAY," WAS PUBLISHED IN 1926. FAULKNER'S SCENES AND CHARACTERS WERE FROM HIS HOME TOWN, OXFORD, WHERE HE LIVED MOST OF HIS LIFE. HE PORTRAYED THE DECAY OF SOUTHERN ARISTOCRACY, ALTHOUGH HE ALSO SHOWED RECOVERY FROM THE DECAY. MANY OF HIS LATER BOOKS DEAL WITH NEGRO RIGHTS. HIS NOVELS SHOW EXCEPTIONAL ELOQUENCE, HUMOR AND REALISM. FAULKNER IS WIDELY CONSIDERED THE GREATEST AMERICAN WRITER OF FICTION OF THE 20th CENTURY.***

HE WAS BORN IN NEW ALBANY, MISS.
KERN

FAULKNER WAS THE VOICE OF THE SOUTH.

"THE SOUND AND THE FURY" AND "SANCTUARY" WON HIM A PLACE AMONG THE MAJOR FIGURES OF AMERICAN LITERATURE. SOME OF HIS OTHER NOVELS WERE "AS I LAY DYING," "LIGHT IN AUGUST," "ABSALOM, ABSALOM!" AND "REQUIEM FOR A NUN." FAULKNER ALSO PUBLISHED "COLLECTED STORIES."

IN 1948 HE WAS ELECTED TO THE ***AMERICAN ACADEMY OF ARTS AND LETTERS, AND IN 1949 HE RECEIVED THE NOBEL PRIZE FOR LITERATURE. IN 1955 HE WON THE PULITZER PRIZE FOR HIS NOVEL OF WORLD WAR I, CALLED "A FABLE."***

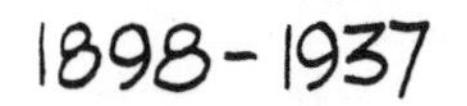

Amelia Earhart

PIONEER AVIATRIX

SHE WENT TO COLUMBIA UNIVERSITY AND HARVARD SUMMER SCHOOL, AFTER RETURNING FROM NURSING DUTY DURING WORLD WAR I. MISS EARHART THEN WENT TO CALIFORNIA WHERE SHE LEARNED TO FLY. **IN 1928 SHE BECAME THE FIRST WOMAN PASSENGER TO FLY THE ATLANTIC WITH WILBUR STUTZ AND LOUIS GORDON, FROM NEWFOUNDLAND TO WALES. IN 1932 SHE WAS THE FIRST WOMAN TO FLY SOLO ACROSS THE ATLANTIC FROM NEWFOUNDLAND TO LONDONDERRY, IRELAND, IN 14 HRS., 54 MIN. IN 1935 SHE WAS THE FIRST WOMAN TO FLY FROM HONOLULU TO THE UNITED STATES AND THE FIRST TO FLY ACROSS THE U.S. IN BOTH DIRECTIONS, ALONE. IN JUNE 1937 SHE BEGAN HER FLIGHT AROUND THE WORLD. FRED NOONAN WENT ALONG AS NAVIGATOR. THEIR PLANE DISAPPEARED JULY 3, SOMEWHERE NEAR HOWLAND ISLAND IN THE PACIFIC. U.S. NAVY PLANES AND SHIPS FAILED TO DISCOVER ANY TRACE OF THE FLYERS.**

SHE WAS BORN AT ATCHISON, KANSAS.

I LOVE FLYING! THIS IS WHY I WROTE "THE FUN OF IT."

IN 1928, SHE DESCRIBED HER FIRST TRANS-ATLANTIC FLIGHT IN THE BOOK **"20 HRS. 40 MIN." "THE FUN OF IT" WAS WRITTEN IN 1931. IN 1937 "LAST FLIGHT" WAS WRITTEN BY HER HUSBAND, PUBLISHER GEORGE PUTNAM, FROM HER DIARY OF THE JOURNEY, TRANSMITTED FROM VARIOUS STOPS ALONG THE WAY.**

KERN

MISS EARHART WAS THE **FIRST WOMAN TO RECEIVE THE DISTINGUISHED FLYING CROSS.**

1898 - 1937

George Gershwin

POPULAR AND CLASSICAL COMPOSER

AT 16, GERSHWIN WAS STUDYING PIANO AND HARMONY, ALREADY CONVINCED OF HIS LIFE'S WORK: TO GIVE POPULAR MUSIC ARTISTIC STATUS. WHEN HE FINISHED HIGH SCHOOL HE ENTERED TIN PAN ALLEY AS A SONG WRITER AND SONG PLUGGER. ***HIS FIRST SUBSTANTIAL MUSICAL COMEDY SUCCESS WAS "LA, LA, LUCILLE." SOON AFTER THIS HE SKYROCKETED TO FAME WITH THE SONG "SWANEE." GERSHWIN WAS NOTED FOR INGENIOUS RHYTHMS AND HARMONY. NEARLY ALL THE LYRICS FOR HIS SONGS WERE WRITTEN BY HIS BROTHER IRA. IN 1935 HE WROTE HIS LARGEST AND PERHAPS HIS GREATEST WORK, THE OPERA, "PORGY AND BESS," WHICH SHOWS SCENES OF NEGRO LIFE NEAR CHARLESTON, S.C. THIS WAS THE FIRST AMERICAN OPERA TO BE A HUGE SUCCESS IN OTHER COUNTRIES AS WELL AS IN THE UNITED STATES. SOME OF HIS MOST MEMORABLE SHOWS ARE "LADY, BE GOOD," "GIRL CRAZY" AND "STRIKE UP THE BAND." GERSHWIN'S "RHAPSODY IN BLUE" HAS BECOME THE MOST INTERNATIONALLY CELEBRATED AND OFTEN PERFORMED ORCHESTRAL WORK EVER WRITTEN BY AN AMERICAN.***

HE WAS BORN IN BROOKLYN, N.Y.

THAT WAS BEAUTIFUL, GEORGE.

SOUNDS LIKE ANOTHER WINNER TO ME.

GERSHWIN, ONE OF AMERICA'S FOREMOST COMPOSERS OF POPULAR SONGS AND MUSICAL COMEDIES, ***WON THE PULITZER PRIZE IN 1932 FOR THE BEST PLAY OF THE SEASON WITH "OF THEE I SING."***

SOME OF HIS BEST-KNOWN SONGS ARE ***"THE MAN I LOVE," "I GOT RHYTHM," "SUMMERTIME," "EMBRACEABLE YOU," "S' WONDERFUL," "BIDIN' MY TIME" AND "A FOGGY DAY." GERSHWIN WROTE 30 MUSICAL COMEDIES FOR STAGE AND FILMS.***

KERN

1898 - 1974

Katharine Cornell

FIRST LADY OF THE AMERICAN THEATER

THIS PART IS JUST MADE FOR YOU, KIT.
WITH YOUR DIRECTION, GUTHRIE, IT WILL BE A GREAT PLAY.

SHE GREW UP IN BUFFALO, N.Y., AND STUDIED DRAMA AT THE OAKSMERE SCHOOL IN MAMARONECK, N.Y. WHEN SHE WAS 18 SHE BEGAN ACTING WITH THE WASHINGTON SQUARE PLAYERS IN NEW YORK CITY, THEN JOINED THE FAMOUS JESSIE BONSTELLE PLAYERS IN DETROIT AND BUFFALO. SHE MARRIED GUTHRIE McCLINTIC, THE NOTED THEATRICAL PRODUCER, IN 1921. HE WAS HER DIRECTOR. *KATHARINE BECAME FAMOUS WHEN SHE APPEARED IN "A BILL OF DIVORCEMENT." MOST OF HER ROLES WERE ROMANTIC AND EMOTIONAL. SHE SOON BECAME A MAJOR STAR. DURING THE THIRTIES AND FORTIES SHE APPEARED ON U.S STEEL'S RADIO SHOW, "THEATRE GUILD ON THE AIR." IN 1957 SHE HEADED THE CAST OF A TV PRODUCTION, "THERE SHALL BE NO NIGHT." FROM 1959 TO 1960 SHE MADE A FAREWELL TOUR IN "DEAR LIAR."*

SHE WAS BORN IN BERLIN, GERMANY.

AS ST. JOAN

SHE PLAYED IN "LITTLE WOMEN," "ROMEO AND JULIET," "SAINT JOAN" AND "THE PRESCOTT PROPOSALS." ***ONE OF HER BEST ROLES WAS AS ELIZABETH IN "THE BARRETTS OF WIMPOLE STREET." DURING WORLD WAR II SHE PRESENTED THIS PLAY FOR THE SOLDIERS IN THE EUROPEAN AREA.***

I MEAN EVERY WORD I SAY, KIT!
YOU FLATTER ME, GEORGE.

GEO. JEAN NATHAN, FOREMOST DRAMA CRITIC, ONCE SAID OF HER, ***"I WOULD GIVE ALL THE OTHER YOUNG ACTRESSES PUT TOGETHER FOR HER—AND THREE-QUARTERS OF THE OLDER ONES."***

KERN

1899-1974

Edward "Duke" Ellington

AMERICAN BANDLEADER, COMPOSER AND PIANO VIRTUOSO

HOW MANY COUNTRIES HAVE GIVEN YOU AWARDS, DUKE?

I NEVER COUNT AWARDS. I ONLY ENJOY!

HE SHOWED AN EARLY TALENT FOR PAINTING AND WON AN ART SCHOLARSHIP TO NEW YORK'S PRATT INSTITUTE. HE REJECTED IT AND EVENTUALLY WENT TO NEW YORK AS A MUSICIAN. ***IN 1927, HE AND HIS BAND WON WORLDWIDE FAME WHEN THEY PLAYED AT HARLEM'S FAMOUS COTTON CLUB. THEY STAYED THERE 5YRS. ELLINGTON WAS KNOWN AS AMERICA'S GOODWILL AMBASSADOR ALL OVER THE WORLD AND ONE OF AMERICA'S GREATEST 20th CENTURY COMPOSERS. HE WAS CALLED "DUKE" BECAUSE OF HIS IMMACULATE ATTIRE. IN LATER YEARS HE WROTE LONGER ORCHESTRAL PIECES, SACRED WORKS, CHORAL PIECES, TONE POEMS DEPICTING THE HISTORY OF THE AMERICAN NEGRO, AND MOVIE, TELEVISION AND BALLET SCORES. "DUKE" ELLINGTON LEFT A GREAT AMERICAN MUSICAL LEGACY THAT WILL LIVE ON THROUGH HIS RECORDS AND BY ALL THE OTHER ARTISTS WHO PLAY HIS MUSIC.***

I WORK AND I WRITE AND THAT'S IT!

YOUR WIT, TASTE, INTELLIGENCE AND ELEGANCE MAKE YOU AMERICA'S FOREMOST COMPOSER.

"DUKE" WAS 17 WHEN HE WROTE HIS FIRST SONG, ***"SODA FOUNTAIN RAG." SINCE THEN HE WROTE MORE THAN 1,000 SONGS.*** SOME OF THE WELL KNOWN ONES ARE ***"MOOD INDIGO," "SOLITUDE," "SOPHISTICATED LADY"*** AND ***"DON'T GET AROUND MUCH ANYMORE."***

KERN

IN 1969, PRES. NIXON PRESENTED HIM WITH THE NATION'S HIGHEST CIVILIAN HONOR, ***THE MEDAL OF FREEDOM. IN 1973, HE WAS PRESENTED WITH THE FRENCH LEGION OF HONOR AND MEMBERSHIP IN THE SWEDISH ACADEMY. HE RECEIVED PRACTICALLY EVERY HONOR THAT COULD COME TO A MUSICIAN.***

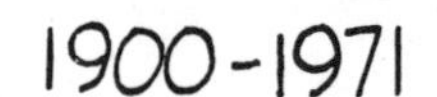

Louis Armstrong

JAZZ TRUMPETER, BAND LEADER AND SINGER

MY PHILOSOPHY? IF YOU DON'T TREAT ME RIGHT, SHAME ON YOU.

BORN ON JULY 4 IN A BLACK GHETTO, HE WAS 9 YRS. OLD WHEN HE LEFT SCHOOL TO GO TO WORK. 4 YRS. LATER, HE WAS PLACED IN A COLORED WAIFS' HOME, WHERE HIS MUSICAL CAREER BEGAN. *BY THE TIME HE LEFT THE HOME, HE WAS PLAYING THE CORNET AND LEADING THE BAND. HE SAILED FOR A YEAR ON THE MISSISSIPPI RIVERBOAT "SIDNEY," PLAYING WITH AN ORCHESTRA. ONE OF THE BAND MEMBERS TAUGHT HIM TO READ MUSIC. HE WAS THEN INVITED TO PLAY WITH KING OLIVER'S BAND IN CHICAGO. HERE HE WAS ALLOWED TO SING IN HIS DEEP, WARM HUSKY VOICE AND WAS AN IMMEDIATE SUCCESS. ARMSTRONG, WHO WAS KNOWN AS "SATCHEL MOUTH" OR "SATCHMO," ORGANIZED HIS OWN BAND IN 1925 AND TOURED THE WORLD. HIS TRUMPET PLAYING DISPLAYED A GREAT ENERGY, IMAGINATION AND INSTANTLY RECOGNIZABLE TONE THAT INSPIRED MANY OTHER JAZZ MUSICIANS. FROM THE POVERTY-STRICKEN SLUMS, LOUIS ARMSTRONG ROSE TO FAME AND IS RECOGNIZED AS THE MOST INFLUENTIAL MUSICIAN IN THE HISTORY OF JAZZ.*

HE WAS BORN IN NEW ORLEANS, LOUISIANA.

HE COMPOSED MANY POPULAR SONGS, SUCH AS *"SWING THAT MUSIC," "WHERE DID YOU STAY LAST NIGHT," "SATCHEL MOUTH SURVEY," "I GOT A HEART FULL OF RHYTHM"* AND *"SUGAR FOOT STOMP."*

KERN

ARMSTRONG MADE *OVER 1500 RECORDS, MANY OF WHICH ARE COLLECTORS' ITEMS. HE WAS A MEMBER OF THE AMERICAN SOCIETY OF COMPOSERS, AUTHORS AND PUBLISHERS.*

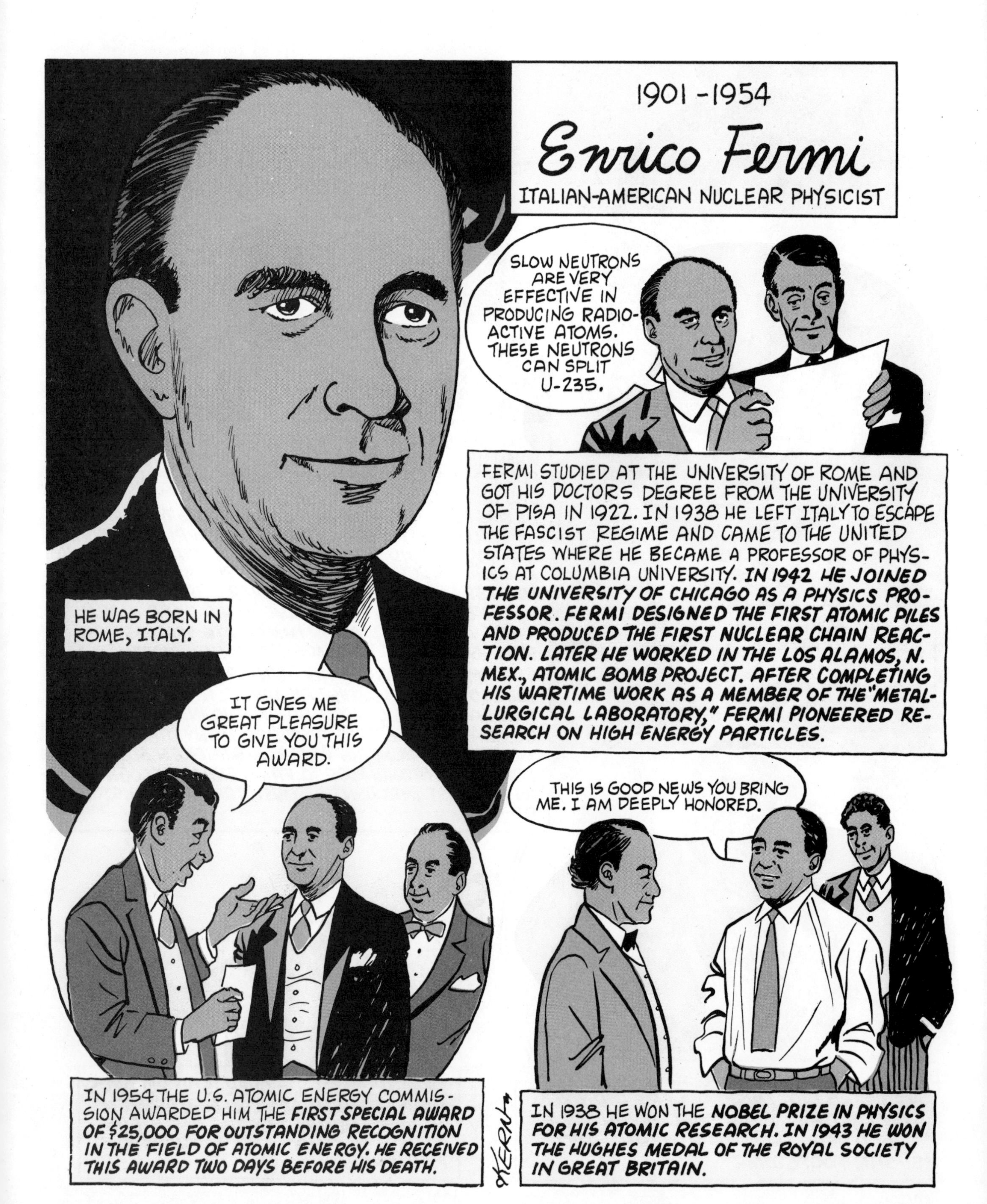
1901 - 1954
Enrico Fermi
ITALIAN-AMERICAN NUCLEAR PHYSICIST
SLOW NEUTRONS ARE VERY EFFECTIVE IN PRODUCING RADIO-ACTIVE ATOMS. THESE NEUTRONS CAN SPLIT U-235.
FERMI STUDIED AT THE UNIVERSITY OF ROME AND GOT HIS DOCTORS DEGREE FROM THE UNIVERSITY OF PISA IN 1922. IN 1938 HE LEFT ITALY TO ESCAPE THE FASCIST REGIME AND CAME TO THE UNITED STATES WHERE HE BECAME A PROFESSOR OF PHYSICS AT COLUMBIA UNIVERSITY. IN 1942 HE JOINED THE UNIVERSITY OF CHICAGO AS A PHYSICS PROFESSOR. FERMI DESIGNED THE FIRST ATOMIC PILES AND PRODUCED THE FIRST NUCLEAR CHAIN REACTION. LATER HE WORKED IN THE LOS ALAMOS, N. MEX., ATOMIC BOMB PROJECT. AFTER COMPLETING HIS WARTIME WORK AS A MEMBER OF THE "METALLURGICAL LABORATORY," FERMI PIONEERED RESEARCH ON HIGH ENERGY PARTICLES.
HE WAS BORN IN ROME, ITALY.
IT GIVES ME GREAT PLEASURE TO GIVE YOU THIS AWARD.
IN 1954 THE U.S. ATOMIC ENERGY COMMISSION AWARDED HIM THE FIRST SPECIAL AWARD OF $25,000 FOR OUTSTANDING RECOGNITION IN THE FIELD OF ATOMIC ENERGY. HE RECEIVED THIS AWARD TWO DAYS BEFORE HIS DEATH.
THIS IS GOOD NEWS YOU BRING ME. I AM DEEPLY HONORED.
IN 1938 HE WON THE NOBEL PRIZE IN PHYSICS FOR HIS ATOMIC RESEARCH. IN 1943 HE WON THE HUGHES MEDAL OF THE ROYAL SOCIETY IN GREAT BRITAIN.
KERN

1902-1968

John Steinbeck

NOBEL-PRIZE NOVELIST

"GRAPES OF WRATH" CHARACTERS LEAVING FOR CALIFORNIA.

STEINBECK WENT TO STANFORD UNIVERSITY BUT LEFT IN 1926 WITHOUT GETTING HIS DEGREE. HE WORKED AT VARIOUS JOBS, THEN PUBLISHED HIS FIRST NOVEL, "**CUP OF GOLD**." IN 1930 HE SETTLED NEAR MONTEREY, CAL., AND WORKED FULL TIME ON HIS WRITING. ***MOST OF HIS NOVELS HAVE A CAL. SETTING AND NEARLY ALL DEAL WITH THE POOR AND DOWNTRODDEN. HIS SIXTH NOVEL, "OF MICE AND MEN," WRITTEN IN 1937, BECAME A BEST SELLER. THIS STORY ABOUT THE TRAGIC FRIENDSHIP BETWEEN TWO MIGRANT LABORERS WAS MADE INTO A PLAY AND A MOVIE. IN 1939 HE WROTE "THE GRAPES OF WRATH," THE STORY OF A FAMILY OF POOR FARMERS FROM THE OKLAHOMA DUST BOWL, WHOSE DREAM WAS TO FIND SECURITY IN CAL. THIS NOVEL IS ONE OF THE MOST FAMOUS OF OUR TIME. SOME OF HIS OTHER WORKS INCLUDE "THE MOON IS DOWN," "CANNERY ROW," "THE WAYWARD BUS," "THE PEARL" AND "BURNING BRIGHT."***

HE WAS BORN IN SALINAS, CAL.

HOW ARE THINGS GOING, SOLDIER?

IN 1943, HE WAS EUROPEAN WAR CORRESPONDENT FOR THE NEW YORK "***HERALD TRIBUNE***." ***IN 1948 HE PUBLISHED "RUSSIAN JOURNAL," AN ACCOUNT OF HIS TRIP TO RUSSIA.***

YOUR "GRAPES OF WRATH" IS CALLED THE TWENTIETH CENTURY "UNCLE TOM'S CABIN."

IN 1940, HE WON THE PULITZER PRIZE FOR ***"GRAPES OF WRATH." IN 1962, HE WON THE NOBEL PRIZE FOR LITERATURE FOR HIS "THE WINTER OF OUR DISCONTENT" AND OTHER WORKS WHICH SHOW HIS SYMPATHY FOR POOR AND OTHER SOCIAL OUTCASTS.***

KERN

1902–1971

Robert "Bobby" Jones

"GREATEST GOLFER OF ALL TIME"

YOU MEN DO ME GREAT HONOR AND I THANK YOU FOR IT.

JONES ATTENDED THE GEORGIA INSTITUTE OF TECHNOLOGY, THEN STUDIED LAW AT HARVARD UNIVERSITY. HE WAS ADMITTED TO THE GEORGIA BAR, PRACTICING IN ATLANTA. *JONES WAS THE ONLY GOLFER TO TO WIN THE U.S. OPEN, BRITISH OPEN, U.S. AMATEUR AND BRITISH AMATEUR TOURNAMENTS--"THE GRAND SLAM"-- ALL IN ONE YEAR. HE RETIRED IN 1930 TO A LAW BUSINESS AND APPEARED IN SEVERAL MOVIES ON GOLF. IN 1950 THE AMERICAN SPORTS EDITORS VOTED HIM THE OUTSTANDING GOLFER OF THE YEARS 1900-49.*

HE WAS BORN IN ATLANTA, GA.

AFTER HIS RETIREMENT, *HE WAS VICE-PRESIDENT OF A. G. SPAULDING SALES CORP., SPORTING SUPPLIERS. "BOBBY" AUTHORED "DOWN THE FAIRWAYS," "GOLD IS MY GAME," "BOBBY JONES ON GOLF" AND "BOBBY JONES ON THE BASIC SWING."*

GOLF IS THE ONE GAME I KNOW WHICH BECOMES MORE AND MORE DIFFICULT THE LONGER ONE PLAYS IT.

KERN

OFTEN CALLED *THE GREATEST GOLFER OF ALL TIME. HE WON THE U.S. OPEN 4 TIMES, THE BRITISH OPEN 3 TIMES AND THE U.S. AMATEUR 5 TIMES. IN 1944 HE SERVED AS A COLONEL WITH THE USAAF.*

1902-1974

Charles A. Lindbergh

PIONEER FLYER AND ENGINEER

ST. LOUIS

RAISED IN LITTLE FALLS, MINN., LINDBERGH LEFT THE UNIVERSITY OF WIS. AFTER 2 YRS. AND TOOK A COURSE IN FLYING AT LINCOLN, NEB. HE BOUGHT A PLANE FOR $500 IN 1923 AND MADE HIS FIRST FLIGHT ALONE. HE FLEW BETWEEN CHICAGO AND ST. LOUIS FOR THE U.S. AIRMAIL SERVICE. WHEN *$25,000 WAS OFFERED TO THE AVIATOR WHO COULD FLY FROM NEW YORK TO PARIS, LINDBERGH ACCEPTED THE CHALLENGE AND, LEAVING ON MAY 20, 1927, HE SUCCESSFULLY FLEW ACROSS THE ATLANTIC IN A SINGLE ENGINE MONOPLANE, "SPIRIT OF ST. LOUIS," IN 33 HRS., 29 MIN. 100,000 PEOPLE GREETED THE "LONE EAGLE" AT THE PARIS AIRFIELD WITH WILD ENTHUSIASM. DURING WORLD WAR II LINDBERGH WORKED AS A TECHNICAL ADVISOR TO MANUFACTURERS OF MILITARY AIRCRAFT, THEN BECAME SPECIAL CONSULTANT TO THE CHIEF OF STAFF, U.S. AIR FORCE.*

HE WAS BORN IN DETROIT, MICH.
TO YOU, LINDY, WITH OUR SINCEREST CONGRATULATIONS.

PARIS
NEW YORK
AMERICA IS PROUD OF YOU.!
KERN

PRES. COOLIDGE PRESENTED HIM WITH THE DISTINGUISHED FLYING CROSS. *"SLIM" LINDBERGH WAS THE NATION'S HERO!*

THE NEW YORK "TIMES" PAID HIM *$250,000 FOR HIS STORY OF THE FLIGHT. HIS BOOK "WE" BECAME A BEST SELLER. "THE SPIRIT OF ST. LOUIS" WON THE PULITZER PRIZE FOR BIOGRAPHY IN 1954.*

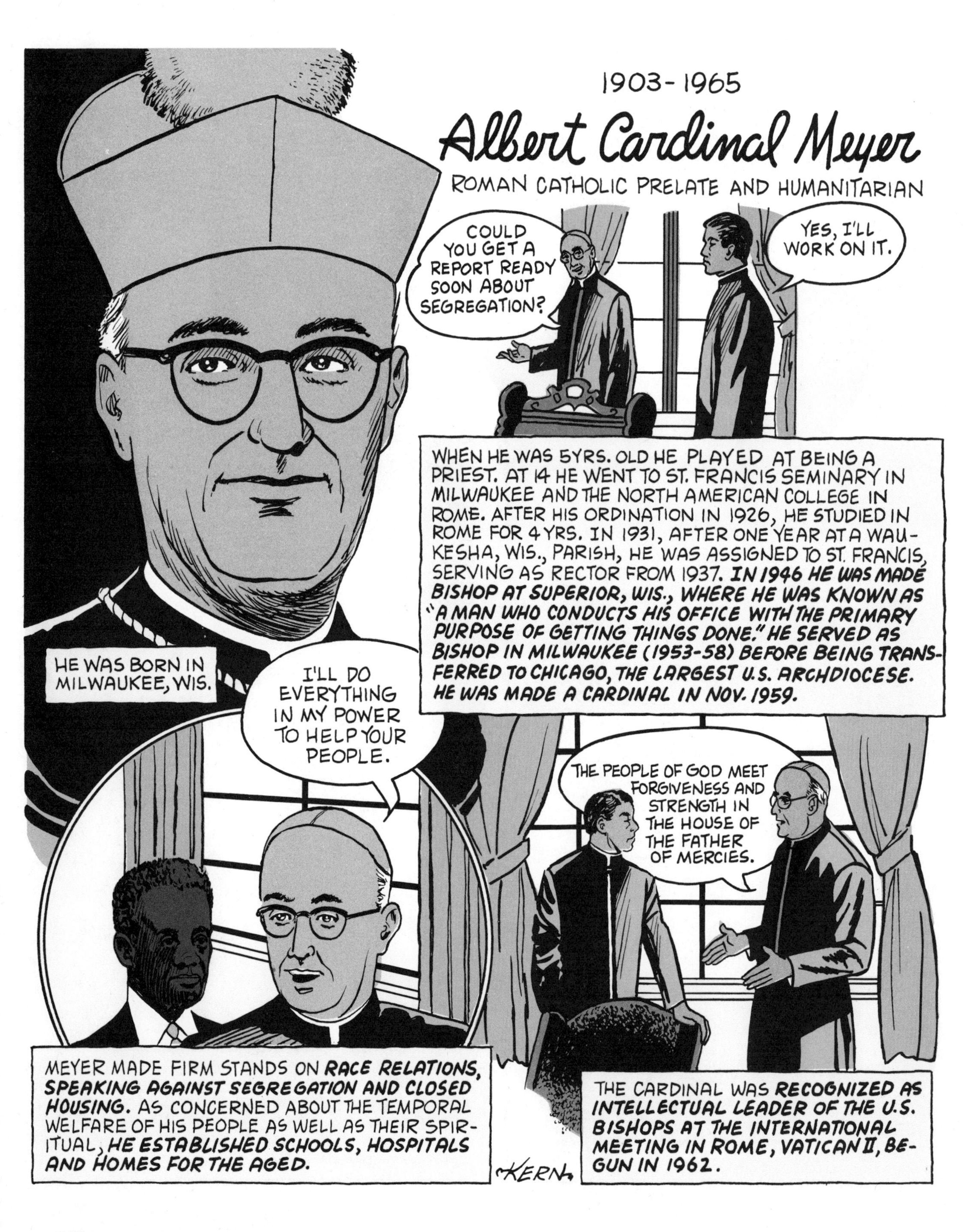
1903-1965
Albert Cardinal Meyer
ROMAN CATHOLIC PRELATE AND HUMANITARIAN
COULD YOU GET A REPORT READY SOON ABOUT SEGREGATION?
YES, I'LL WORK ON IT.
WHEN HE WAS 5 YRS. OLD HE PLAYED AT BEING A PRIEST. AT 14 HE WENT TO ST. FRANCIS SEMINARY IN MILWAUKEE AND THE NORTH AMERICAN COLLEGE IN ROME. AFTER HIS ORDINATION IN 1926, HE STUDIED IN ROME FOR 4 YRS. IN 1931, AFTER ONE YEAR AT A WAUKESHA, WIS., PARISH, HE WAS ASSIGNED TO ST. FRANCIS, SERVING AS RECTOR FROM 1937. IN 1946 HE WAS MADE BISHOP AT SUPERIOR, WIS., WHERE HE WAS KNOWN AS "A MAN WHO CONDUCTS HIS OFFICE WITH THE PRIMARY PURPOSE OF GETTING THINGS DONE." HE SERVED AS BISHOP IN MILWAUKEE (1953-58) BEFORE BEING TRANSFERRED TO CHICAGO, THE LARGEST U.S. ARCHDIOCESE. HE WAS MADE A CARDINAL IN NOV. 1959.
HE WAS BORN IN MILWAUKEE, WIS.
I'LL DO EVERYTHING IN MY POWER TO HELP YOUR PEOPLE.
THE PEOPLE OF GOD MEET FORGIVENESS AND STRENGTH IN THE HOUSE OF THE FATHER OF MERCIES.
MEYER MADE FIRM STANDS ON RACE RELATIONS, SPEAKING AGAINST SEGREGATION AND CLOSED HOUSING. AS CONCERNED ABOUT THE TEMPORAL WELFARE OF HIS PEOPLE AS WELL AS THEIR SPIRITUAL, HE ESTABLISHED SCHOOLS, HOSPITALS AND HOMES FOR THE AGED.
KERN
THE CARDINAL WAS RECOGNIZED AS INTELLECTUAL LEADER OF THE U.S. BISHOPS AT THE INTERNATIONAL MEETING IN ROME, VATICAN II, BEGUN IN 1962.

1907-1964

Rachel Carson

AMERICAN MARINE BIOLOGIST AND SCIENCE WRITER

THERE IS REAL BEAUTY IN NATURE, RACHEL.

SHE RECEIVED HER PRECOLLEGE EDUCATION FROM SPRINGDALE AND PARNASSUS, PA., PUBLIC SCHOOLS. HER MOTHER INSTILLED IN HER A LOVE OF NATURE TEACHING HER AS A CHILD THE JOY OF THE OUTDOORS. SHE WENT TO THE PENNSYLVANIA COLLEGE FOR WOMEN AT PITTSBURGH, INTENDING TO BE A WRITER. SHE CHANGED FROM AN ENGLISH TO A SCIENCE MAJOR, RECEIVING HER DEGREE IN 1929. ***SHE ENTERED JOHN HOPKINS UNIVERSITY FOR POST GRADUATE STUDY, RECEIVING HER MASTER'S DEGREE IN ZOOLOGY. IN 1931 SHE JOINED THE ZOOLOGY STAFF OF THE UNIVERSITY OF MARYLAND AND STAYED FOR 5 YRS. IN 1936 SHE ACCEPTED A JOB AS AQUATIC BIOLOGIST WITH THE U.S. BUREAU OF FISHERIES IN WASH, D.C., AS EDITOR-IN-CHIEF OF THE BUREAU. HER MAIN OBJECTIVE WAS TO INSURE THE CONSERVATION OF THE NATION'S WILD BIRDS, MAMMALS, FISH AND OTHER FORMS OF WILDLIFE, AND PREVENT THE DESTRUCTION AND DEPLETION OF OUR NATURAL WEALTH.***

SHE WAS BORN IN SPRINGDALE, PA.

I AM KNOWN AS A RELUCTANT CRUSADER BUT I HAD TO SPEAK ON THE DEGRADATION OF THE WORLD'S ENVIRONMENT.

I TRIED TO SIMPLIFY A DIFFICULT SUBJECT.

RACHEL CARSON HAD AN "***ECOLOGICAL CONSCIENCE.***" IN 1962 SHE WROTE "***SILENT SPRING.***" ***THIS BOOK JOLTED AMERICA AND PROMPTED THE FEDERAL GOVERNMENT TO TAKE ACTION AGAINST WATER AND AIR POLLUTION, DDT AND OTHER DANGEROUS PESTICIDES.***

KERN

SHE WROTE "***THE SEA AROUND US***" IN 1951 WHICH DESCRIBES THE CHEMISTRY, BIOLOGY, HISTORY AND GEOGRAPHY OF THE SEA IN PLAIN, SIMPLE TERMS FOR THE LAYMAN TO UNDERSTAND. ***THIS BOOK BECAME A BEST SELLER.***

1908 - 1965

Edward R. Murrow

AMERICAN RADIO AND TELEVISION COMMENTATOR

GOOD EVENING.

MURROW MOVED WITH HIS PARENTS TO BLANCHARD, WASH., WHEN HE WAS 5 YRS. OLD. HE GRADUATED FROM WASHINGTON STATE IN 1930 WITH A B. A. IN SPEECH. AFTER VARIOUS JOBS IN NEW YORK, MURROW JOINED C.B.S. WHERE HE WORKED FROM 1935 TO 1961. *HE WAS DIRECTOR OF TALKS AND EDUCATION, EUROPEAN DIRECTOR, WAR CORRESPONDENT, VICE-PRESIDENT AND NEWS ANALYST. DESPITE MUCH OPPOSITION, HE RAISED THE STANDARDS OF TV JOURNALISM TO NEW HEIGHTS. MANY OF HIS PROGRAMS AROUSED CONTROVERSY. HE LEFT C.B.S. IN 1961 TO BECOME THE HEAD OF THE U.S. INFORMATION AGENCY WHERE HE SERVED UNDER PRES. KENNEDY AND FOR A SHORT TIME WITH PRESIDENT JOHNSON.*

I THANK YOU FOR THIS AWARD.

MURROW LECTURED IN THE U.S. AND ABROAD ON INTERNATIONAL RELATIONS. *IN 1954 HE RECEIVED A FREEDOM HOUSE AWARD FOR A PROGRAM THAT ATTACKED SEN. JOSEPH McCARTHY AS A THREAT TO AMERICAN CIVIL LIBERTIES AND HELPED TO BRING ABOUT McCARTHY'S DOWNFALL. HE ALSO RECEIVED TELEVISION'S EMMY AWARD IN 1956 AND WAS THE AUTHOR OF "THIS IS LONDON."*

HE WAS BORN NEAR GREENSBORO, N.C.

THIS IS LONDON.

POSSESSED OF A DEEP DRAMATIC VOICE, *HE IS REMEMBERED FOR HIS EYEWITNESS ACCOUNTS VIA RADIO OF THE WORLD WAR II BOMBING RAIDS ON LONDON. AFTER THE WAR MURROW BECAME A NARRATOR AND INTERVIEWER ON TV PROGRAMS: "PERSON TO PERSON," "SEE IT NOW," "SMALL WORLD" AND "C.B.S. REPORTS."*

KERN

1908-1973

Lyndon B. Johnson

CONGRESSMAN, SENATOR, VICE-PRESIDENT AND **THIRTY-SIXTH** PRESIDENT OF THE UNITED STATES (1963-69)

I PLEDGE TO PRESS FORWARD THE NEW FRONTIER PROGRAM THAT HAS BEEN BOGGED DOWN BY INACTION IN THE LEGISLATURE.

WHEN LYNDON WAS 5 HE MOVED WITH HIS FAMILY TO JOHNSON CITY, TEXAS, AND STARTED PUBLIC SCHOOL. HE EARNED SPENDING MONEY SHINING SHOES AND PICKING COTTON. AFTER A VARIETY OF JOBS HE WENT TO SOUTHWEST STATE TEACHERS COLLEGE IN SAN MARCOS, TEX. HE GRADUATED IN 1930 AND TAUGHT PUBLIC SPEAKING AND DEBATE. ***HE THEN SERVED AS A CONGRESSIONAL SECRETARY, DIRECTOR OF THE NATIONAL YOUTH ADMINISTRATION IN TEX., U.S. REPRESENTATIVE FROM TEX., A LT. COMMANDER IN THE NAVY DURING WORLD WAR II, AND, WHILE U.S. SENATOR FROM TEXAS, HE SERVED AS MAJORITY LEADER FOR 15 YRS. FROM 1961-63 HE WAS VICE-PRESIDENT OF THE U.S. UNDER PRES. KENNEDY. HE SUCCEEDED TO THE PRESIDENCY AFTER THE TRAGIC DEATH OF PRES. KENNEDY IN DALLAS, TEX.***

HE WAS BORN NEAR STONEWALL, TEXAS.

IT'S THE DUTY OF AMERICA TO TAKE CARE OF THE AGED!

I BEAT GOLDWATER BY THE LARGEST POPULAR VOTE IN AMERICA'S HISTORY!

JOHNSON ENACTED ***MORE PROGRESSIVE LEGISLATION THAN ANY OTHER PRESIDENT IN OUR HISTORY.*** A 6FT.-3IN. TEXAN, HE SPOKE IN A FOLKSY MANNER AND REGARDED HIMSELF AS A SOUTHWESTERNER RATHER THAN A SOUTHERNER.

DURING HIS "GREAT SOCIETY" ADMINISTRATION, JOHNSON OBTAINED NEW CIVIL RIGHTS LAWS, TAX REDUCTIONS TO STIMULATE THE ECONOMY, A STRONG ANTI POVERTY PROGRAM, FEDERAL AID FOR ALL EDUCATIONAL PROGRAMS AND INCREASED SOCIAL SECURITY BENEFITS WHICH INCLUDED MEDICAL CARE FOR THE AGED.

KERN

POLLOCK GREW UP IN ARIZONA AND SOUTHERN CALIFORNIA. EARLY GEOGRAPHICAL IMPRESSIONS PLAYED AN IMPORTANT PART IN THE DEVELOPMENT OF HIS PAINTINGS. **AS A YOUTH HE OBSERVED THE SPLENDOR OF THE WESTERN LANDSCAPE AS IT UNVEILED ITSELF BEFORE HIM FROM FREIGHT TRAINS OR HIS FORD CAR. POLLOCK STUDIED WITH THOMAS HART BENTON, FAMOUS REGIONALIST ARTIST FROM MISSOURI, BEFORE DEVELOPING HIS OWN STYLE. HE BECAME ONE OF THE MOST CONTROVERSIAL ARTISTS OF HIS TIME. HIS PAINTINGS SHOW SPEED, POWER AND EMOTIONAL INTENSITY. HE WAS KILLED IN A TRAGIC AUTOMOBILE ACCIDENT IN 1956.**

HE WAS BORN IN CODY, WYOMING.

POLLOCK AND HIS STUDIO

HIS MOST ADMIRED WORKS WERE PAINTED BETWEEN 1946 AND 1951. **HE USED THE "DRIP" METHOD IN WHICH PAINT TRICKLED FROM A BRUSH OR STICK ONTO A CANVAS LAID ON A FLOOR. THIS METHOD INSPIRED THE TERM "ACTION PAINTING."**

POLLOCK WAS THE CRITICAL FIGURE IN THE EVOLUTION OF A NEW MODE OF PAINTING CALLED "**ABSTRACT EXPRESSIONISM,**" **A MOVEMENT WHICH GREW AFTER WORLD WAR II. THIS WAS AMERICA'S FIRST ART MOVEMENT TO BE FOLLOWED AND ADMIRED WORLDWIDE.**

KERN

1913 - 1970
Vince Lombardi
GREAT PRO FOOTBALL COACH
ONE MORE, MEN, AND WE HAVE IT!
LOMBARDI GRADUATED FROM FORDHAM UNIVERSITY IN 1937. HE TAUGHT AND COACHED AT ST. CECELIA HIGH SCHOOL, ENGLEWOOD N. J., THEN COACHED AT WEST POINT, NEW YORK, FOR 5 YRS. MOVING TO PROFESSIONAL FOOTBALL, HE WENT WITH THE NEW YORK GIANTS FOR 5 YRS. FROM 1959 TO 1968 HE COACHED THE GREEN BAY (WIS.) PACKERS FROM LOSERS TO WINNERS. HE BECAME NATIONALLY FAMOUS AND REGARDED AS THE TOP FOOTBALL COACH OF THE '60'S. HE COACHED THE PACKERS FOR 9 SEASONS AND THE WASHINGTON REDSKINS FOR ONE, A TOTAL OF 204 GAMES. HIS TEAMS WON 6 WESTERN CONFERENCE CHAMPIONSHIPS, 5 NATIONAL FOOTBALL LEAGUE CHAMPIONSHIPS AND TWO SUPER BOWL CHAMPIONSHIPS. IN 10 SEASONS, WINNING FOR LOMBARDI WAS INDEED THE ONLY THING.
HE WAS BORN IN BROOKLYN, N.Y.
WINNING ISN'T EVERYTHING! IT'S THE ONLY THING!
YOU NEED THIS MORE THAN I DO.
THANK YOU, MR. LOMBARDI.
DURING THE DEPRESSION HE HAD A JOB WITH THE SEABOARD FINANCE CO. HIS JOB WAS TO FORECLOSE LOANS, BUT HE ENDED UP GIVING PEOPLE CASH OUT OF HIS OWN POCKET.
STERN
LOMBARDI'S SPEECHES TO HIS TEAM WERE INSPIRING, CHALLENGING HIS PLAYERS TO ALWAYS BE READY TO WIN. HE WAS A STERN AND HARDWORKING COACH, MANY TIMES PUSHING HIS PLAYERS BEYOND ENDURANCE IN DAILY PRACTICE SESSIONS.

B. 1913

Richard M. Nixon

NAVY OFFICER, CONGRESSMAN, SENATOR, VICE-PRESIDENT AND ***THIRTY-SEVENTH*** PRESIDENT OF THE UNITED STATES (1969 – 74)

HE WAS BORN IN YORBA LINDA, CAL.

NIXON GRADUATED SECOND IN HIS CLASS FROM WHITTIER COLLEGE, CAL., IN 1934, AND THEN ATTENDED DUKE UNIVERSITY LAW SCHOOL IN DURHAM, NORTH CAROLINA. ***DURING WORLD WAR II HE SERVED AS OPERATIONS OFFICER FOR A NAVY TRANSPORT UNIT FOR 15 MONTHS IN THE SOUTH PACIFIC. HE ADVANCED TO THE RANK OF LT. COMMANDER. AFTER THE WAR HE WAS ELECTED TO CONGRESS FROM CAL., SERVING 3 YRS. FROM 1950-53 HE WAS U.S. SENATOR FROM CAL., AND FROM 1953-61 HE WAS VICE-PRESIDENT OF THE U.S. JOHN F. KENNEDY DEFEATED HIM FOR THE PRESIDENCY IN 1960. NIXON THEN TRIED FOR THE GOVERNORSHIP OF CAL., BUT WAS DEFEATED BY PAT BROWN. FROM 1963-68 HE PRACTICED LAW IN NEW YORK CITY. IN ONE OF THE GREATEST POLITICAL RECOVERIES IN OUR HISTORY, HE WON THE 1968 PRESIDENTIAL ELECTION OVER VICE-PRESIDENT*** HUBERT HUMPHREY.

I HAVE DECIDED, FOR THE GOOD OF THE COUNTRY, TO RESIGN!

IN 1974, DUE TO REVELATIONS ABOUT HIS INVOLVEMENT IN ***COVERING UP THE WATERGATE AFFAIR, NIXON, FACING CERTAIN IMPEACHMENT AND PROBABLE REMOVAL FROM OFFICE, RESIGNED THE PRESIDENCY ON AUG. 8, THE FIRST PRESIDENT TO DO SO.*** AS PRESIDENT HE PROPOSED SOME GOOD PROGRAMS BUT WAS UNABLE TO GET THEM THROUGH A DIVIDED CONGRESS.

HISTORY WILL REMEMBER NIXON ESPECIALLY FOR HIS FOREIGN ACCOMPLISHMENTS. ***WITH THE HELP OF DIPLOMAT HENRY KISSINGER, THEY STARTLED THE WORLD WITH THEIR DETENTES WITH RUSSIA AND CHINA.*** THEY GOT THE U.S. OUT OF VIETNAM ***WITH HONOR AND CALMED MIDDLE EAST TENSIONS WITH A BALANCED APPROACH BETWEEN THE ARAB WORLD AND ISRAEL.***

KERN

B. 1913

Gerald Ford

ATHLETE, CONGRESSIONAL LEADER, VICE-PRESIDENT AND *THIRTY-EIGHTH* PRESIDENT OF THE UNITED STATES (1974-)

HE WAS BORN IN OMAHA, NEB.
WELCOME! MY NEW VICE-PRESIDENT.

THE LONG NIGHTMARE IS OVER.

FORD WAS BORN LESLIE LYNCH KING. HIS FATHER WAS A MONTANA WOOL TRADER. HIS PARENTS DIVORCED, AND AT AGE 2 HE WENT WITH MOTHER TO GRAND RAPIDS, MICH., WHERE SHE MET AND MARRIED GERALD R. FORD, A PAINT SALESMAN. JERRY TOOK HIS STEPFATHER'S NAME AND WENT TO SCHOOL IN GRAND RAPIDS. *HE WAS ALL-CITY FOOTBALL CENTER AND MADE THE ALL-STATE FOOTBALL TEAM. AT THE UNIVERSITY OF MICHIGAN HE WON THE MOST VALUABLE PLAYER AWARD FOR FOOTBALL. FROM 1935 TO 1941 HE WENT TO YALE WHERE HE STUDIED LAW AND COACHED FOOTBALL. IN JUNE 1941, HE WAS ADMITTED TO THE MICHIGAN BAR. 1ST ELECTED FROM MICHIGAN IN 1948, FORD SPENT 25 YRS. IN THE HOUSE OF REPRESENTATIVES. HE BECAME HOUSE MINORITY LEADER IN 1964. HIS PERFORMANCE IN CONGRESS WAS OUTSTANDING. WHEN HE TOOK OVER THE PRESIDENCY HE WAS THE FIRST NON-ELECTED VICE-PRESIDENT TO SUCCEED TO THE PRESIDENCY.*

ON DEC. 6, 1973, GERALD FORD BECAME VICE-PRESIDENT OF THE U.S., *APPOINTED BY PRES. NIXON UNDER THE NEWLY ENACTED 25TH AMENDMENT TO THE CONSTITUTION. ON AUG. 9, 1974, FORD WAS SWORN IN AS PRESIDENT OF THE UNITED STATES WHEN NIXON RESIGNED.*

KERN

FORD JOINED THE NAVY IN 1942, WHERE HE TAUGHT PHYSICAL TRAINING TO CADETS. *HE THEN SHIPPED ABOARD THE "MONTEREY" WHICH WAS WITH THE 3RD FLEET OF ADMIRAL "BULL" HALSEY IN THE SOUTH PACIFIC.*

1917 - 1963

John F. Kennedy

WAR HERO, CONGRESSMAN, SENATOR, AUTHOR AND ***THIRTY-FIFTH*** PRESIDENT OF THE UNITED STATES (1961 - 63)

LT. KENNEDY

HE WAS BORN IN BROOKLINE, MASS.

JOHN ATTENDED CHOATE ACADEMY, CONNECTICUT, AND PRINCETON, BEFORE GRADUATING CUM LAUDE FROM HARVARD IN 1940 WHERE HE MAJORED IN GOVERNMENT AND INTERNATIONAL RELATIONS. HE WAS COMMISSIONED AS A NAVAL OFFICER AND IN 1942 WAS ASSIGNED TO A P.T. BOAT SQUADRON. ***A JAPANESE DESTROYER CUT HIS BOAT IN HALF. HIS HEROIC RESCUE OF HIS CREW WON HIM THE PURPLE HEART AND THE NAVY AND MARINE CORPS MEDAL. AFTER THE WAR HE SERVED AS A REPORTER FOR A SHORT TIME, THEN BECAME A CONGRESSMAN. IN 1952 HE WAS ELECTED SENATOR, SERVING UNTIL 1960 WHEN HE DEFEATED VICE-PRES. NIXON IN ONE OF THE CLOSEST ELECTIONS IN U.S. HISTORY. IN NOV. 1963 HE WAS ASSASSINATED IN DALLAS, TEXAS. KENNEDY WAS THE YOUNGEST MAN ELECTED PRESIDENT AND THE FIRST ROMAN CATHOLIC. HE WON GREAT PRAISE FOR HIS COURAGEOUS STAND AGAINST RUSSIA DURING THE CUBAN MISSILE CRISIS IN 1962.***

THOMAS HART BENTON

EDMUND G. ROSS

COURAGE: "GRACE UNDER PRESSURE"

GEORGE W. NORRIS DANIEL WEBSTER ROBERT A. TAFT

WE CHOOSE TO GO TO THE MOON IN THIS DECADE, AND DO THE OTHER THINGS, NOT BECAUSE THEY ARE EASY BUT BECAUSE THEY ARE HARD.

WHILE PRESIDENT, KENNEDY FOUGHT FOR CIVIL RIGHTS, ESTABLISHED THE PEACE CORPS, ***WHICH BECAME ONE OF KENNEDY'S MOST SUCESSFUL ACHIEVEMENTS, AND PRESSED THE NATION'S SCIENTISTS TO MASTER OUTER SPACE.***

HIS BOOK, "***PROFILES IN COURAGE,***" PUBLISHED IN 1956, WAS A BIOGRAPHICAL SERIES ABOUT ***SENATORS WHO HAD TAKEN COURAGEOUS STANDS THROUGHOUT AMERICAN HISTORY. THIS BOOK BECAME A BEST SELLER AND WON THE PULITZER PRIZE FOR BIOGRAPHY.***

KERN

1924 - 1971

Audie Murphy

MOST DECORATED WORLD WAR II HERO

ONE OF 9 LIVING CHILDREN OF A TEXAS SHARE-CROPPER, HE WAS STILL IN HIS TEENS WHEN HIS FATHER LEFT HOME. HIS MOTHER DIED LEAVING AUDIE TO SUPPORT THE REST OF THE FAMILY. HE WORKED THE FARM AND DID ODD JOBS. MURPHY HAD NEVER BEEN MORE THAN 100 MILES FROM HOME WHEN HE ENLISTED IN THE INFANTRY IN WORLD WAR II. *HE WAS NOT YET 21 WHEN HE RETURNED AS THE MOST DECORATED SOLDIER IN U.S. HISTORY. MURPHY WON THE CONGRESSIONAL MEDAL OF HONOR AND 23 OTHER CITATIONS FOR HIS BRAVE DEEDS WHILE SERVING IN FRANCE. IN 1955 HE REENACTED HIS WAR EXPERIENCES FOR HOLLYWOOD IN "TO HELL AND BACK." MURPHY WAS IN 40 MOVIES, EARNING $2.5 MILLION. BECAUSE OF POOR INVESTMENTS HE FILED BANKRUPTCY IN 1968. HE WAS KILLED IN A PLANE ACCIDENT.*

1970

HE WAS BORN IN KINGSTON, TEXAS.

US 1946

SOMETHING LOOKS MIGHTY SUSPICIOUS OVER THERE, CAPTAIN.
POLICE

MURPHY WON THE *MEDAL OF HONOR FOR HIS BRAVERY IN THE BATTLE FOR THE COLMAR POCKET IN EASTERN FRANCE. HE MOUNTED A BURNING TANK DESTROYER. USING ITS .50-CAL. MACHINE GUN, HE HELD OFF A NAZI FORCE OF 250 MEN AND 6 TANKS.*

©KERN

HE HAD A POWERFUL AVERSION TO THE DRUG TRADE. *AS A SPECIAL OFFICER, HE RODE AROUND WITH THE LOS ANGELES POLICE, HELPING TO BREAK UP DRUG DEALINGS. THIS WAS IN THE EARLY '60'S.*

1926 - 1967

Virgil "Gus" Grissom

U.S. AIR FORCE MAJOR, ASTRONAUT AND SECOND MAN IN SPACE

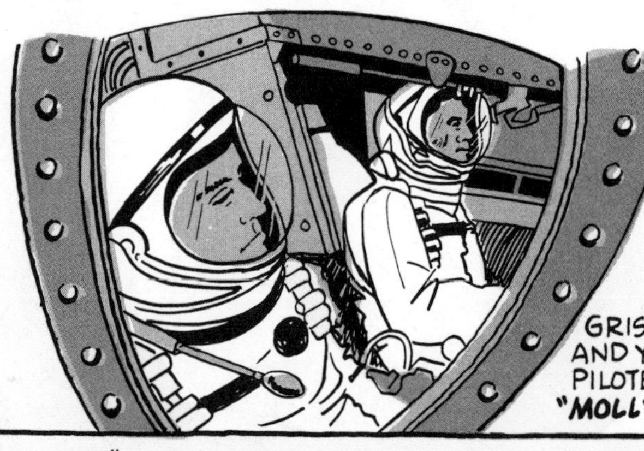

GRISSOM AND YOUNG PILOTED THE **"MOLLY BROWN"**

IN 1950, "GUS" GRADUATED FROM PURDUE UNIVERSITY IN MECHANICAL ENGINEERING, THEN WENT TO AVIATION CADET TRAINING SCHOOL WHERE HE WAS AWARDED HIS WINGS IN MAR. 1951. ***GRISSOM FLEW 100 COMBAT MISSIONS IN KOREA. HE WAS AWARDED THE DISTINGUISHED FLYING CROSS AND AIR MEDAL WITH CLUSTER FOR HIS SERVICE. AFTER THE WAR GRISSOM BECAME A JET PILOT INSTRUCTOR AND LATER A TEST PILOT. HE HAD FLOWN MORE THAN 3,500 HRS. AND 2,500 HRS. IN JET AIRCRAFT. IN 1965 GRISSOM AND JOHN W. YOUNG MADE THE FIRST 2-MAN GEMINI SPACE FLIGHT.***

HE WAS BORN IN MITCHELL, IND.

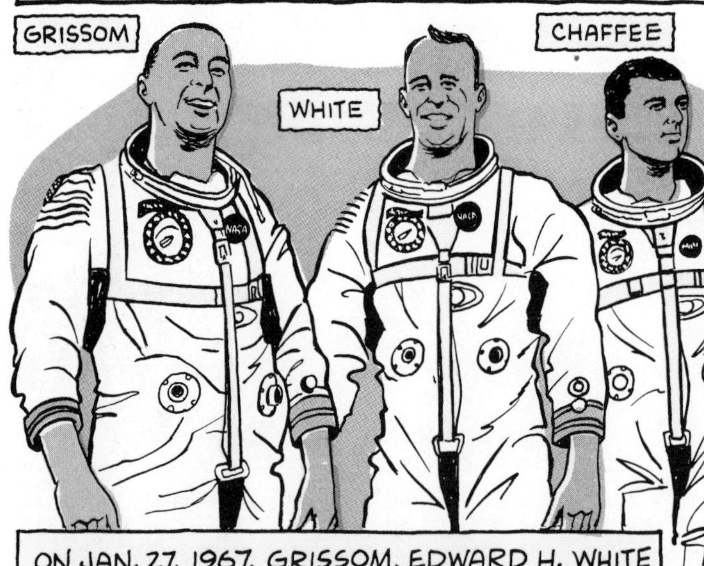

ON JAN. 27, 1967, GRISSOM, EDWARD H. WHITE II AND ROGER B. CHAFFEE ***WERE BURNED TO DEATH IN A FIRE ABOARD THEIR APOLLO CRAFT DURING A COUNTDOWN REHEARSAL.***

IN 1959 "GUS" WAS ASSIGNED TO THE NASA MANNED SPACE CENTER AND STAYED WITH THE SPACE PROGRAM UNTIL HIS DEATH. ***HE MADE A SUBORBITAL FLIGHT AS PART OF PROJECT MERCURY JULY 21, 1961. HIS CAPSULE, "LIBERTY BELL 7," ROCKETED TO AN ALTITUDE OF 116 MILES AND TRAVELED 254 MILES DOWN THE ATLANTIC MISSILE RANGE.***

1929-1968

Martin Luther King, Jr.

BAPTIST MINISTER AND CIVIL RIGHTS LEADER

KING WAS EDUCATED AT MOREHOUSE COLLEGE AND CROZER THEOLOGICAL SEMINARY, WHERE HE EARNED THE PLAFKNER PRIZE FOR SCHOLARSHIP. IN 1955 HE RECEIVED HIS PH.D. DEGREE FROM BOSTON UNIVERSITY AND HIS D.D. DEGREES FROM BOTH BOSTON THEOLOGICAL SEMINARY AND THE UNIVERSITY OF CHICAGO THEOLOGICAL SEMINARY. ***AS A BAPTIST MINISTER HE ASSUMED THE LEADERSHIP OF THE CIVIL RIGHTS REVOLUTION, USING THE METHOD OF NONVIOLENCE. IN 1955 HE LED A BOYCOTT OF THE MONTGOMERY, ALA., BUS LINE TO PROTEST THE PRACTICE OF SEATING NEGROES IN THE BACK OF THE BUS. THE BOYCOTT CONTINUED FOR 382 DAYS. IT ENDED WITH VICTORY. KING WAS AN ADVOCATE OF CHRISTIAN LOVE. THE 1963 MARCH ON WASHINGTON BROUGHT MORE THAN 200,000 NEGROES AND WHITES TO THE NATION'S CAPITOL. KING'S MOVING SPEECH, "I HAVE A DREAM," LED TO THE PASSAGE OF THE CIVIL RIGHTS ACT OF 1964.***

HE WAS BORN IN ATLANTA, GA.

THIS LAW IS GREAT FOR YOUR PEOPLE, MARTIN.

WE ARE GRATEFUL TO YOU, MR. PRESIDENT.

KING WAS PLANNING A POOR MAN'S MARCH ON WASHINGTON, D.C., ***BUT BEFORE HE COULD LEAD IT A SNIPER'S BULLET CUT HIM DOWN APR. 4, 1968, IN MEMPHIS, TENN.***

KERN

THROUGH KING'S EFFORTS ***A LAW WAS PASSED AND SIGNED BY PRES. JOHNSON TO SWEEP AWAY ALL RACIAL BARRIERS TO VOTING. HE WAS AWARDED THE NOBEL PEACE PRIZE IN 1964, THE YOUNGEST MAN EVER TO RECEIVE THIS.***

INDEX